IS THIS A PRIVATE FIGHT OR CAN ANYBODY JOIN?

To My Family

Is This a Private Fight or Can Anybody Join?

The Spread of Interstate War

ZACHARY C. SHIRKEY
St. John Fisher College, USA

ASHGATE

Published by
Ashgate Publishing Limited
Wey Court East
Union Road
Farnham
Surrey, GU9 7PT
England

Ashgate Publishing Company
Suite 420
101 Cherry Street
Burlington
VT 05401-4405
USA

www.ashgate.com

British Library Cataloguing in Publication Data
Shirkey, Zachary C.
Is this a private fight or can anybody join? : the spread of interstate war.
1. Interstate relations. 2. National interest. 3. Military policy. 4. Escalation (Military science)
I. Title
327.1'6-dc22

Library of Congress Cataloging-in-Publication Data
Shirkey, Zachary C.
Is this a private fight or can anybody join? : the spread of interstate war / by Zachary C. Shirkey.
p. cm.
Includes bibliographical references and index.
ISBN 978-0-7546-7585-3 (hardcover) -- ISBN 978-0-7546-9690-2 (ebook)
1. Intervention (International law) 2. Intervention (International law)--Case studies. I. Title.
JZ6368.S47 2009
341.5'84--dc22

2009011728

ISBN 9780754675853 (hbk)
ISBN 9780754696902 (ebk)

Mixed Sources
Product group from well-managed forests and other controlled sources
www.fsc.org Cert no. SA-COC-1565
© 1996 Forest Stewardship Council
FSC

Printed and bound in Great Britain by
MPG Books Group, UK

Contents

List of Tables and Figure

Tables

Figure

Acknowledgements

I would like to thank Emily Copeland, Kara Drebitko, Page Fortna, Erik Gartzke, Robert Jervis, Paul MacDonald, Jack Levy, Peter Liberman, Justine Rosenthal, Ivan Savic, David Schmitt, Charles Tilly, Harrison Wagner, Nicole VanGorder-Pratt, Gregory Wawro, Alex Weisiger, and several anonymous reviewers for their comments, help, and advice on this and earlier drafts as well as on the data collection. Any mistakes are my own.

List of Abbreviations

CENTCOM—United States Central Command

COW—Correlates of War

CUP—Committee of Union and Progress

EC—European Community

EUGene—Expected Utility Generation and Data Management Program

GCC—Gulf Cooperation Council

GCFCG—Gulf Crisis Financial Coordination Group

GEE—Generalized Estimating Equation

IMPMIL—Importance of an Unexpected Military Event

IMPPOL—Importance of an Unexpected Political Event

MAP—Military Assistance Program

MIL—Military Unexpected Event

MLE—Maximum Likelihood Estimation

NATO—North Atlantic Treaty Organization

POL—Political Unexpected Event

UAE—United Arab Emirates

UNEXP—Unexpected Event

WEU—Western European Union

Chapter 1
The Puzzle of Why States Join Ongoing Wars

> We must remember that so long as war exists on the earth there will be some danger that even the nation that most ardently desires peace will be drawn into war
>
> Franklin D. Roosevelt

As Roosevelt's quotation suggests, national leaders, statesmen, diplomats and political scientists have long been concerned about the spread of war. While rare, the spread of war from one state to another has led to some of the largest, costliest, and deadliest conflicts the world has seen, and therefore, is viewed as a real threat to the state. Wars which significantly altered the international system have almost always involved joining. Both the First and Second World Wars, the Crimean War, and the Korean War all began as bilateral conflicts, but then spread to include other states. Truman feared the Korean War might spread further still. Fear of the spread of war in part led the United States and the Soviet Union to pay attention to and attempt to stop or at least contain several of the Israeli-Egyptian conflicts, though ironically this attention increased the probability the wars would draw in the great powers. Thus, wars often spread to include or threaten states that were initially non-belligerents and even conflicts that remain bilateral are often fought with and influenced by the possibility that other states will join. Indeed, some wars may not be fought at all due to the fact they would draw in additional belligerents. Additionally, the odds an existing war will expand are often greater than the initial odds that a war would occur at all. Finally, the outcomes of wars are altered by joining. For example, the Crimean War and Russo-Turkish War of 1877 had the same initial belligerents and similar causes, yet due to the entries of France and Britain, the former resulted in a Russian defeat, while the later resulted in a Russian victory, though even here Russia had to limit its gains due to the possibility of foreign intervention. Therefore, understanding why and when states join ongoing wars is important, as it is essential to understand how and why wars are initiated, prosecuted, and terminated.

When national leaders speak of the spread of war they often discuss it as though it were driven by some force completely beyond their control, as is exhibited by Roosevelt's quotation. While this might be convenient for political reasons, it is dissatisfying for the political scientist. To think of states being arbitrarily and almost mystically pulled into wars is unhelpful. Surely there must be some reasons why particular states get drawn into wars, while others remain neutral, and why some wars end up involving many states, while others remain bilateral conflicts. Additionally, the timing of when states join is likely not random and is certainly not determined by the stars. Surely, national leaders must have some sort of control over the spread of war and they should be able to discover, comprehend, and react to, if not necessarily control, the forces that may lead them into war. Leaders make conscious decisions about whether or not to enter a war, rather than being dragged into a war by some sort of mystical force. Events must occur in order to cause these leaders to decide to take their states into war. Given this, political scientists should be able to understand why and when leaders decide to involve their states in wars while others choose to remain neutral and what events or forces lead them to make these decisions. This work will argue that information generated and revealed by wars, such as surprising battlefield results, holds the key to why and when non-belligerents join ongoing wars.[1]

Previous attempts to understand the spread of war have been largely unsuccessful. Even the terminology has proven difficult. The spread of war has been called infectiousness, diffusion, spillover, and most often, contagion. All of these terms unfortunately connote that the spread of war is some sort of involuntary process, much like the spread of disease from one person to another, while in truth as argued above it is driven by conscious decision-making.[2] In order to avoid this misleading connotation, the term "joining" will be used in this work to describe a state voluntarily entering an ongoing war. True, states are sometimes referred to as having joined a war even if they were invaded and became a belligerent involuntarily, but such difficulties of nomenclature are sadly unavoidable.[3] Let it suffice to say, that within this work joining will always connote the voluntary entry of a state into a war, unless the phrase "involuntary joining" is used.

Two other terms will be used throughout the work in exactly the same manner as joining for the sake of readability. These are entering and intervening. Entering is a straightforward synonym of joining and requires no explanation. Intervening, however, may be seen as conflating the concept of voluntarily joining a war with humanitarian efforts. The term, intervention, however, has been applied to third parties entering wars since at least the mid 19th century, while armed mediation was used for what we now commonly call intervention. Intervention has the advantage of conveying the voluntary aspect of entering the war. When confusion is likely, a distinction can always be made between military and humanitarian intervention.

1 Information that is unobservable antebellum, at least by one side, is what causes war (Gartzke 1999). Thus, though as scholars we should be able uncover why leaders decided to join wars, it does not mean we will be able to predict when states will go to war *ex ante*.

2 See Goertz (1994, 77–82) for an excellent discussion of the difference in terminology used between rational actor approaches and diffusion approaches regarding the spread of war. The two approaches are not inherently in conflict as rational actors respond to outside stimuli and this can look very much like diffusion. Recently, scholars have begun to use the term war expansion, which while somewhat vague, is a major improvement over the use of contagion and diffusion for discussing the rational spread of war.

3 For example, it is often said that the Netherlands joined or entered the Second World War even though the Netherlands became a belligerent because it was invaded by Germany, not because it chose to become an active belligerent.

Besides, the two concepts are in fact but subsets of the larger concept of third party involvement in a conflict. Thus, intervention or military intervention is a satisfactory term with which to label the action of a state voluntarily joining an ongoing war. Therefore, the terms joining, entering, and intervening will be used synonymously throughout the work.

More troubling than the difficulty of nomenclature has been the literature's inability to shed light on the causal mechanisms behind joining. Much of the reason for this failure is that previous approaches have focused either on the premise that one war causes additional wars—a proposition for which little evidence has been found—or they have focused on country specific variables in order to explain the geographic spread of war. These country specific approaches, of which much more will be said in Chapter 2, generally try to explain joining through geographic proximity and the alliance structures of states not involved in a war. While such state specific characteristics help partially explain which states get drawn into wars, they offer little insight into which wars are more likely to experience intervention and none into when non-belligerents will enter a war. It seems likely that the key to these unanswered questions resides within the nature of the war itself.[4]

Napoleon Bonaparte famously said, "War is composed of nothing but surprises."[5] While this is clearly hyperbole, the point is important nevertheless. The outcome and course of a war are difficult to predict. Surprises in war change not only the course of the war, but also the way that non-belligerent states perceive that war. The information revealed by these events holds the key to understanding why and when states join ongoing wars. Information revealed during the course of wars can cause third parties to decide to join those wars and it dictates the timing of their entry.

As will be shown in Chapter 3, revealed information changes the perceived costs and benefits of joining an ongoing war. This is crucial, as any rational change in a state's decision to enter a war should be driven by a change in that state's expected utility for joining. Prior to any significant new or revealed information in a war, the expected utility of going to war will generally be the same for a given non-belligerent as it was for that same state at the outbreak of the war.[6] Thus, unexpected battlefield results and surprising political events that occur in

4 The reasons for the spread of wars exist within wars, including the benefits of a war and the effect these benefits have on balancing and extended deterrence (Blainey 1973; Werner 2000). More will be said of this in Chapter 2.

5 Scheina 2003.

6 There are some exceptions, primarily where expected events reduce the uncertainty associated with a state's expected utility and where states are waiting for some expected process, such as rearmament, to be completed. These will be discussed in more detail below and in Chapter 2. Additionally, changes within non-belligerents, such as the restructuring of a government, could lead to a decision to join. While such factors are considered in the case studies, a systematic collection of such events was not possible in the statistical portion of the work.

a belligerent are the key to understanding why and when states will join ongoing wars because these sort of events reveal information during a war and change the expected utility for joining. Unexpected events in particular and revealed information more generally, therefore, should logically dictate the timing of state intervention.

Using revealed information to explain the spread of war is rooted in the wider learning and bargaining theory literature. As was argued above, without the presence of uncertainty and states' ability to learn from information revealed by wars, there would be little reason for states to join wars well after they had begun. Rather, states would join very quickly or not at all. Thus, this work serves not only as an investigation of intervention, but also as a test of bargaining theory in general. If bargaining theory fails to help illuminate why states become belligerents mid-war, it is unclear why it should help explain the initial outbreak of war. Thus, this work has important implications for the study of war in general and bargaining theory specifically, in addition to its obvious relevance to the literature on the spread of war.

Of course, not all non-belligerents will react to new or revealed information in the same way. Some will be more likely to join than others. First, states that are geographically proximate to the conflict will join at a higher rate than more distant states (Richardson 1960; Siverson and Starr 1991). This is because nearby conflicts will be more salient to states and because geographically proximate states will have a greater ability to join wars since they do not have to project power over great distances in order to intervene. Second, great powers will also join wars at a higher rate than less powerful states (Pearson, Baumann, and Pickering 1994; Wright 1965). This is likely because great powers can project their power more effectively and thus have the ability to influence more wars than do smaller states. Third, alliances should also transmit wars from one ally to another (Siverson and Starr 1991), though this mechanism should operate quite quickly or not at all. Fourth, United Nations involvement should also raise the likelihood of intervention (Betts 1992). Finally, while some information may make joining a war more attractive by revealing opportunities to pick up spoils or a need to balance, other information may make joining the war less attractive. This is because revealed information may indicate defeat is now more likely if the state joins or that a potential enemy that was earlier perceived to be a growing threat has been sufficiently contained and there is, therefore, less of a need to balance against it. These causes and correlates of intervention will be derived and fleshed out in the next chapter.

The body of the work is laid out in the following manner. In Chapter 2, a new theory of joining is laid out, but first the existing state of the joining literature is discussed. Specifically, the three main theoretical approaches to understanding why states join wars, Siverson and Starr's (1991) "opportunity and willingness" framework, Haldi's (2003) political costs approach, and Altfeld and Bueno de Mesquita's (1979) rational actor model will be presented and their strengths and flaws examined. All three approaches have strengths, but ultimately fall short. Siverson and Starr's approach is able to show that states with allies in a conflict and geographically proximate states are more likely to join an ongoing war. These findings are helpful, but they do not explain the underlying question of why states join, nor when they join. Geography and often alliance structures remain constant throughout a conflict, yet states often do not intervene initially. What causes this change in behavior? Haldi's approach offers that states join when political costs are low and they remain neutral when costs are high. This approaches tautology and Haldi does not develop the concept further. The only variation Haldi finds in political costs is that prior to the Napoleonic wars they were low and afterward they were high. While this may be true, it means that the theory provides absolutely no indication about which states are more likely to join and in which wars states are more likely to intervene since 1815. Obviously, this is dissatisfying, as the level of intervention has varied since 1815. Finally, Altfeld and Bueno de Mesquita focus on the fact that joiners can alter the probability of which side will win a war and to a lesser extent on the reputational benefit that accrues to states that honor their alliances. Altfeld and Bueno de Mesquita argue that states will join in order to increase the odds their preferred outcome for the war will occur and that states will be careful to avoid joining the losing side as to avoid bearing unnecessary costs. While these factors are undoubtedly very important to understanding joining, Altfeld and Bueno de Mesquita look at joining only in the first two months of a war and do not attempt to explain when states join wars. As this work's focus is late joining and the timing of joining, it can help answer questions that are not addressed by Altfeld and Bueno de Mesquita.

After Chapter 2 illustrates that despite their strengths existing explanations are ultimately insufficient, the chapter develops a new theory of military intervention. The goal of this new theory is to explain which states will intervene, which wars are most likely to grow in size, and most especially when states will join. It builds upon the concepts of revealed information and unexpected events and is based chiefly upon the works of Blainey, Goemans, Iklé, Wagner, and Wittman. Specifically, the theory argues that something in the war itself must change in order for a non-belligerent to decide to join. This is because if conditions had remained constant, the non-belligerent would have stuck with its initial decision to remain neutral. Non-belligerents incorporate the information revealed by events in the war into their calculations about the benefits of entering the war. These changes are what explain when states join and why certain wars experience intervention while others do not. Obviously, this framework is not applicable to states that join very soon after a war begins, as such delays may be due to mechanical aspects of declaring war or waiting for news of the outbreak of hostilities rather than uncertainty about whether belligerency is wise given the occurrence of the war.

In Chapter 3, the theory advanced in Chapter 2 is tested using a large statistical study. All interstate wars in the Correlates of War (COW) database from 1816-1995 are included. Additionally, two more recent interstate wars were included: Kargil and Eritrea-Ethiopia. This results in only two interstate wars since 1815 not being included: US-Afghanistan and US-Iraq. Both wars are ongoing and while they clearly began as interstate wars, have both morphed into civil wars.[7] Additionally, while both wars are multilateral, states not among the initial belligerents have yet to involve themselves in either war to a sufficient degree to warrant labeling the action joining, though there is an outside possibility that bordering states' actions may eventually escalate to such a level.[8] Whether states voluntarily joined an ongoing war—as opposed to being attacked by a belligerent—is regressed against variables derived from previous approaches and the hypotheses advanced in Chapter 2. Tests are run to see if unexpected events can predict when states enter wars and also when they leave. The tests use generalized estimating equations (GEEs). GEEs, a subset of generalized linear models, are better able to control for temporal effects in models involving lagged variables than are the more common maximum likelihood estimation (MLE) models.[9] The interpretation of GEE coefficients is identical to the interpretation of MLE, so the results can be easily understood by anyone familiar with logistic regression techniques.[10]

Extra-systemic wars were excluded from the study because state intervention almost never occurs in such wars. Out of a total of 108 extra-systemic wars, state intervention occurred in only two of them.[11] These two wars are the Uruguayan Dispute, 1845–52, and the Riff Rebellion, 1921–26. The former is best viewed as an Uruguayan civil war—though Uruguay is not considered a state by the Correlates of War project at that point in its history—in which Argentina, Brazil, France, and Britain all intervened. As such, it is best excluded from this study along with all other civil wars for reasons discussed below. The second, the Riff Rebellion, is a more classic case of joining. The Spanish, in attempting to occupy all of Morocco allotted to them per their agreement with the French, brought on a war with the Riffian tribesmen. This war went disastrously for the Spanish, much to the surprise of the Spanish, tempting the Riffs to overreach.[12] They attacked the French part of Morocco—the French were not expecting an attack—and though this attack was initially successful, it brought upon the Riff the combined forces of France and Spain, which eventually crushed them.

---

7 Of course, it could be argued the US intervened in an ongoing Afghan civil war, but then this would have been excluded on the grounds it was a civil war as discussed below. It is assumed COW will code Kosovo and the conflict in the Democratic Republic of the Congo as civil wars, which as will be discussed below, are excluded from the study on theoretical grounds.

8 This assumes non-US NATO members are seen as an initial belligerents in Afghanistan and not late joiners. The difficulty in answering such questions in a manner free of bias is one of the main reasons these ongoing wars have been excluded.

9 Liang and Zeger 1986.

10 Zorn 2001. This is addressed in detail in Chapter 3.

11 These numbers are taken from the Correlates of War Two project at Penn State rather than the original Correlates of War project at the University of Michigan, which has a somewhat different and larger list of extra-systemic wars. The COW Two project has coded a number of wars as civil wars rather than as extra-systemic.

12 Perry 1996.

Extra-systemic wars are likely fundamentally different from interstate wars. It is not at all clear that states view the colonial wars of others in the same manner as they do the interstate wars of others. Certainly, the French did not care about Spain's misfortunes in Morocco until they, too, were attacked. The outcomes of such wars are generally less salient to other states and thus it takes an exceptional one to lead to third party involvement.[13] More importantly, this work examines why states voluntarily join ongoing wars. As the French were attacked, their entry was not voluntary and would be beyond the scope of the study even if the Riff Rebellion were classified as an interstate war. Thus, even if extra-systemic wars are similar to interstate wars, there would never be an instance of a state entering a war prior to being attacked, provided the Uruguayan War is seen as a civil war. Thus, given the absence of a positive value for the dependent variable, the inclusion of extra-systemic wars would add very little statistical leverage.

As alluded to above, civil wars were also excluded from the study. They are excluded not because such wars do not lead to third party involvement; they do (Gleditsch 2003; Gleditsch and Beardsley 2004). Rather, they are excluded on theoretical grounds. Such wars generally have issues of contested sovereignty, which greatly complicate the wars themselves and the issue of why third parties join.[14] Also, intervention in such wars often follows ethnic lines, while ethnic motivations for joining are rare in interstate wars.[15] Still, the ideas advanced in this work should apply to civil wars, even if their application would be complicated by these additional factors. States which do not join a civil war immediately likely would join later only if something caused their expected utility for joining

13 Why states interfered so rarely in the extra-systemic wars of the 19th and 20th centuries is not abundantly clear as outside involvement was fairly common in the 18th century. It may be that states simply came to agreements, tacit or explicit, such as the Berlin Conference of 1884 , that it would be in the best interests of all to allow each others' imperial projects to go forward without interference provided they respected each others' spheres of influence. This is not to say there was never tension, the two Moroccan and the Fashoda crises highlight that there was. It also may be that the rewards to be had through interference in the extra-systemic wars of others were never worth the risk of bringing on a war between two great powers in Europe. Additionally, COW does not record intervention by non-state or extra-systemic actors, so the lack of joining does not mean these wars did not spread at all, but rather that did not spread to include other states as recognized by COW.

14 Haldi 2003.

15 Ethnic conflicts may spread in a manner distinct from non-ethnic conflicts (Lake and Rothschild 1998). Specifically, states which have "risk populations" and are, therefore, already vulnerable to ethnic tensions are more susceptible to the spread of ethnic conflicts. This is similar to the more general risk population argument (Strang and Tuma 1993). Domestic ethnic politics in non-belligerents also play a large role in the spread of ethnic conflicts (Saideman 2001). Ethnic ties are crucial in understanding the spread of civil wars to the point that such ties account for most or all of any geographic clustering of civil wars (Buhaug and Gleditsch 2008).

to change. Just as in interstate wars, such a change would likely be driven by revealed information. However, while it is likely possible to form a grand theory that explains the growth of both interstate and civil wars, it seems practical to first attempt to understand the phenomena independently, rather than jointly. The field would do well to examine civil wars in the future, either separately or jointly with interstate wars, but undertaking such a study is not practical at present. The same can be said of extra-systemic wars as well.

Chapters 4 through 7 are case studies that explore in depth the findings presented in Chapter 3. The cases were selected to provide variation over time as well as theoretical leverage. Some cases look at balancers while others examine bandwagoners. States that do not join are also examined. One case examines a world war, one looks at a war that grew, but did not become general, while the third examines a war that no one joined. This variation in the size of the war examined is important, since the phenomenon of intervention is what explains the difference in the size of these and most other wars. Thus, it is vital to examine wars of different sizes to avoid bias. Finally, the fourth case looks at how the dynamics which affect late joining have changed since 1945.

Chapter 4 examines the Crimean War. The Crimean War is an intriguing case because two major powers, Great Britain and France, and one minor power, Sardinia, entered the conflict, while several other states that could reasonably have been expected to join the conflict, including Austria, Sweden, Persia, and Greece, did not. Thus, the case allows for contrasts between joiners and non-joiners to be drawn. While Britain and France intervened in order to balance against Russia, Sardinia had other motivations. Thus, contrasts across motivations can be drawn as well.

Chapter 5 looks at the First World War. This case was chosen for several reasons. First, some argue the dynamics that lead to world wars are distinct from those that operate in smaller wars. By including a world war in the study, it can be compared to other wars to see if this proposition is true. Second, most of the countries that joined after August 1914 were looking to pick up spoils, rather than to balance. This offers a contrast to the Crimean War. The First World War is also interesting as the US did not join the war for traditional reasons of bandwagoning or balancing, but rather to defend the rights of neutrals as generally accepted antebellum. Such an entry should provide a difficult hurdle for hypotheses derived in part from Realist principles. Finally, the First World War examines two states, the Ottoman Empire and Greece, which joined the war, but whose decisions to join were greatly complicated by internal divisions.

Chapter 6 analyzes the Franco-Prussian War. This war remained a bilateral conflict even though a reasonable observer in 1870 might have expected the war to involve many more states. This lack of intervention is a bit of a mystery and makes it an interesting case. Also, it will be argued in Chapter 3 that certain types of revealed information should actually dissuade states from joining. The Franco-Prussian War provides an opportunity to test this hypothesis. In general, negative cases are often as informative as positive ones and should not be ignored.

Chapter 7 explores how the motivations which drive late joining have changed to some degree since 1945. Most notably, the chapter explores the growing role international organizations have played in the spread of war and how the decline in availability of territorial spoils has altered the nature of bandwagoning. The chapter specifically looks at the Vietnam War and the 1990–91 Gulf War.

Chapter 8 concludes the work and summarizes its findings. The chapter examines how the various hypotheses and counter-hypotheses derived in Chapter 2 fared. The different ways in which states looking to balance and those looking to pick up spoils react to revealed information is also explored. Finally, the chapter proposes potential avenues for future research.

Late joining is an important and previously inadequately explained phenomenon in international relations. This work will propose and test a new explanation of why states abandon neutrality and enter wars in the manner laid out above. Before this can be done, however, the previous research on intervention must be reviewed.

Chapter 2
Previous Findings and a New Theory of Joining

> Every decision to wage war is influenced by predictions of how outside nations will affect the course of war
>
> Geoffrey Blainey (1973)

Previous attempts to explain the spread of war have taken two separate tracks. The first track examined the possibility that a war increases or decreases the chance that another war will occur at some point in the future. This is known as temporal spread. Such wars might include states involved in the first war or entirely new belligerents. The second track looked at the possibility that a war will widen to include additional states—in other words, states join an ongoing war or use the window of opportunity created by the first war to start a second war, thereby creating the spatial spread of war.[1] In addition to the idea that a war may lead to further conflict, the exact opposite, that a war will reduce the likelihood of future conflicts, must also be considered. The idea that a war may reduce the likelihood of a future war has been examined, but the negative spatial spread of war, in other words states leaving wars, has generally not been considered in the joining literature. It has been addressed in the war termination literature; however, while it is clearly related to war termination, and the case of all belligerents leaving a war is war termination, a state leaving a war should also be seen as the inverse of joining even if the departure results in the end of the war. Viewing war termination in this manner has important theoretical implications that are explored in Chapter 2.[2]

Work focusing on the temporal track found that it is unlikely that a positive or negative correlation exists between the outbreaks of wars. Richardson (1960), who

---

1 Though spatial spread has a temporal component, this work defines temporal spread to not include such phenomena. Thus, as defined here the concepts of spatial and temporal spread do not overlap. Spatial spread includes only states joining ongoing wars or states using the window of opportunity created by the first war to initiate a second war. Spatial spread incorporates both the initiation of new wars and non-belligerents joining ongoing wars (Most and Starr 1981; Most and Starr 1990). Temporal spread, however, includes two states going to war because of the example of the first, a war changing the international environment to make the system more war prone in the future, and enduring rivals re-igniting a conflict at a later time.

2 The war termination literature can greatly inform the joining literature in much the same way as it has informed the literature on the outbreak of war.

examined interstate and civil wars together for the preceding 400 years, determined that the outbreaks of wars were independent of each other and that they fit a Poisson distribution.[3] Wright (1965), however, suggests a 50-year cycle, but concludes that the evidence simply is not sufficient to support such a finding. In particular, he states that long term prediction based on periodicity is impossible.[4] Richardson also hints that there might be some long term periodicity to the frequency of war. He bases this on the work of Moyal (1949), which indicates that there may by long cycles of 50 to 200 years. Moyal, however, concluded that over shorter periods of time the outbreaks of wars are independent of each other. He and Richardson both suggest that the apparent long-term cycles may be an artifact of the way Wright collected his data.[5] Sorokin (1937) found no regular periodicity of war in either the ancient Greek or modern European state systems. Using Wright's own data, he concluded that the evidence did not even support Wright's cautious suggestion of a 50-year cycle. Singer and Small (1972) confirmed this lack of periodicity and the independence of the outbreaks of wars using the Correlates of War dataset.[6] Additionally, Levy (1982) found that wars from 1495 to 1975 with a great power on each side neither increased nor decreased the likelihood of future wars. Finally, Beck (1991) concludes that there simply is not compelling evidence that long cycles exist, and that even if they do, they are so mild as to not distort the results of studies which ignore their possible existence.

Contrary to these findings, the enduring rivalries literature argues that some dyads fight a series of wars that are causally linked (Goertz and Diehl 1995; Diehl and Goertz 2000). However, the number of enduring rivalries as enumerated by Goertz and Diehl, is nearly the same as if wars occurred randomly between state dyads.[7] Thus, again there is strong reason to doubt the existence of temporal causal links between wars. These strong, consistent, and mutually supporting results suggest that it is unlikely that either a positive or negative relationship exists between a given war and a potential future war. Certainly if such relationships do exist, their nature has yet to be well understood. Still, the enduring rivalries literature suggests that a state might be more likely to join a war if one of its enduring rivals is already in the war. Therefore, this possibility needs to be considered by any study on joining.

Scholars have had more success on the spatial track. This literature has generated four main causal reasons why states join ongoing wars.[8] First, a state's pre-existing adversary may already be engaged in war, therefore, encouraging the

---

3 Richardson 1960, 128 and 140–1. He used Wright's dataset.

4 Wright 1965, 228 and 1263.

5 Like Richardson, Moyal used Wright's dataset.

6 Similarly, Davis, Duncan and Siverson (1978) showed that what temporal clustering there is in the incidence of war is best explained by the geographic and not the temporal spread of war.

7 Gartzke and Simon 1999. They show the data fit a Poisson distribution.

8 Kadera 1998.

state to join the war to fight its adversary.[9] Second, an ongoing war provides a window of opportunity for third party states to engage in opportunistic aggression. This aggression may be against other third parties—without the threat of interference from one of the states engaged in the initial war—or bandwagoning with the successful state in the ongoing war.[10] Third, a state may join the ongoing war to protect an ally, protect its own interests, maintain the balance of power, or demonstrate its credibility.[11] Finally, the expansion of the conflict may be seen as necessary to victory, and therefore, a non-belligerent may be invaded by one of the belligerent states.[12] For example, a neighboring state may possess or lay across a supply route for raw materials vital to the war effort such as Norway and Denmark in 1940, may be seen as the most practical invasion route such as Belgium in 1914, or may be serving as a base for enemy combatants such as Greece from 1915 to 1917.[13] On top of this, Rosen (1970) and Starr (1972) claim states in wars will seek out allies not only to the extent new allies will help them win, but even to a point of vast preponderance to make the war shorter and cheaper. Clearly, this list is not theoretically driven. Rather it is a fairly exhaustive laundry list of reasons why states may join wars. As such, it provides limited leverage for understanding why and when wars spread. Indeed, this has been a problem with most joining studies. They have been primarily exploratory or purely descriptive with only limited theoretical content. This naturally makes understanding the spread of war difficult, if not impossible, since it leads to an exploration of correlations rather than focusing on the underlying causal mechanisms. Additionally, the first two reasons listed are essentially carryovers from the stalled temporal track. Still, the literature has generated some robust and useful correlations.

---

9 Houweling and Siccama, 1985. This is essentially the enduring rival hypothesis.

10 Gartzke and Gleditsch 2001; Haldi 2003; Houweling and Siccama 1985; Houweling and Siccama 1988. Actual incidences of a state using this window of opportunity to start a new war are exceedingly rare in the post-1816 period (Diehl 1991; Most, Starr, and Siverson 1989). This book does not examine this type of the spread of war, as it would require a very different type of data collection.

11 Gartzke and Gleditch 2001; Haldi 2003; Levy 1982.

12 Levy 1982.

13 Germany relied on Sweden for most of its iron ore. The delivery of this vital material could be interrupted by the Allies if they occupied Norway and Denmark. When it became apparent that they intended to do just that, Germany preemptively invaded both countries to secure the supply of Swedish iron ore (McEvedy 1982, 74). Also, the example of Greece is imperfect since the government of Greece did eventually initiate hostilities with the Central Powers. Prior to that time the Central Powers had violated Greek territory to combat Allied troops located in Greece, but Greek troops had not been actively engaged in the fighting. See Chapter 5.

Correlates of Joining

In particular, scholars have found that a state's geographic proximity to an ongoing war affects the likelihood that it will enter the war. Specifically, the nearer a state is to a war, the likelier it will join the war. Richardson (1960) found that wars tend to be geographically localized.[14] Starr and Most (1976) found evidence that the closer a state was to a war, the more likely it was to join that war. Raknerud and Hegre (1997) found that geographic contiguity increased the odds that a state would join an ongoing war six-fold. The importance of contiguity has been confirmed by many additional studies.[15] These findings fit with more general studies which determined that proximity results in more interactions and relations between entities.[16] Colonial geographic proximity, however, is less important. Siverson and Starr (1991) found that colonial borders were less likely to transmit war than were other forms of contiguity and Wright (1965) found that colonial disputes tend to remain bilateral in nature.

Being in the same region as a war was also found to be highly correlated with states joining that war. Houweling and Siccama (1985, 1988) determined that the spread of war was regional in character, rather than purely a function of distance. Others have confirmed this.[17] Additionally, Gleditsch and Ward (2000) found that understanding the regional spread of war is vital for understanding the democratic peace. The importance of being in the same region is consistent with the work of Buzan and Waever (2003). They argue that only great powers frequently interact at the global level and that the regional level is the pertinent security level for most states.[18] Most states, even great powers, primarily interact with states within their region and connections between regions are far fewer in number than those within

---

14 Specifically, "infectiousness," Richardson's word for a process similar to the popular notion of contagion, can not by itself account for the spread of war. Geography has to be considered (Richardson 1960, 270–3, and 287). It is possible to model the territorial acquisitions of states based on Richardson's findings regarding geography and the spread of war (Cederman 2003).

15 Faber, Houweling and Siccama 1984; Leeds 2005; Most and Star 1980; Siverson and Starr 1989; Siverson and Starr 1990; Siverson and Starr 1991; Vasquez 1993; Ward and Gleditsch 2002. Additionally, geographic proximity to conflicts was found to play a role in the initiation of conflicts in Africa in the 1960s and 1970s (O'Laughlin and Anselin 1991; Starr and Most 1983; Starr and Most 1985).

16 Tobler 1979; Zipf 1949.

17 Bremer 1982; Faber, Houweling and Siccama 1984; Gleditsch 2002; Pearson, Baumann, and Pickering 1994; Wallensteen and Sollenberg 1998. Even approaches arguing that conflict spreads through domestic linkages and learning rather than more Realist explanations found that the expansion of conflict had a regional character (Hammerström 1993a; Hammerström 1993b; Hammerström 1994; Hammerström 1995) or that contiguity was important (Hammerström and Heldt 2002).

18 Buzan and Waever 2003, 43.

a region.[19] Finally, even when great powers do engage in conflicts beyond their own region, those conflicts tend to stem from factors inherent to the region where the conflict originated.[20] Thus, it is reasonable to assume states will put a higher priority on conflicts within their own region and will be more likely to enter such conflicts rather than more distant conflicts.

In sum, regional proximity and contiguity can be thought of as capturing several factors. First, more proximate states are likely more concerned about the outcome of a war than are more distant states. This should be true both for states in the same region as a war and for contiguous states, though perhaps more so for contiguous states. Also, geographically proximate states should have lower costs for entering the war, as it will be less costly for them to deploy their forces.[21] Again, this should be true both for states in the same region as the war and for contiguous states, though again more so for contiguous states. Finally, contiguous states may become involved in a war because the conflict physically spills across their borders, perhaps deliberately to draw them into the conflict, including direct invasion, or accidentally, as was the case of Russian troops violating Romania's frontier in 1916.[22]

The literature also argues that great powers are more likely to join ongoing wars. Woods and Baltzly (1915) and Wright (1965) find that great powers are more likely to go to war and Wright (1965) finds they are more likely to join wars than are other states, especially if another great power is involved. Richardson (1960) finds evidence that sea powers are more likely to join wars than are other states. Richardson's list of sea powers closely matches the Correlates of War's list of great powers, with the notable exception of Austria-Hungary.[23] Altfeld and Bueno de Mesquita (1979), Pearson, Baumann, and Pickering (1994), and Siverson and Starr (1991) also find that great powers are more likely to join wars than are lesser powers. As great powers have greater capabilities, it logically follows that they would be more able to affect the outcome of a wider range of wars than lesser powers both because they have the logistical capacity to join more wars and the military power to alter the outcome of more wars. Thus, it is not surprising they would be more likely to join a greater number of wars than would other states. Interestingly, the literature finds no relationship between being a great power and

---

19 Ibid, 45.

20 Ibid, 47.

21 Boulding 1962.

22 See Chapter 5. Contiguous states also have to deal with refugee flows, whereas this is less common for states simply in the same region as a conflict. Such flows do have the potential to draw states into wars, though this seems to be more characteristic of intervention in civil wars rather than interstate wars.

23 Richardson excludes Austria-Hungary from his list until just prior to the First World War.

the propensity to balance versus bandwagon,[24] though Yamamoto and Bremer (1980) do find that great power's decisions are often contingent on whether other great powers join or not.

Alliances have also been found to aid the spread of war. Siverson and King (1979) found that having an ally in a war increased the chance of a state being drawn into the war fivefold. Raknerud and Hegre (1997) found defense pacts and ententes raised the chance a war would spread by a factor of 21. This correlation between alliances and the expansion of war likely exists because, as Leeds (2005, 121–30) argues, alliances involve more states in the bargaining process. Additional studies by Most, Siverson and Starr as well as Huth and Russett (1984) found that alliances tended to transmit wars from one ally to another.[25] Siverson and Starr (1991) suggest alliances may help overcome geopolitical constraints that would otherwise limit joining. Furthermore, Snyder (1997) argues alliances generally reflect underlying interests and often serve as proxies for such interests. In other words, states may join wars not because they are required to do so by their terms of alliance, but rather because they share interests, such as opposing an aggressor, with a belligerent that happens to be their ally.

Interestingly, despite the apparent strong connection between alliances and joining, alliance reliability has been found to be remarkably low. Sabrosky (1980) and Siverson and King (1980) both found that states come to the aid of their alliance partners only about a quarter of the time. The literature, however, does not discriminate between states honoring the actual terms of the alliance and states entering a war on the same side as an ally for other reasons. Leeds, Long, and Mitchell (2000) suggest this accounts for the low level of alliance reliability. Thus, states often are not bound by treaty to come to their ally's aid in the specific situation brought on by the given war or need only offer assistance short of joining the war.[26]

Additionally, it may be that there is a selection effect at work. Fearon (1994), Gartner and Siverson (1996), Smith (1995), and Smith (1996) all argue that aggressors should be far more inclined to challenge alliances they suspect are unreliable. Alliances that are deemed reliable by aggressors help deter war, and therefore, are effective.[27] However, because of this they do not necessarily lead to

24 Jones 1994. Jones also finds that balancing is only slightly more common than bandwagoning for all states. The weaker side of a conflict is no more likely to get aid than is the stronger side (Cusack and Stoll 1991).

25 Most and Starr 1980; Siverson and Starr 1989; Siverson and Starr 1990; Siverson and Starr 1991. See Vasquez (1987) for a good summary of the literature on the connection between alliances and the spread of war. The more flexibility there is in alliances, the less likely war is to expand (Kegley and Raymond 1994).

26 Belligerents may also dissuade allies from joining a war in order to avoid further complicating the war's diplomacy. More will be said of this later.

27 This effect of successful general and immediate deterrence has been widely discussed in the literature at large. See Leeds (2005) for a discussion of how defensive alliances lower the probability of dispute initiation and why such alliances, if known

joining or war and thus do not show up in alliance reliability studies. Thus, alliances that are deemed suspect by aggressors, and therefore prone to fail, are the ones that primarily show up in reliability studies, which in turn makes alliances appear less reliable than they are. In fact, this selection effect is one reason why joining is a fairly rare phenomena. Many wars that are likely to experience joining simply do not occur because aggressors are deterred by potential joiners.[28] Unfortunately, there is another effect working here as well. A particularly credible commitment may actually embolden the threatened state into more bellicose actions versus its rival. It is, therefore, possible that some alliances may actually increase the likelihood of war.[29] Thus, the overall effect of credible alliances on the initial outbreak of war is unclear as these two effects—emboldening the third party's ally and deterring its ally's rival—work in opposite directions. Regardless, of whether alliances are in fact more reliable than they initially appear, they do appear to be strongly correlated with joining.

Even this finding, however, is not completely unchallenged. First, Kadera (1998) shows that Siverson and Starr's coding of alliances is problematic. They code non-aggression pacts as a mild form of alliance in between entente and defense pacts. While this might be proper for true neutrality pacts, many non-aggression pacts are actually a result of tensions between two states and are a sign of enmity, not of friendship or shared interests.[30] Thus, they may actually be good predictors of future conflict.[31]

Second, Haldi (2003) claims that alliances do not matter at all, coding problems or not, and that any relationship between alliances and intervention is entirely

antebellum, should not affect the likelihood of conflict after general deterrence fails. Known alliances affect the likelihood of dispute initiation, but not necessarily the likelihood of war, though they may lead to wider wars (Leeds 2003; Leeds 2005).

28 Gartner and Siverson (1996).

29 Crawford 2003; Jervis 1994; Leeds 2005; Leng 1993; Smith 1995; Smith 1996. The fundamental problem is that the third party wants to deter both its ally's enemy and its ally from going to war. This problem is nicely illustrated in Chapter 4 on the Crimean War. Furthermore, states are more likely to be deterred by threats if they are acting opportunistically, rather than out of vulnerability. In particular, threats of intervention are more likely to be successful when the threat of intervention is an attempt to deter opportunism (Davis 1995; Davis 2000). Thus, threats may often be sufficient to deter predatory behavior, but not behavior that the aggressor perceives as actually being defensive. For this reason, predatory wars are more likely to be censored than are other wars.

30 Kadera 1998. Neutrality pacts may also indicate friendship, while failing to aggregate power (Snyder 1997). If only defense pacts and ententes are examined, alliances are correlated with joining (Altfeld and Bueno de Mesquita 1979). While this further suggests Siverson and Starr's coding is problematic, it suggests their results may be sound despite their suspect treatment of alliances.

31 Kadera 1998. Neutrality pacts might still indicate a state is likely to be drawn into conflict, but against its erstwhile alliance partner.

spurious.[32] In fact, Haldi suggests that a desire to enter a war may in fact lead to alliances. Haldi cites the "Diplomatic Revolution" just prior to the outbreak of the Seven Years War in Europe as evidence of this. Jones (1994) also finds that defensive pacts are not correlated with wars widening. Haldi concedes Siverson and Starr's finding that alliances are correlated with intervention in the post-Napoleonic era, but found no evidence for the transmission of interstate conflict by alliances in the 18th century, nor in the Napoleonic era.[33] One reason for this discrepancy may be that Haldi examined alliances as a whole, while Siverson and Starr weighted the different types of treaties. This possibility will be examined in Chapter 3.

Another potential source of the discrepancy is that Haldi and Siverson and Starr examined different time periods. It may be that for the earlier periods in Haldi's study, the conclusions about alliances are correct. There is no compelling evidence to suggest otherwise as the data in this study and Siverson and Starr's studies cover only the post-Napoleonic period. It is possible that alliances in the period studied by Haldi were simply different from more recent alliances.[34] Alliances, like many other things, have changed in character over time and Haldi does not examine any cases of intervention more recent than World War One. Many and perhaps most formal alliances since the Second World War have been long-term in nature rather than temporary expedients. Such pacts are neither easily nor quickly made. Perhaps this trend toward more permanent, and therefore, more politically meaningful alliances has been a long one. If so, this hypothesized changing nature of alliances may help to explain the discrepancy between Haldi's findings and the rest of the literature. Certainly, such a study would prove interesting, though it is beyond the scope of this book. Additionally, assume for the moment that in the 18th and very early 19th centuries alliances did not transmit war. As will be discussed in more detail later in this chapter, Haldi claims that the political costs of joining a war were much lower prior to the Napoleonic Wars, and therefore, joining was far more common. This finding and the change in the importance of alliances may in fact be related. An increase in political costs would make joining any conflict, but especially a conflict in which a state did not have a prior commitment, unattractive. Prior to the rise in political costs, it could very well be that joining was attractive

---

32 Even if Haldi is correct that alliances do not transmit wars between alliance partners, this does not mean alliances are irrelevant more broadly speaking. They may be formed to influence diplomatic outcomes, rather than military outcomes.

33 Haldi did not run a robust statistical analysis on pre-Napoleonic and Napoleonic era alliances, so it is possible a small, but significant relationship between alliances and joining in these time periods was missed.

34 Prior to the Franco-Russian alliance in the late 19th century, alliances were almost always of short duration and formed for a specific purpose—the British-Portuguese alliance is a partial exception—rather than the "permanent" alliances we see today. Such short-term, issue specific alliances might be very poor predictors of alignment in a war that is unrelated to the reason why the alliance was formed.

irrespective of alliances, and thus, any tendency for alliances to transmit wars was hidden by the general willingness of states to join ongoing wars.

Despite the findings of Haldi and Jones, there are sufficient reasons to think that alliances, especially defense pacts and ententes, do increase the likelihood of joining. Most likely, any effect alliances have on joining should happen rather quickly. If, soon after the conflict begins, third parties decide not to enter a war in which their ally is embroiled, it is unlikely that the alliance will affect their decision later. Any subsequent decision to join will have to be based on some new factor. Thus, it seems likely that having an alliance with a belligerent increases a state's likelihood of joining in the early stages of that war.

The relationship between regime type and a state's propensity to join ongoing wars has to be considered as well. While Reiter and Stam (2002) found that democracies are no more likely to come to the aid of their fellow democracies than any other regime type once other relevant factors are taken into account, other studies have reached the opposite conclusion. Gleditsch and Hegre (1997) find that democracies are four times more likely to fight along side fellow democracies than with other regime types. Werner and Lemke (1997) show this propensity cannot be explained by alliance portfolios alone. This tendency to come to the aid of other democracies results in democracies joining wars involving fellow democracies at a higher rate than autocracies do.[35]

So far the impact of geography, alliances, regime type, and great power status on the likelihood that non-belligerents will join ongoing wars has been discussed. The impact of institutions has been neglected. In general, the literature on the spread of war has ignored the role of institutions, though truthfully, alliances can be viewed as a type of institution. Indeed, much of the international security institutions literature focuses on alliances.[36] Even so, the treatment of institutions in the literature has been scanty. This is not the glaring omission it first seems, as most international institutions focus on economics or issues of so called "low politics" such as public health. There is no compelling theoretical reason to think such institutions affect the spread of war. Other international institutions, like NATO, are simply highly organized alliances and as such have already been addressed.[37] Still, there are genuine international institutions that deal with security issues. As Keohane, Haftendorn, and Wallander (1999) argue, international security is an institutionalized domain. There is evidence that such institutions reduce the likelihood of conflict between members and that on occasion they can reduce the scope of a conflict, but it is difficult to spin out concrete hypotheses about joining from these findings.[38] This results from the tendency of the literature to focus on how institutions affect the likelihood of the initial outbreak of war. Such

35 Gleditsch and Hegre 1997; Raknerrud and Hegre 1997.

36 Gelpi 1999; Richardson 1999; Tams 1999; Tuschhoff 1999.

37 While NATO is sometimes described as a collective security arrangement, it is really a traditional alliance (Betts 1992).

38 Richardson 1999; Russett and Oneal 2001.

studies have found that institutions can reduce uncertainty, reduce transaction costs, facilitate side payments and policy coordination, help form coalitions, shape norms, and coerce norm-breakers.[39] Many of these attributes should allow regimes and institutions to reduce or mitigate conflict, though some, such as coercing norm-breakers, as well as aiding policy coordination and the formation of coalitions, may exacerbate conflicts. In general, institutions often fail to get involved in conflicts directly.[40] Still, institutions often do attempt to mediate conflicts. Such mediation efforts might reduce the chance conflicts will spread by shortening their length and by mediating between belligerents and non-belligerents. However, at present there is little evidence that such attempts significantly affect the likelihood non-belligerents will enter a war. In fact, it seems possible that mediation efforts might increase the likelihood that a conflict will spread by drawing additional states into the bargaining process.[41]

This is particularly a danger in collective security arrangements. Betts (1992) and to a lesser extend Claude (1962) argue that collective security arrangements may cause wars to spread. At first this seems perverse, but it is a logical result of collective security arrangements. These arrangements mandate that members of the institution act militarily to punish any aggressor. They are not aimed at any specific state. Thus, collective security requires states to join wars to punish aggression, thereby turning what might have been a small war into a large war.[42] This was precisely one of the criticisms by the American opponents of the League of Nations. Senator Henry Cabot Lodge asserted the League's "decisions are to be carried out by force ... This league to enforce peace does a great deal for enforcement and very little for peace."[43] True, effective collective security will deter wars from occurring in the first place, but if war does break out, the norm of collective security makes it impossible for disputes to remain localized. Additionally, Morgenthau (1973) argues some states might come to the aid of the initial aggressor due either to prior treaty obligations, enmity toward one of the states acting in the name of collective security, or out of a desire to keep the initial aggressor from being crushed.[44] These motives could further spread the conflict beyond the members of the collective security organization. This hypothesis, though logical, has yet to be rigorously tested. Additionally, by sanctioning intervention, legitimate security organizations like the United Nations undoubtedly lower the political costs for

---

39 Axelrod and Keohane 1985; Keohane 1982; Keohane and Nye 1974; Russett and Oneal 2001; Wallander and Keohane 1999.

40 Keohane, Haftendorn, and Wallander 1999, 333.

41 This is similar to the argument put forward by Leeds (2005) about why alliances may broaden conflicts.

42 Betts 1992.

43 Claude 1962, 99. Similar views were held by Secretary of State Robert Lansing and Senator Arthur Capper.

44 The aggressor, if it is clear who that is, may not be one state but a coalition (Claude 1962, 195–7, and 203).

joining a war and perhaps create some political costs for not joining.[45] Thus, a collective security organization, something the UN on occasion approximates, can increase the likelihood states will enter a war.

Since 1815 there have been only three institutions, two formal, one informal, which can reasonably be claimed as collective security institutions. They are the Concert of Europe, the League of Nations, and the United Nations. The Concert of Europe was not a true collective security arrangement—nor did the great powers ever want it to be a collective security organization—not because it was informal, but rather because it was really a selective security arrangement.[46] It sought to preserve peace between the great powers by satisfying their interests at the expense of the lesser powers and aimed to avoid major wars by allowing great powers to win minor wars as long as their aims remained limited. The Concert allowed France's invasion of Spain in 1823 and Russia's invasion of the Ottoman Empire in 1828.[47] Never did the Concert mobilize states to punish aggression. The Concert fell apart as a result of France and Britain aiding the Ottomans in the face of Russian aggression, though this was not the result of the norm of collective security, but rather the result of France and Britain each acting in their own interest.[48] Obviously, collective security can be in the national interest, however, there is no evidence that Britain and France were acting out of a concern for collective security. Rather, Britain wanted to prevent Russia from controlling the Dardanelles and France saw it as an opportunity to end her diplomatic isolation.[49] Prussia and Austria never entered the conflict, reinforcing the notion that France's and Britain's entries into the war were not the result of collective security. The League of Nations did aspire to be a true collective security organization, but its failure to achieve this is infamous. When faced with the crises of the 1930s, the League proved ineffective and the norm of collective security was never effectively enforced.

The United Nations has also had its difficulties in bringing about collective security. For much of the Cold War, the UN was paralyzed by the rivalry between the US and the USSR. More recently, it has proven ineffective when faced with wars in the Balkans and with the recent US invasion of Iraq. On two occasions, however, the UN has acted in a manner that reasonably approximated that of a true collective security arrangement: the Korean War and the 1990–91 Gulf War.[50]

---

45 Altfeld and Bueno de Mesquita (1979) argue that the UN's involvement in the Korean War altered states' utilities for joining that war. Unfortunately, this leads them to drop the case, rather than test the proposition that UN actions can alter the expected utility of states' for joining ongoing wars. In the same study, they show that intervention in the nuclear era looks very much like intervention in the pre-nuclear era.

46 Betts 1992.

47 Ibid.

48 See Chapter 4.

49 Haldi 2003.

50 On both of these occasions, great power rivalry within the UN was muted. It was muted during the Korean War because the USSR was boycotting the UN at that time and the

Many states became involved in these wars that would not have done so if not for the UN. Intervention in both wars would have remained almost exclusively American with perhaps an ally or two. Instead, through the auspices of the UN, many states became involved to support the norm of punishing aggression. Admittedly, the actions of these states likely aligned with their interests, but it is highly unlikely that they would have become active belligerents if not for the involvement of the UN. Additionally, though some states' contributions were more symbolic that substantive, many states that would not have otherwise participated sent significant forces to these wars. Clearly, in these two cases the role of collective security arrangements needs to be considered as a control variable. Looking at only these two cases is obviously insufficient for testing Betts' hypothesis as it is a case of selecting on the dependent variable. Despite this limitation, it is important to consider the UN's role in the growth of these two wars as a control variable.

Thus, the literature suggests that geographic proximity, alliances, and collective security arrangements should all be positively correlated with joining. Though these correlations are informative, there remains a gaping void in understanding why wars spread. A theory that explains which states join, when they join, and why they join is needed. Three theoretically based attempts at understanding such behavior have been made; however, none sufficiently explains the motives for joining, especially late joining.

Previous Theories of Joining

The best known of the two is the "willingness and opportunity" framework (Siverson and Starr 1990; Siverson and Starr 1991). Siverson and Starr argue that states need both the opportunity and the willingness to join an ongoing war.[51] In their framework, opportunity is captured by the variable "warring border nations" and willingness is captured by the variable "warring alliance partners." A "warring border nation" is a state currently at war that is contiguous to the non-belligerent under consideration. A "warring alliance partner" is a state at war that is allied to the non-belligerent under consideration. Their theory has several strengths. First, it recognizes that both strategic interaction and conscious decision-making influence the likelihood states will join ongoing wars. In doing so, they correctly argue both that it is necessary to distinguish states that voluntarily join wars from those that do so because they were invaded and that the passage of time alone cannot explain

---

Chinese seat was still held by the Nationalists. On the second occasion, great power rivalry was muted by the end of the Cold War.

51 Their approach cannot explain the fourth type of intervention found in the literature: that occupying a state may be seen as necessary to victory. In such a case, the non-belligerent is forced into the war against its will, usually because it is invaded. Siverson and Starr's testing of geographic proximity, however, should capture this type of intervention even if their theory does not.

why states join wars. Instead, states have to decide to join. Second, it captures the idea that geographic proximity plays an important role, which has been shown to be important by many previous studies.

The theory has two main drawbacks. First, willingness—the strategic interaction component of the theory—is captured only through states having allies already involved in war. Though it is logical that alliances would affect the likelihood of a non-belligerent entering a war—and there is evidence to this effect—it clearly is not the only component of willingness, nor probably the most important. States may join ongoing conflicts in which their allies are not involved and states also frequently fail to come to the aid of their allies. Also, as will be shown in the next chapter, alliances tend to be correlated with joining only in the first month of a war. This makes sense as alliance portfolios tend to remain fairly steady over the course of wars. If having an alliance with a belligerent does not cause a state to voluntarily join initially, it is not clear why the continuing existence of that alliance should cause that state to join voluntarily at a later date. Thus, Siverson and Starr do not explain the willingness component behind late joining. Clearly, there is much more to willingness than just alliances. Second, their explanation for the timing of entry is insufficient. They find that states with more warring alliance partners and more warring border nations join sooner than those with fewer such treatments. While it makes sense that a state with more treatments should be more likely to join, it is not clear why a state that has sufficient treatments to join, but fewer than another joiner should take longer. What sort of decision-making process is occurring in a state that joins later? Why are the number of treatments not sufficient in the first few months of the war, but causal of voluntary entry later in the war? Siverson and Starr do not provide an answer. Simowitz and Sheffer found that their approach so utterly failed to advance the understanding of the spread of war that they claimed the field had become degenerative in a Lakatosian sense.[52] While this judgment is obviously far too harsh,[53] the "willingness and opportunity" framework as operationalized by Siverson and Starr clearly leaves much unanswered about why states voluntarily join ongoing wars, especially after the early stages. What they present is not wrong, but further explanation of joining is needed.

The second approach is Haldi's (2003) political costs explanation. Haldi claims that the political costs of entering a war, which are based on risks of losing influence, territory, and the fall of the regime, determine the likelihood that wars will spread. If the political costs of entering are low, intervention will be more common and it will most often take the form of predation. If costs are high, few states will join ongoing wars and when they do, they will balance. Smaller powers, however, should still join only for purposes of predation. Such an assertion is logical and Haldi's case studies do offer evidence to support this assertion, but the

52 Simowitz (1998); Simowitz and Sheffer (1998).

53 Starr and Siverson (1998) offers a strong rebuttal to the charge that research on joining has become degenerative.

logic begs the question of why the political costs are high or low in the first place. Also, Haldi finds that the only true variation in the level of political costs is that prior to the Napoleonic Wars costs were low and after the Napoleonic Wars they were high.[54] Thus, Haldi's theory offers no help in understanding why intervention occurs in some wars and not in others in the post-Napoleonic era. Obviously, this is unsatisfying. Additionally, Haldi's explanation of what drives political costs is problematic. Haldi reasonably argues that if wars are limited wars, there are few risks to joining, and thus political costs are low, while if wars are total, there are many risks to joining, and therefore, political risks are high. Haldi argues that wars prior to 1803 were limited and since 1803 they have been total. While the trend may have been towards total wars since 1803, it seems very difficult to argue that all wars since 1803 have been total and that all wars before 1803 were limited. On top of this, Haldi's claim that states will join for predation in limited wars seems suspect if, as she argues, there are few changes in territorial alignments or influence. True, the risks associated with joining such wars are low, but so are the rewards. Haldi's logic holds only if states are very risk averse. Even if this is true, the theory's inability to predict variations in levels of intervention since 1803—or before 1803 for that matter—is troubling. Moreover, in the post-Napoleonic era, large wars with many participants, especially both world wars, are precisely the wars that have entailed the greatest risks for participants. It is puzzling from the viewpoint of Haldi's theory why so many states would have joined such wars despite the high risk. Clearly, this is a serious problem for Haldi's theory. Finally, like Siverson and Starr, Haldi offers little in the way of explanation for the timing of when states join wars. Haldi's work does at least suggest that the causes of intervention changed significantly during the Napoleonic era and thus the 1816 cutoff used by this study and many others is not arbitrary, but is in fact substantively justified. In *toto*, however, Haldi's work adds very little to our understanding of when states join ongoing wars.

The final approach is that of Altfeld and Bueno de Mesquita (1979). They argue that rational states benefit from joining wars by mainly changing the probability one side will win. They also suggest there should be a small benefit directly related to honoring alliance commitments as this would improve a state's reputation. Thus, rational states need to be concerned with which side will win and whether their contribution can alter the war's outcome. Potential joiners will have a preferred outcome for a war and may want to bear costs to increase the likelihood that their preferred outcome occurs. There will be uncertainty, however, about the distribution of power in the international system, and thus, about both the likely outcome of any given war and any potential joiner's ability to change that outcome. For this reason, it may often make sense for states to join the side they think will win to increase the probability that side will in fact win, rather than staying on the side lines and hoping that the preferred, and apparently stronger, side wins. Since great powers are more likely to be able to significantly influence

54 Haldi estimates the exact tipping point to be 1803.

the probability one side will win, they should be more likely to join than lesser powers. Altfeld and Bueno de Mesquita also find that nuclear weapons have not significantly altered the joining dynamic.

Altfeld and Bueno de Mesquita's use of a rational actor model and their focus on war outcome and uncertainty are strengths of the approach. However, in order to avoid complications with bandwagoning motives, they look at joining only in the first two months of a conflict. Additionally, their approach also does not attempt to explain the timing of joining. Thus, their model raises a number factors affecting willingness to join which should be included in theories of joining, but it cannot explain late joining, the timing of joining, nor does it address how events within wars affect states' estimates about the outcome of those wars.

Given these existing theoretically driven explanations of the spread of war, a new theoretically driven, causal explanation is needed in order to understand the process of states joining ongoing wars in the modern era. Such an explanation should be able to incorporate the correlations established in the existing literature and it should be able to explain not only which states join wars, but when they do so. It should also be able to incorporate the idea that late joiners are acting on perceived opportunities to revise the status quo, the desire to join one side for their own protection, or a need to balance,[55] but also explain what causes them to perceive or act on such needs and opportunities months or years after a war began, but not at its outset. To this end, this work offers a new theoretical approach for explaining interstate military intervention in general and its timing in particular, based on the proposition that wars are a bargaining process and a mechanism for revealing information.

War, Peace, and Revealed Information

At the beginning of wars all states decide whether to fight or not. Rationally, in order for states to change that decision, they must be privy to new information which changes the expected benefits of belligerency relative to peace. This information changes their perceived costs and benefits of joining and ultimately can change states' calculations about whether to enter. Wars are in essence strategic learning processes from which both belligerents and non-belligerents gather information.[56] Non-belligerents react to information generated or revealed by the war. Thus, states should enter wars shortly after new or private information that changes their calculations is revealed. This is not to say that all states will react to new information. New information is not a sufficient cause; states will need to have a great deal at stake and be able to react militarily in order for new information to trigger belligerency. New information can be thought of as a loosely necessary cause. In other words, while there maybe other paths to war, in the revealed

55 Schweller 1994; Walt 1985.

56 Goemans 2000.

information path, the information acts as a necessary cause. Thus states which do join, whether to balance or pick up spoils, most of the time should be reacting to new information and the revelation of this information should dictate the timing of their entry.

To understand why information drives joining, it is necessary to realize that wars are dynamic, evolving processes which rational states expect to lead to negotiated settlements,[57] not one-shot costly lotteries.[58] States continue to bargain and make decisions after wars have begun.[59] In other words wars are a continuation of bargaining, albeit in a tacit and much more costly form, in which information is revealed and costs imposed causing the range of acceptable bargains for all parties, including non-belligerents, to shift.[60] States continuously weigh the value of proposed offers against the value of no agreement and the expected value of continued bargaining.[61] Wars clarify the distribution of power, goals, and reservation prices of the combatants, thereby bringing about peace. As these factors become clearer due to new and revealed information, the belligerents will alter their demands until an agreement acceptable to both sides is reached.[62] The lack of such an agreement, tacit or otherwise, causes war.[63] Just like onset of a new war, an ongoing war will widen if an agreement, tacit or otherwise, between a belligerent and a non-belligerent unravels.[64]

This is because states obtain information about themselves and other states not only from wars in which they are involved, but also from wars in which they are not yet involved. Any event, even an outside event, causing unanticipated changes in relative military capabilities is a reason for states to change their expectations and hence their actions.[65] While it is more difficult for an outsider to obtain

57 Kecskemeti (1958). Settlement, as used here, indicates an end to a conflict through negotiation rather than conquest, not necessarily a resolution of the issues that led to war in the first place. Most wars, especially since 1945 have led to negotiated settlements rather than total military defeats (Fazal 2004; Fazal 2007).

58 This is consistent with the conclusion that war is the continuation of diplomacy by other means (Blainey 1973; Clausewitz 1976; Downs and Rocke 1994; Goemans 2000; Iklé 1971; Pillar 1983; Simmel 1904; Smith 1998a; Wagner 2000). While it may seem obvious that war is not a one shot costly lottery, it is not uncommon for game theoretic articles to view war as just such a one-shot process. See especially Fearon (1995), but also Powell (1999), Schultz (1999), and Smith (1998a). Powell (2004) is the best example of newer game theoretic work which returns to the older tradition of seeing war as a form of bargaining, but Filson and Werner (2002a, 2002b), Kim (2002), Slantchev (2002, 2003), Smith (1998b) and Smith and Stam (2004) are also good examples.

59 Smith 1998a; Wagner 2000.

60 Goemans 2000; Wagner 2000.

61 Iklé 1964.

62 Blainey 1973.

63 Goemans 2000; Wittman 1979.

64 Blainey 1973.

65 Pillar 1983.

information than for a combatant, wars should reveal significant information to non-belligerents through such sources as military observers, intelligence services, journalists, and refugees.[66]

Because of this ability to gather and react to information, the actions of one pair of states are not independent from those of outside states.[67] Thus any bargaining between two states, including war, can affect third parties and their settlements with the initial two parties.[68] For example, the defeat of the Swedes by the Imperial forces at the battle of Nordlingen in 1634 made it clear the Imperial forces had seized the upper hand in the Thirty Years War. Yet, instead of leading to peace, it quickly resulted in an increase in Austrian demands and the eventual entry of France into the war. France's involvement was a direct result of the unexpectedly decisive Imperial victory at Nordlingen and France's unwillingness to accept a decisive Habsburg victory.[69]

Similarly, third parties can affect the bargaining of the initial states. This is because belligerents may wish to attract other states to their side and almost always will want to avoid having states enter against them.[70] There may be actions belligerents can take, or avoid taking, that will influence a third party decision-making. For instance, limiting the stakes of the war may reduce the incentives for third parties to join due to balancing concerns.[71] In essence, such limiting of demands can be seen as undermining the potential joiner's resolve by greatly reducing the costs it would suffer for remaining neutral. This is not to say the potential joiner did not affect the course of the war. Such a conclusion would be precisely wrong. Thus, the possibility of intervention causes belligerents to fight and choose the stakes of war *strategically*, not only to influence their current opponents, but also to affect the likelihood that third parties will join.

Prussian actions in the Seven Weeks War demonstrate this selection effect. Bismarck intentionally limited Prussian demands, especially territorial demands, when negotiating a settlement with Austria for the express reason of discouraging French involvement.[72] Thus, though the possibility of intervention did not deter the

66 This is not to say non-belligerents will be able to gather perfect information on the embattled states. They clearly cannot, nor can the belligerents.

67 Richardson 1960.

68 Iklé 1964.

69 McEvedy 1972, 42.

70 This, however, is not a given. There are clearly cases in which a state, C, joining a war on the same side as state, A, actually hurts A. This may be because C's participation opens up new avenues of attack that were not available when C was neutral, such as Romania in 1917, that C may have supply problems and would be a drain on A's resources, such as Italy in 1940, or that the entry of C may lead to the entry of other states into the conflict against A or to the desertion of A's allies, such as Israel if it had entered the 1990–91 Gulf War. Also, A may wish to avoid having to share the spoils with C. See Chapter 5 for details on Romania and Chapter 7 for Israel. See Murray (1984) for Italy.

71 Werner 2000.

72 McEvedy 1982.

Table 2.1 Probable Settlements and State Motives for Joining

	C is Worried about B's Expansion	C has Predatory Motives versus B
A is Doing Better	C is less likely to join—A is in less need of aid	C is more likely to join—Can more easily acquire spoils from B
A is Doing Worse	C is more likely to join—Needs to balance unless B moderates demands	C is less likely to join—Scared off by B's success

war itself, it did deter Prussia from inflicting a more severe defeat on its opponent. Additionally, credible threats should cause belligerents to alter their war-fighting strategies. For example, in the First Schleswig-Holstein War, Prussian forces advanced beyond the duchies in question and occupied the whole of Jutland. This additional advance worried Sweden and led the Swedes to threaten war unless Prussia withdrew. The Prussians soon withdrew back to the duchies and Sweden did not enter the war.[73]

Thus, events within wars change the range of acceptable settlements for all parties, including non-belligerents. If antebellum peace is seen as a form of tacit agreement, then a third party's willingness to remain a non-belligerent should also be seen as a form of tacit agreement. For example, take a scenario where C may intervene on A's side, in A's war with B. Events in the war between A and B can change the probability of C having military success if it were to join the war on behalf of A. Such events can also change the probable settlement of that war. This new probable settlement may be more or less acceptable to C than the previously anticipated settlement. Therefore, events in the ongoing war between A and B should change the range of acceptable settlements between C and B that would keep C out of the war and hence the likelihood that C will join.

What sort of events should be most likely to bring about these shifts? Sudden, dramatic changes in battlefield fortunes or similar changes in the dominant indicators by which strategies are evaluated should be especially likely to bring about shifts in states bargaining ranges.[74] As Goertz posits, "What if those beliefs [about power relationships] change because of a dramatic power shock? Then a country's expected utility may jump; hence it may become rational to intervene

73 Longmans, Green, etc. 1848–49 .

74 Gartner 1997; Iklé 1971.

in an ongoing conflict."[75] Similarly, in referring to the Molotov-Ribbentrop Pact, Wright stated that:

> A single unexpected change in relations, such as that of the Soviet-German pact, had an influence on many relations ... Probably such changes, altering at least temporarily the entire international configuration, are the least predictable elements in the probability of war between two states.[76]

Thus, information that is unexpected or surprising should be particularly well suited as an indicator of when states will join ongoing wars.[77] New information may reveal a new power distribution as Goertz suggests or it may indicate the need to balance due to the revelation of a commitment problem, an opportunity to pick up spoils, or a chance to obtain a seat at the conference table. The information may also indicate that joining a war now would allow the joiner to tip the balance of the war. Thus, a smaller state's decision to join may affect the war's outcome far beyond what its proportional contribution would suggest.[78] Such a state would get spoils far larger than what its power and degree of fighting would normally warrant.[79]

This is not to say all new or revealed information will cause states to join wars—the revelation of information in not a sufficient cause of war. Only if the revealed information makes joining the original war or initiating a second war appear more attractive, will the probability that war will spread increase. Despite this uncertainty, it is still possible to test the proposition that revealed information will lead to intervention. This is because it is reasonable to assume that if a non-belligerent has not joined the war, it finds the prospects of entering the war unappealing. If the non-belligerent found joining attractive, it would have joined at some prior point. If no information is revealed, it is safe to presume that intervention will remain unattractive and that the state will not enter the ongoing war. New information, however, may make joining the war attractive. Thus, when information is revealed, joining will be attractive some positive percentage of the time, while joining should never be attractive without new information. Thus, *ceteris paribus*, there should be a positive correlation between unexpected events and states joining ongoing wars.

75 Goertz 1994, 83; Most and Starr 1980. Unexpected events play the role of "agents of contagion" (Siverson and King 1979).

76 Wright 1965, 1281.

77 While military innovation is particularly hard in war, militaries often do reevaluate their strategies and try to improve the success of their strategies over the course of a war (Rosen 1991). Organizations are able to evaluate if events are proceeding as expected and if they are performing as expected.

78 Russett 1968, 296.

79 Starr (1972).

There are two main potential objections to the proposition that new or revealed information causes non-belligerents to join war which need to be addressed. First, because events not only reveal information, but also change the probability of winning, they therefore change the range of acceptable settlements for all parties.[80] This would seem to cause a problem, as any event within a war would cause the demands of both the belligerents and any potential joiners to shift simultaneously, thereby preventing a rupture in relations from occurring. It does not. Though the shifts of each side's settlement range are not independent of each other, they need not shift by exactly the same amount. This is because, although events reveal information to all parties, they do not necessarily reveal the same amount of information to everyone. For example, an event may reveal a great deal of private information about belligerents' relative capabilities. The event may reveal that one side is doing better than anyone, including the potential joiners, expected; but the potential joiners may have learned more because the belligerent already had information about, and more accurate expectations for, its own capabilities. Just because multiple states are updating their expectations based on the same event does not mean that they will learn the same amount. Since states will update their expectations based on different amounts of new information, their bargaining ranges will shift by different amounts. This in turn will lead toward a greater convergence or divergence of demands thereby potentially destroying existing settlements or allowing new ones to form. Thus, revealed information can cause non-belligerents to join ongoing wars.

In Figure 2.1, states A and B—solid and dashed lines respectively—are at peace, but A is at war with a third state. Initially, as shown in Set 1, their bargaining ranges overlap. Information revealed in A's war causes both A and B to assume A will do better than expected leading A to increase and B to lower its demands

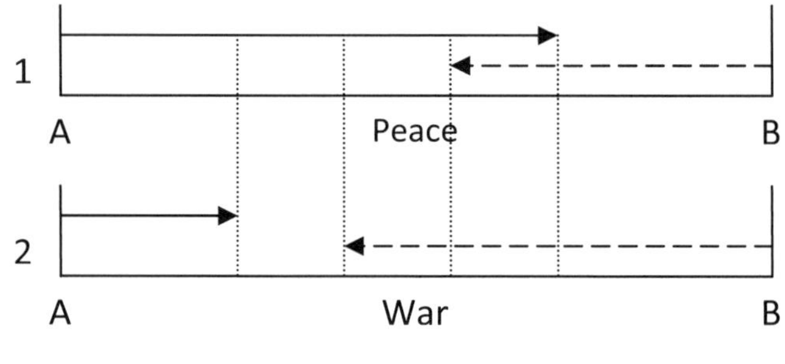

Figure 2.1 Revealed Information and Shifting Bargaining Ranges

80 Wittman 1979.

respectively. This is shown in Set 2.[81] A, however, increases its demands by more than B lowers its demands, causing B to join the war against A.

A second potential objection, arising out of Fearon (1995), is that since private or unknown information are necessary causes of rational war and that rational war is impossible with complete information,[82] revealing information should lead to peace, not joining. In fact, these two propositions are not at odds with one another because even after new information is revealed, much uncertainty remains. The apparent tension stems from the false notion that given war is a mechanism for revealing information, *ceteris paribus*, the less private information there is, the less likely war is to occur. [83] This can easily be shown to be false. For example, the discovery of Soviet missiles in Cuba in 1962 was clearly a case of private information being revealed, but it increased rather than reduced the likelihood of war as it raised questions about US, and especially, Soviet intentions. Thus while some uncertainty is necessary for war to occur, it does not follow that the less uncertainty there is, the less likely war is to occur.[84] Additionally, new information may create new types of uncertainty, as illustrated by the Cuban Missile crisis above.

Smith and Stam (2004) argue that with the exact same information different states could have different estimates about the likely course of a war. This could result from psychological or bureaucratic biases, but need not. Rather two rational actors can have different frameworks for analyzing information and thus believe that the same data leads to different conclusions.[85] Like the example of the Cuban Missile Crisis, this helps show that the apparent deduction that the more information that is revealed the less likely there will be conflict is false. However, the role of battles becomes different using Smith and Stam's analytical framework. Where previously battles and other events in war revealed private information, when viewed through this lens they test the veracity of the analytical

81 Longer arrows indicate lower demands as the range of acceptable settlements is further from the state's ideal point.

82 Side payments can solve the problem of indivisibility and commitment problems are just a special type of private information. This makes private information and information that is unknowable by either side antebellum necessary causes of all rational wars (Gartzke 1999). Additionally, private information is a necessary cause of crises (Bueno de Mesquita, Morrow, and Zorick 1997).

83 Information regarding a state's reservation price, however, should always reduce the likelihood of conflict.

84 Supporting that more uncertainty does not necessarily mean a higher likelihood of war is the finding that uncertainty is not a sufficient cause of war in formal models (Leventoğlu and Tarar 2008).

85 This sort of rational disagreement in the face of identical information is not uncommon in debates among social and natural scientists (Smith and Stam 2004). Bargaining rigidities and bargaining costs can also bring about conflict with complete information (Chadefaux 2005). Interestingly, Chadefaux also concludes that sudden changes in things like relative power can cause bargains to break down resulting in war.

frameworks states were using to draw conclusions based upon the information available prior to the event. In other words, battles generate new information and act as sort of experiment which can help confirm or refute a state's calculations. Thus, belligerents and non-belligerents will still update their calculations and change their strategies based on events within the war, but the focus becomes new information rather than revealed private information. Likely both processes are at work in actual wars.

Thus, new and revealed information changes non-belligerents' calculations about the merits of joining ongoing wars or it tests held beliefs. Such information reveals potential threats and opportunities to non-belligerents and changes their expected utility for war. Most importantly, the revelation of such information, especially if it is new and dramatic, can motivate non-belligerents to join and explains when they do so.[86] Of course, revealed information may not actually convey anything new. Instead, the information might be consistent with non-belligerents' original estimates, and therefore, would not affect the probability they would engage in warfare.[87] One way to avoid this problem is to look at unexpected events, which are a subset of revealed information.[88] Unexpected events are military or political events within a war that reveal information that is contrary to what most neutral observers expected antebellum or up to that point in the war. They can include not only surprising events that happened, but also the surprising absence of an event. Much more will be said of unexpected events in Chapter 3 and in the Appendix.

Based on these arguments and the literature's previous findings, several specific hypotheses can be generated. First, unexpected events in a war change a state's expected utility for joining the war. As was argued above, the occurrence of an unexpected event will increase the chance that a state will join an ongoing war a positive percentage of the time. Thus, if an unexpected event has occurred in an ongoing war in a given month or the previous two months, all states are more likely to join that war—H1. Also, the greater the magnitude of the unexpected event, the higher the likelihood a given state will join the war and the sooner it will do so—H2.

86 This mechanism can account for all of the motivations for late joining listed earlier in this chapter except for the last one—that states are viewed as necessary to victory either because of their natural resources or because they are an invasion route—but neither is it in opposition with it. The factors driving this last cause would likely be unique to a given war and thus are difficult to incorporate into a general theory. The literature's finding that contiguity increases the chance a state will join that war is likely partially driven by this hypothesis of necessity. As long as this cause is accounted for through geographic control variables when testing the revealed information hypothesis, it should not pose a significant problem.

87 This may not hold for sufficiently risk averse third parties as will be discussed later in the chapter.

88 The concept that events within wars are responsible for joining is not entirely new (Yamamoto and Bremer 1980, 199–200).

Second, alliances should transmit wars from one ally to another, at least in the initial stage of the conflict. Specifically, if a state has an ally that is actively engaged in a war, it is more likely to join—H3. The effect should be greatest for defensive pacts and least for neutrality pacts. This is because an alliance is a signal that two states share many interests, such as the containment of a third state or the survival of the states in the alliance. Of course, this correlation may be weaker than suggested by some of the literature because, as discussed above, some states might not even initiate a war because they are certain of intervention by an allied power and because neutrality pacts may indicate enmity. Additionally, the effect of alliances should be strongest in the first month of the war—H4.

Third, previous findings suggest geographic proximity should also affect the likelihood that a state will enter an ongoing war since the closer a state is to the ongoing conflict, the more able that state will be to join and the more likely it will be invaded because control of its territory will be seen as necessary to victory. Thus, it is important to control for geography. Specifically, states that are contiguous by land to a war will be more likely to join and states in the same region as a war will be more likely to join—H5 and H6.

Fourth, states' power also needs to be considered. Specifically, great powers should be more likely to join ongoing wars—H7. Great powers have greater logistical capabilities to intervene than do lesser powers. They are also more likely to be able to influence the outcome of a given war. Also, if a great power is involved in a war, all states, but especially other great powers, should be more inclined to join as more will be at stake in the war—H8.[89]

Fifth, the strategic situation caused by the war must also be considered—specifically what states are already involved in the war and their relationship to the non-belligerent in question. In particular, democracies may come to the aid of fellow democracies, making them more likely than other regime types to join wars in which other democracies are already involved—H9. Also, states with enduring rivals in the war should also be more likely to enter that war and states already involved in other wars should be less likely to join— H10 and H11. Lastly, prior joining, especially by great powers may increase the odds the war will spread still further—H12 and H13.

Sixth, the existing literature suggests that collective security arrangements should also increase the odds of joining. Though this is difficult to test, it must at least be considered for the purposes of a control variable. As the UN is the best proxy for collective security, it is proposed that if the UN passes a resolution endorsing the use of force against an aggressor, all states are more likely to join that war—H14. Finally, it is proposed that the more time that has passed since the outbreak of the war the less likely a state is to join—H15. Like the UN variable, this is a control variable and is discussed further in the next chapter. Yamamoto and Bremer (1980) argue that typically no one factor will have an overwhelming

89 This suggests an interaction term between major power status and a major power being in the war is appropriate in a statistical study.

impact on a state's decision to join a war. Rather the decision will be a result of a composite of factors. In other words, though individually none of the above factors is likely to cause a state to join even though they will increase the odds of this occurring, the confluence of several factors—especially the confluence of both geographic and revealed information factors—may well cause states to join ongoing wars. Thus taken as a whole, these hypotheses form a coherent theory of the reasons a state may join an ongoing war, however, the connection between states leaving wars and revealed information, as well as potential counter-hypotheses, must still be considered.

Revealed Information and Leaving Wars

Blainey (1973) suggests that states joining wars should have much in common with states leaving wars. If, as was proposed above, unexpected events—which by definition reveal information—make entry into a war more or less attractive, it follows that such events should make remaining in a war more or less attractive as well. This is true for several reasons. First, the decision to continue fighting is a political decision, just like the decision to initiate or join a war.[90] Second, wars continue until there is a change in the calculations of one of the actors.[91] Only changes to states' demands can lead to the termination of war as the benefits of war are endogenous to the war and cannot change; only state demands can change.[92] In other words, in rational war, war termination is endogenous.[93] Third, changes in such calculations should come about only if something contrary to the belligerents' expectations is revealed.[94] States learn from new information and react to the new probable outcome of the war by changing both their strategy within the war and their proposals for settlement.[95] As revealed information can cause states' expected utility, and therefore, their demands to change, such events can make remaining in the war less appealing. Hence, unexpected events should result, on average, in some states deciding that it is in their interest to leave ongoing wars.[96] Even though not all unexpected events will lead to states viewing remaining in the war as less attractive than exiting, the assertion that unexpected events should at times make remaining in a war unattractive is testable for the same reasons that the assertion

90 Bennett and Stam 1996.

91 Fox 1970.

92 Filson and Werner 2002b, 821; Goemans 2000, 20.

93 Slantchev 2004.

94 Filson and Werner 2002b.

95 This is simply stating that war is a strategic learning process. This is consistent with an older line of literature. For example, see Kecskemeti (1958), Pillar (1983), or Schelling (1966).

96 Of course, no state can leave a war unilaterally, but rather can exit only with the approval, tacit or explicit, of its opponents (Goemans 2003).

that unexpected events should at times make joining a war attractive was testable. Thus, if an unexpected event has occurred in an ongoing war in that month or the previous two months, all states will be more likely to leave a war and the greater the magnitude of an event the more likely it is that a given state will leave the war and the sooner it will do so—H16 and H17.

These deductions help rectify the earlier apparent disagreement with the notion that the revelation of private information should reduce the likelihood of conflict. Yet, this work has previously argued the revelation of private information can actually increase the likelihood of conflict. The proper conclusion, however, is that revelation of private information shifts the range of acceptable settlements of the parties involved. New information causes belligerents to change their demands and how they pursue their goals.[97] These shifts may either reduce or increase the likelihood of conflict. Thus, revealed information should lead to both the positive and negative spread of war.

Of course, unexpected events are not the only considerations that determine when a state will leave a war. Regime type must also be considered when examining why states leave wars. Downs and Rocke (1994) argue publics have an incentive to punish leaders that perform badly during wars in order to discourage future leaders from involving the country in wars which are either unduly costly or that have very low probabilities of success. Due to asymmetric information, it is often difficult or impossible for publics to assess how well leaders performed given the constraints they faced. Thus, in order to maintain a credible deterrent on reckless behavior, publics must punish all leaders that are associated with failed war policies.[98]

While this incentive to punish failed leaders exists across regime types, the sort of punishment leaders likely will face varies by regime type. Goemans (2000) argues that leaders in different regime types face significantly different kinds of punishment for failure in war and this affects the way leaders respond to negative information revealed by a war. Specifically, Goemans argues that leaders in democracies and dictatorships will likely face severe punishment only if they lose a war very badly.[99] Thus, such leaders are willing to end wars even if they are faced with a mild defeat. Leaders of mixed regimes, however, are often severely punished even after mild defeats. Such leaders, therefore, have an incentive to gamble for resurrection when faced with negative information in hopes that the war will turn around even though such a possibility is unlikely and continued fighting likely will cause significant damage to their state. This is because such leaders' personal fates are equally grim in the face of both minor and major defeats, and therefore,

---

97 Goemans 2000, 28. Only new information will cause rational belligerents to change their strategies.

98 Downs and Rocke 1994.

99 Goemans' defines severe punishment as incarceration, exile, or death. Leaders in dictatorship may be able to avoid domestic punishment entirely in the face of mild defeats.

they have nothing to lose personally by continuing the fight. Downs and Rocke argue that this incentive to gamble for resurrection exists across all regime types, however, they assume there is no variation in the severity of punishment—all removals from office are equally costly to the leader. As Goemans illustrates, this is not the case. Therefore, while leaders of democracies and dictatorships may have some incentive to gamble for resurrection, this incentive exists only to the extent that such gambling will not greatly increase the severity of defeat and the scale of punishment they will receive from their domestic publics. Thus, while most regime types should be more likely to exit a war after both positive and negative unexpected events, mixed regimes should only be more likely to exit after positive events and should actually be less likely to exit after negative events—H18.

Strategic Delay and Risk Aversion

It is also important to consider alternatives to the work's hypothesis. Other than revealed information, what might explain the timing of late joining? Why would a state voluntarily enter a war well after its outbreak, rather than join initially, other than because the war is not proceeding as expected? Certainly bureaucratic inefficiencies could delay joining to some extent,[100] but it is not clear that such inefficiencies can explain states joining months or even years after wars begin. Also, many states faced with such obstacles declare war before the delays are resolved even though it may take many months before they can make substantive contributions to the war effort.[101] The most likely possibility is that the state was waiting for some anticipated process to be completed.[102] For example, a state may wish to wait until at least some, if not all, of the combatants have worn themselves out through attrition making spoils more easily available. Another possibility is that a state may want to wait until its potential enemies' forces have been moved away from the frontier and engaged elsewhere. Italy in 1940 may have had such a motive in mind when it delayed declaring war on France, though undoubtedly Mussolini wanted to see how the initial battles between France and Germany would go as well.[103] Finally, a state may be waiting to complete rearmament or the delivery of armaments. Peru delayed declaring war on Spain during the Spanish-Chilean War of 1865–66 because it was waiting for the warships it had purchased to sail from Britain. At the time, British law prevented the delivery

100 Chayes and Chayes 1993; Downs, Rocke, and Barsoon 1996.

101 The US's entry into the First World War is a good example of this.

102 Other possibilities arise if we relax the assumption that states are unitary actors. Shifts in the composition of governments, which may or may not be related to events within the war, could cause non-belligerents to join an ongoing war. See the Greek and Turkish cases in the First World War in Chapter 5 as well as Bueno de Mesquita and Lalman (1992).

103 Murray 1984.

of armaments to belligerents, so if Peru had declared war on Spain before the ships were completed, they would have been impounded for the duration of the war.[104] Thus, strategic delay presents a counter-hypothesis to the idea unexpected events will cause states to join ongoing wars. This counter-hypothesis, however, is not entirely in conflict with the revealed information framework—though it is in opposition to the unexpected events hypotheses—as wars can reveal that an anticipated action has taken place or an expected process has been completed.

This counter-hypothesis logically could operate in some wars, while the unexpected events hypothesis would operate in others. There is, however, a major problem with the alternate hypothesis: it is not clear why belligerents should allow late joining to occur at the time that suits their foes. In such cases, preemption should occur.[105] If it is better for state C to declare war on state A in two months rather than now, logically A would be better off striking C now. Unless A was uncertain about C's intentions, it would be illogical for A not to attack immediately. Such logic has led states to initiate wars; the Six Day War is the classic example. Thus, it is reasonable to assume the same logic should lead to wars widening. Interestingly, Reiter (1995) demonstrates that this sort of preemption almost never occurs. This suggests states rarely wait for an expected chain of events to be completed prior to joining, which in turn limits the number of cases in which states would have an incentive to preempt. Alternatively, states may be unable to extrapolate a sufficient number of steps down the road in order to conclude that they would be better off if they engaged in preemptive or preventive warfare. Much like a chess player, there may be a limit to how many moves ahead states can see. It is also possible that leaders assume the situation will change before their potential enemy attacks. Thus, even though it may be better to preempt now if all goes as expected, if the situation is sufficiently fluid, it might be still wiser to wait and see if something turns up due to high levels of uncertainty down the game tree.[106] Thus, either states rarely wait for an expected chain of events to play out before joining or belligerents fail to launch preventive or preemptive attacks against such states for yet unexplained reasons. Thus, though potential problems exist for the counter-hypothesis, they are not sufficient to dismiss the hypothesis entirely. This discussion reinforces the earlier point that belligerents try to manipulate the course of wars to induce neutrals to join or stay out. Most, perhaps all, wars are fought with the fact that other states may join in mind. The possibility of third party involvement strongly influences the course of many wars, including those that never experience intervention. This becomes particularly apparent in the case studies.

---

104 Burr 1980.

105 Murray 1984, 314–15 and 362–3.

106 Large scale discounting of the future by states could produce similar results, but given the short time frames involved in preemptive decisions, discounting is unlikely to significantly impact the preemption dynamic in this way as states are unlikely to discount the very near future that heavily.

Risk aversion may also play a role in keeping states from initially entering a war. So far the discussion has assumed that states are risk neutral. This, of course, is likely not true. Most states are probably risk averse to some degree and this may affect the likelihood that wars will spread. Revealed information should make intervention appear more attractive to risk averse states and cause them to join wars just as it caused risk neutral states to join. A risk averse state, however, should need a more positive assessment or greater certainty about such an assessment than a risk neutral state would. Oddly, the need for greater certainty might lead a risk averse state to join for reasons that would not cause a risk neutral state to join. Ex ante, a risk averse state could determine it has a positive expected utility for joining a war, but the variability of its estimate could be quite high. In other words, despite the fact that on average entering the war would lead to a positive outcome, the state's best estimate suggests with a reasonably high probability—though less than 50%—that it would not benefit from joining. Given the state's aversion to risk, it might be unwilling to take the significant chance that war would be a mistake. In this scenario, information revealed by the ongoing war that confirmed the state's initial estimate, thereby reducing the uncertainty associated with the assessment, could cause the state to join. This could never happen for a risk neutral state, but it is entirely possible for a risk averse state because new information can reduce the level of uncertainty associated with joining. It may seem perverse that a risk averse state will join a war in a scenario that would not cause a risk neutral state to join, however, the risk neutral state would have already entered the war since it would not have been deterred by the high variability in its original estimate. Thus, it is a selection effect and not a direct effect that leads risk aversion to be associated with joining after a certain point in war. In other words, the more risk averse a state, the more information it will need to be convinced it should join.

There is a rebuttal to the claim that risk averse actors will join simply if their original estimates are confirmed—provided those estimates were positive. Even though such states will be more certain about the probability of victory, the reward for intervention should decrease as states on the probable winning side will now be less willing to offer significant spoils as it is clearer their side will win. Thus, they will have fewer incentives to court potential allies. In other words, there would be less uncertainty, but also less reward. Therefore, it is ambiguous whether a risk averse actor would be more likely to join. Even given this uncertainty, there still should be a selection effect operating in favor of seeing more risk averse states joining than risk neutral states after a certain amount of time. This is because the same declining rewards for joining would apply to the entry of risk neutral states as well as risk averse states. Thus, the payoff for risk neutral states would decline, while the overall effect on risk averse states is ambiguous. In sum, though it is unclear whether a confirmation of a positive estimate will cause a risk averse state to join, such confirmation could cause a risk averse state to join, while it should never cause a risk neutral state to join.

Thus, there are two competing reasons why states voluntarily join ongoing wars after the initial stages of the war.[107] First, they do so because information revealed by wars has led them to decide that, though involvement was not attractive before, it is now. Second, they join when some expected process or chain of events is completed—such as rearmament or attrition—or their antebellum estimates have received adequate confirmation to overcome their risk aversion. Though undoubtedly both mechanisms can logically lead to intervention, it is this work's contention that the former will be predominant. Chapter 3 will test this and the other hypotheses enumerated above using Generalized Estimating Equations on a dataset collected by the author. They will be further explored in cases studies on the Crimean War, Franco-Prussian War, First World War, and the post-World War Two era.

---

107 It is possible to conceive of states joining wars in three stages. In the early period of the war, states may join because they essentially share the expectations of the initial belligerents and simply did not join at the outset due to bureaucratic delays. Also, states may join in the very early stages of a war because they are compelled to do so by an alliance—either to honor the commitment to uphold their reputation or out of a need to militarily protect an ally. After these initial stages, states that have yet to join will not join later simply because of the event of the war or due to alliance considerations. Instead, they will join only in response to new or revealed information as is argued in this chapter. Finally, states may join after some expected process has been completed or after their initial estimates have less risk associated with them. In particular, states may join very late in the war after one or both sides have been exhausted in the expectation of easy spoils, though the above discussion of states joining after completing rearmament will also fall under this rubric. It seems likely that this last logic driving joining would be dominant in the last stages of a war, while the unexpected events logic would be the predominant cause behind entries after a war's initial stages until the very late stages of the war.

Chapter 3
Statistical Analysis of the Spread of War

> No matter how enmeshed a commander becomes in the elaboration of his own thoughts, it is sometimes necessary to take the enemy into account
>
> Winston Churchill[1]

The above quotation applies just as well to scholars in relation to empirical evidence as it does to military commanders, though of course, no scholar should see evidence as the enemy. Statistics are very useful for determining a theory's general accuracy and the overall validity of its hypotheses. Chapter 2 laid out a theory of why states join ongoing wars. Its various hypotheses will now be tested using Generalized Estimating Equations on a dataset collected by the author.

The dataset includes all interstate wars in the Correlates of War (COW) database from January 1816 through January 1995. This time period includes all 79 interstate wars from the Franco-Spanish War of 1823 through 1990–91 Gulf War. To these were added the 1999 Kargil conflict between India and Pakistan and the 1998–2000 war between Ethiopia and Eritrea, bringing the total to 81 wars. Two recent wars were excluded due to a lack of definitive data on which states COW would code as participants: the ongoing US-Iraq and US-Afghanistan wars.[2] Each war was broken down into war-months. Each case was a war-month for each state not in the war. Thus for any given war, there would be a case for every state in the state system except for those states in the war, multiplied by the number of months the war lasted. Given a hypothetical war involving two states, lasting ten months, with a total of 202 states in the system—thus 200 not in the war—2,000 cases would be generated. When a state joins an ongoing war, it drops out of the dataset for that particular war until it leaves the war. Thus, in the previous example if a state had joined in the fifth month and remained in the war until its conclusion, only 1,995 cases would have been generated. If more than one war occurs at the same time, states are included in the database for each war in which they are not involved. Thus, although Germany was in World War Two during the winter of 1939–40, it is included in the database for the Winter War between Finland and the Soviet Union. This methodology results in 91,942 cases. Additionally, World War Two was split into two wars with the Pacific theater being treated as a continuation of the Sino-Japanese War which began in 1937 and expanding beyond a bilateral conflict after Pearl Harbor.

---

1 Edwards 2004, 54.

2 This assumes the recent war in the Democratic Republic of the Congo will be coded by COW as a civil war with outside involvement, while US-Afghanistan will be seen as a new interstate war and not a civil war with US intervention.

Variables

The dependent variable in the study is whether a state voluntarily joined an ongoing war in a particular war-month after the war's first month. The COW dataset on interstate wars is the source for the dependent variable, though it was modified to exclude states that entered wars because they were attacked. States entered a war only 102 times after the war's initial outbreak and only 68 joined voluntarily after the war's first month. Thus, though there are 91,942 cases, the dependent variable is positive only 68 times. Of course, looking at each non-belligerent separately greatly inflates the number of cases. There are only 1,276 war-months in the dataset. Thus, though joining is exceptionally rare when looked at from the perspective of all possible states that could join in all possible war-months, it is substantially more common when looked at from the perspective of how often any state joins in a given war-month, and almost common place when it is realized late joining happened 68 times in 81 wars.

The independent variables are of two sorts: non-belligerent specific and war-month specific variables. In the first category are whether and what type of alliance a non-belligerent had with a belligerent, if the non-belligerent was contiguous to the war or in the same region as the war, if the non-belligerent was involved in another war, if the non-belligerent had an enduring rival in the war, if the non-belligerent was a great power, and if the non-belligerent was a democracy during a war involving a fellow democracy. The war-month specific variables indicate whether an unexpected event happened in a given war and the nature of that event, if the United Nations' was approximating a collective security organization during the war, if a great power was involved in the war, if a great power had already joined the war, and how long the war has lasted up to that point.

The detailed descriptions of the non-belligerent specific variables are as follows. The alliance variables were derived from the COW dataset. In that dataset a defense pact between two states is coded as a one, a neutrality pact as a two, and an entente as a three. As it is inappropriate to treat alliance types as an ordinal variable, the variable was dummied out into the three separate dichotomous variables, one for each type of alliance between a non-belligerent and warring state.[3] The absence of an alliance is represented by all three variables being equal to zero. Whether a given non-belligerent is a great power or not is also indicated by a dichotomous variable. This variable was taken directly from the COW database. Whether the non-belligerent was contiguous to the conflict by land is indicated by a dichotomous variable and was taken from the EUGene dataset. Whether or not the state was in the same region as the conflict was coded by the author and is indicated by a dichotomous variable.[4] The EUGene coding was not used

3 All dichotomous variables in the dataset are recorded zero/one.

4 See the Appendix for a list of where each war is coded as having occurred. For wars that occurred over a large area, only areas of major fighting were considered. For example, even though the Graf Spee was sunk off the coast of South America during the Second

because the regions in EUGene are too large and often include states that are not in effective political contact with each other.[5] Whether the non-belligerent had an enduring rival in the war was determined using Diehl and Goertz's list of enduring rivalries and was coded as a dichotomous variable.[6] These non-belligerent specific variables, with the exception of the enduring rivalry variable, are consistent with the hypotheses advanced by Richardson, Most, Siverson, and Starr in Chapter 2 regarding the spread of war. Whether the non-belligerent was in another war was coded as a dichotomous variable and was derived directly from the COW dataset.

The detailed descriptions of the war-month specific variables are as follows. The unexpected events variables indicate whether an unexpected event happened in a given month, whether it was political or military in nature, and the magnitude of the event. Only unexpected events that occurred in the given war or to one of the belligerents were recorded.[7] Limiting unexpected events to those that happen within a war and not including those that happen to potential joiners, should if anything, mute the effect of unexpected events on joining. Overall, 206 unexpected events were recorded as happening in 192 months.[8] The magnitude of an event is measured on a scale of zero to three, with a zero indicating that no event occurred, while a three indicates an event of the highest magnitude. When the magnitude of an event is considered, the variable is dummied out as the effects of increasing one step in magnitude is likely not uniform across the scale. In other words, the effect of moving from no event and to an event of magnitude one may be different from

---

World War, the war was not considered to have been fought in South America. Naturally, the area where a particular war is listed as occurring can change over the course of the war. Again, using the Second World War as an example, it began as a European affair and came to be fought for a time in North Africa. While most countries are listed only in one region, Russia is always considered as part of both Europe and Northeast Asia, while Turkey is considered as part of Europe until 19 April 1913, the end of the First Balkan War, and always as part of the Middle East.

5 See the appendix for a list of which states are in each region. EUGene has five regions: Europe, Middle East, Sub-Saharan Africa, Asia and Oceania, and the Western Hemisphere. The coding used in the study has 10 regions: Europe, Middle East, West Africa, Southern and East Africa, Southern and Central Asia, Northeast Asia, Southeast Asia, Oceania, North America and the Caribbean, and South America. These regions are strongly suggested by the COW country codes, though the match is not exact.

6 Diehl and Goertz 2000, 145–6.

7 If an event occurred in the same month a state joined, but after it entered the war, no event was recorded as having occurred in that month for that non-belligerent. For example, if Russia joined a war on 1 May 1850 and an unexpected event occurred on 10 May 1850 the event would not be recorded as having occurred for the case of Russia in May of 1850, though it would be recorded as having occurred for all other non-belligerents in May of 1850—provided of course that they had not also joined in May prior to the event.

8 Thus, 1,084 months did not contain an unexpected event. This puts the small size of the dependent variable into a more proper perspective. 68 late entries is much more comparable to 192 months with unexpected events than it is to the total number of cases. In twelve of the months both a military and political event were coded as having occurred.

the effect of moving from a magnitude two to a magnitude three event. Events were recorded as being either political or military in nature. In the models, lags are included indicating if an unexpected event happened in the current month or the previous two months, as it likely takes states some time to digest and act upon new information. A two-month lag was chosen as this should be enough time for a state to learn about, analyze, and act upon an unexpected event, even during the earlier part of the nineteenth century when information traveled more slowly. A longer lag was not used to avoid conflating state responses to the unexpected event with state responses to later stimuli.

As the unexpected events variables were coded by the author, it is important to discuss the coding procedures in detail, but that is not possible here. The coding procedures, therefore, are thoroughly discussed in the Appendix. The exact coding and a description of each unexpected event are also available in Table 9.1 in the Appendix. Still, it is helpful to briefly discuss the coding here to give a sense of the nature of unexpected events. Unexpected events are non-trivial events which surprised contemporary leaders of non-belligerents. Military events on the level of a three are surprising, severe battlefield defeats—or large victories depending on the point of view—that result not just in a retreat but the destruction of a very large portion of the defeated side's forces. Level three political events are unexpected changes in regime type, not just unexpected changes in the composition of a government or riots. Level two events include large, unexpected victories—or defeats, again depending on the point of view—widespread, unexpected rioting, and surprising, large changes in the composition and expected direction of a government. Level one events include surprising, small protests, unexpected deaths of leaders that at the time do not appear to significantly change government policy, and one side doing slightly better or worse than expected in a war. An example of each type of event can be seen in Table 3.1. The examples were selected from events in one of the case studies later in the book or from events that will be familiar to most readers.

The other four war-specific variables are as follows. First, a dichotomous variable records if the United Nations was acting similarly to a collective security organization in that month. Obviously, prior to the founding of the UN this variable always equals zero. Since its founding, the UN has acted as a collective security organization in only two wars: the Korean War and the 1990–91 Gulf War. The UN variable is coded as a one for these two wars in all war-months after the UN endorsed military action in the war in question.[9] This variable does not test the proposition that collective security institutions cause wars to spread, but rather acts as a control variable for the UN's role in these two wars. Second, a dichotomous variable records whether one of the belligerents was a great power.

9 The relevant resolutions are Security Council Resolution 83—passed 27 June 1950—and Security Council Resolution 687—passed 29 November 1990—that authorized the use of force in Korean and 1990–91 Gulf Wars respectively. The UN variable is coded as a one in each war from June 1950 and November 1990 onward.

Table 3.1 Examples of Types of Unexpected Events

Type of Event	Example
Political–Level One	Death of Tsar Nicholas I during the Crimean War—March 1855
Political–Level Two	Fall of Mussolini in an Administrative Coup—July 1943
Political–Level Three	Bolshevik Revolution—November 1917
Military–Level One	Breakout from the Normandy Beachhead in WWII—August 1944
Military–Level Two	US landings at Inchon in the Korean War—September 1950
Military–Level Three	Rapid German defeat of France in WWII—May 1940

Third, a dichotomous variable indicates if at least one great power has joined the war either voluntarily or because it was attacked. Finally, the duration of the war up to the point being examined is measured in months.

Methods

As the dependent variable is dichotomous—as are many of the independent variables—care is required when selecting the appropriate model. Dichotomous dependent variables are best treated using logistic regressions. As the focus of the study is the likelihood that a given state will join a war in a given month, maximum likelihood estimation (MLE) with a binomial functional form—either logit or probit—would seem the obvious choice. Certainly MLE would be preferable to a hazard model. Hazard models are not appropriate as they operate on the assumption that an event will happen given enough time. This assumption is legitimate for a great many issues, but whether states join a war is not one of them. States are not guaranteed to join, even if the war lasts a very long time. Thus, a hazard model is inappropriate on theoretical grounds.

There are problems, however, with an MLE based model as well. States' decisions about whether to join are likely neither temporally nor spatially independent of each other. For example, it is reasonable to assume that the decision of a state to not join in January affects the likelihood it will enter the war in February.[10] This lack of temporal independence violates a key assumption of binomial models, and therefore, is a serious problem. Normally this could be

10 Additionally, one state entering the war affects the probability another will enter (Leeds 2005, 125).

controlled for by using temporal splines as is suggested by Beck, Katz, and Tucker (1998). This correction, however, is impossible as the unexpected events variables in this work are lagged. The lagging of variables prevents the use of the Beck, Katz, and Tucker correction.

For this reason, generalized estimating equations (GEEs) were chosen. GEEs were developed out of generalized linear models and have several advantages.[11] First, they are able to control for temporal dependency while still incorporating lagged variables.[12] GEEs can also cluster a set of observations to control for within group dependence. This allows for the partial controlling of spatial dependence. These advantages are gained while retaining many of the strengths of MLE models. The coefficients returned by GEE models are interpreted in exactly the same manner as coefficients in any logistic regression. Also, the Huber-White method of calculating robust standard errors can be closely approximated by GEE models, though as it is only an approximation, the standard errors are best labeled as semi-robust. This work uses a GEE model with a binomial functional form and clusters the observations for a given non-belligerent over a particular war. For example, cases in which the US was a non-belligerent during the Franco-Prussian War would constitute a cluster. Logit rather than probit was used as the functional form because logit based models are more likely to converge than probit based models. As there is very little substantive difference between the two functional forms, the greater ability to converge is a significant advantage for logit based models.

Results: Unexpected Events and Joining

The first test of the work's hypotheses was conducted by running a regression examining the effect of an unexpected event occurring in that month or the previous two months on the likelihood of joining. The regression included all non-belligerents in the world for each war. The results are listed in Table 3.2. The most important result from this first model is that unexpected events were positively correlated with joining and were statistically significant.[13] Holding the dichotomous variables at their mode and all the other variables at their mean, an unexpected

11 See Hardin and Hilbe (2003), Liang and Zeger (1986), or Zorn (2001) for a comprehensive description of the properties of GEE models.

12 Zorn 2001, 472. The asymptotic consistency of the βs estimated by GEE models holds even if the exact nature of the intra-cluster relationship is unknown. Thus, it is not necessary to know precisely how certain observations are causally linked to control for interdependence. Rather, it is simply necessary to know that the observations may be causally linked. See Oneal and Russett (1999) for an example of the use of GEE models to control for temporal dependence in the international relations literature.

13 This result held if the lag was lengthened to three months, but it did not hold if the lag was shortened to one month.

event in that month or the previous two months more than doubles the likelihood a given state would join the war—from 0.011% to 0.028%.[14] The overall likelihood remains very low, but this is to be expected, as most states will not join an ongoing war, let alone in a given month. The finding helps confirm the main hypothesis laid out in Chapter 2 and helps explain the timing of intervention. When the effect

Table 3.2 Joining War: Unexpected Events as One Variable

	Marginal Effect on Likelihood of Joining*	**Coeff.**	**Semi-Robust Standard Error**	**P > |z|**
Unexpected Event in Given or Prior Two Months	1.66e-4	0.943	0.302	**0.002**
Non-belligerent in the Same Region as the War	3.99e-4	1.561	0.384	**0.000**
Non-belligerent is Contiguous to the War	1.83e-4	1.002	0.385	**0.009**
UN is Involved	1.28e-3	2.571	0.602	**0.000**
Non-belligerent is a Great Power	6.16e-4	1.919	0.615	**0.002**
Great Power in War	-5.82e-5	-0.795	0.544	**0.144**
Great Power Previously Joined the War	2.66e-4	1.256	0.626	**0.045**
Non-belligerent has Defense Pact w/ a Belligerent	-1.81e-6	-0.017	0.450	**0.969**
Non-belligerent has Entente with a Belligerent	1.24e-4	0.773	0.456	**0.090**
Non-belligerent has Neutrality Pact w/ a Belligerent	-7.48e-5	-1.222	0.752	**0.104**
Fellow Democracy in the War	1.30e-4	0.798	0.463	**0.085**
Non-belligerent has an Enduring Rival in the War	-3.22e-5	-0.362	0.643	**0.574**
Non-belligerent is in Another War	8.29e-5	0.578	1.038	**0.578**
Duration of the War up to this Point	3.73e-8	0.000	0.000	**0.443**
Constant	-------	-9.158	0.381	**0.000**

* Holding all variables at their median

N = 91,942

Wald Chi Squared = 207.74

ROC Area = 0.9172

14 It is appropriate to hold dichotomous variables at their mode as their means have no meaningful interpretation.

of unexpected events is limited to states more likely to join a war—major powers and geographically proximate states—rather than for all states, the importance of unexpected events remains strong and the overall likelihood of joining increases. For example, an unexpected event increases the odds that a great power in the same region of the war will join in a given month from 0.350% to 0.893% and for a lesser power in the region the odds increase from 0.051% to 0.132%. The effects of events on contiguous states are similar, though the overall likelihoods are somewhat lower.

Consistent with this, the geographic proximity variables were also statistically significant on their own and positively correlated with joining. Again holding the other variables at their mode, being contiguous to a war tripled the likelihood a state would join in a given month—0.011% to 0.029%, while simply being in the same region as the war more than quintupled the chance the state would join—0.011% to 0.051%. These results are consistent with and help confirm the previous findings that geographic proximity is an important determinant of which states, if any, will join an ongoing war.

The UN and great power variables generally behaved as expected. UN involvement was also statistically significant and positively correlated with joining. UN actions that approximated collective security norms increased the likelihood of joining twelve-fold—0.011% to 0.141%. This finding, however, does not confirm Betts' (1992) hypothesis that collective security institutions widen wars as the variable was structured as a control variable to account for the unusually high levels of intervention in the Korean War and 1990–91 Gulf War rather than as a test for Betts' hypothesis. It does suggest that such a control variable is needed when studying joining and that a true test of Betts' hypothesis would prove interesting. Likewise, the possession of great power status by the non-belligerent and having a great power join the war are also both significantly correlated with states joining ongoing wars and increase the odds of joining to 0.074% and 0.038% respectively. These findings are consistent with Richardson (1960) and Yamamoto and Bremer (1980). Simply having a great power in the war as opposed to a great power joiner, however, does not increase the odds a state will join.[15]

The remaining variables produced several surprising null results. The results for the three alliance variables are particularly interesting. None of the three alliance variables are significantly correlated with joining and what little effect defense and neutrality pacts have is negative rather than positive. Given the very large number of cases, it is unlikely the lack of significance results from insufficient leverage due to limited data. Therefore, we can be confident in the result that defense pacts, ententes, and neutrality pacts do not transmit wars given the constraints of this

15 Other regressions were run using an interaction term between a non-belligerent being a great power and there being another great power already involved in the war and being a great power and having another great power already join. Also, regressions were run with variables indicating whether any state had already joined the war and the number of states that had already joined. All of these interaction terms were statistically insignificant.

regression. As will be shown in Table 3.5 below, the lack of a result for defense pacts is due to the fact that states that joined in the first month of the war were excluded from this regression. Such early joiners are what drove Siverson and Starr's (1991) and others' findings, at least as they relate to defense pacts.

Similarly, the duration of the war, the non-belligerent being in another war, and having an enduring rival in the war are not significantly correlated with late joining. The finding for the enduring rivalries variable runs counter to what one would expect based on the enduring rivalries literature and lends support to, though it certainly does not prove, the literature that questions the role such rivalries actually play in causing interstate wars.[16] The lack of significance for non-belligerents being in other wars may be because two distinct effects cancel each other out. States in other wars may have fewer resources available for another war and thus be less likely to join, but because they are engaged elsewhere, they may be attractive targets for aggressors who are engaged in the initial ongoing war. Even though states that are actually attacked are not counted as joiners, it may be some states that are engaged elsewhere are more aggressively pressured by belligerents on the assumption they will be unable to respond. This attempt to squeeze additional concessions out of states that are engaged elsewhere may induce them to decide that fighting two wars simultaneously is better than making substantial concessions to avoid being draw into a second war. Alternatively, it may also be that many states are not sufficiently constrained by already being in a war to alter their calculations about another war. Finally, there is no evidence that democracies come to the aid of other democracies in late joining.

While it is interesting to know that unexpected events increase the likelihood of joining, this raises other questions. Do events of a greater magnitude have more of an effect? Do both political and military events affect the likelihood of joining? In order to answer these questions, the unexpected events variable was broken up based on its type, political or military, and its magnitude, one to three. Regressions were then run with these disaggregated unexpected events variables and the control variables used above. The results can be seen in Table 3.3 and 3.4.

The findings for the control variables remain essentially the same as they were in the previous regression. Geographic proximity, UN involvement, and great power status all remain significantly correlated with late joining. The size of the effects of these variables remain essentially the same, though in the model which examines event intensity—Table 3.3—the marginal effects of being in the same region as a war and being contiguous to a war become noticeably larger. In the model where events are broken down by their type—political or military—the effects of these variables are essentially the same as in the original model where unexpected events were left undifferentiated. Alliances, joint democracy, enduring rivalries, being in another war, and the duration of the war all remain statistically insignificant. Also, of some interest is that whether or not a great power already joined the war just misses being significant at the 0.05 level in the model which

16 See Gartzke and Simon (1999).

Table 3.3 Joining War: Unexpected Events by Intensity

	Marginal Effect on Likelihood of Joining*	Coeff.	Semi-Robust Standard Error	P > |z|
Level One Event in Given or Prior Two Months	8.82e-5	0.535	0.267	0.045
Level Two Event in Given or Prior Two Months	8.85e-5	0.537	0.297	0.071
Level Three Event in Given or Prior Two Months	2.48e-4	1.095	0.486	0.024
Non-belligerent in the Same Region as the War	4.48e-4	1.526	0.387	0.000
Non-belligerent is Contiguous to the War	2.16e-4	1.006	0.387	0.009
UN is Involved	1.75e-3	2.713	0.627	0.000
Non-belligerent is a Great Power	7.01e-4	1.891	0.622	0.002
Great Power in War	-6.82e-5	-0.793	0.550	0.149
Great Power Previously Joined the War	3.00e-4	1.227	0.646	0.058
Non-belligerent has Defense Pact with a Belligerent	9.56e-6	0.074	0.470	0.875
Non-belligerent has Entente with a Belligerent	1.57e-4	0.815	0.454	0.073
Non-belligerent has Neutrality Pact w/ a Belligerent	-8.71e-5	-1.201	0.730	0.100
Fellow Democracy in the War	1.49e-4	0.787	0.466	0.090
Non-belligerent has an Enduring Rival in the War	-3.87e-5	-0.372	0.652	0.568
Non-belligerent is in Another War	9.77e-5	0.579	1.029	0.578
Duration of the War up to this Point	3.71e-8	0.000	0.000	0.514
Constant	-------	-8.996	0.321	0.000

* Holding all variables at their median

N = 91,942

Wald Chi Squared = 230.23

ROC Area = 0.9186

Table 3.4 Joining War: Political vs. Military Events

	Marginal Effect on Likelihood of Joining*	Coeff.	Semi-Robust Standard Error	P > |z|
Military Event in Given or Prior Two Months	7.03e-5	0.493	0.250	0.049
Political Event in Given or Prior Two Months	1.81e-4	0.973	0.232	0.000
Non-belligerent in the Same Region as the War	4.30e-4	1.590	0.386	0.000
Non-belligerent is Contiguous to the War	1.82e-4	0.976	0.394	0.013
UN is Involved	1.27e-3	2.531	0.580	0.000
Non-belligerent is a Great Power	6.35e-4	1.911	0.623	0.002
Great Power in War	-5.90e-5	-0.766	0.552	0.166
Great Power Previously Joined the War	2.79e-4	1.261	0.610	0.039
Non-belligerent has Defense Pact w/ a Belligerent	5.45e-6	0.048	0.441	0.913
Non-belligerent has Entente with a Belligerent	1.26e-4	0.763	0.450	0.090
Non-belligerent has Neutrality Pact w/ a Belligerent	-7.77e-5	-1.220	0.761	0.109
Fellow Democracy in the War	1.40e-4	0.818	0.464	0.078
Non-belligerent has an Enduring Rival in the War	-3.52e-5	-0.385	0.655	0.557
Non-belligerent is in Another War	1.01e-4	0.650	1.059	0.540
Duration of the War up to this Point	4.46e-8	0.000	0.000	0.387
Constant	-------	-9.120	0.371	0.000

* Holding all variables at their median

N = 91,942

Wald Chi Squared = 207.37

Roc Area = 0.9196

examines event intensity, though the size of its effect increases very slightly. In the model which disaggregates political from military events, the effect of prior great power joining is essentially the same as it was in the undifferentiated model. Given the nearness of the miss and the constancy of the substantive effect, it seems likely that having a major power already join a war does in fact increase the likelihood of further joining.

These regressions show that both political and military unexpected events are significantly correlated with late joining and that higher intensity unexpected events have a great effect on the likelihood of intervention than do lesser events. Both level one and two events doubled the likelihood of joining from 0.013% to 0.022%. Level three events had the biggest effect as predicted, tripling the likelihood to 0.038%. Interestingly, while both military and political effects increase the likelihood of joining, the effect of political events is much larger. While military events increase the odds of joining from 0.011% to 0.018%, political events triple the odds of joining to 0.030%.

Of course, all of these likelihoods remain quite low. This is the case for several reasons. First, the likelihoods are the odds that a particular state will join a war in a particular month, rather than the odds that any state will join a war. Given that the vast majority of states never join a given war, even world wars, the low likelihood makes sense. Second, the dataset is looking at all states, not just states that are more likely to join. When the data is limited to politically relevant states—defined as great powers and contiguous states—the likelihood for entry in the month after any unexpected event rises to 0.492% and to 0.786% after a magnitude three unexpected event.[17] Third, the likelihoods are determined holding the dichotomous variables at their modes, which in all cases is zero. Thus, they reflect the likelihood of only one variable being more likely to bring about joining. What are the odds of joining if using the universe of all cases, multiple factors are considered? As expected, the likelihoods increase. Great powers in the same region as the war join 0.893% of the time after any unexpected event and 1.750% of the time after a magnitude three event. Similarly, great powers in the same region join 1.409% of the time after an event if another great power has already joined and great powers not in the same region join 2.42% of the time after an unexpected event if there is also UN involvement. Thus, the likelihoods do increase noticeably, though they remain low as the great majority of states do not join a war in any given month.

One surprising result from these regressions is that alliances have not been correlated with states joining ongoing wars. This finding runs counter to many

17 Unexpected events and unexpected political events remain significantly correlated with late joining for politically relevant states. This is true even if the definition of politically relevant states is changed to select on region instead of contiguity or on both region and contiguity. The magnitude of the effects vary slightly. Somewhat troubling, however, is that out of all unexpected military events only magnitude three military unexpected events remain correlated with joining. Magnitude three military events increase the odds of joining by slightly more than magnitude three events in general.

strong findings in the literature. As was mentioned above, this discrepancy is a result of the exclusion of joining in the first month of wars in the previous regressions. Table 3.5 shows that alliances do transmit wars between alliance partners, but that this happens mainly in the first month of a conflict. The dependent variable in this model includes all states that joined an ongoing war regardless of when they joined or if they joined because they were invaded.

Table 3.5 Joining War: Alliance Variables Including First Month Joiners

	Marginal Effect on Likelihood of Joining*	Coeff.	Semi-Robust Standard Error	P > |z|
Unexpected Event in Given or Prior Two Months	1.83e-4	0.814	0.235	0.001
Non-belligerent in the Same Region as the War	6.11e-4	1.647	0.310	0.000
Non-belligerent is Contiguous to the War	1.71e-4	0.775	0.349	0.026
UN is Involved	5.49e-4	1.562	0.539	0.004
Non-belligerent is a Great Power	1.21e-4	2.235	0.408	0.000
Great Power in War	-2.13e-5	-0.158	0.398	0.692
Great Power Previously Joined the War	3.90e-4	1.302	0.439	0.003
Non-belligerent has Defense Pact with a Belligerent	3.02e-4	1.124	0.381	0.003
Non-belligerent has Entente with a Belligerent	-5.17e-6	-0.036	0.415	0.931
Non-belligerent has Neutrality Pact w/ a Belligerent	-8.76e-5	-0.921	0.611	0.132
Fellow Democracy in the War	9.38e-5	0.497	0.376	0.186
Non-belligerent has an Enduring Rival in the War	-2.66e-5	-0.202	0.480	0.674
Non-belligerent is in Another War	8.57e-5	0.463	0.769	0.547
Duration of the War up to this Point	-6.81e-8	-0.000	0.000	0.286
Constant	-------	-8.825	0.312	0.000

* Holding all variables at their median

N = 91942

Wald Chi Squared = 273.82

ROC Area = 0.9255

As would be expected from previous research, defense pacts are strongly correlated with states joining wars. They raise the likelihood a state will enter the war from 0.014% to 0.043%, about a threefold increase. The other alliance variables, however, are not correlated with states entering ongoing wars. Neither ententes nor neutrality pacts significantly affect the likelihood of joining and to the extent there is an effect, it is in the opposite direction of what was anticipated. Thus, defense pacts must have been the driving factor behind the results in the previous literature.[18]

Outside of the defense pact variable, none of the other variables changed whether they were significant or not. However, several variables had large changes in their marginal effects. The importance of region increased by one and a half, as did the impact having a great power already join the war. Similarly, the effect of a non-belligerent being a great power doubled, while the importance of UN involvement was almost halved. Thus, it seems that classic Realist variables—alliances, state power, and proximity—have their greatest impact in the first month of the war. While outside of alliances, they remain important past the first month, non-Realist variables like institutional involvement increase in importance. The effects for the other variables, including unexpected events, remained essentially the same.

From the previous four regressions several overarching conclusions can be drawn. Most importantly, it is clear that unexpected events are correlated with the timing of joining both for the pool of all non-belligerents and also for the smaller set of politically relevant non-belligerents. This is true for both military and political events.[19] These results strongly support the overall theory that revealed information causes states to join ongoing wars. Equally clear is that events of great magnitude are more likely to cause states to enter a war than events of a lesser magnitude. This finding is fairly intuitive. The regressions also confirm findings in the literature that geographically proximate states are more likely to join than are more distant states and that great powers are more likely to join than are other states. As these were the strongest and most consistent findings in the preexisting literature, these results are not surprising. Finally, it was found that the presence of a great power in a war did not increase the likelihood states would join, however, having a great power join that war did increase the likelihood other states would subsequently join. This suggests that great powers often are among the initial belligerents in small, likely bilateral wars that do not threaten the interests of non-belligerents sufficiently to induce them to join, but wars which attract great powers

18 A variable that indicated whether a non-belligerent had any form of alliance with a belligerent was found to be significant when substituted for the three alliance variables. Thus, the results for defense pacts alone are sufficient to make it appear that any form of alliance will increase the likelihood of joining in the first month of a war.

19 Additional regressions not shown in this chapter found results very similar to those for politically relevant non-belligerents for the pool of all non-belligerents when unexpected events were disaggregated by magnitude and type.

as joiners, however, are the sorts of wars that can become system wide wars or at least greatly affect and draw in many non-belligerents. While this is generally consistent with previous findings about great powers and the spread of war, the findings clarify and refine that relationship.

Also important is that some variables were not at all correlated with late joining. Perhaps most notably, having an enduring rival already engaged in the war did not increase the likelihood that a state would enter the war. As the models in this study did not even check to see if the non-belligerent would join to oppose its rival—as would be expected based on the enduring rivalries literature—it was artificially biased in favor of the enduring rivalries hypothesis and yet rivalries still did not matter. While this does not disprove that enduring rivalries exist, the finding does run counter to the logic of the enduring rivalries literature and casts some doubt onto its claims. Second, the duration of the war was not correlated with joining. States were no more or less likely to join after many months had passed. This lack of a relationship was true even if first month joiners were included. Third, being engaged in another war was not significantly correlated with joining. To the extent a relationship existed, it was negative as expected, but it was not significant. This was true even if non-belligerents which were attacked and "forced" to join were excluded. This suggests that states engaged in other conflicts may still find joining in their interest even though their resources are strained. It is possible this is because belligerents attempt to extract too much from these states and ultimately make fighting two wars more attractive than fighting one and conceding a great deal to avoid the second. Finally, the presence of a fellow democracy in a war did not make democracies more inclined to join. This finding does not run counter to the democratic peace literature in general and in fact confirms the findings of Reiter and Stam (2002), though it does differ with Gleditsch and Hegre (1997) and Werner and Lemke (1997).

On the other hand, the results for the alliance hypotheses were less clear. The regressions showed the relationship between alliances and the transmission of war from one alliance member to another is more complicated than indicated in the literature. Defense pacts are correlated with drawing alliance partners into wars, but only in the very early stages of the war—roughly the first month of a conflict. Such pacts cease to be correlated with joining thereafter. Thus, if antebellum alliances are not honored quickly, they are unlikely to be honored at all. Interestingly, neither neutrality pacts nor ententes were significantly correlated with states joining ongoing wars regardless of whether the first month of combat was included or excluded. The finding of support for defense pacts, but not for entente and neutrality pacts may be explained by two factors. One, it could be argued that defense pacts are a stronger form of alliance and indicate stronger ties between two states than do the other types of alliances, and therefore, are more likely to be honored. Two, it could be that the nature of ententes and neutrality pacts complicates the relationship between allegiance and joining. Ententes call for action only in a specific set of circumstances. Thus, one member of the entente may become involved in a war without triggering the *casus foederis*. For this reason, the finding may not indicate that ententes are not honored, but rather that members of ententes are frequently embroiled in wars that do not involve the conditions stipulated to activate the treaty. Similarly, the finding that neutrality pacts do not transmit war may actually suggest that, though such treaties indicate tension between two states,[20] they may actually be somewhat successful in resolving those tensions. In other words, if neutrality pacts are successful, they should reduce the incidences of states joining ongoing wars. However, because they indicate tension between two states, they may be a sign, though not a cause, of an increased likelihood of joining. These two effects would tend to cancel each other out, and this is likely why no relationship between neutrality pacts and joining can be discerned.

Results: Unexpected Events and States Leaving Wars

In addition to these hypotheses on joining, it was posed in Chapter 2 that revealed information should also make remaining in a war less attractive. Cox proportional hazards models were used to determine whether unexpected events were correlated with states leaving wars.[21] Unlike with joining, all states eventually leave wars, thus a hazard model is appropriate.

The variables used in the first model, with the exception of the number of belligerents, are all the same as variables used in the joining models and thus do not need to be described again. The number of belligerents was taken directly from the COW database and is simply the number of countries actively participating in a war in a given month. In this first model—see Table 3.6—unexpected events were treated as one variable. The results show that as predicted, unexpected events are correlated with belligerents leaving wars. States were 41.8% more likely to exit the war after an unexpected event occurred. This is important, as the logic underpinning the hypothesis that unexpected events cause states to join wars also strongly suggests that unexpected events should cause states to leave wars. Thus, this finding is additional support for the joining hypothesis or at least the logic underpinning it.

The findings for the control variables are interesting as well. The presence of a great power in a war and the presence of a great power on each side of the war both decrease the odds a belligerent will exit the war by 34.6% and 44.4% respectively. This is likely because the presence of great powers, especially on both sides of a conflict, means that there are more resources available to each side and they

20 Kadera (1998).

21 States that left a war and then later rejoined were counted as having exited and then treated as a new case after they again became a belligerent. The dependent variable and the number of belligerents were taken directly from the COW dataset. The other variables, with the exception of regime type which will be covered later, were operationalized in the same manner as discussed in the previous section.

Table 3.6 Leaving War: Unexpected Events as One Variable

	Hazard Ratio	Robust Standard Error	P > |z|
Unexpected Event in Given or Prior Two Months	1.418	0.164	0.002
Belligerent is a Great Power	1.299	0.175	0.053
Great Power in the War	0.636	0.102	0.005
Great Powers on Each Side	0.556	0.104	0.002
Number of Belligerents	1.000	0.015	0.980

* Holding all variables at their mode

N = 5360

Wald Chi Squared = 64.31

will be able to continue the war for a longer time. Also, the presence of a great power on each side reduces the chance that either side will be swiftly overrun. The number of belligerents, however, does not seem to affect the likelihood of exit by a state. This is counterintuitive as it seems likely that larger wars should last longer. This may well be true, but such large wars often involve some of the belligerents exiting early through defeat. For example, World War Two was a long war involving many belligerents, but many of the states involved left quite quickly due to being overrun by the Wehrmacht. Thus, the effects of longer wars and the overrunning of some belligerents may cancel each other out and thus result in the null finding. Finally, great powers were 29.9% more likely to exit a war than other states, however, this finding just misses being significant at the 0.05 level. As great powers' correlation with quicker exits is statistically significant in the next two models, it is worth exploring why this may be. The key is to remember that other control variables are already capturing the lengthening effect great power involvement can have when they are on both sides of a conflict. By definition, anytime a belligerent is a great power it means that there is a great power in the conflict. This is important as the effect of a great power being in a conflict more than cancels out the effect of a belligerent being a great power. Thus, the finding that great powers leave sooner than other states indicates only that great powers leave conflicts involving other great powers sooner than do lesser powers. A conflict involving only minor powers will still likely be shorter than one involving a great power. The marginal effects of the great powers variables vary from being about three quarters the size of the effect of the unexpected events variable to being slightly more than one and a quarter times as large. Thus, the magnitudes of the effects of the variables are about the same.

The finding that unexpected events lead to quicker exit, however, cannot be taken on face value. Recall, it was argued in Chapter 2 that regime type must be considered when examining when states exit wars. Goemans (2000) argues that mixed regimes should respond differently to negative events than they do to positive events. Specifically, mixed regimes will try to gamble for resurrection when faced with negative events. Thus, though unexpected events, whether positive or negative, should make most regimes more likely to exit the war, negative unexpected events should not make mixed regimes more likely to exit. Additionally, any other regime in the war with the mixed regime will not be more likely to exit either, as the mixed regime's refusal to negotiate an end to the war will force both its allies and enemies to continue to fight. For this reason, unexpected events were broken down into events which hurt mixed regimes and those which did not.[22] Events were deemed positive for a belligerent if they shifted the relative balances of forces in their favor, strengthened the belligerent or its allies internally, or weakened an opponent internally. Conversely, events that shifted the relative balance of forces against a belligerent, weakened the belligerent or its allies internally, or strengthened an opponent were deemed to be negative. All events were coded as being either positive or negative for a given belligerent. Internal disturbances and changes of government were always coded as negative, unless the change of government clearly and quickly increased the internal stability of the belligerent. States are classified as democracies, mixed regimes, or dictatorships using Goemans' classification based on the Polity IV dataset. The regime type variables were derived using Goemans' typology that created a twenty-one point scale created by subtracting the autocracy index from the democracy index in the Polity IV database. Regimes with a score of seventeen or greater are democracies, while regimes with a score of six or less are dictatorships. Regimes scoring from seven to sixteen are coded as mixed regimes.[23] In order to be viewed as hurting a mixed regime, the event did not have to directly impact the mixed regime, but could have been detrimental to its allies. However, coalitions were only considered to include mixed regimes if those regimes were major belligerents. States were deemed to be major belligerents if they suffered at least 50% of their proportional share of casualties as recorded by COW. Thus, in a war with ten belligerents on one side, a state would have to have suffered 5% of its alliance's total casualties to be considered a major belligerent. In practice, the effect of this rule is very small. It excludes mixed regimes in only two wars: the Sino-Japanese War and World War Two. These belligerents are South Africa in both wars and Yugoslavia, Finland, and Hungary in World War Two. Military events were deemed to have

22 Events could not be categorized as positive or negative for the regressions related to joining as it is not always clear whether an event in a war is positive or negative for a non-belligerent. In fact, some unexpected events in a war may be viewed by a non-belligerent as irrelevant to their interests, rather than either positive or negative.

23 Additionally, France was coded as a dictatorship during the Franco-Mexican war based on Goemans' research.

hurt a mixed regime if the unexpected event was a poorer than expected military showing for the mixed regime or its allies or if the states were subjected to a military mutiny. Political events were deemed to have hurt mixed regimes if the unexpected event was an assassination, coup, protests, or weakening of the ruling government as such events destabilize states and at least temporarily reduce their ability to wage war successfully. These results can be seen in Table 3.7.

The effects of the control variables remain about the same as before. The number of belligerents is not significant, but the great power variables do affect the likelihood of exit. Being a great power increases a state's odds of exit by 33.8%, but having a great power in the war or a great power on both sides of the war, decreases the odds of exit by 39.1% and 45.0% respectively.

The main findings are the two unexpected events variables. Events which did not hurt mixed regimes led to states exiting wars sooner, just as both the revealed information and Goemans regime type hypotheses would predict. An event of this type increased the likelihood of a state's exit by 42.4%. As predicted, these events are strongly correlated with states exiting. Just as in the decision to join wars, states use information revealed or generated by these events to recalculate their anticipated benefits from remaining at war. While this will not always cause a state to leave a war, it often will, as is shown by the results. Also as predicted, events which hurt regimes were not statistically speaking significantly correlated with exit. They do not clearly lead to either quicker exits, nor to mixed regimes gambling for resurrection, thereby delaying both their and their opponents' exit. The reason no systematic gambling for resurrection can be seen is that high magnitude unexpected events can force even mixed regimes to sue for peace.

Table 3.7 Leaving War: Unexpected Events and Regime Type

	Hazard Ratio	Robust Standard Error	P > |z|
Event Hurt Mixed Regimes	1.036	0.123	0.765
Event Did Not Hurt Mixed Regimes	1.424	0.189	0.008
Belligerent is a Great Power	1.338	0.180	0.030
Great Power in the War	0.609	0.098	0.002
Great Powers on Each Side	0.550	0.101	0.001
Number of Belligerents	1.006	0.015	0.704

* Holding all variables at their mode

N = 5360

Wald Chi Squared = 60.57

Thus, they gamble for resurrection after lower magnitude events and collapse after higher magnitude events.

This dynamic can be seen in Table 3.8, where unexpected events are further broken down by their magnitude and whether they were political or military in nature. The results generally support both the revealed information hypothesis and Goemans' regime type hypothesis.[24] Level two and three military events which did not hurt mixed regimes worked exactly as expected. They increased the likelihood of exit by 128% and 169% respectively. Similarly, level two military events which hurt mixed regimes reduced the likelihood of exit by 56.1%. As predicted, unexpected events that hurt mixed regimes cause mixed regimes to gamble for resurrection. Interestingly, level three military events that hurt mixed regimes slightly increased the odds of exit, but the relationship was not statistically significant. Likely this is because after such an event mixed regimes would prefer to gamble for resurrection, but the scale of the defeat suffered often makes this impossible. Thus, no relationship between the event and exit is discernable as is consistent with the regime type hypothesis. While none of the level one events, political or military, were significantly correlated with exit, this is not surprising as they are the smallest scale events. This merely indicates that larger events are what drove the earlier findings and what cause states to exit wars. Thus, overall military events work as predicted. Those events above level one that did not hurt mixed regimes greatly increased the likelihood of exit, while those that hurt mixed regimes did not increase the likelihood of exit likely due to attempts by mixed regimes to gamble for resurrection.

The results for political events are less clear. As predicted, level two political events that hurt mixed regimes significantly reduce the likelihood of exit—by 88.4%—thus showing evidence that mixed regimes are gambling for resurrection. Level three political events which hurt mixed regimes, however, increase the likelihood of exit by a whopping 1,147%! While this is consistent with the revealed information hypothesis, it is not consistent with the regime type hypothesis. Likely after such events mixed regimes, though they would prefer to gamble for resurrection, simply cannot and are forced to sue for peace or collapse. The massive increase in the likelihood is in part because level three political events are extremely rare. There are only four of them in the entire dataset—see the Appendix—and all of them adversely affect mixed regimes. This is why there are no findings for level three political events which did not hurt mixed regimes. They simply do not exist. Given the rarity of such events and that they are correlated with exit even when they hurt mixed regimes, their absence in the "did not hurt mixed regimes" category should not be seen as particularly harmful to the revealed information hypothesis. What is troubling is that level two political events that did not hurt mixed regimes are not correlated with exit. In fact, to the extent that there is any relationship, it is negative. This does not fit with either the revealed information hypothesis or the regime type hypothesis.

24 The results for the control variables remain essentially the same as before.

Table 3.8 Leaving War: Disaggregated Unexpected Events and Regime Type

	Hazard Ratio	Robust Standard Error	P > |z|
Level 1 Military Event Hurt Mixed Regime	1.134	0.276	0.607
Level 2 Military Event Hurt Mixed Regime	0.439	0.153	0.018
Level 3 Military Event Hurt Mixed Regime	1.123	0.441	0.768
Level 1 Political Event Hurt Mixed Regime	1.450	0.331	0.104
Level 2 Political Event Hurt Mixed Regime	0.116	0.092	0.007
Level 3 Political Event Hurt Mixed Regime	12.4740	4.577	0.000
Level 1 Military Event Did Not Hurt Mixed Regime	0.994	0.200	0.977
Level 2 Military Event Did Not Hurt Mixed Regime	2.280	0.463	0.000
Level 3 Military Event Did Not Hurt Mixed Regime	2.688	1.049	0.011
Level 1 Political Event Did Not Hurt Mixed Regime	0.905	0.284	0.752
Level 2 Political Event Did Not Hurt Mixed Regime	1.24	0.559	0.636
Belligerent is a Great Power	1.275	0.155	0.046
Great Power in the War	0.631	0.103	0.005
Great Powers on Each Side	0.481	0.094	0.000
Number of Belligerents	1.000	0.016	0.976

* Holding all variables at their mode

N = 5360

Wald Chi Squared = 180.79

On the whole, however, the results support the revealed information and regime type hypotheses. Large scale events are generally correlated with an increase in the likelihood of exit unless the event hurt a mixed regime. In such cases, mixed regimes attempt to gamble for resurrection. This is often successful for level two events and thus reduces the likelihood of exit, but the level three events are often too devastating and thus mixed regimes are often unable to gamble for resurrection and such events may actually increase the likelihood of exit.

Conclusions

There are several overarching conclusions to be drawn from these statistics. The first and most important is that unexpected events are an important cause of states voluntarily joining ongoing wars. This is true of military and political events and especially higher magnitude events. This finding is important because it explains when and why late joining occurs and lends strong support to the revealed information hypothesis. The previous findings in the literature helped to illuminate which states were likely to join ongoing wars, but not when or necessarily why they would do so. In the previous literature it was unclear why states waited to join wars well after they began, rather than simply joining at the wars' outset.

Prior to the findings supporting the unexpected events hypotheses, one might reasonably suppose that states were simply waiting for the adversaries to wear each other out in order to pay a smaller cost in terms of lives and material than they would have paid had they joined at the outset. Such a hypothesis implies that states which waited to join wars were somehow cleverer than their fellow states and had found a way to reduce the cost of war. The findings of this study suggest that such a line of reasoning is likely wrong. It is improbable that unexpected events would be so highly correlated with states joining wars if states were just waiting for the combatants to fight themselves out. There is no reason to expect that such a process would be highly correlated with unexpected events, as attrition is not necessarily unexpected. Indeed, for the strategy of waiting for combatants to exhaust themselves to be rational, attrition would have to be expected. It is more reasonable to conclude that the hypothesis advanced by this work is correct and that states join wars primarily due to changes to the expected outcome and implications of wars.[25]

The statistics also confirmed the importance of geography in explaining the spread of war. They confirmed both the hypothesis that contiguity increases the likelihood of joining and the hypothesis that being in the same region as an ongoing war increases the likelihood a state will join. Also, great powers were found to be more likely to join ongoing wars than were minor powers. The presence of a great power in a war, however, was not found to be significant unless that great power had joined the conflict, rather than having been an initial belligerent. Finally, the study also found that institutions must be accounted for when attempting to explain why wars widen. UN involvement seems to have played an important role in why non-belligerents, especially minor powers that were geographically removed from the conflict, joined the Korean and 1990–91 Gulf Wars. Though these findings do not prove Betts' theory, they do suggest it is wise to at least consider and control for the effects of international institutions.

Just as interesting as confirmation of these hypotheses was the need to modify or discard other hypotheses. Specifically, alliances were found to transmit war

25 This is not to say that the attrition hypothesis is never correct. Rather, the claim is that the revealed information hypothesis predominates.

from ally to ally only in the early stages of a war and even this more limited correlation applied only to defense pacts. Also, states with enduring rivals already engaged in a war were no more likely to join that war than any other state, nor were democracies anymore likely to join to aid their fellow democracies. The enduring rivalries finding runs counter to what one would expect based on the existing literature. Finally, the length of the war did not help explain the likelihood of joining.

In addition to the findings on joining, the findings on states leaving wars were important as well. Unexpected events are clearly correlated with states leaving wars. This was most clearly true of higher magnitude events. The finding held for both military and political events, though the relationship was clearer for military events in part due to the extreme rarity of level three political events. This finding, combined with findings that unexpected events lead to joining, strongly supports the theory that states decide if they want to join or leave wars based on what they learn from those wars.

The regime type hypothesis also held up well. In general, moderate to severe unexpected events which did not hurt mixed regimes increased the likelihood that any state would exit. Events which hurt mixed regimes, however, caused them to gamble for resurrection which in turn reduced the likelihood of exit for all states in those wars. The exception to this was level three political events in the face of which mixed regimes were unable to continue and thus attempts at resurrection did not lengthen states' involvement.

It was also found that having a great power in a war or on both sides of a war lengthened wars and reduced the likelihood of exit. This finding makes sense intuitively, as great powers have more resources and if they are on both sides of a conflict, they can draw that conflict out. More surprising was that the number of belligerents had no effect on the likelihood of exit. This is likely due to the fact that although many wars with a large number of belligerents are long, even within these wars, some belligerents exit the wars quite quickly due to being overrun. The fate of states like Poland or Belgium in World War Two are examples of quick exits by belligerents in what are otherwise long wars. Also, some wars with a great many belligerents are short. The 1990–91 Gulf War is a prime example. Despite these occasional surprises in the control variables, states behaved generally as expected in the models exploring when states exit wars, especially in relation to the unexpected events variables.

Thus, the basic theory and key hypotheses advanced in Chapter 2 were supported by the large n study. Unexpected events were shown to be important in explaining when and why states join and leave wars, though the latter process is complicated by regime type. It is now necessary to flesh out these findings. The next four chapters are case studies designed to do exactly that. Two of the cases examine instances of joining—the Crimean War and First World War—while the third looks at an instance where states seemingly should have joined, but did not—the Franco-Prussian War. Finally, the fourth case looks at joining in the post-World War Two era.

Chapter 4
The Crimean War: Public Opinion, Divided Cabinets, and the Partial Spread of War

The conqueror is always a lover of peace;
he would prefer to take over our country
unopposed—Karl von Clausewitz[1]

The Crimean War was an important watershed in European history. It destroyed the diplomatic system that had been set up by the Congress of Vienna. In particular, the war destroyed the Holy Alliance and, along with the revolutions of 1848, helped to unleash a period of instability and war in European politics. Its important place in history, however, is only a minor reason why the Crimean War was chosen as one of the case studies. The Crimean War began as one in the long series of Russo-Turkish wars of the 18th and 19th centuries, but unlike the other Russo-Turkish wars, grew to become a major European war. Two great powers and one minor power joined the war and several others considered joining or were thought likely to join by contemporaries. Thus, the war provides a contrast between those that joined and those that did not. The war is also interesting because of how long it took the British and French to join the Turkish side. Finally, the war illustrates quite clearly that the actions of belligerents in any war are to a large extent shaped by the possibility that outside states may join the war, even if those states never actually enter the war. Belligerents craft policies both to react to the actions of potential interveners and to influence the decisions of those potential interveners.[2]

The chapter is structured in the following manner. First, the antebellum goals of the states that joined or reasonably could have joined are explored. This is necessary as it provides a base from which the later actions of the states involved can be understood. Second, the crisis leading to the war and the diplomatic exchanges during the war itself are reviewed. This discussion shows why certain states joined the war and why they joined when they did. Third, the events and causes that led to peace are reviewed. Finally, conclusions are drawn about the role unexpected events played in the spread and termination of the war.

1 Edwards 2004, 25.

2 Belligerents will craft policies both to reduce the likelihood of hostile intervention and to increase the possibility of the entry of potential allies.

State Goals and Beliefs

To understand why states behaved as they did during the crises leading up to the war and during the war itself, it is first necessary to understand the goals of the relevant states, beginning with the original belligerents: Russia and the Ottoman Empire. Russian goals prior to the Crimean War were very straightforward and were almost exclusively set by Nicholas I. Though he did listen to the advice of his councilors, especially that of his foreign minister Count Karl Nesselrode, Nicholas always made the final decision. Nicholas wanted first to resolve the crisis that had resulted from the Holy Places Question and second to obtain a legal protectorate over all the Orthodox subjects residing within the Ottoman Empire. The second goal, if achieved, would result in a *de facto* protectorate over the empire itself. These were strictly political goals, despite the involvement of religious issues in the Holy Places Question.[3] He and his councilors were more than willing to go to war with the Ottomans to achieve these goals, though of course if they could be achieved without bloodshed that was preferable. Whether Nicholas would have been deterred at this stage by the prospect of a general European war is less clear, though it is clear he saw such a war as far less attractive than a war with the Ottomans alone and worth taking greater care to avoid provoking.

Unlike these rather straightforward goals, the beliefs of Nicholas and his advisors about the status of European politics prior to the crisis were more complicated. First, Nicholas believed that Austria and Prussia were loyal allies, and thus, the only threat he faced was from Britain and France.[4] He stated to Sir Hamilton Seymour, the British ambassador in St. Petersburg who had queried Nicholas about Austria's likely reaction to Russian plans in the Balkans: "Oh, but you must understand that when I speak of Russia, I speak of Austria as well. What suits one, suits the other. Our interests, as regards Turkey, are perfectly identical."[5] This statement seems not so much a bluff, but an actual belief.[6] To believe this, was to ignore true Austrian interests in the Balkans. Such erroneous beliefs as to the interests of others seem to have been somewhat commonly held by Nicholas. He often believed that Russia's interests were the same as those of what

3 Wetzel 1985, 77. The Tsar's policy was probably not driven by economic issues in the Danube delta and in the Straits. Of course, in regard to the Straits, it is nearly impossible to disentangle Russian economic interests from Russian political interests as control of the Straits would have greatly furthered both types of interests. The Holy Places Question grew out of debates between Orthodox and Latin Catholic priests and pilgrims over their right of access to the Christian holy sites in Palestine. France backed the Catholics, while Russia backed the Orthodox. The issue was resolved in part with the Ottomans, who controlled Palestine at the time, granting additional privileges to the Catholics. This set a dangerous precedent for expanding the millet system in the Ottoman empire, which the Russians sought to exploit via the Menshikov Mission—see below.

4 Taylor 1969, 103.

5 Troubetzkoy 1986, 103.

6 Ibid.

he called "Europe," the great powers other than France: namely Prussia, Austria, and Britain.

More reasonably, Nicholas believed that France would not oppose Russia without British backing and that such backing was unlikely.[7] First, Nicholas believed his good personal relationship with Lord George Aberdeen, the British prime minister, would limit British hostility. Nicholas's faith in his relationship with Aberdeen was such that he told Seymour:

> If I could hold but ten minutes conversation with your Ministers – with Lord Aberdeen, for instance, who knows me so well, who has full confidence in me, as I have in him — [the issue could be resolved]. A general understanding is all I require — that between gentlemen is sufficient.[8]

This is not to suggest the Nicholas advanced his plan only because he thought he could rely on his personal relationship with Aberdeen. He had originally suggested the partition of the Ottoman Empire to Seymour before he knew Aberdeen had become prime minister.[9] Nicholas based much of this belief of British neutrality on the secret Anglo-Russian agreement of 1844 in which Britain and Russia promised to cooperate in the event of the dissolution of the Ottoman Empire.[10] The agreement was not the clear statement of British support Nicholas believed it to be. It had been only a private agreement and the British cabinet had not been informed of it at the time. Though later foreign ministers were aware of it, they clearly were not bound by it.[11] Thus, the agreement was not necessarily a reflection of current British policy.

Even if Anglo-Russian understanding and Nicholas's relationship with Aberdeen fell through, Anglo-French cooperation seemed unlikely for many reasons. First, France was ruled by a Bonaparte who had helped overthrow both a constitutional monarchy and a republic, hardly a traditional candidate for a British ally.[12] Second, France and Britain had been involved in a naval building race and there was even an invasion scare as recently as early 1853. Third, Lord John Russell, a minister without portfolio in Aberdeen's cabinet and both a former prime minister and former foreign secretary, had raised no objections when in late 1852 Filipp Brunnov, the Russian ambassador in London, had said Russia planned to take a tough stance to limit French influence at the Sublime Porte.[13] Russell had

7 Goldfrank 1994, 123–7 ; Saab 1977, 14; Taylor 1969, 98.

8 Saab 1977, 15; Seaman 1969, 2; Troubetzkoy 1986, 97 and 102. Though Aberdeen wished to avoid war and viewed Nicholas as an honorable man, it is not at all clear that the relationship between Nicholas and Aberdeen was as warm as Nicholas believed it to be.

9 Henderson 1969, 15.

10 Troubetzkoy 1986, 97.

11 Henderson 1969, 13.

12 Troubetzkoy 1986, 97.

13 Puryear 1969b, 8.

also rebuffed a French offer of an alliance in January of 1853.[14] Fourth, Brunnov had sent word to St. Petersburg in early 1853 that British public opinion would not support maintaining the Ottoman Empire.[15] Fifth, Nicholas could also feel confident in the fact that Britain and Russia had coordinated their policies against France from 1844 until just before the present crisis.[16] Finally, Britain and France had not fought on the same side in a war in more than two hundred years.[17] Thus, Nicholas' confidence that an Anglo-French entente would not materialize was not without solid grounds.

In contrast, Nesselrode feared that a long war with the Ottoman Empire would become general even given these difficulties to Anglo-French cooperation.[18] Both he and Nicholas wanted a quick and decisive war, not a drawn out affair.[19] The Russians realized that quick wars offer far less opportunity for outside interference than do longer wars. As Russia's military was clearly superior to that of the Turks, Russia could only be hurt by outside involvement, and thus, it was important to prosecute the war with all possible speed. Nesselrode also warned that Britain and Austria would not support Russia in a war against France.[20] Nesselrode should have been able to get this point across, especially as Seymour had tried to dissuade the Tsar from his proposed plan.[21] In the Russian system, however, Nicholas had the final say and Nesselrode did not conceive his duty as anything more than giving the Tsar advice and executing the Tsar's wishes to the best of his ability. This is not to say the Tsar thought he could succeed in the face of united opposition from the other great powers. He knew he could not.[22] Rather, he did not expect to face united great power opposition.

Of course, the secret agreement with Britain obliged both Russia and Britain to uphold the status quo in the Ottoman Empire unless it was on the point of disintegration. Thus, it would seem quite obvious that Russia was violating this agreement, and therefore, should have expected British opposition. The reason the Russians did not see the situation this way stems from a pair of mistaken beliefs. First, Nicholas seems to have believed quite firmly that the empire was "a sick man" and was on the verge of collapse.[23] It was his *idée fixe*. Nicholas

14 Ibid, 9.

15 Ibid, 8. In hindsight, it would be difficult to think of how the ambassador could have been more incorrect in his assessment of what British public opinion would allow.

16 Ibid.

17 Wetzel 1985, 78.

18 Saab 1977, 13.

19 Ibid, 155.

20 Henderson 1969, 14–16; Taylor 1969, 98. Nicholas appears to have believed this warning from Nesselrode, but only to the extent that it indicated that he would not have active allies in a war with France. He did not fear a war with an apparently isolated France.

21 Henderson 1969, 14.

22 Wetzel 1985, 77.

23 Henderson 1969, 16; Seton-Watson 1969, 36.

believed allowing the empire to disintegrate without taking swift action would be a disaster. He interpreted Ottoman attempts at reform as death throes.[24] Adding to this impression were the revolts in Montenegro and other parts of European Turkey and the inept Turkish efforts to suppress them. On top of this, Austria had recently been able to dissuade the Ottomans from campaigning against the Montenegrans simply by dispatching a diplomatic mission. Nicholas felt not only that the time was ripe to pressure the Turks, but that it was imperative it be done immediately. Second, Nicholas and his chief advisors, including Nesselrode, believed the treaty of Kutchuk-Kainardji in 1774 had already given Russia a legal protectorate over the Ottoman's Orthodox subjects. Thus, they were doing nothing more than insisting on their *de jure* treaty rights. Unfortunately, the treaty had done no such thing and the Turks knew it. The actual wording, however, was somewhat vague and may help explain the Russian misinterpretation. The clause in question read as follows:

> The Sublime Porte promises constant protection to the Christian religion and to the Churches of this religion. She allows the Minister of the Imperial Court to make, at all times, representations to the Porte, either for the church built at Constantinople ... or for those ministering in it, and she promises to pay heed to these observations as coming from a person of importance and belonging to a neighboring and sincerely friendly Power.[25]

The text gave Russia only the right to lodge protests at the Sultan's court on behalf of his Christian subjects, rather than any actual authority to protect those subjects. Nicholas' and Nesselrode's misunderstanding of the treaty—neither bothered to reread the treaty at this stage in the crisis—allowed them to believe their demands for an actual protectorate were quite moderate and were not a significant departure from the status quo when in fact they were.[26] This in turn allowed the Russians, especially Nicholas, to deceive themselves as to the likelihood of their demands leading to a general European war.

Opposing the Russians' aims were the Ottoman Turks. They had two straightforward goals. First, the Turks wished to avoid conceding a Russian

24 Simpson 1969, 74.

25 Troubetzkoy 1986, 99.

26 Saab 1977, 27. Both had read the treaty previously, but neither had a clear recollection of it when the Russian demands were presented to the Turks. A more cynical interpretation might be that Nesselrode and Nicholas failed to review the treaty not because they were sure of the authority it granted them, but rather because they did not want to learn that the treaty did not give them the authority they claimed. Nicholas certainly refused to ever be drawn into discussions of the text by foreign diplomats. Saab, however, claims both Nesselrode and Nicholas were later somewhat embarrassed by how far they stretched the treaty. Whether or not this is the case, the Russians proceeded from the premise, and especially in Nicholas' case seemed to believe, that they were simply insisting on their *de jure* rights.

protectorate over the Ottoman Empire. Second, they wanted to maintain the territorial integrity of the Ottoman state. The Turks also realized that going to war with Russia without the aid of Britain or France would be a disaster.[27] Such a military disaster would lead to a far worse outcome than what Russia was demanding. The Ottoman leaders, however, were somewhat constrained by domestic public opinion. The reforms that had been undertaken in the last decade and a half at the instigation of the British, among others, had given the masses to some extent, and the religious classes to a larger extent, a say in Ottoman politics. The masses could make their weight felt only through protests and riots, but the religious classes had some *de jure* power through the *Meclis-i Umumî*, which was similar to an extremely limited parliament. These two classes were very hostile to the Russians and to any concessions. The Ottoman leadership could concede only so much to the Russians without risking significant domestic fallout. Thus, the goals of the Russians and Ottomans conflicted significantly with each other.

Given the uncertainty of whether aid would be forthcoming from Britain and France, the Ottomans found themselves in a very difficult spot. Both war and conceding to the Russian demands were unattractive. In the past, the Turks had obtained moderate success in negotiations with foreign powers simply by stalling for time. This tactic allowed foreign interest to wane or become distracted by events elsewhere. It also gained time to elicit the interest and aid of allies. Years of practice had allowed the Ottomans to perfect delaying tactics and not surprisingly they resorted to them when the Russians presented their demands by dispatching Prince Menshikov to Constantinople. Their ability to delay had the effect of drawing out the crisis as will be seen below.

In addition to the goals of the initial belligerents, the goals of those states that did join the war or could have been expected to join the war must also be examined. These states are Britain, France, Sardinia, Austria, Prussia, the lesser German states, Sweden, Persia, and Greece. It is difficult to speak of British goals, as Britain's cabinet was badly divided prior to and during the crisis caused by the Menshikov Mission. Additionally, Lord George Aberdeen was a weak prime minister who could not force his views on his fellow ministers.[28] Thus, two camps formed. On one side were the Peelites. They were led by Aberdeen and supported by William Gladstone. They wished to avoid war and felt Nicholas was an honorable man with whom the British could strike a bargain. On the other side were the Whigs, led by the home secretary, Lord Henry Palmerston, and to a lesser degree the Foreign Secretary, Lord John Russell. They viewed Russia as a threat to the Straits, India, and liberalism. Russell in particular was driven by Whig idealism and concern for India.[29] Also holding a strong antipathy toward Russia was the powerful British ambassador in Constantinople, Lord Stratford Canning

27 Small clashes along the border could be handled without overly serious consequences, but Ottoman prospects if Russia launched a full-scale invasion were grim.

28 Seaman 1969, 2.

29 Ibid, 1.

de Redcliffe. Lord Stratford in particular wanted to oppose Russian designs and deal Russia a sharp diplomatic reverse. In part because of the divisions within the cabinet and parliament as a whole, public opinion was able to play a very large role in the formation of British policy and it formed along lines very different from those anticipated by Ambassador Brunnov.[30]

Despite the division among the British ministers about the threat Russia posed and the desirability of war, some common goals can be derived. Primarily, the British wanted to preserve the balance of power within Europe, and believed this required preserving Ottoman control over the Straits.[31] No British minister wanted to see the Ottoman Empire descend into chaos nor did they want to see Constantinople and the Straits under the control of a European power. Most importantly, no one in the cabinet believed that an immediate crisis existed in the Ottoman Empire, and thus, there was no perceived need for an immediate and drastic solution to the Eastern Question. This contrasted sharply with Nicholas' view of the Ottoman Empire's health and his belief that there was a pressing need for a solution to the Eastern Question. The British ministers felt that the Ottoman Empire might collapse eventually, but as Russell stated in a letter to Seymour, the collapse was not imminent but "may happen in 20, 50 or 100 years hence."[32] This is not to say the British were enamored with the Ottoman government, far from it. Reforming the Ottoman Empire was a long running British project, albeit one with limited success. The British believed the Porte was viable for the time being and with proper reforms who knew who long it could last.[33] The British also wanted to maintain their dominant influence in the Ottoman Empire. This required, in part, opposing any strengthening of the millet system for dealing with Christian minorities. Britain feared that the millets might become vehicles for separatist movements and for further Russian influence.[34] Nicholas's demands threatened to turn the entire Ottoman Empire into a giant millet under his protection. British commercial interests would also be hurt by Russian dominance of the region.[35] British opposition to such a plan, therefore, is not surprising, though whether the issue would result in war was not clear until late in the crisis.

Discovering French motivations is also difficult. French policy lacked central direction, as Napoleon III remained detached from foreign affairs.[36] French policy was plagued by bureaucratic infighting. French ministers and diplomats often worked at cross-purposes. Édouard Thouvenel, the deputy foreign minister, went as far as to tell Adolphe de Bourqueney, the French ambassador to Austria, to

30 Ibid, 2.

31 Taylor 1969, 103.

32 Troubetzkoy 1986, 100.

33 Seton-Watson 1969, 36.

34 Saab 1977, 150–1. The millets were a system of granting special rights to minority confessional communities within the Ottoman Empire.

35 Ibid, 157.

36 Saab, Knapp, and Knapp 1986, 475–7.

ignore the official dispatches sent by the foreign minister, Édouard Drouyn de Lhuys.[37] The lack of a unified policy became such a problem that de Lhuys, said in exasperation, "We never have a plan. Everything is done by instinct."[38]

Despite these difficulties, French motives for joining the Crimean War can be discerned. French involvement had both domestic and international sources. Domestically, Napoleon III needed the support of the Clericals, an important pro-Papist faction. Napoleon had already intervened on the behalf of the Pope during the revolutions of 1848. This action was clearly done for domestic reasons, as Napoleon opposed the status quo in the Italian peninsula and had as a long-term goal the breaking of the conservative and Austrian hegemony over the peninsula.[39] Clearly, his intervention against the Roman Republic ran counter to these aims and can only be explained by his need to curry favor with Clericals.

Napoleon continued this policy by becoming the champion of the Latin monks in their clash with the Orthodox monks in the debate over the control of the Holy Places. Both the Latin and Orthodox monks wanted the Ottomans to grant them exclusive control of these religious sites in Palestine. Nicholas I championed the cause of the Orthodox monks. This drew France and Russia into conflict in their attempts influence Ottoman policy. The dispute, however, did not cause France to go to war with Russia. Though it did cause a strain in Franco-Russian relations, the question was solved diplomatically prior to the outbreak of the Crimean War. The issue, however, did draw France deeply into Ottoman politics.

Napoleon III's foreign policy goals also led to conflict with Russia. He wanted to destroy the diplomatic arrangements associated with the Congress of Vienna. These arrangements kept France diplomatically isolated and prevented France from pursuing most of its major foreign policy goals. Napoleon felt this isolation keenly, but realized the confusion caused by the recent revolutions had created opportunities for France provided the confusion could be brought to light.[40] He saw destroying the Holy Alliance and establishing an alliance with Great Britain as the keys to escaping the straight jacket that had been imposed on France at the Congress of Vienna.[41] De Lhuys supported Napoleon in his desire to ally with Britain.[42] The Balkans offered the perfect area to achieve these goals. It was the one of the few areas in which Russia and Austria could be brought into conflict and it was also an area where British and French interests could be aligned. The Menshikov Mission and the 1841 Straits Convention gave France an opportunity to turn a Russo-Turkish dispute into a European affair.[43]

---

37 Ibid, 477 and 495.

38 Ibid, 496.

39 Bourgeois 1969, 42; McEvedy 1982, 14.

40 Saab 1977, 150.

41 Jomini 1969, 65; Saab 1977, 150; Seaman 1969, 3.

42 Wetzel 1985, 73. De Lhuys and Bourqueney also pushed for an alliance with Austria.

43 Ibid, 74.

This is not to say Napoleon sought a war with Russia. He did not. If French goals could be met short of war, this was preferable.[44] Ideally, he wished to threaten Russia, destroy the Holy Alliance and then reach an accommodation with the Tsar prior to the outbreak of war.[45] Napoleon felt that, long-term, an alliance with Russia was the best course to pursue and naturally any war with Russia would make this long term goal more difficult to achieve.[46] An alliance with Russia, however, would not be productive until after the Holy Alliance had been destroyed and Russia was shaken from its desire to maintain the European status quo. Napoleon did not want war if the destruction of the Holy Alliance and an alliance with Great Britain could be achieved without it, but he was willing to risk war in order to obtain those goals. His desire to avoid alienating the Tsar is shown by his replacement of the bellicose French ambassador in Constantinople in early 1853 with a more moderate figure. Still, war itself might have benefits. It would allow France to restore honor to its arms—an important consideration in the 19th century—and it would bring much needed prestige, both internationally and domestically, to the Second Empire. Thus France had strong reasons for opposing Russia diplomatically and for risking, if not actually seeking, war.

Austria's situation could not have been more different. The coming of the Crimean War put Austria in an almost impossible bind. Overall, its interests aligned with the conservatism of Russia, but in the Eastern Question, its interests were aligned with liberal Britain and France.[47] Any change, foreign or domestic, was bad for the Austrians, and therefore, profound conservatism had underscored Austrian policy since 1815. Austria was allied with Prussia and Russia, both of which had monarchs that supported the conservative order. Austria was dependent on Russia in particular. In the Balkans, however, Russian and Austrian interests diverged, though Nicholas I seemed oblivious to this. Austria wanted no political changes in the Balkans, while Russia, convinced the collapse of the Ottoman Empire was imminent, wanted greater control over the affairs of the Balkans. This Russian desire was contrary to Austria's interests as any disturbances in the Balkans were likely to lead to disturbances in Austria itself—disturbances that Austria did not have the resources to combat in the wake of the revolutions of 1848. Even those revolutions had been put down only with Russian help. In an attempt to prevent further change Austria had dispatched the Leiningen mission to pressure the Ottomans to stop their campaign against the Montenegrans. The Austrians clearly assumed the less disorder there was in the Balkans, the less reason the Russians would have to intervene. The Ottomans yielded to the Austrian pressure, but this

44 Saab 1977, 150.
45 Saab, Knapp, and Knapp 1986, 469.
46 Taylor 1969, 102.
47 Puryear 1969a, 93; Wetzel 1985, 81.

success backfired as it convinced Nicholas that the Sublime Porte was weak and about to collapse.[48]

An additional source of conflict was that Austria wanted a freely navigable Danube while Russia had an economic interest in diverting trade, especially grain exports, from the Danube to Odessa.[49] Russia controlled the mouth of the Danube, and therefore, could bottle up Austrian exports. In 1853, Russia had deliberately failed to dredge the Sulina channel in the Danube delta despite Austrian and British protests.[50] This meant that goods had to be transferred from river boats to ocean going ships, rather than having one ship navigate both the river and Black Sea. This raised the cost of Austrian grain and caused enough economic hardship that even the most conservative of Austrian ministers came to oppose Russian domination of the Danube delta.[51] Despite these areas of conflict, Russia was Austria's closest ally. A war with Russia would be disastrous militarily, diplomatically, and financially. Even just breaking ties with Russia could lead to dangerous diplomatic isolation.

Austria could also ill afford to offend the western powers. France, in particular, was dangerous to Austria. France could support Sardinian efforts to liberate the Austria portions of Italy and create a united Italian kingdom. Austria, likely would need Russian or Prussian aid to hold northern Italy. Thus, Austria found itself in a position where it was dependent upon Russia, could be easily hurt by either France or Russia—and perhaps Prussia—and was greatly threatened by Russian aims in the Balkans. If Austria backed the Russians, it risked increased domestic disturbances among the Slavs and in its Italian possessions and greater dependence on Russia. Austria would bear the brunt of the fighting while Russia would pick up the spoils, much as had happened in the Napoleonic wars. Such a situation was hardly an attractive proposition. If Austria backed Britain and France, it would lose the friendship of its most valuable ally, Russia, and perhaps that of Prussia as well, as it was known that King Frederick Wilhelm IV was favorably disposed toward Russia. Thus, Austria's only rational course was to attempt to prevent the war. It needed to restrain both Russia in the Balkans and the liberal impulses of France and Britain.[52]

Similarly to Austria, Prussia and the lesser German states all wanted to prevent the war from becoming general, though unlike Austria they were not concerned

48 Goldfrank 1994, 115–20 and 122–3; Temperley 1969, 56. Leiningen did not achieve all of his goals. Notably, he failed to gain control over several small enclaves in the Western Balkans. This unwillingness on the part of the Ottomans to cede sovereignty over even small enclaves should have served as a partial warning to Nicholas that the Ottomans would not simply capitulate to his demands. Nicholas had been planning to pressure the Ottomans prior to Leiningen's mission, so while Leiningen failed in reducing the likelihood of Russian involvement in the Balkans, his actions did not cause the Menshikov Mission.

49 Puryear 1969a, 93. In wanting a freely navigable Danube, Austrian commercial interests were aligned with those of Britain.

50 Ibid, 94.

51 Wetzel 1985, 85.

52 Seaman 1969, 4; Wetzel 1985, 82.

about a Russo-Turkish war. The states that had territory along the Rhine, including Prussia, feared a French attack if the war became general, but none of the German states outside of Austria had interests in the Balkans.[53] The German states also had great respect for the Russian army, stemming from the Napoleonic wars and the suppression of the recent Hungarian uprising. Thus, none of these states could see any advantage from joining either side as such a move would ensure either a French or Russian attack. This said, the smaller German states and Prussia were in general led by conservatives who respected Nicholas I. This was especially true of Frederick Wilhelm IV of Prussia. He, like Franz Joseph of Austria, was not a great strategic thinker and the great Prussian minister, Otto von Bismarck, had yet to rise to power.[54] Still, Frederick Wilhelm knew Prussia's interests lay in remaining neutral and, as Austria's rival in Germany, Prussia stood to gain from any decline in Austria's position, including damage to the Austro-Russian alliance.[55] For the most part, the rest of the German states initially followed Prussia's lead and strove to remain neutral during the war.

Sardinia's main and almost only foreign policy goal had nothing to due with the Eastern Question at all.[56] Almost all of Sardinia's ministers and King Victor Emmanuel II had as their primary objective the unification of Italy under Sardinian rule. Camillo Paolo, conte di Cavour also had as an important goal the maintenance of his relatively liberal—at least by contemporary Italian standards—government. Victor Emmanuel desired to have his troops bring martial glory to his kingdom, perhaps in part to redeem the defeats of his father. Certainly, war was the king's favorite occupation and throughout his reign he sought out every opportunity to make war.[57]

Sweden, Greece, and Persia all had similar goals prior to the outbreak of war. All three wanted territory held by either Russia or the Ottoman Empire. Sweden desired to obtain large parts, if not all, of Finland from Russia. Finland had been held by Sweden prior to the Napoleonic Wars and a dispute over Finmark in northern Finland had recently soured Russo-Swedish relations. Still, King Oscar I was fairly risk averse and Sweden did not have any direct interests in the Eastern Question. Oscar worried that Sweden would not be able to hold any territory gained from Russia after the war unless Russia was thoroughly defeated. Similarly, Persia wanted to obtain several Ottoman provinces. The Persians and Ottomans were historically enemies and it should not be surprising that the Persians would

53 Wetzel 1985, 82. This also included Bavaria and Baden.

54 Seaman 1969, 1. At this point in his career, Bismarck was the Prussian delegate to the German Confederation at Frankfurt.

55 Wetzel 1985, 82.

56 The Kingdom of Sardinia consisted of the island of Sardinia itself and its three mainland—and contiguous—territories: Liguria, Savoy, and the Piedmont. Its capital, Turin, and most of its resources were on the mainland. Thus, even though the state's proper title is Sardinia, it should not be thought of as an island state.

57 Halperin 1963, 60.

have considered taking advantage of the Ottomans' weakness. Of course, Persia had also clashed in the past with both Russia and Britain and the Shah feared both powers. Persia desired to regain its lost Caucasian provinces from Russia and had designs on western Afghanistan that were contrary to British interests.[58] Finally, Greece had interests in obtaining Turkish territory as well. Many ethnic Greeks lived within the Ottoman Empire in 1853 and the Greek government wanted to either incorporate their fellow Hellenes within their kingdom or at a minimum aid their rebellions against the Ottoman authorities.[59] In the spring of 1853, Greece had resisted Ottoman claims to return two villages that the Greeks had occupied illegally. A visit from Admiral Kornilov of Russia had strengthened Greek resolve.[60] Though the matter was resolved through arbitration in favor of the Ottomans, Greek forces remained mobilized.[61] Additionally, Greece and Russia had a natural affinity due to their common Orthodoxy. Thus, Sweden, Persia, and Greece all had incentives to intervene in order to pick up spoils and aggrandize their territory if the opportunity presented itself.

The Drift to War and its Spread

The outbreak of the Crimean War was preceded by a long crisis, full of diplomatic maneuvers. The antebellum crisis began with the dispatch of Prince Alexander Menshikov, a popular figure among the pious Orthodox in Russia but a novice in foreign affairs, to Istanbul by the Tsar in order to resolve the Holy Places Question, obtain full rights for all Orthodox Christians throughout the Ottoman Empire, and have the Tsar recognized as their protector.[62] It was hoped that Menshikov would have as much success as the recent Leiningen mission. Unlike Count Christian von Leiningen, Menshikov attempted little diplomacy and did not seek a compromise, but rather attempted to intimidate and bully the Ottomans into conceding. Though it was not the Tsar's goal to provoke war, Menshikov's instructions made compromise impossible and made it clear he was not to settle for less than his full set of demands.[63] Stratford, in Britain being knighted, warned London that Menshikov's mission carried the risk of war between the Ottomans and Russians.[64]

58 Hobkirk 1992, 287.

59 Saab 1977, 103–104.

60 Wetzel 1985, 106.

61 Saab 1977, 31.

62 Ibid, 25; Troubetzkoy 1986, 106.

63 Goldfrank 1994, 133.

64 Seton-Watson 1969, 27. Stratford Canning had been relieved as ambassador to the Ottoman Empire and had returned to Britain to be knighted. At the time of the Menshikov Mission a replacement had yet to be selected. With a crisis looming, Canning was rushed back to Istanbul freshly titled Lord Stratford de Redcliffe.

Menshikov, negotiating with the Porte and the French ambassador in Istanbul, succeeded in quickly bringing the Holy Places Question to a mutually satisfactory conclusion. On the larger issue of granting full rights to all of Orthodoxy in the empire and placing the Tsar as their protector, however, the Ottomans stalled and appealed for aid from France and Britain.[65] The British and French *charges d'affaires*—neither had an ambassador in Istanbul at this crucial juncture—issued requests for the fleets from Malta and Toulon respectively to be dispatched.[66]

Most of the French cabinet, led by the minister of the interior, Comte Jean de Persigny, favored dispatching the fleet.[67] France knew that the British *charge d'affaires* had requested the aid of the British fleet in Malta.[68] With hopes of coordinating with Britain, the French fleet was dispatched on 22 March, though only as far as Salamis to avoid making a tense situation worse.[69] The dispatch of the fleet was less intended as a threat to Russia, but as a way to force the British into cooperation.[70] On the same day, the French threatened to invade Belgium if Russia and Austria invaded the Ottoman Empire.[71] Similar to the dispatch of the fleet, this threat was designed not to deter Russia, but to influence Britain's decision.[72] Clarendon, the British foreign secretary, perceived this but he took the threat seriously enough to warn the Russians that their actions in the east would open up settlements in the west.[73]

Still, the British cabinet was hesitant to act as they feared dispatching the fleet would make the Turks inflexible and, therefore, decided against sending the fleet.[74] Nesselrode saw this as a sign of division between France and Britain.[75] Drouyn de Lhuys had opposed sending the French fleet without coordinating with the British out of fear of this exact situation.[76] The British cabinet had hoped that Clarendon's note would be enough to make their position clear, but sending the note while withholding the fleet muddled the message. The Russians, perhaps in part because of the positive spin put on events by Brunnov, viewed these actions as signs of British acquiescence and that Britain would not back the Ottoman Empire and France.[77]

65 Saab 1977, 33

66 Troubetzkoy 1986, 108. The French ambassador had been recalled in early 1853 and his replacement had yet to arrive.

67 Wetzel 1985, 71 and 74. Persigny claimed public opinion demanded it.

68 Taylor 1969, 99.

69 Puryear 1969b, 10; Saab 1977, 33. The French fleet arrived off Salamis on 4 April 1853.

70 Gochal and Levy 2004, 317; Goldfrank 1994, 136.

71 Puryear, 1969b, 10.

72 Troubetzkoy 1986, 111–13.

73 Puryear 1969b, 10–11.

74 Wetzel 1985, 70.

75 Ramboud 1969, 50; Simpson 1969, 74.

76 Ramboud 1969, 49.

77 Puryear 1969a, 11; Saab 1977, 16–17.

The failure to send clear signals resulted both from Aberdeen's reluctance to go to war over the Eastern Question and because at this point the extent of Russia's demands was not apparent. Nicholas had stated in his conversations with Seymour that maintaining the Porte was preferable to partition. Nicholas may have indeed meant what he said, but his conviction that the Porte was about to collapse made his reassurances meaningless and undid the secret agreement of 1844, if it had not been undone already.[78]

At the beginning of his mission, Menshikov engineered the fall of the Ottoman foreign minister, Mehmet Ali, who was seen as hostile to Russian demands.[79] However, the new foreign minister, Reshid Pasha, proved no more willing to make concessions. As instructed to do if progress proved impossible, Menshikov broke relations with the Porte and left Istanbul in late May.[80] At this point Nicholas began to realize the extent of the opposition he faced.[81] It was clear that the Ottomans were not going to yield to all of his demands and that France was firmly behind the Ottomans. Britain too, was a concern. Thus, the Russians became more willing to actually negotiate rather than simply make demands upon the Ottomans.[82] This did not make settlement more likely, as the Ottomans were emboldened by the belief that the French would aid them in the case of a Russian attack.[83] The Turks continued negotiations, but only so they could gain the necessary time to complete their military preparations.[84]

In order to pressure the Turks, Russia announced at the end of May that it would occupy Moldavia and Wallachia, though the troops did not actually enter the principalities until early July.[85] Shortly thereafter, Britain finally accepted the offer of an entente with France and dispatched their fleet from Malta to Besika Bay on 1 June.[86] It arrived at Besika Bay on 13 June, with the French fleet joining it from

78 Puryear 1969a, 11. Puryear argues that the 1844 agreement was still robust in 1853, while Henderson argues it had little value after the Peel government left office in 1846. Either way, the disagreement over the viability of the Ottoman government hid from the British cabinet the severity of the Tsar's demands.

79 Saab 1977, 41.

80 Ibid, 47 and 49.

81 Ibid, 51.

82 Gochal and Levy 2004, 319; Rich 1985, 72; Wetzel 1985, 85–6. It is not clear that Nicholas would have settled for much less than his initial demands, but Russian diplomacy did become far less preemptory. A war with the Ottoman Empire was not a serious concern, but the growing danger of a war with Britain and France was.

83 Saab 1977, 53. This nicely illustrates Wittman's (1979) claim that agreement that one side is going to do better than originally expected does not necessarily lead to the creation of a bargaining space since as one side lowers its demands the other raises its demands.

84 Saab 1977, 51.

85 Wetzel 1985, 77.

86 Ibid, 78.

Salamis the next day.[87] This move has traditionally been seen as a response to the Russian threat to occupy the principalities.[88] Word of the Russian threat, however, did not reach London until after the fleet had been ordered to Besika.[89] If it was not in response to the Russian threat, why did the British change their position and dispatch the fleet? The cabinet was still thoroughly opposed to war, but had to act because of public opinion.[90] Clarendon told Aberdeen that dispatching the fleet was "the least measure that will satisfy public opinion and save the government from shame hereafter, if, as I firmly believe, the Russian hordes pour into Turkey from every side."[91] Palmerston had wanted to move the fleet to the Bosporus, but this plan had been rejected by Aberdeen and his fellow Peelites.[92] Thus, the decision to send the fleet to Besika Bay was a compromise crafted by Clarendon. It was enough of a move to satisfy public opinion and was somewhat of a middle ground between the positions of Palmerston and Aberdeen.

Faced with the opposition of Britain and France, the Russians began to search for allies. Persia was offered a £10 million subsidy.[93] The Shah was momentarily encouraged and did mobilize a large portion of the Persian army. British threats and the dispatch of a warship from India to the Persian Gulf, however, proved sufficient to cause the Shah to reconsider.[94] Persia remained neutral throughout the war. An attempt to woo Austria by promising territorial gains in the Balkans proved equally unsuccessful. Given Austria's fear of upheaval in the Balkans and of a Russian dominated Balkans, this is not surprising. Austria did not want to offend the Tsar and claimed plausibly, not that it opposed the Tsar, but that it was too poor and had too many domestic problems to be able to afford a war.[95]

At this point, everyone except the Turks wanted to avoid a great power war, though the Russians were willing to risk one. Diplomatic efforts took two paths, with Austria playing a major role in both. The Turks with the British, French, and Austrian ambassadors in Istanbul drew up a proposal that came to be called the Turkish Ultimatum. In this, the Ottomans agreed to maintain in perpetuity the concessions previously given to the Orthodox millets and promised to extend to the Orthodox millets any concessions granted in the future to any other millet.[96] The Ultimatum also stated that the Ottomans, despite these concessions, "reserved

87 Saab 1977, 54. The French were much relieved that the British had decided to dispatch their fleet.

88 Ramboud 1969, 49.

89 Seton-Watson 1969, 28.

90 Rich 1985, 66; Saab 1977, 54.

91 Rich 1985, 64.

92 Bell 1969, 36; Temperley 1969, 57.

93 Saab 1977, 53.

94 Hobkirk 1992, 287.

95 Saab 1977, 53. Much of the Austrian military did want to annex the Western Balkans, but they never managed to obtain control of Austrian affairs during the Crimean War.

96 Ibid, 59.

the sacred rights of sovereignty in relation to its own subjects."[97] Concurrently in Vienna, under the leadership of Count Karl Ferdinand von Buol, the Austrian foreign minister, representatives of Austria, France, Prussia, and Britain—with some secret input from the Russians—drew up a proposal called the Vienna Note. Not surprisingly, the Vienna Note was more favorable for the Russians than was the Turkish Ultimatum. It stipulated the same guarantees as the Turkish Ultimatum, but contained some additional passages that were deemed necessary by the diplomats in Vienna to assuage the Tsar. Indeed, the Vienna Note had been crafted to almost guarantee Russian acceptance and as expected the Russians quickly accepted it. Ottomans acceptance was assumed. Surely, the Porte, given its military weakness, would not reject the mediation of the combined powers. Everyone in Vienna thought the crisis was over.

It was not. The Turks rejected the Vienna Note after some consideration. Its rejection shocked almost everyone and seemed inexplicable. Contemporaries, early historians, and especially the British cabinet believed that Stratford must have engineered its rejection.[98] Stratford's influence, however, was more apparent than real and the Porte would have rejected the Vienna Note without any outside influence as the Turkish Ultimatum was the extreme limit of its possible concessions.[99] From the Turks' point of view the Vienna Note deviated significantly from what they had agreed to in the Turkish Ultimatum and contained some truly objectionable passages. It required the Turks to honor the "letter and spirit of the stipulations of the treaties of Kutchuk-Kainardji and of Adrianople relative to the protection of the Christian cult."[100] Given the conflicting interpretations of Kutchuk-Kainardji, this was ominous. The Note also had a clause stipulating the resolution of the Holy Places Question could not be modified by the Ottomans without Russian or French approval, but it was vaguely worded and it would not have been too difficult to suggest the clause prevented the Ottomans from modifying any religious arrangements within Ottoman Empire without French and Russian approval.[101] Given the current government's secularization drive, the Vienna Note could be construed as requiring the Porte to turn over the direction of some of its most important policies to foreign control. The Ottomans refused to budge from the Ultimatum in part because they did not feel the Vienna Note reflected a united position of the great powers; they were confident of French and British support.[102] Additionally, the populace and *Meclis-i Umumî* were solidly

97 Ibid.

98 Bourgeois 1969, 46; Seton-Watson 1969, 29–30; Simpson 1969, 80.

99 Jomini 1969, 6; Ramboud 1969, 53; Simpson 1969, 78; Temperley 1969, 55; Wetzel 1985, 87.

100 Saab 1977, 61.

101 Ibid.

102 Rich 1985, 7; Saab 1977, 71. The Ottoman foreign minister, Reshid, believed he had British support in large part because of overly optimistic reports from his ambassador in London, Constantine Musurus.

pro-war.[103] There were pro-war riots in Istanbul that required part of the combined British and French fleets to be moved up from Besika Bay to the capital to help the Ottoman elites maintain control and avoid being forced into a declaration of war.[104]

Faced with Ottoman intransigence, Nicholas and Nesselrode refused to budge from the Vienna Note. The Note had been accepted by the European powers, so the Russians saw little reason to offer further concessions. Still with the Turks insisting upon changes to the Vienna Note to bring it more in-line with the Turkish Ultimatum, war became almost certain, though British and French participation was not assured. Aberdeen especially wanted the Ottomans to yield. At this crucial juncture, the Russians' explanation to the Prussians of why they refused to accept the proposed modifications to the Vienna Note was leaked. This set of reasons became known as the "violent interpretation." The "violent interpretation" argued that the modifications would unduly limit Russia's right to act on behalf of Orthodox citizens within the Ottoman Empire. Of course, this is exactly what the Turks wanted the modifications to do and this disagreement should have been clear from looking at the differences between the Vienna Note and Turkish Ultimatum. In essence, it just made explicit the disagreement between the Ottomans and Russians over how the Treaty of Kutchuk-Kainardji should be interpreted. Thus, the "violent interpretation" did not reveal anything new and did not suggest a Russian departure from what had been agreed to in the Vienna Note.[105]

While the British and French claimed the reasons Nesselrode had given showed Russia's true expansionist aims, the interpretation was not really violent nor particularly unexpected.[106] The Austrians were unfazed by the leak. The violent interpretation did, however, give the British and French governments an excuse to take a harder line with the Russians, a decision that had already been made for reasons having nothing to do with Nesselrode's interpretation of the proposed modifications to the Vienna Note.[107] The allies had already decided that they would back the Ottoman Empire and felt there was a good chance the Porte would reject the Vienna Note even if Britain and France pressured the Porte to accept it.[108] If this scenario occurred, Britain and France would find themselves in the ridiculous position of having to militarily back a state that had rejected their diplomatic advice. In order to avoid this embarrassment the allies seized on the violent interpretation as an excuse to back the Ottomans diplomatically.[109] Public opinion also played an important role in the British decision. After this diplomatic

103 Saab 1977, 56.
104 Ibid, 85.
105 Schroeder 1972, 68.
106 Rich 1985, 80; Schroeder 1972, 63.
107 Rich 1985, 80–1.
108 Schroeder 1972, 61–7.
109 Ibid, 63–7.

exchange events moved quickly with the Ottomans declaring war on 9 October and the allied fleet moving up to Constantinople to protect it from a Russian attack.

Thus, it would seem that Britain and France were drawn in before the war even began and that they were not drawn in by revealed information. This is not the case. Even at this late point, the allies still hoped to stay out of war and obtain a diplomatic solution during the winter.[110] It was hoped, given the lateness of the season, that the Ottoman Empire and Russia would engage in only limited fighting allowing diplomatic attempts to continue virtually unaffected. The British cabinet and public opinion were still divided over the question of war.[111] The British cabinet reassured the Russians that the British fleet would not enter the Black Sea unless it was needed to defend Ottoman territory or the Russian fleet left Sevastopol.[112] As the Tsar promised the Russian military would refrain from offensive actions, hope remained for avoiding a clash between great powers.[113] The standoff between the allies and Russia lasted through November even as reports of successful Ottoman raids along the Danube reached western capitals.

The news of the overwhelming Russian naval victory at Sinope and an equally crushing land victory at Bashkadyklar shattered the status quo. Thouvenel, the French deputy foreign minister, said the battles had the "effect of an elephant in a spider's web."[114] The Russians were no longer remaining on the defensive and the previous Ottoman successes were shown to be flukes. The battles made it clear that without allies the Ottomans would lose badly. They also showed the Tsar would not settle for less than his original demands outlined by Menshikov. Diplomacy having failed, he would defeat the Turks by force of arms. If this meant war with Britain and France, so be it.[115] Interestingly, fear of an Ottoman defeat and Russian expansion was only part of what drove the British and French to enter the war. More important were French hopes of cementing the British alliance and a sense of military honor, while Britain entered due primarily to public pressure.

Sinope provided Napoleon III with both an opportunity and a problem. It created an opportunity for France to cement its alliance with Britain. There were strong reasons to believe that Britain would be forced to respond to Sinope. Britain had issued an ultimatum in October that it would respond to aggressive actions by the Russian fleet and had extracted from the Tsar a promise to avoid all offensive operations. Sinope had violated the ultimatum and Bashkadyklar had broken the Tsar's promise. If the French and British responded with joint military action, the entente between the two powers would be cemented. Therefore, Napoleon favored a quick French military response to Sinope that would in all likelihood force the British to take an equally hard-line response. This was the opportunity

110 Saab 1977, 96–7.
111 Ibid, 98–9.
112 Goldfrank 1994, 227; Saab 1977, 99.
113 Troubetzkoy 1986, 137.
114 Saab, Knapp, and Knapp 1986, 485
115 Gochal and Levy 2004, 322–4; Goldfrank 1994, 228–9 and 271–3.

provided by Sinope. There was, however, a problem as well. The Ottoman Empire had been loosely under France's military protection and the crushing blow at Sinope, if unavenged, might reflect poorly on French arms. Napoleon felt that as a Bonaparte he could not be associated with military defeat and still retain legitimacy.[116] This problem worked in conjunction with the opportunity to cement the British alliance and encouraged Napoleon to respond forcefully and militarily to Sinope. Thus, Sinope influenced French policy both directly through military honor and indirectly through the more important opportunity to cement its alliance with Britain as Napoleon was able to predict Britain's reaction to the battle. Thus, French policy was formulated largely on an anticipated reaction of another third party to an unexpected event and only partially composed as a direct response to the event itself.

Unfortunately, there simply is not enough information on Napoleon's thinking to know if the battles surprised him or not. There is no evidence that he anticipated them, but neither can it be concretely shown that they surprised him. All that can be done in attempting to determine if Sinope surprised the Bonaparte government is to draw inferences from Napoleon's policy choices after Sinope and Bashkadyklar. French policy did change significantly after the battles. Thouvenel's quote alone suggests a significant departure from the previous policy. Napoleon chose to move France closer to military conflict with Russia. Given that he wanted to avoid such a conflict—though he was willing to risk it—and had previously taken several steps to avoid such a conflict, it seems reasonable to conclude that the battles altered his thinking to some degree and that likely they were at least somewhat surprising to the French government.

Sinope affected Britain in more complex ways than France. The battles had violated the British ultimatum that the Tsar not use the Black Sea fleet in an offensive capacity and ran contrary to the Tsar's promise to remain on the defensive. Still, for the most part the cabinet was initially unphased by Sinope, though Palmerston and his fellow hawks called for war even louder than before. More importantly, the effect of Sinope on British public opinion was electric.[117] The *Morning Chronicle* headlines urged the cabinet to, "Strike down the aggressor" while the *Times* claimed peace was "was no longer compatible with the honor and dignity of the country."[118] Nor were such sentiments confined to small portions of the populace. Clarendon observed that, "The feelings of honour which this dreadful carnage could not fail to create, have been general throughout all ranks and classes of Her Majesty's subjects in this country."[119] Similarly the First Lord of the Admiralty, Sir James Graham, noted that,

116 Saab 1977, 26.

117 Rich 1985, 97; Saab 1977, 127; Schroeder 1972, 118; Simpson 1969, 81; Seton-Watson 1969, 31; Taylor 1969, 102; Wetzel 1985, 94.

118 Troubetzkoy 1986, 144.

119 Ibid.

> The attack on Sinope has produced an immense effect on the public mind … It is difficult to put any restraint on the national desire to avenge what is regarded as a contempt and defiance of our flags. I have been one of the most strenuous advocates of peace with Russian until the last moment; but the Sinope attack and recent events have changed entirely the aspect of affairs. I am afraid rupture with Russia is inevitable.[120]

Given the political weakness of Aberdeen and the internal divisions within the ministry, this public opinion was sure to affect the ministry's actions.

Public opinion was further heightened by Palmerston's resignation. He had resigned from the cabinet shortly after Sinope, though it was as much, if not more, over differences with Russell regarding election reform as with Aberdeen over war. The public, however, saw it solely as a result of differences over war. The calls for his return were so loud that he quickly rejoined the government, his power much increased. Public opinion also turned on Prince Albert, an advocate of peace with Russia. He was falsely accused of having forced Palmerston from office and of being in league with the Tsar.[121] Even wilder rumors flew that both he and Queen Victoria had been arrested for treason and had been imprisoned in the tower. Public opinion grew so hostile, that Victoria even briefly considered abdication.[122] Of course, public opinion eventually blew over, but while it was still running hot, word arrived that the French wanted to enter the Black Sea in conjunction with the British fleet. The British ambassador in France, Lord Henry Cowley, stated that Napoleon was "prepared should it become necessary, to carry it out alone."[123] Given that Russell was now threatening to resign unless a harsher line was taken against Russia and that Clarendon was now also clearly for war, Aberdeen had little choice but to yield and agree to joint action.[124] To do otherwise and allow the French to act alone, would have been political suicide given the state of public opinion and likely would not have kept Britain out of war as the Conservatives in opposition were pro-war.[125]

The growing public pressure, combined to a lesser extent with the direct effect of the Russian actions caused Clarendon to convert to the pro-war position.[126] Prior to Sinope, he had previously given up on trying to avoid war, but he had been content to allow events to dictate the course of British policy. Now, after

120 Parker 1907, 79.

121 Saab 1977, 126.

122 Ibid, 127.

123 Troubetzkoy 1986, 144. The French may have been bluffing, but it would have been highly risky for Aberdeen to call the bluff given the state of British public opinion. Cowley generally favored war and might have overstated Napoleon's willingness to act unilaterally.

124 Temperley 1969, 58.

125 Gochal and Levy 2004, 331.

126 Ibid, 329; Peterson 1993, 117–22.

Sinope he was willing to take more energetic steps and convince Aberdeen to go along with Palmerston's and Russell's proposals. As Clarendon represented the center position between the peace and war factions in the cabinet, this small shift was as decisive as the increased public calls for war.[127] Had Aberdeen been a stronger prime minister or his cabinet more united, it might have been possible to withstand the public pressure. As it was, the weak ministry combined with Napoleon's aggressive reaction to Sinope and the slow pro-war drift within the cabinet created a situation in which the cabinet had no choice but to yield to public pressure and agree with the French proposals. Given the British ultimatum in October, not acting with the French would have made it seem that Britain was not honoring its word, while France was in fact enforcing British threats. Lord James Malmesbury, a former foreign secretary, aptly noted that, "Public opinion had been so universally aroused by the manner in which the Russians had behaved at Sinope that war had become inevitable."[128]

The fleet was duly ordered into the Black Sea on 22 December and the joint British and French fleets actually entered the Black Sea on 4 January. Though the allies did not declare war until March, the combined fleet was operating on a war footing from the moment it entered the Black Sea.[129] War had become unavoidable unless Russia backed down completely, an event most unlikely to happen prior to a military defeat. Thus, the chain of events from Sinope to the allied intervention fits very well with the hypothesis that revealed information leads third parties to join wars, even if in large part the information operated through public opinion rather than directly on the British government.

But were the battles truly unexpected? British advocates of peace, notably Prince Albert, had warned that the Turks might try to lure the Russian fleet out by sailing in the Black Sea, thereby dragging Britain into war.[130] While there is no concrete evidence that this is why the Turks sent their fleet into the Black Sea, it does suggest that the British cabinet could have reasonably anticipated Sinope.[131] Indeed, neither French public opinion nor the British cabinet were initially greatly moved by Sinope. Of course, the fact the battle could have been anticipated does not mean it actually was anticipated. More importantly, though Albert warned about Sinope, no one expected the Russian offensive in the Caucasus that resulted in the battle of Bashkadyklar. This battle, as much as Sinope, showed the hopelessness of the Turkish position and clearly violated Nicholas' promise to refrain from offensive action. Also, most of the decisiveness of Sinope was its effect on public opinion. While elites might have expected something like Sinope, the British

127 Peterson 1993, 129.

128 Saab 1977, 127.

129 Rich 1985, 104; Schroeder 1972, 131–3. The Russians did not take the entry of the fleets as an act of war as they wished to avoid war with Britain and France. Instead, they asked for clarification. This merely delayed the inevitable.

130 Simpson 1969, 80–1.

131 The official reason for the foray was to re-supply forces in the Caucasus.

public at large most certainly did not. As their reaction drove British policy, their perception of Sinope is what matters. Also, the British cabinet seems to have been caught off guard by both the French government's reaction and the British public's reaction. Thus at a minimum, the battles were unexpected by the British public and the British cabinet was surprised by others' reactions to the battles.

The entry of Britain and France into the war opened up the prospect that the war would become general. The prospect of additional states entering the war seemed good. Persia briefly mobilized, but as previously discussed, the threat of British naval actions in the Persian Gulf convinced the Shah to remain neutral. Greece, too, initially looked likely to enter the war on the Russian side. The Greek government backed several revolts in Ottoman possessions in Europe, going as far as sending non-uniformed troops to aid the rebels and foment rebellion where there was none. The revolts were initially successful and King Otto was ready to lead the Greek army into war. The British and the French sent supplies to the Ottomans to suppress these revolts and also quickly occupied Athens with an amphibious landing.[132] They forced the Otto to dismiss his pro-war ministers and bring in a pro-allied cabinet.[133] This ended the possibility Greece would enter the war. The allies had hoped that Austria would help deal with the Greek rebellions and, thereby, be drawn into the war but Austria remained wary and did little to help fight the revolts.

The allies also hoped to bring Sweden into the war. They offered substantial territorial gains and promised a Baltic offensive, but King Oscar remained unconvinced. He feared Sweden would not be able to hold any potential territorial gains unless Russia was badly beaten. He also feared retribution from the German states. Only if Austria joined the war, could Oscar be sufficiently confident of a decisive victory and protection from the other German states.[134] Thus, British and French hopes for military assistance hinged upon Austria.

Austria had no intention of joining. Its hopes of preventing the war dashed, Austria aimed to localize it and find a way to mediate it. Austria mobilized 55,000 troops on the Serbian border and leaked to Russia that it might occupy Serbia in hopes of forestalling Russian plans for fomenting revolution in the western Balkans.[135] This move proved a success. Serbia quickly declared its neutrality and the Russians confined themselves to prosecuting the siege of Silestra in the eastern Balkans. Austria also threatened Montenegro and got Prince Danilo to limit his activities to minor raids on Ottoman territories.[136]

The western Balkans quiet, Austria tried to calm the eastern Balkans. The key to preventing major fighting in the Balkans was to get Russia to withdraw

132 Saab 1977, 143.

133 Wetzel 1985, 106–7.

134 Ibid, 107; Schroeder 1972, 174–5 and 198. Prussia, in particular, was a potentially dangerous enemy for Sweden, especially if Swedish forces were already engaged in Russia.

135 Saab 1977, 134–5.

136 Ibid, 139.

from Moldavia and Wallachia and have these principalities occupied by Austrian troops.[137] This would allow Austria to serve as a buffer between Russia and its enemies. The Russians were reluctant to leave; therefore, on 3 June 1854 Austria threatened war if the Russians did not agree to withdraw. The threat worked, and the Russians began to withdraw in early August. Austrian troops quickly occupied the principalities.[138]

Though Austria had successfully prevented a disaster in the Balkans, its diplomatic position was tenuous. The war continued and had strained Austria's relations with Russia without getting much in return from France and Britain. Austria needed to bring the war to a conclusion. Buol asked the British and French their terms for peace. These were vaguely outlined in the Four Points and amounted to a repudiation of the Tsar's special role as protector of the Orthodox in the Ottoman Empire and the neutralization of the Black Sea. The demands were obviously more than Russia would accept, and indeed they were promptly rejected. This led to an Austrian mobilization in October. The Russians accepted the Four Points as a basis for negotiation in November, but the vagueness of the Points prevented them from becoming an actual basis upon which to negotiate.[139] Thus, Austria had gained nothing and had become diplomatically isolated. The British also gained nothing, as Austria steadfastly remained out of the war, though the French did benefit long-term from the increasing rift between Russia and Austria.[140]

This was not the only diplomatic activity underway. Ever since the initial failure to capture Sevastopol in the autumn of 1854, Britain and France had been seeking additional allies. The British in particular wanted to find some way to augment their small army. Hopes centered on Sardinia, which had a small, but good army. The Sardinians were willing to join the war if they were given promises about acquiring Austrian territory in northern Italy.[141] This would naturally anger Austria and as the allies were wooing Austria simultaneously, the entry of Sardinia had to be refused, at least initially.[142] The British, fed up with the Austrians, were willing to lose any hope of an Austrian alliance to get Sardinia, but the French were not.[143]

137 Rich 1985, 121.

138 The Austrians did not occupy all of the principalities; the Turks occupied portions as well. The Turks and Russians even faced off across the Pruth, but Austria controlled the main invasion routes and effectively prevented campaigning in the Balkans.

139 The British and French made the Points intentionally vague in order to avoid having to make peace prior to capturing Sevastopol and in hopes of luring Austria into the war.

140 Recall, creating such a rift was one of the main goals of Napoleon's foreign policy. Of course, as much as this rift helped the French, they would have preferred Austria to join the war against Russia.

141 This sort of behavior—bandwagoning to obtain spoils not directly tied to the outcome of the war itself—will be explored in detail in Chapter 7.

142 Rich 1985, 148.

143 Wetzel 1985, 135.

The French won out and the allies refused the Sardinian conditions. This should have ended the matter, but Sardinia suddenly decided to enter the war in January of 1855 even without any understanding on Italian unification. The decision angered many in Italy and seemed to gain Sardinia nothing.[144] Why would Cavour, a shrewd politician, make such a decision? It was driven in large part by intra-governmental politics. The Sardinian king, Victor Emmanuel II, wanted to enter the war to gain military honor for Sardinia and himself, perhaps in order to erase the disgrace of his father's defeats. Whatever his underlying motives, he was always eager to lead his country into war. Victor Emmanuel realized that the cabinet was unlikely to support entering the war, and therefore, he was secretly planning to throw out his relatively liberal ministers and replace them with more conservative, pro-war ministers. Cavour was alarmed to learn of this. He convinced his fellow ministers of the necessity of declaring war to save the cabinet.[145] Additionally, entering the war would get Cavour a seat at the post-war conference table. This at least held out the possibility Sardinia might be able to extract the sort of concessions in the post war peace treaty it failed to obtain in exchange for entering the war. Thus, Sardinia primarily entered the war because of Victor Emmanuel's willingness to dissolve his cabinet.

The Decision for Peace

The spring and summer of 1855 saw few military developments. Much of the year was spent rebuilding the allied army in the Crimea, which had suffered severely during the winter. The siege of Sevastopol dragged on and a Russian offensive to capture Kars in the Caucasus neared success as the garrison slowly starved and the allies failed to mount a relief effort. Diplomatic efforts similarly failed to produce any significant results.

In September of 1855, Sevastopol, weakened by siege and bombardment, finally fell to the allied armies. Its fall had been the goal of the allies for almost two years and had been anticipated by belligerents for some time.[146] Still, it encouraged the Austrians to try to get peace negotiations going again, but without much success. The Russians simply were no more willing to agree to allied demands than before. Given that the loss of Sevastopol had been expected, its actual capture changed nothing. Tsar Alexander II, who had ascended to the throne after his father's death in early 1855, took a tour of the remaining Russian fortifications in the Crimea

144 Ibid, 136.

145 Ibid, 135.

146 Obviously, the British and French had expected Sevastopol to fall soon after their landing on the Crimean peninsula in 1854, but they had revised this expectation after the battles of Inkerman and Balaklava. The British had been planning for how to deal with the fall since Russia had been defeated in its last chance to relieve the port during the summer. Rich 1985, 135 and 158.

in October. He found both the fortifications and the army's morale to be in good shape. There were also exaggerated reports of war-weariness in France. Alexander II was confident in Russia's eventual, if difficult, victory and in November he instructed all peace feelers to be rejected.[147] His optimism can be seen in a message to one of his generals:

> Let not your courage fail, but think of the year 1812 and trust in God. Sevastopol is not Moscow, and the Crimea is not Russia. Two years after Moscow burned, our victorious armies entered Paris. We are still the same Russians and God is with us.[148]

The overdue Russian capture of Kars also did little to further peace, as it did not moderate allied demands. France and especially Britain pressed ahead with plans for a Baltic campaign to capture the fortress of Kronstadt the following spring. There were also hints of campaigns in Bessarabia.

Austria believed that if the war continued into 1856 it would become general.[149] In particular, the Austrians believed Sweden, Prussia, and several of the lesser German states would enter the war and that the focus of the fighting would shift from southern Russia to Russian Poland, much nearer Austrian territory. This belief was shared by the other German powers. Count Buol became desperate to achieve peace. As nothing could budge the Russians, Austria finally issued an ultimatum that unless Russia agreed to preliminary peace terms, Austria would become an active belligerent against the Tsar. Buol did so fully expecting the Russians to refuse. He believed Austria would have to enter the war, though given Austria's financial difficulties it was unlikely Austria would be able to put a large force in the field.[150] It was a remarkable and surprising change of course in Austrian policy. The change caught the other German states completely off guard. They grudgingly consented to not oppose what they saw as an Austrian *fait accompli*.[151]

The Russians first got word that an Austrian ultimatum was likely in late November. For the first time, Alexander became troubled and worried about the coming campaign. He immediately let his ministers know that he was now willing to accept limitations on the size of Russia's fleet in the Black Sea.[152] The actual ultimatum arrived on 16 December. The next day the Russians learned of the treaty that had been signed between Sweden and Russia's enemies in September. The treaty clearly indicated Sweden would participate in the Baltic campaign

---

147 Baumgart 1981, 47 and 58.
148 Ibid, 58.
149 Ibid, 47.
150 Ibid, 52.
151 Ibid, 53.
152 Ibid, 62–3.

against Russia in the coming year and shocked the Russians. Upon learning of its existence Nesselrode exclaimed, "What! There is a treaty?"[153]

The twin shocks of the ultimatum and Swedish alliance greatly influenced Alexander and his ministers.[154] Given Russia's difficult financial situation and the impossibility of further enlarging the army without abolishing serfdom, there was nothing to do but agree to a peace conference on allied terms.[155] Alexander believed Russia could have continued despite the financial and manpower difficulties against Britain, France, the Ottoman Empire, and Sardinia, but Austria and Sweden would make victory impossible. Hostilities were soon suspended. Though negotiations proved somewhat difficult, major combat operations never resumed. The Austrian threat to enter the war coupled with the Swedish alliance effectively ended the conflict.

Conclusions

The case clearly provides support for the hypothesis that revealed information causes non-belligerents to join ongoing wars. The entries of Britain and France were clearly driven by the twin shocks of Sinope and Bashkadyklar. Though both states were already hostile to Russia, neither had determined upon war, nor was it certain that they would do so. Neither was simply looking for an excuse to declare war; the British cabinet still hedged briefly after Sinope. The most interesting part of the case is how the revealed information operated through public opinion. As was discussed above, Sinope should not have come as a complete shock to British and French elites, though it appears it did surprise some of them. However, it clearly came as a surprise to the British public at large and turned what had been strong public pressure to back the Ottoman Empire—though not necessarily to go to war—into irresistible calls for war. Thus, it would appear that events that surprise the public can be as important as events that surprise leaders, provided these events lead to significant shifts in public opinion. It is also important to note that the British and French entry into the war was not recorded as an entry due to an unexpected event in the statistical portion of the work as they did not enter the war for more than three months after the event, in large part due to the difficulty of campaigning in winter. Thus, the earlier statistical finding may somewhat understate the importance of unexpected events if such long lags between an event and joining are common.[156]

The entry of Sardinia does not support the hypothesis. Though the unexpected difficulty in investing and taking Sevastopol caused the British and French to

153 Ibid, 70.

154 Ibid.

155 Ibid, 72–5 and 79.

156 Bulgaria's entry into the First World War is another example of a lengthy lag between an event, the Gorlice-Tarnow offensive, and joining. See Chapter 5.

seek out new allies, nothing in the war itself caused Sardinia to join. Rather the longstanding goal of uniting Italy caused Cavour and others to seek the favor of great powers by entering the war. Had Sardinia gotten specific concessions from the British and French, Sardinia's entry might have fit with the alternate hypothesis that states wait for an anticipated event or chain of events to be completed, in this case negotiations for concessions. This did not happen. Sardinia joined prior to receiving concrete concessions largely because of the desire of Victor Emmanuel to join and the fear that he would dismiss the cabinet if they did not vote to enter the war. The revelation of the king's willingness to dismiss the cabinet certainly surprised Cavour and was revealed information of a sort, though not analogous to what had been theorized earlier in this work. Thus, the Sardinian case is primarily a failure for the hypothesis.

The secondary hypothesis, that revealed information leads to states leaving wars, also receives solid support. The fall of Sevastopol and the Russian capture of Kars, both widely anticipated, did not lead to peace. The Austrians attempted to jump start negotiations after these two events, but the two sides were as far apart as ever. Britain and France continued with plans for a Baltic campaign for the coming spring. Buol decided upon the gamble of threatening Austrian intervention unless Russia agreed to peace. This unexpected reversal of Austrian policy, described as a betrayal by the Russians for years, did the trick. Sweden's willingness to go to war also played a role. The Russians, who were intransigent prior to the Austrian ultimatum, promptly agreed to a peace conference at which they met the allies' minimal demands. Clearly, the unanticipated Austrian ultimatum was instrumental in bringing about peace.

Some themes emerge from the case that are not related to the central hypotheses. The first is the ability of states to drag their allies into war. Britain did not want war with Russia, but it also did not want to see the Ottoman Empire destroyed. The ideal outcome in the British cabinet's mind—Palmerston excepted—would have been for the Porte to make some concessions, and thereby, avoid both war and Russian control of the Straits. The Ottomans, however, felt confident of western support and chose to pursue a harder line than their allies wished. This eventually led to war, a war the Porte could not win without assistance. This put the British and to a lesser extent the French into the position of having to choose between war and an overwhelming Russian victory. Given those limited options, war became the obvious choice.

The second theme is that the entry of certain states can lead to additional entries. Had Austria joined, Sweden would have also. This would have greatly widened the conflict and made it very difficult for Prussia and the other German states to remain neutral. Compare the potential entrance of Austria to the entries that did occur. Britain's and France's entry made additional entries somewhat more likely, but they led to only Sardinia joining the war. Sardinia's entry had very little effect on additional entries, though it did hurt relations between the allies and Austria. This suggests that great power entrants are much more likely to cause additional entries when compared to small power entrants. Also, and perhaps more importantly, the entry of centrally located states such as Austria may significantly increase the chance that the war will spread still further.

Finally, the notion that belligerents can take actions to discourage other states from entering received strong support. Both Greece and Persia were dissuaded from joining the Russian side because of allied threats and naval deployments. Sweden remained neutral out of fear of Russian retaliation post-bellum. Russia also kept Austria from joining on several occasions, although through appeasement rather than threats. The Tsar first agreed to withdraw from the principalities and shortly thereafter accepted the vaguely worded Four Points as a suitable place to begin negotiations. Finally, the Russians agreed to a cease-fire and the negotiations that ended the war to avoid having to fight Austria. Austria, while remaining a non-belligerent was also able to dissuade Montenegro and Serbia from becoming involved through the use of threats. In short, the states looking to pick up spoils, Persia, Greece, Sweden, Serbia, and Montenegro, were dissuaded from joining by threats, while Austria, which was looking to balance, was dissuaded by appeasement. Also, Russia's half-hearted attempts to appease Britain and France antebellum were more favorably received than were bellicose pronouncements. Thus, threats worked well against potential bandwagoners, while appeasement was more successful against potential balancers. This theme, which is consistent with Davis (1995, 2000), will recur in Chapter 5 and especially in Chapter 6.

Overall, the Crimean war lends solid support to the main hypotheses and several of the lesser hypotheses. Revealed information significantly influenced the timing of the entry of Britain and France into the war and played a lesser role in the Sardinian entry. Another surprise, Austria's ultimatum to Russia, also led to the opening of the negotiations that ended the war. The case also shows how belligerents can manipulate their own actions to discourage other states from joining. Likewise the case shows how a non-belligerent, such as Austria, can influence the likelihood that other states would join the war. These two findings are consistent with the ideas that underpin the theory of joining proposed in Chapter 2: that war is an ongoing bargaining process and that the absence of war is at a minimum a tacit agreement between two states.

Chapter 5
The First World War: The Growth of a World War

Nations do not commonly join in wars,
once the wars have started, out of pure
idealism—Cyril Falls[1]

The states that joined the First World War after August 1914 went through very similar calculations as those that joined the Crimean War. Potential joiners watched the course of the war and decided whether it would be in their interest to join or not. The decisions of those states that initially remained neutral were thereafter influenced by information revealed by the war. The type of decisions that were made and the information used to make them was the same as in smaller wars, even though the war they were considering joining was a world war. As they relate to voluntary joining, world wars are different only in scale.[2]

The main substantive difference between the First World War and the work's other case studies is that many states initially entered the First World War due to complex antebellum alliance structures, though as is consistent with the statistical findings, after August 1914 pre-existing alliances had little effect on how the war spread. The war's origin and its initial spread through alliances has been recounted many times and in far greater detail than is possible here. It is not this work's intent to shed light or pass judgment on the many debates about why the Austro-Serbian dispute initially grew into a great power war or why diplomacy failed in July 1914. Rather, this work seeks to explain why, after the war became general in August 1914, seven additional states joined over the next three years, as it is this behavior of late joining that the hypotheses advanced in Chapter 2 attempt to explain. A detailed retelling of the events of July and August 1914, therefore, is not appropriate. Before the work can focus on the later interventions of the Ottoman Empire, Italy, Bulgaria, Portugal, Romania, the United States, and Greece, however, some background regarding the war's outbreak and how it became general is necessary.

The assassination of the Archduke Franz Ferdinand on 28 June 1914 provided Austria-Hungary with an excuse to punish Serbia. When the Serbs rejected the Habsburg ultimatum as expected, the Austrians declared war on 29 July. Russia

1 Falls 1959, 98.

2 World wars do seem to have far more incidences of neutrals being attacked, resulting in involuntary joining. This is likely a result of the high stakes of such wars which makes the risks of attacking neutrals appear more acceptable.

quickly mobilized to keep its Serbian ally from being crushed. At first, Russia considered mobilizing against only Austria-Hungary, but anticipating a German mobilization to protect the Habsburgs, Russia mobilized against Germany as well, though they insisted they did not want war with Germany. Russia still hoped to avoid war and did not declare war on either power, but the Russians knew mobilization almost certainly meant war with both powers.[3] In truth, a partial mobilization against only Austria-Hungary would have been very difficult to pull off as the Warsaw military district abutted both Austrian and German territory and due to railroad timetables and other technicalities it would have been very difficult to switch from a partial to full mobilization.[4] The Germans naturally mobilized in response to the Russian mobilization. The Russians may very well have been right that the Germans would have mobilized in any case to protect their Habsburg ally; the point has been contentious ever since. As it was, Germany declared war on Russia on 1 August, plunging both countries into the war.

Russia was now in real danger of being crushed by Germany and Austria-Hungary. France, therefore, quickly mobilized to protect Russia in accordance with the longstanding Franco-Russian alliance. The Germans insisted the French declare neutrality, which was impossible for the French to do. To absolutely no one's surprise, including the Germans, France entered the war on 3 August. Faced with the long anticipated two-front war, Germany decided to execute the Schiefflen plan, or at least a slightly modified version of it. This required the German army to move through Belgium, but the Belgian government refused permission for this maneuver. This meant war and Belgium was duly invaded on the 4 August.[5] Britain's Liberal government was slow to react to the initial crisis. Not until late on 23 July did Sir Edward Grey, the foreign secretary, realize the risk of war. Despite his late start, by 27 July he was doing his best to express to the Germans that Britain would side with France and Russia. Kaiser Wilhelm II, however, may have ignored Grey's clear warnings and instead focused on the much less ominous words of the British king, George V.[6] Whether or not the Germans expected the British to intervene has been widely debated and a consensus on the issue has yet to form.[7] Other European states, however, seemed to get the message. San Giuliano, the Italian foreign minister, was certain of British involvement by the 28 August, though in truth the British cabinet was still undecided.[8] The gross violation of

3 Trachtenberg 1990, 124–9.

4 Ibid, 125–6; Levy 1990, 179; Rich 2003, 223.

5 Luxembourg also had to be occupied in order for the Germans to execute the Schiefflen plan, though as Luxembourg had no army outside of the palace guard, war was not necessary. Germany occupied Luxembourg on 2 August, one day before war broke out with France. The Germans had forced France to make a decision in part so that they could determine if they should execute their plans for a one or two front war.

6 See Levy (1990) and Trachtenberg (1990) for an overview of the debate.

7 Harris 2003, 278–81.

8 Renzi 1987, 76.

Belgian neutrality got the cabinet to back war. However, if the government had not decided to enter the war, it likely would have fallen and have been replaced by a pro-war Unionist government.[9] Thus, San Giuliano's belief in the certainty of British intervention was sounder than it might initially appear. Britain declared war on 5 August.[10] Shortly after Britain's entry, one of Serbia's traditional allies entered the war. Montenegro declared war on both Austria-Hungary and Germany on 7 August. Though its forces contributed little to the Entente effort, Montenegro's entry plunged the Balkans a little deeper into war.[11]

Japan was the last power to enter the war in its first month. Japan was allied to Great Britain, but the terms of the treaty did not obligate Japan to join the war.[12] Many in Japan, especially foreign minister Katō Takaaki saw the European war as an opportunity to reinforce Japan's position in China.[13] Domestic opinion, however, was largely neutralist. More importantly, Katō saw the war as an opportunity to weld Japan to the British alliance and to further the domestic power of the rising political parties against the remaining Meiji era samurai elites.[14] Katō managed to persuade the Japanese cabinet to enter the war on behalf of the British even though many of the members were pro-German.[15] Even these leaders saw the advantages of taking German territory in China, though long-term they favored a more radical solution to the China question than did Katō. The Japanese cabinet voted for war on 8 August, only one day after Britain's request for aid. On 15 August, an ultimatum effectively demanding that Germany surrender its possessions in China to Japan within eight days was delivered to the Germans. The Germans failed to reply satisfactorily and Japan duly declared war on 23 August. Japan would prove a fickle ally. The Japanese rarely acted outside of the Pacific sphere, flirted with a separate peace, and even with a German alliance at various points in the war, but they never actually abandoned their British allies.

Thus, within a month the bilateral conflict between Serbia and Austria-Hungary ballooned into a world war. The war, however, would get larger still. Over the course of the next three years, seven states—the Ottoman Empire, Italy, Bulgaria, Portugal, Romania, the United States, and Greece—would join the war. Excluding the unusual case of Portugal, none favored war in August 1914. All would come to change their positions as events in the war provided them with opportunities or

9 Harris 2003, 287–8.

10 Britain's entry automatically brought about the entry of the other parts of the British Empire such as Canada, South Africa, India, Australia, and New Zealand.

11 Montenegro's neighbor, Albania, played almost no active role in the war. At the time, it was in chaos and controlled by competing warlords and governments. Portions were also occupied by various neighboring states. In short, Albania was the classic failed state and had no central policy during the war.

12 Dickinson 2003, 306–7.

13 Ibid, 313–15.

14 Ibid, 306–12.

15 Ibid.

necessitated their entry. They would do so for a variety of reasons, though most were looking to pick up spoils. The United States, however, had no territorial aims, while Portugal had only very slight territorial aims. The seven states' decisions to intervene will be presented in thematic rather than in chronological order. The first three cases—Bulgaria, Romania, and Italy—are states that were looking to pick up spoils and joined in response to revealed information about the relative balance of military forces. The fourth case is of a state, the US, which had no territorial aspirations, but responded to revealed information about a belligerent's intentions. The fifth and sixth cases—the Ottoman Empire and Greece—are cases which are complicated by intra-governmental disagreements and explore how domestic politics alters the revealed information hypothesis. The last case, Portugal, is a study of a state that honored its alliance obligations at the outset, but did not become an active belligerent for several years.

Bulgaria

Bulgaria's entry into the First World War can be understood only in light of its role in the First and Second Balkan wars. For more than 30 years, Bulgarian foreign policy had as its goal the reacquisition of the borders granted to it in the Treaty of San Stefano, which ended the Russo-Turkish war of 1877–78. The other European powers, however, had refused to recognize the treaty, and in concert at Berlin, they had reduced the size of Bulgaria by half.[16] With the aid of its Balkan allies in the First Balkan War from 1912–13, Bulgaria had defeated the main Turkish army, captured Adrianople, and had been stopped by the Turks only at the gates of Constantinople. Bulgaria captured much of Thrace and part of Macedonia. Greece and Serbia, however, had gained far more territory with far less fighting and both had occupied portions of Macedonia to which Bulgaria felt it was entitled. In an attempt to get a larger share of Macedonia, Bulgaria attacked its erstwhile allies in what became the Second Balkan War in 1913. This misfired badly. The combined Serbian and Greek forces quickly defeated the Bulgarians. Defeat turned into disaster when the Romanians and Turks joined to pick up spoils. The Treaty of Bucharest, which ended the war, reflected Bulgaria's military humiliation. Serbia acquired more of Macedonia, Greece picked up parts of Macedonia and Thrace, Romania got the southern Dobrudja, and Turkey regained Adrianople. These losses nearly canceled out Bulgaria's gains from the First Balkan War.

The Second Balkan War had also destroyed the Russo-Bulgarian understanding. Prior to the war, Russia had backed Bulgaria in the Balkans.[17] Russia also had amicable relations with Serbia, but many Bulgarians felt Russia could be counted on and these Russophiles led the government. Russia's decision to support Serbian

16 McEvedy 1982, 34. This reduced Bulgaria was split into two states, Bulgaria and East Rumelia, until 1885.

17 Hall 1996, 241.

claims and the Treaty of Bucharest shattered the Russo-Bulgarian relationship. The disaster of the Second Balkan War and the equally disastrous Treaty of Bucharest revealed the apparent fecklessness of Russia, drove the Russophiles from office, and led to the rise of Russophobe politicians. As Vasil Radoslavov, a prominent Russophobe, put it:

> At Bucharest we clearly realized that Russia had turned away from us; a word ... would have been enough for us to obtain Macedonia and Kavalla. The word was not spoken and therefore we find ourselves in our present melancholy position.[18]

Tsar Ferdinand agreed and elevated Radoslavov to the office of prime minister.[19]

Thus, in 1914, Bulgaria had revisionist territorial claims against all of its neighbors and was without its traditional ally of Russia. Bulgaria's leaders, however, were very wary of war due to both their diplomatic isolation and the disastrous Second Balkan War.[20] Still, revision of the Treaty of Bucharest was Bulgaria's major foreign policy objective.[21] Thus, the crisis resulting from the assassination of Archduke Franz Ferdinand offered Bulgaria an opportunity for revenge against Serbia. Since the Second Balkan War, Bulgaria had drawn closer to Serbia's enemy, Austria-Hungary, but they were not allies. In particular, Bulgaria had obtained a major loan from German and Austro-Hungarian banks, rather than from its traditional French creditors.[22] Initially, Radoslavov sought to correct this. On 16 July, Radoslavov and the Bulgarian government asked the Austro-Hungarian government for admission into the Triple Alliance.[23] They were initially intrigued, but declined out of a desire to keep the upcoming war with Serbia localized.[24] Also, as Romania was a member of the Triple Alliance, this made it difficult to admit Bulgaria, Romania's enemy, to the alliance. The Bulgarians, too, quickly thought better of the alliance. Fears of attacks from Turkish, Romanian, and Greek forces made a war with Serbia, even on the side of Austria-Hungary, look unattractive.[25] Romanian intervention was particularly feared and the Romanian Prime Minister had warned the Austro-Hungarian ambassador that Romania would act if Bulgaria

18 Ibid, 251. Kavalla, a strategic Aegean port in Thrace, had been occupied by Greece.

19 Ibid.

20 Petkov 1991, 23.

21 Ibid, 24.

22 Holden 1976, 57–78.

23 Hall 1996, 269.

24 Ibid, 286; Holden 1976, 89–92, and 99. The Germans were more enthusiastic as they oddly thought a Bulgarian entry would cause Romania to join the Central Powers despite ample evidence to the contrary. In August 1914, Bulgaria refused to sign a defense pact with the Ottomans unless Romania signed as well.

25 Hall 1996, 286–7 and 295; Holden 1976, 86.

joined the Central Powers; at this stage Bulgarian intervention was in part contingent on the attitude of Romania.[26] No further serious diplomatic activities occurred antebellum.

When war did break out, Bulgaria adopted a wait and see attitude. Charles Vopicka, the American ambassador to Bulgaria as well as Serbia and Romania, neatly summarized the Bulgarian position:

> My opinion is that Bulgaria is trying to get through her diplomacy what she lost on the battlefield. She is waiting for developments in the war … If the chances of war favor Germany and Austria, Bulgaria will join them, against the will of her people whose sympathies are with Russia, because the present Bulgarian Government believes that it can obtain more from Germany and Austria than from Russia.[27]

There are two important points in this dispatch. One, the Central Powers were in position to offer more to Bulgaria than was the Entente. Second, and more importantly, Bulgaria was waiting on events even though it was clear which side would offer more. The Bulgarian leadership would enter the war on the side of the Central Powers only if it began to look as though the Central Powers would win. The British Ambassador to Bulgaria, Henry Bax-Ironside, agreed that Bulgaria's policy would be "one of opportunism."[28]

Bulgaria remained divided internally between the Russophobes and Russophiles.[29] Most felt a strong connection to Russia, but for many this was insufficient in itself. As one of Radoslavov's aides put it "Our natural place was with Russia. Yet after 1885, … and the Bucharest Peace Treaty, how could Bulgaria take Serbia's side?"[30] Most of the peasants were weary of war, but they had little power.[31] Still, the strength of the Russophiles was a serious check on Radoslavov's desire to join the Central Powers. Radoslavov told General Fichev, the Bulgarian Chief of Staff, "If we stand on the side of the Triple Alliance against Russia, the people will stone us."[32] Radoslavov did have Tsar Ferdinand on his side. Ferdinand had been an Austrian officer in his youth and he feared for his Coburg dynasty in the event of an Entente victory.[33]

26 Hall 1996, 290–2.

27 Petkov 1991, 24–5.

28 Holden 1976, 93.

29 Hall 2003, 391; Holden 1976, 37.

30 Hall 2003, 397. Serbia had attacked Bulgaria in 1885 with loose Russian backing in a failed attempt to prevent the unification of Bulgaria and East Rumelia.

31 Petkov 1991, 27–8.

32 Hall 1996, 292. Some Bulgarians even served as volunteers in the Russian army.

33 Ibid.

Everyone, including Radoslavov, agreed that it was vital to be on the winning side, but yet join early enough to acquire valuable spoils.[34] The results in 1914 were mixed. Germany initially looked like it would win a stunning victory in the west, but was soon checked at the battle of the Marne. Events in the east—and Bulgaria was always more interested in eastern events—were also mixed. Austria-Hungary had done poorly, being rebuffed by Serbia and driven out of Galicia by Russia. The Habsburg ambassador at Sofia, Adam Tarnowski, warned his government that offers of Serbian territory to entice Bulgaria to join the Central Powers lacked credibility due to the recent defeats.[35] Russia, however, had been badly beaten by Germany at Tannenberg and around the Masurian Lakes in East Prussia. Thus, though Radoslavov allowed Germany to send six hundred advisors to the Ottoman Empire and quietly encouraged guerilla activity against Serbia in Macedonia, Bulgaria remained on the sidelines throughout 1914 waiting for the situation in the East to become clearer.[36]

Both the Entente and the Central Powers very much coveted an alliance with Bulgaria. Bulgaria had the best military of the remaining neutral Balkan states. Additionally, if Bulgaria joined the Central Powers, it would create the opportunity for a two-pronged attack on Serbia and would allow Austria-Hungary and Germany to establish direct communications with the Ottoman Empire. In addition to denying the Central Powers these advantages, an alliance with Bulgaria would provide the Entente with a land base for attacking Constantinople and reopening the Straits. The Entente also hoped that Bulgaria's entry would lead to the entry of Romania and Greece.

Each side was somewhat constrained in what it could offer Bulgaria. Neither side wanted to go to war with Greece or Romania, thus Bulgaria could not be offered territory of either of these states as long as they remained non-belligerents. The Central Powers were additionally constrained in that they could not offer much Turkish territory. They could and did, however, offer significant amounts of Serbian controlled Macedonia. The Entente was in an even tighter bind. It could offer Turkish territory, but as Russia wanted to acquire Constantinople and its hinterland for itself, only small sections of eastern Thrace could be promised to the Bulgarians. Serbian territory was much more difficult to offer. The Entente suggested that Bulgaria could be compensated in Serbian Macedonia provided Serbia made significant gains in Austria-Hungary. Given that Serbia would have to agree to these concessions, they always remained conditional on Serbian gains in the north and were never as large as those promised by the Central Powers.

34 Ibid, 291; Hall 2003, 389; Holden 1976, 85. This fits in part with Russett's (1968) notion that states entering at crucial times can extract spoils out of proportion to the size of their military capabilities. If Bulgaria waited until after it was clear who would win, it would not receive as many spoils as it would if its entry significantly contributed to the defeat of the Entente. Romanian leaders engaged in similar calculations.

35 Holden 1976, 99.

36 Ibid, 101–102; Hall 1996, 288.

Additionally, the Bulgarians wondered if the Entente would actually be able to deliver on its promises as Serbia might refuse to honor them after Bulgaria joined the war.[37] Perhaps, in part to offset this inherent disadvantage, Entente offers to Bulgaria were often coupled with threats that Bulgaria would be militarily punished if it remained neutral or joined the Central Powers.[38] The Entente also failed to coordinate its policies toward Bulgaria; France, Russia, and Britain often pursued different and incompatible diplomatic efforts in Bulgaria. Still, the Bulgarians always entertained Entente proposals through the end of 1914.

Radoslavov remained convinced of a Central Power victory throughout 1914, and therefore, rejected the Entente offers of alliance.[39] As Grey put it, "until Bulgaria believes that Germany is not going to win the war, she will not be moved by any promises of other people's territory which we may make her."[40] Radoslavov, however, was unable to bring Bulgaria into the war on the side of the Central Powers. He lacked enough evidence of an eventual Central Powers victory to sway the Russophiles. Beginning in 1915, however, Radoslavov began to waiver in his support of a pro-Central Powers policy, despite the granting of a German loan worth 150 million francs.[41] From December 1914 to February 1915, the Entente had a string of successes. The Turks were crushed in the Caucasus and rebuffed at the Suez Canal. The Russians were making headway in pushing from Galicia into the Carpathian passes. If they cleared the passes, Austria-Hungary would have nothing with which to meet the Russian advance. Finally, it was becoming apparent that Britain was going to launch a major offensive against the Dardanelles. Early naval operations looked promising and it was widely expected throughout the Balkans that the main operation would be a success as well.

These events led Bulgaria to curtail its guerilla operations against Serbia, though they were resumed in the spring.[42] Radoslavov pondered the question of further Entente successes in his writings: "If Constantinople falls what shall we do? We shall decide according to how events dictate. It is still too early for a decision."[43] He made it clear to the Austrians that Bulgaria could not act until the results of Austria-Hungary's campaign against Serbia were clear, while at the same time hinting to the Russians that Bulgaria might aid the Entente.[44] He also

37 Holden 1976, 120–126, and 157–162. The Entente also tried to get the Greek government to cede Kavalla to the Bulgarians in return for a Greco-Bulgarian advance on Constantinople in conjunction with a British naval attack up the Dardenelles. The Greeks consistently refused these offers, though they did briefly flirt with the idea in March 1915 (Theodoulou 1971, 53–4, 97–102, and 155–65).

38 Hall 1996, 289–90.

39 Ibid, 290.

40 Dewing 1924, 47.

41 Hall 2003, 397–98; Holden 1976, 137. The antebellum loan had not actually been delivered as it had contained a clause that it would be cancelled in the event of war.

42 Hall 1996, 296–97.

43 Ibid, 296 nt. 77.

44 Ibid, 296 nt. 75.

indicated he was interested in a Serbo-Bulgarian agreement in early February. Radoslavov was willing to act against his preference for the Central Powers if it would serve Bulgarian aims.[45] He was carefully analyzing the course of the war, trying to determine which side would win.

The Entente successes continued in March, with the Russian capture of Tarnow and the fall of the great fortress of Przemysl, the last Austro-Hungarian possession in Galicia. This shook both Radoslavov and Ferdinand. Additionally, Radoslavov believed Italy's entry was imminent and would strengthen the Entente still further.[46] The possibility of Bulgaria joining the Entente became very real, especially if the Gallipoli campaign went well.[47] The Entente powers, flushed with success, failed to meet Bulgaria's demands for an alliance. The Entente powers were convinced either that their successes meant they could do without Bulgaria or that their successes would force Bulgaria into their camp on lesser terms.

Either way, the Entente powers' refusal to give Bulgaria as much of Macedonia as Radoslavov wanted proved disastrous. On 4 May Germany and Austria-Hungary launched the Gorlice-Tarnow offensive against Russia. The offensive was stunningly successful, forcing the Russians to retreat from the Carpathian passes and western Galicia. The affect of this did not register immediately, in no small part because the worst defeats for the Russians did not occur until June. Radoslavov even engaged in serious negotiations to join the Entente during May. He did this apparently in hopes of using the newly started offensive to extract maximal concessions and out of a belief that the success so far of the Gorlice-Tarnow offensive did not offset the Russian gains the previous winter and Italy's recent entry.[48] At the time, Britain's Gallipoli offensive still seemed to be going well. All of this changed in June. The Russians began to suffer catastrophic defeats in Galicia, it became apparent Italy's offensive would not be able to make any headway, and at about the same time it became apparent that Britain's Gallipoli campaign was failing. These Entente defeats made a Bulgarian attack on the Ottoman Empire unattractive.[49] As Turkish territory was the most attractive feature of the Entente's offer, the British failure greatly weakened the Entente's hopes of wooing Bulgaria, but the Russian defeats in Galicia were more important. They, along with additional Russian defeats in July and early August convinced the Bulgarian government, and especially Ferdinand, that the Central Powers would win the war.[50] As Ferdinand had at least as much say over Bulgarian policy as Radoslavov,[51] the change in his thinking was crucial. Though as the Entente's position weakened their diplomats worked harder and promised more Serbian territory to Bulgaria, attracting Bulgaria to the Entente

45 Ibid, 297.
46 Holden 1976, 139–143.
47 Petkov 1991, 25.
48 Holden 1976, 145–147.
49 Hall 1996, 300.
50 Ibid, 302; Holden 1976, 168–170.
51 Theodoulou 1971, 52.

side was now a forlorn hope.[52] When on 14 June 1915 the Bulgarians asked for clarifications to the Entente's formal offer of 29 May, the offer had ceased to be attractive.[53] The offer might have been acceptable in May before the series of Russian and British defeats, but it was no longer viable given the turn of events. Russia suffered further defeats in June and July in Galicia and Poland. Russia had to eventually abandon the whole of Galicia and in August German forces occupied Warsaw. These successes of the Central Powers convinced Radoslavov that the Central Powers would win and he began to energetically pursue an alliance.

Even before the fall of Warsaw, Bulgaria had opened formal alliance negotiations with Germany on 22 July. The Germans offered larger portions of Macedonia than had the Entente, as well as parts of Greece and Romania if either of those powers were to join the Entente.[54] They also got the Turks to transfer a small enclave to the Bulgarians. The railroad from Sofia to Bulgarian Thrace ran through a small section of Turkish territory known as the Maritza enclave. The lack of a continuous railroad to the Aegean seriously weakened the Bulgarian government's communications with the coast. The district itself, however, was not of tremendous value to the Ottomans, though they were naturally somewhat reluctant to cede any territory. As an alliance with Bulgaria would make it much easier for Germany to send supplies to the Ottoman Empire and the British had landed fresh troops at Gallipoli from 6–7 August 1915, the Turks ultimately agreed to a German brokered deal to cede the district to Bulgaria though the transfer was not to occur until Bulgaria mobilized.[55] In addition to these territorial concessions, the Germans' willingness to contribute German forces to the offensive against Serbia was crucial in winning Bulgaria's alliance, as the Austro-Hungarians' failure the year before—as well as their overall military ineptness in the war so far—was still fresh in the Bulgarians' minds.[56] The Greek government had also promised to remain neutral if Bulgaria invaded Serbia, despite Greece's alliance with Serbia.[57] Romania, too, was shrinking from its desire to join the Entente, though whether this was apparent to the Bulgarian leadership is unclear.[58] Even given these enticements and positive developments, talks stalled in August after the sinking of the *Arabic*.[59] The Bulgarians feared the sinking might result in the United States joining the Entente which would offset the gains made by the Central Powers. The Germans saw this and quickly repaired relations with the US in part to bring Bulgaria into the fold.

---

52 Petkov 1991, 25.
53 Hall 2003, 398.
54 Petkov 1991, 26.
55 Holden 1976, 163–165; Leontartis 1970, 218; Morgenthau 1918, 269–71.
56 Hall 2003, 398
57 Hall 1996, 304; Mitrakos 1982, 9; Seligman 1920, 65. See the Greek case.
58 See the Romanian case.
59 May 1959, 219. See the US case.

With this last complication resolved, Bulgaria signed a treaty of alliance with the Central Powers on 6 September and mobilized its forces on 21 September 1915.[60] Bulgaria attacked Serbia on 11 October, entering the First World War on what would ultimately be the losing side. Vopicka, the US ambassador, believed Bulgaria joined the Central Powers for four reasons.[61] First, the Entente's diplomacy had been disorganized and uncoordinated. Second, Ferdinand firmly believed that the Central Powers would win the war. Third, Germany was willing to offer greater spoils than was the Entente. Finally, Russia suffered a crushing defeat due to the Gorlice-Tarnow offensive. Given that the offensive is what convinced Ferdinand that the Central Powers would win the war, the offensive takes on added causal significance. Hall (1996, 303), too, believes that the Entente defeats in 1915 were crucial to Bulgaria's entering the war on the side of the Central Powers. Even though Radoslavov had been favorably disposed to the Central Powers from the outset, he was willing to work with whichever side was most likely to help Bulgaria overturn the Treaty of Bucharest and achieve the borders it had been given at San Stefano.[62] His negotiations with the Entente in early 1915 made that clear. The Gorlice-Tarnow offensive and Germany's larger offers of Serbian territory convinced Radoslavov that the Central Powers were the side that would win and would support a greatly enlarged Bulgaria.

Without a doubt, Radoslavov's decision-making was greatly influenced by revealed information, most especially the Russians' success in Galicia from August 1914 to March 1915, Britain's failure at Gallipoli, and the Central Powers' success in the Gorlice-Tarnow offensive. The last of these led directly to Bulgarian intervention. Clearly, the Bulgarian case provides very strong support for the hypothesis that revealed information causes states to reconsider their decision for neutrality and often causes them to join ongoing wars.

Romania

Romania's entry into the First World War provides strong support for the hypothesis that revealed information causes states to join ongoing wars. Though Romania's Prime Minister Ion Brătianu was favorably disposed to the Entente from the outset, he approached the decision to join with great caution and even instituted polices favorable to the Central Powers after they won at Gallipoli and Gorlice-Tarnow. Only the surprising success of Russia's Brusilov Offensive in 1916 convinced Brătianu to lead Romania into war. The Brusilov Offensive changed Brătianu's calculations about the benefits of entering the war by convincing him Austria-Hungary was near collapse and that the war was nearly over. The decisive role the

60 The mobilization on the 21 September was only partial. Full mobilization occurred three days later.

61 Petkov 1991, 26.

62 Hall 1996, 334.

offensive played becomes apparent when tracing Brătianu's decision-making from 1914 through 1916.

Romania entered 1914 as a secret member of the Triple Alliance, but had few interests in common with Austria-Hungary or Germany. Romania's main interests were retaining the slice of the Dobrudja obtained from Bulgaria in the Second Balkan War and in satisfying its irredentist claims in Transylvania, Bukovina, and Bessarabia. The first two were part of the Austro-Hungarian Empire, while Bessarabia was part of the Russian Empire.

The Hungarians actively repressed the three million Romanians in Transylvania through voting restrictions, educational restrictions, limits on the freedom of association, and the suppression of the press, the Orthodox religion, and the Romanian language.[63] The situation of the million or so Romanians in Bessarabia was somewhat better, but its occupation aroused strong feelings as Bessarabia had been independent of Russia prior to 1878.[64] These feelings had subsided over time, especially as the repression of the Transylvanian Romanians became more severe. In addition to the lower level of repression in Bessarabia as compared to Transylvania, Romanians were also more favorably disposed toward Russia than Austria-Hungary for reasons of Balkan politics. Austria-Hungary had intervened diplomatically on Bulgaria's behalf after the Second Balkan War, whereas Russia had supported Serbia. The ability of Romania to hold onto the gains achieved in the Second Balkan War depended on the containment of Bulgaria by Serbia, Greece, and Romania. Austria-Hungary's support of Bulgaria created the possibility that the whole settlement could be overturned, and thus, was a significant source of friction in Austro-Romanian relations.[65] This strain led the Romanians to focus on the irredentist claims in Transylvania and Bukovina rather than those in Bessarabia.[66] Given the relative weakness of Romania compared to both Austria-Hungary and Russia, barring a general war, Romania could do little to satisfy either set of irredentist claims, nor could it confront Austria-Hungary about its support for Bulgaria. It was far safer to lie low and remain loyal to the Triple Alliance.

Of course, the crisis arising from Archduke Franz Ferdinand's assassination and the resulting war provided just such an opportunity, but it also brought dangers. As stated above, much of Romania's security depended on Serbia balancing against Bulgaria. An Austro-Serbian war threatened to destroy that balance. Naturally, most of the Romanian government, led by Prime Minister Brătianu, was favorably disposed to the Entente cause. Brătianu not only viewed the Entente powers more favorably, but he also believed that the Entente would win, as evidence by his interest in Russian, but not Austro-Hungarian inducements to join the war.[67]

63 Petrescu-Comnène 2000, 46–7, 51 and 53–7; Torrey 1982, 25–8.

64 Petrescu-Comnène 2000, 25.

65 Torrey 1998, 76.

66 Ibid, 10.

67 Ibid, 49 and 96; Vopicka 1921, 79.

This pro-Entente disposition did not mean Brătianu wanted to intervene immediately on the Entente's behalf. Brătianu believed that intervention would be difficult, no matter which side Romania joined. Given Romania's geographic isolation from the Entente powers it would be highly dangerous to intervene before Austria-Hungary was in dire straits. This concern about proper timing would remain central to Brătianu's calculations. Romania also suffered from serious military deficiencies. In addition to simply having fewer and poorer weapons than its potential enemies, Romania's armaments industry could produce only one cartridge per day per rifle owned by Romania antebellum and only two artillery shells per artillery piece per day.[68] Such a level of production was grossly insufficient to replenish armament stocks during a war. To make matters worse, Romania's fortresses were located along the Russian frontier and not along the frontier with Austria-Hungary as military planners had assumed adherence to the Triple Alliance.[69] Premature intervention, or even worse, joining the losing side would be disastrous for Romania. Brătianu saw this and as a result crafted a very deliberate and cautious policy. He told Ottokar von Czernin, the Austrian ambassador, that Romania would wait on events in the east and explained to the French that he would wait to join until Romania had "75 chances out of 100 of winning."[70]

Brătianu, who exercised almost exclusive control of Romanian foreign policy, therefore, initially favored a policy of neutrality. Parliament had very little say in foreign affairs and the public had even less.[71] Only King Carol, a Hohenzollern who favored joining the Central Powers, was an obstacle to Brătianu's preferred policy. He, however, easily yielded to the preferences of his ministers for neutrality especially after the Battle of the Marne shook his belief in German invincibility.[72] He died in October 1914 and was succeeded by his son, Ferdinand, removing any significant potential opposition to Brătianu.[73]

The initial Russian victories in Galicia and Bukovina in 1914 electrified the Romanian public and many called for Romania to join the Entente cause.[74] Brătianu, however, was not convinced Austria-Hungary was in danger of collapse and Bulgaria's pro-Austrian leanings presented a real problem. These concerns, coupled with German threats after their victory over the Russians at Tannenberg, reinforced Brătianu's belief that joining at this point would be premature.[75] Until

68 Torrey 1982, 26.

69 Ibid, 26.

70 Hitchins 1994, 252; Torrey 1998, 96.

71 Hitchins 1994, 255–7; Silberstein 1970, 179; Torrey 1998, 96 and 110.

72 Hitchins 1994, 254–5; Marie 1935, 50–1; Torrey 1998, 10; Vopicka 1921, 78.

73 Ferdinand had familial ties to Germany, but believed his duty as king of Romania required him to support joining the Entente. Marie 1935, 7; Torrey 1998, 17 and 96–7; Vopicka 1921, 78 and 86.

74 Torrey 1998, 11.

75 Ibid, 53–6.

the Entente's military situation improved and he received written guarantees from the Entente regarding Romania's promised territorial gains, Brătianu was not prepared to go to war; he much preferred to wait on events.[76] He told opposition leaders he favored neutrality because, "The war will be long; wait for the march of events. We will have the chance to say our word."[77] His strategy was to join early enough to greatly benefit from the dismemberment of Austria-Hungary, but late enough to not pay many of the costs.[78]

Brătianu, however, was not inactive. He attempted to coordinate Romania's policy with that of Italy. He hoped coordination would make Romania a more attractive ally for both sides, as it would appear that Romania could deliver Italy. Additionally, coordination would allow Romania to obtain a friend while still neutral and would not necessarily threaten either the Central Powers or the Entente. Romania and Italy seemed to have much in common. Both were formally part of the Triple Alliance, but their interests diverged with those of Austria-Hungary. An agreement was reached on 23 September 23 1914 in which both sides pledged to coordinate their policies and give the other eight days warning if neutrality was to be abandoned.[79] Though Romania tried to honor the agreement, Italy ignored both it and a second agreement signed 6 February 1915.[80] On the whole, the negotiations with Italy hurt Romania's position as the Entente tended to believe that if it could induce Italy to enter, Romania would follow suit without difficulty, rather than the other way around. Though previous Russian promises of Transylvania remained valid, the western powers did not actively pursue Romania in 1914 and early 1915.

The Central Powers offered Romania Bessarabia, but none of Transylvania. The Hungarians, led by their premier, Count István Tisza, had a great deal of influence in Vienna and were naturally reluctant to cede any Hungarian territory to Romania. In addition to his reluctance to cede Hungarian territory, Tisza agreed with Czernin that the Romanians were opportunistic aggressors who, therefore, would be influenced by the course of the war rather than by territorial concessions.[81] As Czernin put it, "decisive victories or decisive defeats are more important than the Transylvanian question" and "Romania's neutrality would end the moment a decisive victory in the war seemed about to be realized."[82] The German ambassador, Hilmar von dem Bussche, shared Czernin's view saying, "If we are victorious they will remain neutral."[83]

76 Ibid, 15; Hall 1996, 293; Spector 1962, 25–30.
77 Spector 1962, 23.
78 Silberstein 1970, 195–6.
79 Spector 1962, 25; Torrey 1998, 50 and 90.
80 Torrey 1998, 20 and 91–3.
81 Silberstein 1970, 181–5; Spector 1962, 22; Torrey 1998, 40.
82 Torrey 1998, 39.
83 Silberstein 1970, 200.

The belief in the primacy of military results was proved correct in 1915. From conversations with Ferdinand and Brătianu in early 1915, the Central Powers' ambassadors deduced that Romania was weighing the Russian victories in Galicia against the German successes in East Prussia and that Romania was waiting on further events, especially whether Italy would join.[84] If Austria-Hungary suffered serious reverses and Italy joined, Romania might do so as well. Austrian defeats in Galicia in March did finally prompt Italy to join in May. Though Romania engaged in a flurry of negotiations with Russia,[85] by the time Italy joined, the tide began to go against the Entente. The crushing Austro-German victory over the Russians at Gorlice-Tarnow, beginning in early May 1915, combined with the knowledge the Germans and Bulgarians planned to aid Austria-Hungary in a new attack against Serbia in the fall, deterred Romanian intervention.[86] Brătianu, however, still believed the Entente would win the war, even if its fortunes were at a low point. Indeed, the difficult straits in which the allies found themselves provided Romania with an opportunity to extract its maximal demands from the Entente. The Romanians insisted upon acquiring not just Transylvania, but also certain districts along the Tisza River, Bukovina to the Pruth, and the Banat to the Theiss. Sergei Sazonov, the Russian foreign minister, initially thought these demands were excessive, but after Gallipoli and continued Russian defeats in Poland he agreed.[87] These same factors naturally made Brătianu want to delay joining.[88] The Romanians stated they were no longer interested in a military alliance, but only a political accord. The fall of Warsaw ended the Romanians' interest in even the political accord.[89] Czernin and Bussche reported the Romanians remained fearful through early 1916.[90] With the Central Powers dominant in the Balkans and the Russians badly battered, Romania would not join unless the Entente's situation dramatically improved. Romania even resumed exporting grain and oil to the Central Powers, though oil exports remained well below their antebellum levels.[91]

During first half of 1916, not only was Romania uninterested in joining the Entente, but also the Entente became uninterested in Romania. After Gallipoli, Britain had lost interest in the Balkans and France was focused on its force at Salonika and Greek politics. Russia, its forces stretched to the limit, was wary of adding the 600 kilometer long Romanian front to its lists of commitments. Nothing happened, therefore, until the Brusilov offensive in June 1916.

---

84 Ibid, 201–11.

85 Queen 1997, 60–1.

86 Ibid, 61–2; Salandra 1932, 368; Silberstein 1970, 196–97, 219–20, and 247.

87 Renzi 1968, 1414–32; Torrey 1998, 20–1.

88 Renzi 1968, 1414–32.

89 Torrey 1998, 21.

90 Silberstein 1970, 228 and 231.

91 Torrey 1998, 23–5; Silberstein 1970, 233–4; Vopicka 1921, 80–1. The grain exports also pleased Romanian landowners.

The Russians launched the offensive, named by historians after its commander Alexei Brusilov, against the Austro-Hungarians in Galicia. The offensive was designed both to improve the situation on the Eastern Front and to take pressure off the French who were hard pressed at Verdun. The attack was wildly successful; the Austro-Hungarian forces were routed and roughly 350,000 prisoners were taken. Its success was well beyond the expectations of the Entente, and as reported by the British ambassador, caught Brătianu quite off guard.[92] Even the Russians were surprised by success on such a vast scale. Brătianu, though pleased by the Russian success, was not initially convinced that the offensive was general. He believed that the Russians lacked the ability to sustain the offensive long term, that Germany would bail out its junior partner, and based on inaccurate reports from the Romanian ambassador in London, that the offensive was designed solely to relieve pressure on Verdun and Italy.[93] These doubts, the first two of which were to prove correct, caused Brătianu to remain cautious. However, he did greet Entente officials much more warmly in June than he had in recent months.[94]

The offensive's success continued through the end of June convincing Brătianu that Austria-Hungry was in danger of collapse and might soon sue for peace. On 1 July, he told Czernin, "The war is coming to an end" which caused Czernin to warn Vienna to expect war with Romania.[95] At the end of July, Czernin cabled Vienna that Brătianu believes "our collapse is imminent. He wishes to fall on us."[96] Given this conclusion, it was imperative Romania join immediately to secure the territory promised by the Entente. Delay would mean the exclusion of Romania from the peace settlement and the loss of a great opportunity for territorial gain. On 29 June, Brătianu told French officials, "Up to now, when you have said to me that it is time to act, I have always said that I am not of this opinion. Today I will no longer tell you the same thing. I believe the hour has come."[97] Similarly, he told the British, "I do not wish to miss my train and I shall not do so".[98] Five day later he said he was ready to sign a military convention. This prompted a British diplomat to comment, "The game is won … the allies can have Romania now if they want her."[99] Queen Marie of Romania, who was more aware of Brătianu's thinking than most, noted the significance of the Brusilov offensive in her diary, "the Russian advance … was the sign that our hour was approaching, our great hour."[100] Even the US ambassador, Charles Vopicka, stated that the Brusilov offensive had increased

92 Torrey 1998, 98–101 and 119.
93 Ibid, 101.
94 Ibid, 99.
95 Silberstein 1970, 234.
96 Ibid, 238.
97 Torrey 1998, 105.
98 Ibid, 103.
99 Ibid, 95.
100 Marie 1935, 49.

the Romanians' belief in an Entente victory.[101] Thus, the unexpected success of the Brusilov offensive prompted and guaranteed Romania's intervention.[102]

Intervention, however, was not immediate. Brătianu had several conditions he wanted met.[103] First, Russia and France would supply Romania with 300 tons of munitions per day. Second, Russia would continue its general offensive and at least maintain its current position in Galicia and Bukovina. Third, Romania would be secured against a Bulgarian attack, most likely by an allied offensive from Salonika. Finally, the previous Entente offers of Austro-Hungarian territory would be honored. Haggling over these conditions, especially the supplying of munitions, which due to the logistics involved proved to be nearly impossible, delayed Romanian intervention until 27 August. Further delay was avoided not only because, as indicated by the repeated warnings of the Entente diplomats, the patience of Romania's would-be allies was wearing thin, but because Brătianu feared Romania might miss a golden opportunity.[104] Brătianu was convinced of the near collapse of Austria-Hungary in part because the Central Powers had put out a great many peace feelers in 1916 and Russia had removed Sazonov as foreign minister and replaced him with Boris Stürmer, who was seen as more amenable to peace. Just prior to entering the war, Brătianu told his fellow ministers, "The moment before us is decisive. If peace is concluded without us, we will be crushed between a great Hungary and a great Bulgaria. The world must be forced to see what we want …"[105]

As it turned out, Romania's window of opportunity was already rapidly closing. Though the Romanians easily advanced into Transylvania, pushing aside the limited forces the Habsburgs had at their disposal, the Romanian army was doomed. The Bulgarians easily held the small allied offensive from Salonika. This allowed the Bulgarians, with German aid, to attack Romania from the south. Brusilov's offensive had become hopelessly stalled, freeing large numbers of Austro-Hungarian and German troops to be transferred to Transylvania. The attack from the south caught the Romanian army in its flank, easily routing it. The Central Powers quickly overran two-thirds of the country. The remnants of the Romanian army regrouped in Moldavia, shielded by a Russian relief force. Though the army regrouped and hung on grimly until the end of 1917, Romania's entry had proved more of a burden than a benefit to the Entente.

Even though Brătianu ultimately miscalculated, the case provides strong support for the work's main hypothesis. Brătianu reacted to information that battles revealed about the relative balance of forces and the likelihood of an Austro-Hungarian collapse. He was scared off by unanticipated Entente reverses,

101 Vopicka 1921, 81–2.

102 Hitchins 1994, 261; Queen 1997, 43–5, 71–2, and 89; Silberstein 1970, 232 and 246–7.

103 Torrey 1998, 109.

104 Spencer 1962, 32–3; Torrey 1998, 119.

105 Torrey 1998, 27.

most especially Gorlice-Tarnow and Gallipoli, and was ultimately induced to join by the sudden success of the Brusilov offensive. Romania never did correct the military deficiencies that plagued it in 1914. Almost no improvement in this area occurred, nor did the Entente ever find a way to overcome the impossible logistics and deliver the needed munitions. Thus, a correction of military deficiencies cannot explain Romania's intervention. Rather, the case illustrates how revealed information can make joining less attractive, as was the case with the Gorlice-Tarnow offensive, or more attractive to the point of actually entering the war, as was the case with the Brusilov offensive.

Italy

Italy's situation at the beginning of the war was fairly straightforward, though Italy's membership in the Triple Alliance made it appear more convoluted than it actually was. Italy was one of the three founding members of the Triple Alliance along with Austria-Hungary and Germany, but by 1914, Italy's interests had seriously diverged from those of its allies, especially Austria-Hungary. Italy had irredentist ambitions in the Trentino, which was under Austrian rule. Italy also desired territorial gains in Dalmatia and Albania, both of which Austria-Hungary opposed.[106] Serbia, with Russia's backing, also opposed the desired gains in the Balkans, but overall Italy's territorial ambitions were much more in line with the Entente's goals than those of its formal alliance partners. On top of this, in intra-alliance negotiations and meetings, Germany and Austria-Hungary tended to treat Italy as a junior member at best. They certainly did not treat Italy as a great power and frequently not even as an ally.[107] Even an ardent Germanophile like Ricardo Bollati, Italy's ambassador to Germany, admitted, "In fact, there is, perhaps not one single question where the interests of Italy coincide with those of Austria."[108] This straightforward picture was only slightly muddled by Italy's extensive territorial ambitions in Asia Minor and in Africa. The former became a difficulty with the Central Powers after Turkey joined them in October 1914 and also led to conflict with Greece and to a lesser extent Russia, while the latter were a potential sticking point with Britain and France.[109]

On the whole, however, Italian relations with the Entente were good in 1914. For years, maintaining good relations with Britain had been one of the cornerstones of Italian diplomacy.[110] Relations with France had been cordial since an understanding had been reached in 1902 regarding past grievances and every

106 Like the Trentino, Dalmatia was under Austrian control.

107 Bosworth 1983, 122; Hamilton and Herwig 2003, 356.

108 Salandra 1932, 38. Salandra's memoirs are valuable but they must be taken "*cum grano salis*"—with a grain of salt—(Renzi 1968, 1427).

109 Hess (1963) covers Italy's African ambitions in detail.

110 Renzi 1968, 1416.

time Austria-Hungary acted aggressively in the Balkans, Italy and Russia drew closer.[111] Thus, even though Italy was formally allied to Germany and Austria-Hungary, its relations were far better with the Entente than with the Central Powers.

Control of Italian foreign policy in 1914 was straightforward as well. Marquis Antonio di San Giuliano, the experienced foreign minister, effectively controlled Italy's foreign policy. Constitutionally both King Victor Emmanuel III and Prime Minister Antonio Salandra had significant *de jure* powers in the making of foreign policy, but for various reasons both had effectively abdicated those responsibilities and were content to let San Giuliano direct matters. Victor Emmanuel III, unlike his grandfather Victor Emmanuel II, preferred to reign, but not rule. He was content to let his ministers control all affairs, foreign and domestic, and did not involve himself in the decision-making process after the assassination of Franz Ferdinand.[112] Salandra had only recently become prime minister and had not previously been a major player in Italian politics. He had almost no experience in foreign affairs, and therefore, felt it best to allow San Giuliano to control Italy's international policy with only minimal input from the rest of the cabinet.[113] Salandra kept himself up to date, but left the creation of policy in San Giuliano's able hands.

There was no immediate sense of crisis in Italy after the assassination. Many actually felt relief, as Franz Ferdinand had been a staunch Italophobe and many feared what his foreign policy would look like when he succeeded Franz Joseph to the Austro-Hungarian throne.[114] Both the public and government saw Franz Ferdinand's death as the removal of a threat, not the creation of one. Matters assumed the character of a crisis only when it became apparent Austria-Hungary would use the incident to punish Serbia. The Habsburg ultimatum went down particularly badly in Rome, both because of its severity and because Italy had not been informed of its contents prior to its public announcement, as was required by the Triple Alliance.[115] San Giuliano believed the Austrian ultimatum put Italy in great danger. Austrian gains in the Balkans would forever close Italy's dreams of expansion in that direction. Also, if the Central Powers were to emerge victorious in a war with the Entente, they would likely punish Italy after the war if Italy remained neutral. Yet, even if Italy joined the Central Powers, an Austrian win would be disastrous. As Salandra put it, "Italy, even if a party to their victory, would have been, at best, but the first of the vassal States of the Empire" and that Serbia's defeat would have meant, "The definite hegemony of Austria in the Balkans ... We would have lost all hope of territorial expansion, and we would

111 Ibid.

112 Bosworth 1983, 21; Hamilton and Herwig 2003, 359; Pryce 1954, 221; Renzi 1987, 69.

113 Pryce 1954, 221; Renzi 1987, 69.

114 Renzi 1968, 1417.

115 Bosworth 1983, 121–2 .

have lost the Adriatic in a commercial and military sense."[116] Victor Emmanuel and San Giuliano felt similarly.[117] On 2 August, the latter warned the Italian ambassadors in Berlin and Vienna that:

> Even if it [the Triple Alliance] gained a partial victory, it would not be able to give us adequate compensations; and if the alliance won a decisive victory and reduced France and Russia to impotency for many years, there would be neither the interest nor the desire to give us compensations in proportion to our sacrifices.[118]

Much of this concern stemmed from the aforementioned way in which Austria-Hungary and Germany had treated Italy in the years leading up to and especially during the crisis that preceded the ultimatum. Italy had been neither informed of nor consulted about the terms of the ultimatum. In essence, Germany and Austria treated Italy neither as an ally nor a great power. On top of this, Wilhelm II and Victor Emmanuel III personally despised each other.[119] Relations had been particularly cool since the Italo-Turkish war in 1911; many in Germany had written Italy off as an ally and many of the top Austrian leaders were Italophobes.[120] None of this boded well for how a victorious Austria and Germany would treat Italy. Worse, a Central Powers' victory was a distinct possibility. San Giuliano believed that given the German military's prowess a Central Powers' victory was probable, though by no means guaranteed.[121] He was not alone in this fear. General Luigi Cardona, the new chief of the general staff, warned, "The defeat of Austria and Germany would certainly be advantageous for us. But beware if they win: Then without any apology whatsoever we will have to suffer their vendetta."[122]

Given Italy's conflicts with Austria-Hungary, however, joining the Central Powers was not an attractive option even if they were the likely winners. In addition to the aforementioned political conflicts with the Habsburgs, Italy could not join the Central Powers at the war's outset for four other reasons. First, Italy did not have a powerful fleet, nor were the combined fleets of Germany and Austria a match for the Entente fleet.[123] Given Italy's long and relatively unprotected coastline, it would have been military suicide for Italy to wage a war against the alliance with

116 Renzi 1987, 62; Salandra 1932, 55. Salandra publicly expressed similar sentiments in a speech on 2 June 1915 shortly after Italy entered the war (Hope 1917, 12).

117 Renzi 1968, 1420.

118 Ibid, 1419.

119 Ibid, 1417.

120 Ibid, 1417; Bosworth 1983, 131; Renzi 1987, 62–3.

121 Pryce 1954, 221 and 224.

122 Renzi 1987, 83.

123 Ibid, 76; Hamilton and Herwig 2003, 370. San Giuliano was certain by 28 July Britain would join the war.

the superior fleet.[124] Second, Italy imported 90% of its coal from Britain meaning war with the Entente risked a major collapse of the Italian economy.[125] Third, the vast majority of Italy's population was for neutrality and the government feared a general mobilization could provoke a revolt.[126] Finally, Italy's military was woefully ill prepared for a major war in 1914. The army had been weakened by the recent war with the Ottoman Empire and many of the best units and equipment in the army were still in newly conquered Libya, which had yet to be fully pacified.[127] Adding to the army's difficulty was the death of the chief of the general staff, Alberto Pollio, in July.[128]

The last two reasons, the antiwar attitude of the populace and the poor shape of the military, combined with the might of the German army made joining the Entente at the outset of the war almost as unattractive as joining the Central Powers. Given Italy's weakness, caution was a must. A strong stand against either side could lead to disaster.[129] San Giuliano, therefore, resolved upon a policy of maintaining neutrality initially, while simultaneously trying to obtain compensation from Austria-Hungary through Article VII of the Triple Alliance.[130] San Giuliano felt he could risk neutrality because Italy would be safe post-bellum provided the Central Powers' victory was not decisive.[131] Italy's involvement on the side of the Central Powers would only increase the likelihood of the dreaded decisive victory. Still, he had to leave a way for Italy to enter the war on the side of the Central Powers if such a victory became probable. If it became obvious the Central Powers were going to win the war decisively, Italy could join its allies in hopes of limiting their wrath; indeed it was imperative Italy join its erstwhile allies in such a circumstance.[132] San Giuliano believed that negotiating for compensation through Article VII helped keep the door open for joining the Central Powers at a later date while at the same time making it perfectly clear to the Austrians that Italy did not support their actions.[133] It was this fear of Italy's allies, far more than a desire for territory—though that played a role—which led the foreign minister to resort to Article VII.

Article VII of the Triple Alliance specified that if any member of the alliance acted aggressively and began a war, the other members of the alliance would be due compensation and that the *casus foederis* would not come into effect even if

124 Renzi 1987, 76.
125 Hamilton and Herwig 2003, 371.
126 Dillon 1915, 92; Renzi 1987, 74–5 .
127 Dillon 1915, 88–92 and 98; Hamilton and Herwig 2003, 370; Page 1920, 143.
128 Renzi 1987, 77. He was succeeded by Cardona.
129 Renzi 1968, 1421.
130 Page 1920, 153–5.
131 Renzi 1987, 78.
132 Salandra 1932, 57.
133 Renzi 1987, 67 and 72.

compensation were received.[134] San Giuliano knew Italy was within its legal rights in asking for territorial compensation in the Balkans and in refusing to answer Austria-Hungary's and Germany's calls for mobilization, though of course legal rights alone could not protect Italy.[135] The negotiations also had the possibility of reducing domestic opposition to the war. If the government attempted to achieve its aims without war but found that Austria-Hungary was intransigent, some of those who initially opposed war might be brought around.[136]

Italy declared neutrality on 3 August, while simultaneously negotiating for compensation from Austria-Hungary. San Giuliano informed Italy's ambassador to Russia that, "The Government is decided on maintaining neutrality, save for unforeseen events."[137] In the conflict's first month, Salandra and San Giuliano watched the course of the war and entertained offers of alliance from the Entente and negotiated with Austria-Hungary under the auspices of Article VII. San Giuliano was particularly anxious for the results of the campaign in France.[138] The negotiations with the Austrians went nowhere as they insisted Italy recognize the *casus foederis* in exchange for the compensation.[139] Not only was the Austrian position legally incorrect, but more importantly it ran counter to Italy's interests and San Giuliano's goals. Meanwhile, the Entente offered Italy the Trentino, Trieste, though not its hinterland, the Albanian port of Valona, and hinted at Dalmatia.[140] San Giuliano responded with his terms for an alliance. They included the Trentino, Trieste, the internationalization of Valona, a fair share of the Ottoman Empire provided it was partitioned, the destruction of the Austrian fleet, no separate peace treaties, and a fair share of any postwar indemnity for Italy. Given the closeness of the terms offered and requested, agreement seemed possible.

The German victories in France and at Tannenberg in East Prussia, however, scared the Italians and prompted them to break off negotiations with the Entente.[141] Joining the Entente had become too dangerous. Almost as quickly, however, the Battle of the Marne turned the tide of the war ending the chance of a rapid, decisive Central Powers' victory. It, combined with the successful Russian invasion of Galicia, greatly affected San Giuliano's and Salandra's thinking. Both became convinced that the Entente would eventually win the war and that Italy's best interests lay in joining the Entente at some yet undermined point in the future.[142] Years later, Salandra said, "the battle of the Marne had a more or less decisive

134 Ibid, 63; Hamilton and Herwig 2003, 375; Renzi 1968, 1414, nt. 2.

135 Renzi 1987, 70.

136 Ibid, 108. This was certainly the least of the motivations for San Giuliano policy of negotiation.

137 Salandra 1932, 88.

138 Renzi 1987, 94.

139 Salandra 1932, 63.

140 Renzi 1987, 90 and 92.

141 Hamilton and Herwig 2003, 377; Renzi 1987, 96–7.

142 Bosworth 1983, 123; Pryce 1954, 225; Renzi 1987, 99.

influence on my point of view."[143] By early October, San Giuliano and Salandra had decided to set Italy on a course for possible intervention in the spring of 1915.[144] Salandra seems to have definitely decided on entering the war in the spring, but San Giuliano may have counseled waiting longer, had he lived. After the Marne, San Giuliano foresaw that the war would be long and that there was no need to join quickly. He believed the wisest course was to proceed deliberately and wait on events.[145] He, however, died on 16 October after a long illness that had limited his effectiveness for at least a month, if not since the summer. Whether his death hastened Italy's intervention is difficult to say, but it certainly did not delay it.

Entering the war before the spring was impossible, as the army would not be ready until April at the earliest.[146] The Italian army was in poor shape in 1914. It had 60,000 troops deployed to Libya in an attempt to suppress resistance there and another 20,000 were deployed to East Africa to guard Eritrea and Somalia against a possible Ethiopian attack.[147] Additionally, the army had yet to replace the ordinance spent or lost during the late war with the Ottoman Empire and lacked winter clothing, siege artillery, adequate transport, and other supplies.[148] On top of this, full mobilization would require adding 13,500 officers to the army.[149] At best, the Italian army was prepared for a short, defensive war, not a long, offensive one.[150] Even its defensive preparations were inadequate; its forts along the Austrian frontier were incomplete.[151] The difficulty of crossing the Alps in the winter added to the need for delay. An officer in the military and personal friend of Salandra summed up the situation as follows:

> It is essential that the Prime Minister should be made aware of the exact condition of the Army, and should realize that in its present state it is not fit to take the field. It is therefore to our supreme interest to postpone intervention as along as possible, because every day gained is a day won. To intervene in the meantime, during the winter months, with the Army not ready, with no chance of affording

---

143 Salandra 1932, 94. Though Salandra's own account of Italy's entry into the war is clearly self-serving and at times suspect, his claim here is generally accepted. See the references in the previous note, especially Renzi (1987).

144 Renzi 1987, 101.

145 Bosworth 1983, 129.

146 Renzi 1987, 107.

147 Ibid, 125–7; Bosworth 1983, 125. Renzi (1987) argues the uprising in Libya did not delay intervention, as the government was willing to sacrifice the colony if necessary in order to gain territory in Europe.

148 Page 1920, 181–2; Salandra 1932, 99, 124, 131, and 137.

149 Salandra 1932, 132.

150 Ibid, 130.

151 Bosworth 1983, 125. In the years preceding the war, the general staff, which rarely communicated with the civilian leadership, had assumed Italy would fight on the side of the Central Powers. It had, therefore, focused on completing the forts along the French frontier rather than those along the Austro-Hungarian frontier.

> our Allies the support worthy of a great Power, or of exercising the amount of pressure they have, all this time, been expecting, would be practically to rate ourselves as inferior to Serbia ... But if we carry on our preparations seriously and uninterruptedly, we may be able to intervene in the spring with a real and competent Army, with every chance of being the arbiters of the situation.[152]

San Giuliano had not remained idle after the Battle of the Marne. Shortly before his death, he negotiated an agreement with Romania that required each side to cooperate when possible and give each other eight days warning if they planned to abandon neutrality. San Giuliano and his successors never intended to live up to this agreement, but rather, in hopes of increasing the price each side would be willing to pay in order to obtain Italy's intervention, exploited the agreement to foster an impression that if Italy joined Romania would follow.[153] Thus, the agreement strengthened Italy's position for the coming negotiations with the Entente over the winter. It also created ties to a power that shared Italy's opposition to either Austrian or Slavic domination of the Balkans. The Romanian connection, therefore, gave Italy another way to achieve its goals in the Balkans if the negotiations with the Entente failed. It is unclear whether San Giuliano's successors saw these additional benefits in the Romanian agreement, but they did continue to use it to foster the impression Italy could deliver Romania as an ally.

In addition to possibly hastening intervention and losing some of the value of the negotiations with Romania, San Giuliano's death, combined with the resignation of the Giulio Rubini, the treasury secretary who opposed war preparations on fiscal grounds, led to a reorganization of the cabinet.[154] The main effect of this restructuring was that Baron Sidney Sonnino became the foreign minister and Salandra took a much more active role in determining Italian foreign policy. These two men were almost wholly responsible for Italian diplomatic decisions between October 1914 and Italy's entry into the war in May 1915.[155] Given Salandra's inexperience and that some have described Sonnino as Italy's worst foreign minister ever, this was an unfortunate pairing for Italy.[156]

Sonnino agreed with Salandra's conclusion that Italy should join the Entente in the spring of 1915.[157] This was a shift from Sonnino's position in August 1914. He had originally been in favor of honoring Italian's moral, if not legal, obligations to the Triplice, but he had become in favor of joining the Entente after the Battle of the Marne.[158] The two agreed to continue San Giuliano's policy of negotiating

152 Salandra 1932, 132–3. In hindsight, even this assessment was overly optimistic.
153 Torrey 1998, 88–91.
154 Page 1920, 189; Renzi 1987, 103; Salandra 1932, 146–9 .
155 Salandra 1932, 129.
156 Bosworth 1983, 134
157 Salandra 1932, 147.
158 Dillon 1915, 113; Page 1920, 168; Renzi 1987, 104–105.

with Germany and Austria-Hungary, while they simultaneously began to earnestly negotiate the conditions under which Italy would join the Entente.

The negotiations with Austria-Hungary, under the auspices of Article VII, yielded some fruit. Italy was allowed to occupy the strategic Albanian port of Valona on Christmas Day 1914.[159] Attempts to get the Trentino, however, were not successful. The Habsburg emperor, Franz Joseph, refused to cede any Austrian territory even in exchange for some small slices of German Silesia.[160] Additionally, the Austrians claimed that as they had yet to successfully occupy any Serbian territory, they were not yet obligated to compensate Italy.[161] All that was obtained was a pledge that Austria-Hungary would engage in no further offensives in the Balkans, though Sonnino was able to obtain this concession largely because Count Conrad von Hotzendorf, the Austro-Hungarian chief of staff, felt the troops were needed on the Galician front anyway.[162] Italy made it clear that these concessions were insufficient in themselves. Sonnino turned down offers of French and additional Albania territory and insisted that without the Trentino, Italy would never join the Central Powers.[163] The Austrians, Franz Joseph, and Conrad in particular, refused to budge and even insisted Italy owed them compensation for its occupation of the Dodecanese during the late war with the Ottoman Empire.[164] Talks stalled thereafter until March 1915.

By 8 March, the growing threat of an allied offensive at Gallipoli and sustained Russian pressure in Galicia finally got Franz Joseph to agree that some territorial concessions in the Trentino were acceptable.[165] Two weeks later, the fall of the Przemysl, the largest and last remaining Austrian fortress in Galicia, convinced István Burian, the Austro-Hungarian foreign minister, that significant concessions to Italy were an absolute necessity.[166] Accordingly, on 1 April Austria-Hungary offered Italy not just small sections of the Trentino, but its entire lower portion including the city of Trent itself.[167] These concessions did not meet Italy's current

159 Page 1920, 174–6; Renzi 1987, 122–3; Salandra 1932, 219–21. Italy was allowed to occupy the island of Saseno, which dominates Valona's harbor on 21 October. Italy originally landed 300 marines in Valona, but that figure rose to 6,800 by January. Sazonov had also agreed that Italy could occupy Valona in exchange for neutrality (Renzi 1987, 117). Austria also promised to recognize as *de jure*, Italy's occupation of the Dodecanese (Salandra 1932, 219–21).

160 Renzi 1987, 183–5. Franz Joseph never seriously considered the offer of German compensation.

161 Ibid, 178. This was of course due not to a lack of Austrian ambition but rather military ineptitude.

162 Ibid, 184.

163 Dillon 1915, 149; Salandra 1932, 235.

164 Dillon 1915, 151; Renzi 1968, 1429; Salandra 1932, 229.

165 Renzi 1987, 185–6. German pressure on Austria-Hungary also played an important role.

166 Ibid, 187.

167 Salandra 1932, 238.

demands, which had increased given the weakened position of Austria. Italy wanted the whole of the Trentino, including districts that were predominantly populated by ethnic Germans, plus Trieste, and some districts along the Isonzo.[168] This was more than the Austro-Hungarians were willing to concede and the chance further negotiation would prove fruitful became very slight.

Additionally, Austria-Hungary refused to transfer control of the ceded territories until the end of the war, while Italy insisted upon their immediate transfer.[169] The Habsburgs insisted that the transfers not occur until after the war out of fear that concessions might whet the appetites of other unredeemed nationalities, notably the Romanians in Transylvania.[170] They refused to offer the Italians more, as they believed it would be impossible to satisfy them at a reasonable price. Karl Macchio, the Austro-Hungarian ambassador to Italy, informed his government that he believed Italy would be deterred only by a spectacular victory.[171] By mid April both sides were simply negotiating for time.[172] Austria-Hungary wanted to delay the entry of another enemy into the war as long as possible and certainly until after the Russian pressure on Galicia was hopefully relieved by the upcoming Gorlice-Tarnow offensive. Italy wanted to stall until its army was ready and the negotiations with the Entente were complete; in particular, Italy viewed the talks as an effective vehicle for reducing the likelihood Austria-Hungary would launch a preemptive attack.[173] Indeed, the Italians may have been negotiating for time since early March when Italy's ambassador in Vienna telegrammed Sonnino, "My conversations with [Burian] might be prolonged everlastingly without leading to any practical result seeing that he would go on formulating ever new arguments in support of the contention he is putting forward."[174] To which Sonnino replied on 4 March 1915, "I take it there is nothing to hope from a continuation of the discussion with Baron Burian respecting territorial compensation in connection with Article VII."[175] This certainly would be consistent with the claim advanced below that the Italians stopped updating their calculations in response to new information after March 1915.

Italy's talks with the Entente were initially not much more promising than those with the Dual Monarchy despite the fact the Entente felt Italy's entry might cause several of the non-belligerent Balkan states to join the alliance.[176] Conflicts over how much of the Adriatic coast should go to Italy and general lethargy in Italian

---

168 Ibid, 244–8.

169 Ibid, 240–1; Dillon 1915, 170–1.

170 Renzi 1968, 1428.

171 Salandra 1932, 242.

172 Renzi 1987, 188.

173 Renzi 1968, 1427; Salandra 1932, 244. Cardona was especially worried about preemption.

174 Dillon 1915, 155.

175 Ibid.

176 Renzi 1987, 198.

diplomacy ensured little was done in 1914. Given that Italy could not join until the spring, there was no urgency on the Italian side to get negotiations underway. The early stages of the Dardanelles campaign in February 1915, however, convinced the Italian leadership that Turkey was about to be partitioned and that Italy's bargaining position would be greatly weakened.[177] This, plus the nearing of spring, caused the Italians to get serious about negotiations. Italy presented its conditions to Grey on 4 March.[178] Italy demanded the entire Trentino, South Tyrol to the Brenner Pass, small boundary changes along the Isonzo, Istria including Trieste, all of Dalmatia, and Valona.[179] Though the Entente was more than happy to meet most of Italy's demands, Italian claims on the eastern shore of the Adriatic created difficulties. Sazonov wanted to secure Dalmatia for Serbia and was opposed to Italy's claims there, though the Russian military eventually forced Sazonov to be more flexible.[180] Britain, too, thought a future Yugoslav state needed an outlet to the Adriatic.[181]

While this sticking point was being addressed, Przemysl fell. Though its fall had improved Italy's bargaining position with the Central Powers, it reduced Italy's leverage with the Entente.[182] The Russians in particular felt that they now could get by without Italian aid. Though both sides made some concessions in Dalmatia in late March, the issue remained unresolved.[183] Entente leaders opted to delay the landings at Gallipoli to avoid a costly setback that might hurt their bargaining position with Italy.[184] Even so, difficulties in naval operations in the Straits hurt the Entente's position and made the allied leaders, Grey especially, more pliable.[185] By 16 April, the disagreements over Italy's territorial claims were resolved and only the question of the date of Italy's entry remained.[186] Ten days later, the Pact of London was signed in which Italy promised to enter the war within a month in return for promises of acquiring the whole of the Trentino, Trieste, Istria, some districts along the Isonzo, half of Dalmatia, and Valona.[187]

The signing of the Pact of London did not guarantee Italy's entry into the war. Outside of the small middle class and large sections of the media, there was little support in Italy for entering the war on either side.[188] Because of this, the

177 Ibid, 199–200; Dillon 1915, 153; Hamilton and Herwig 2003, 382.
178 Salandra 1932, 264.
179 Renzi 1968, 1430.
180 Renzi 1987, 204–205; Salandra 1932, 272–3.
181 Renzi 1987, 205.
182 Salandra 1932, 277.
183 Renzi 1987, 207–208.
184 Ibid, 208.
185 Hamilton and Herwig 2003, 382.
186 Renzi 1987, 209.
187 Renzi 1968, 1430. Italy also received vague promises of concessions around Smyrna in Asia Minor.
188 Pryce 1954, 225–6; Renzi 1987, 109 and 240. The Pope also opposed Italian intervention.

government worried it did not have the necessary votes in parliament to carry a war credits bill. Therefore, as a strategic move, Salandra dissolved his government on 13 May fully expecting no one else to be able to form a government and that the king, given his pro-war stance, would return Salandra to power.

Victor Emmanuel first offered the premiership to Giovanni Giolitti, a former prime minister and for over a decade the most powerful politician in the country. Giolitti commanded broad support within parliament and could have formed a government had he so chosen. Giolitti refused, calculating that whatever government was formed would not last long. It was common for Giolitti to relinquish or decline high office in times of expected difficulty to avoid sullying his reputation.[189] In fact, Salandra had become prime minister in the first place because Giolitti had resigned in anticipation of rough times ahead. Though he opposed entering the war,[190] Giolitti had no effective way to oppose it given his reluctance to form a government. As Victor Emmanuel had promised to bring Italy into the war in the Pact of London, Giolitti feared that renouncing the pact would make him appear a tool of the Germans and Austrians, thereby hurting his future political prospects.[191] There was also a real danger that the king might abdicate in favor of his uncle, the Duke of Aosta, if Giolitti publically embarrassed him. Giolitti feared abdication would endanger the growing republicanism in Italy. There was no way for Giolitti to block what he saw as a foolish intervention without hurting his larger interests.

After Giolitti demurred, Victor Emmanuel offered the opportunity to three others: Giuseppe Marcora, Paolo Carcano, and Paolo Boseli. All three were pro-war and Carcano had even served in the Salandra ministry.[192] All were middling political entities who would have had at least as much difficulty controlling domestic politics as the current Salandra government. None saw a need for Salandra's replacement and all declined as Victor Emmanuel, Salandra, and Giolitti expected. During the three days while the king looked, if half-heartedly, for someone to form a government, major pro-interventionist rallies occurred in cities throughout the north. These demonstrations made the strength of the interventionists appear much larger than it was and greatly impressed the neutralist members of the parliament, in no small part because many members were subjected directly to mob violence.[193] When the king returned Salandra to power on 16 May, the prime minister was in a much stronger position than he had been three days before. Four days later, parliament easily approved the war credits, when only a week before there had been no hope that the measure would pass. Deputies changed their positions out of fear of the mob, fear of losing government patronage, and a reluctance to challenge

189 Dillon 1915, 157–8.

190 Ibid, 93–4; Page 1920, 187–8.

191 Renzi 1987, 247–50.

192 Dillon 1915, 219; Page 1920, 212–13 ; Salandra 1932, 353. Carcano had replaced Rubini as the minister of the treasury in the cabinet shake-up after San Giuliano's death.

193 Page 1920, 210–14; Pryce 1954, 226; Renzi 1987, 255–57.

the king.[194] Giolitti's refusal to organize resistance to the bill was also crucial.[195] On 23 October, Italy declared war on Austria-Hungary, but not on Germany, in hopes the Germans would not deploy their troops to the Italian front.[196]

Italy's decision to press ahead with intervention despite the overwhelming success of the Austro-German offensive against the Russians needs some explanation. By any sort of reasoning, the Gorlice-Tarnow offensive should have deterred Italy or at least caused Italian leaders to increase their demands. That neither happened is baffling. Italy joined the war at a most inopportune time. Its leaders were almost asking for defeat. As Richard Bosworth, a leading historian on Italian intervention, puts it:

> Italy had entered a war with a divided elite and a divided society, at a time when her allies were losing, with an underprepared Army, economy and administration … [I]t was a worse moment to choose to join a war than was June 1940.

The inexperience of Salandra and incompetence of Sonnino undoubtedly contributed to this gaff. They correctly estimated that belligerency offered Italy an opportunity, but unlike the late San Giuliano, they worried that the war might end before Italy joined.[197] Both believed it would be over by the winter of 1915–16.[198] This belief was created in early 1915 by Russia's success in Galicia. It had looked for a time that Russia would soon clear the Carpathians and burst into Hungary. Salandra certainly felt pressure to get Italy into the war before Austria-Hungary collapsed.[199]

But while this justified making compromises to get the Pact of London signed in April, by late May it was clear Austria was not about to be knocked out of the war. In fact, it was clear the Central Powers had regained the upper hand on the Eastern Front. The Italian cabinet was aware of the military situation.[200] Why Salandra and Sonnino failed to see that not only did Italy not have to intervene immediately but that it was actually a very bad time to join, is difficult to explain without resorting either to psychological theories about motivated biases or simple incompetence. Salandra's post hoc claim that Italy joined to help offset the Russian disaster seems suspect at best.[201] If the government wanted to balance against the Central Powers rather than just pick up spoils, they logically would have declared war on all of the

194 Hamilton and Herwig 2003, 384–5.

195 Ibid, 385.

196 The Italians also delayed in declaring war on the Ottomans. This double-dealing angered the rest of the Entente, but resulted in little benefit. Germany, however, did avoid deploying troops on the Italian border for months.

197 Renzi 1987, 266.

198 Ibid, 265.

199 Salandra 1932, 371.

200 Ibid, 343.

201 Ibid, 371.

Central Powers, not just Austria-Hungary. If this claim is genuine, Italy certainly failed to achieve this as well as its much clearer aim of picking up easy spoils. The Austrians did not have to divert any troops to the Italian front. Those that had been guarding it as a precaution prior to Italy's entry proved sufficient. Italy had been as helpful militarily to the Entente as a non-belligerent as it was as a belligerent.

In fairness to Salandra and Sonnino, the really crushing Russian defeats in the Gorlice-Tarnow offensive did not occur until June, well after Italy had entered the war. It had not been clear in May that Russia would not be able to recoup the situation on the Eastern Front. Thus, the decision is somewhat more baffling in hindsight than it was at the time. Still, Italy entered the First World War at a most inopportune time and consequently suffered a string of defeats. Though Italy did pick up significant spoils at Versailles, these could have been obtained at a lower price if Italy had entered at a better time. What had been planned as a way to strengthen Italy did just the opposite. In the long run, even given the gains at Versailles, Italy's involvement led to the collapse of Italy's parliamentary system and significantly damaged its military reputation internationally.

The Italian case provides support for both the counter-hypothesis that states wait until an expected chain of events is complete, and also for the work's hypothesis, that revealed information changes the calculus of non-belligerents. Clearly, Italy waited until it believed its military preparations were complete before it joined. Of course, as it turned out, Italy was no more materially prepared for the war than Austria-Hungary was close to being knocked out of the war. Still, based on the beliefs of the Italian government, the timing of Italy's entry is a classic example of what the counter-hypothesis predicts. The military preparations, however, were not all that influenced Italy's decision. The surprising, early German successes definitely scared the Italians off. They halted their negotiations with the Entente. When the course of the war changed, with the allies repulsing the Germans at the Marne and the Russians pushing into Galicia, the Italians again began to think about joining the Entente. Additionally, when in early 1915 it looked like the Entente might be able to knock both Austria-Hungary and Turkey out of the war, something that was unthinkable in 1914, the Italian government rushed to negotiate the terms under which Italy would join. As these later events coincided with the improvement of the Italian army, it is difficult to say that one hypothesis is better than the other. Likely, they worked together and reinforced each other. As was stated in Chapter 2, the two hypotheses are compatible with each other.

The main problem for the unexpected events hypothesis is that the Italians completely failed to factor the Gorlice-Tarnow campaign into their calculations. Its success was unexpected and had the Italians been entering to balance—Salandra's post hoc claim—then the timing would have fit well with the hypothesis. As they were entering to pick up spoils, it fits poorly with the hypothesis. This incongruity, however, seems explainable by the ineptness of Salandra and Sonnino, the fact they remained convinced Austria-Hungary was going to collapse even though the situation had changed, and that the worst defeats for Russia did not come until after Italy entered. San Giuliano likely would have counseled patience. The less experienced team of Salandra and Sonnino wanted to intervene and they thought they had a golden opportunity with the supposedly improved readiness of the army and the sudden weakness of its opponents. The government simply refused to admit that the situation had changed. Ineptitude certainly seems a plausible explanation as the government also thought the military had made sufficient improvements, but in actuality performed miserably on the battlefield. The Italian offensives were easily held by the Austrians, the same Austrians that had been crushed by the Russians and were incapable of defeating the Serbs alone.

Therefore, though the situation in April and May 1915 suggests that the Italian government ignored the most recent revealed information, the same situation also suggests that they ignored the incompleteness of their military preparations. The government had become convinced in March that the situation was favorable and that the preparations would be done on time. After that point, the government either ceased to act rationally or simply was incompetent. A mixture of the two is a distinct possibility. Prior to May 1915, the Italians behaved in a manner consistent with both the revealed information hypothesis and the counter-hypothesis, though their reluctance to talk to the Entente after the early German victories can only be explained by the revealed information hypothesis. After that point, Italian behavior cannot be explained by either hypothesis without factoring in either incompetence or irrationality. Thus on the whole, the Italian case provides as good and perhaps better support for the revealed information hypothesis as for the counter hypothesis.

United States

Like Bulgaria, Romania, and Italy, the United States joined the First World War because of revealed information. Unlike those states, however, the United States joined not because of information being revealed about the relative balances of forces, but rather because of information being revealed about the intentions of one of the belligerents. Specifically, the US joined when Germany resumed unrestricted submarine warfare and the Zimmerman telegram was leaked in the spring of 1917. These events showed that Germany was clearly hostile to the rights of neutrals and unwilling to work with the US.

Compared to the other states that joined the war, the US' strategic position in 1914 was unusual. The US was geographically removed from the conflict, had no allies in the war nor was it initially sought as an ally, and none of the US' relations with the belligerents were particularly difficult. Also, the US was unique among the latter joiners for not looking for spoils. Indeed, the US joined the war neither to balance, nor bandwagon, nor defend American territory from invasion. Even a staunch interventionist like Theodore Roosevelt never mentioned balancing as a reason to enter the war.[202] Rather, the Americans entered for two reasons. First,

202 Cooper 2003, 422.

they entered to uphold their honor and rights as President Woodrow Wilson saw them.[203] Second, Wilson wanted to be able to shape the peace treaty along the lines of a greater respect for international law and to form some sort of collective security institution. Yet, even given these unusual motives for joining a war, the US entry was prompted and timing dictated by revealed information.

Throughout the period, foreign policy was determined almost exclusively by Wilson, though his policies were sometimes undermined by his more pro-Entente aides. Wilson was able to achieve this very unusual high level of control of US foreign policy for several reasons. First, outside of Walter Hines Page, the ambassador to Britain, US ambassadors in Europe were diplomatic nonentities who did little more than relay the messages of the President.[204] Second, during the war's first year Congress was in session for only three months and that was an ineffectual lame duck session.[205] Even when Congress convened more often later in the war, it played little role prior to the actual declaration of war.[206] Congress was as, or more, neutralist than Wilson and as long as he pursued a neutralist course Congress was generally content to remain on the sidelines. Third, Wilson rarely sought the advice of his advisors and they rarely challenged his views, knowing that if they did, he would cut them out of the loop entirely. Only Wilson's first Secretary of State, the pacifist William Jennings Bryan, ever really opposed Wilson's policies and when he did so in 1915, he promptly resigned. Thus, Wilson enjoyed an unusually high level of control over American foreign policy.

Most Americans, including Wilson, were biased in favor of the Entente, but were also deeply neutralist.[207] Wilson wanted to use the US's unique position to promote and protect the rights of neutrals. That Wilson was committed to using the US's position to shape the peace even at an early stage in the war is quite clear. He was interested in the idea of a League of Nations as early as February 1915.[208] In May 1916, Wilson told Grey the US was committed to collective security and that the US wanted the concept of the freedom of the seas guaranteed in any peace document.[209] Again in May 1916 and later in January 1917, Wilson called for the freedom of the seas, popular sovereignty, equality among nations, a general reduction of armaments, and a league to enforce collective security.[210] Thus, even early on Wilson was interested not only in upholding neutral rights, but also in

203 Kennan 1951; Osgood 1953; Questor 1982.

204 Cooper 2003, 430.

205 Ibid, 429.

206 May 1959, 182–90. The issue of armed merchantmen was a notable exception (May 1963, 22–3).

207 Gregory 1971, 11–12; Seymour, 1967, 3. Significant segments of the population also favored the Central Powers. At no time was public sympathy for any of the belligerents strong enough to force Wilson to enter the war.

208 Knock 1992, 35.

209 Ibid, 74.

210 Ibid, 76 and 110.

shaping the peace to come. Wilson wanted peace, but only if it could be achieved without surrendering too many of the rights of neutrals. Reconciling these goals was the trick. Given this, the US naturally declared neutrality when war broke out. Any other course was not considered.

The US's initial difficulties came not with the Germans, but with the British.[211] The British blockade of the Central Powers led to the stopping and searching of neutral ships for contraband cargo. Often the searches required that ships be brought into port and interned for a lengthy time. This was a clear violation of neutral rights. The British had a right to prohibit contraband from being shipped to other belligerents, but they had no right under international law to detain neutral ships in port. The Americans duly protested. The British were unconcerned with international law, but they wanted to avoid offending the Americans.[212] As Grey put it,

> [The] blockade of Germany was essential to the victory of the Allies, but the ill-will of the United States meant their certain defeat … If we quarreled with the United States we could not get supply. It was better therefore to carry on the war without blockade, if need be, than incur a break with the United States.[213]

The issue was resolved amicably with the Americans conceding most points to the British for several reasons. First, Grey treated the Americans with great friendliness and Page, the US ambassador to Britain, was an Anglophile who did his best to prevent the issue from creating friction.[214] Second, the Americans profited greatly under the British system. Britain initially did not prevent all products from going to the Central Powers; that would come later. Though trade was slowed, American ships were always duly released. By 1916, though the value of trade with the Central Powers had fallen to negligible levels, trade with the Entente had quadrupled from its prewar levels.[215] As trade with the Entente had been larger antebellum than trade with the Central Powers, it was hard for the Americans to be overly upset with the British blockade early in the war. Difficulties persisted, but they were always addressed, though not necessarily to the Americans' satisfaction. Third, the British were sensitive to the American difficulties. When the British added cotton, an ingredient in dynamite, to the list of contraband items, they offered to buy a sufficient amount of cotton from the US to keep the market price up and prevent a depression in the South, Wilson's electoral base.[216] Finally, Wilson believed belligerency was the only way to get Britain to abandon the blockade and the temporary detaining of neutral shipping simply was not a great enough offense

211 Ibid, 34; May 1963, 2.
212 Gregory 1971, 37.
213 Ibid, 34.
214 May 1959, 8, 15, and 32.
215 Gregory 1971, 46; May 1959, 66; Seymour 1967, 7–8.
216 Gregory 1971, 73.

over which to go to war.[217] Even when the British decided in March 1915 to stop all goods bound for Germany, the US refused to protest strongly.[218] Thus, through early 1915 all of the difficulties had been with the Entente, not the Central Powers, and the US had found it possible to stay neutral as long as it accepted significant, if not egregious, infringements on the rights of non-belligerent merchants.

Problems with Germany would dominate 1915. In February, the Germans began a submarine campaign in retaliation for the British blockade, though the German leadership was not united behind the idea. [219] The navy, led by Admiral Alfred von Tirpitz strongly supported the campaign, while the army, led by General Erich von Falkenhayn, and the civilian leadership, led by Theobald von Bethmann Hollweg, were more circumspect. Falkenhayn and Bethmann Hollweg were afraid of angering the neutrals, including the US, and Bethmann Hollweg believed that an American entry into the war on behalf of the Entente must be avoided.[220] Neither, however, was convinced that the submarine campaign would cause intervention; therefore, it was allowed to go forward.[221]

The campaign had moderate success in its first months and did not initially lead to significant friction with the Americans, though the US did warn the Germans it would not accept the sinking of neutral ships and would protect American citizens.[222] Many other neutrals, including Norway, Italy, the Netherlands, and Denmark, also issued protests in response to the U-boat campaign.[223] The storm broke on 1 May when the *Gulflight* became the first American vessel to be attacked by U-boats. Six days later the *Lusitania* was sunk. Though the later was not an American ship, it was a passenger liner with many Americans on board. Of the over 1,000 people to die, more than 100 were Americans. The American public was outraged. Not only were the attacks a violation of neutral rights—the *Gulflight* incident more clearly than the *Lusitania*—but Wilson saw the attack on the *Lusitania* as an attack on humanity, which was not the case with the British violations of international law.[224] Such acts were intolerable in both Wilson's and the American public's eyes. To make matters worse for the Germans, the Bryce Report detailing German atrocities in Belgium was released shortly after the attacks. Though much of the report was false, it severely damaged the reputation of the German government in the eyes of the American public.[225] By some estimates the public was so enraged by the attacks and the report that Wilson could have led the US into war at that

217 Ibid, 44.
218 Ibid, 55.
219 United States Department of State 1928, 96–7.
220 Gregory 1971, 49–51; May 1959, 200 and 229.
221 Gregory 1971, 52; May 1959, 120.
222 Gregory 1971, 53–4 .
223 May 1959, 122.
224 Ibid, 65; Seymour 1967, 11–12.
225 Knock 1992, 60.

moment had he so chosen.[226] The attacks also drove American frustration with the British blockade right out the window. Winston Churchill among others noted the benefit Britain derived from the submarine campaign: "The first German U-boat campaign gave us our greatest assistance. It altered the whole position of our controversies with America. A great relief became immediately apparent."[227]

The submarine campaign violated neutral rights in ways the British blockade did not. U-boats failed to distinguish between neutral and belligerent carriers, contraband and legitimate goods, involved the loss of the ship, and often the loss of life.[228] Wilson saw that claims for compensation could be brought against Britain post-bellum to offset US shippers' economic losses, but no post-bellum claims against Germany could compensate for lost lives.[229] It has been argued that the US could have avoided friction by simply withdrawing its merchant fleet from the sea. Pacifists led by Bryan advocated this position. The US merchant fleet was not large and though it would have hurt the US economy, pacifists reasonably argued the cost would have been less than the cost of war.[230] But Wilson was not interested in weighing commercial costs. He wanted peace, but he also wanted to maintain neutral rights as far as possible while at the same time remaining at peace. No position that was consistent with the maintenance of neutral rights could be found in conjunction with unlimited submarine warfare. Wilson refused to surrender accepted neutral rights and American honor by withdrawing US ships from the Atlantic.[231]

Wilson decided to resolve the issue through diplomacy. He pressured the Germans in a series of diplomatic notes over the course of the summer insisting the attacks be halted and requesting compensation for the loss of life and property.[232] Bryan resigned in protest to the harsh line and was replaced by Robert Lansing. The pressure was sufficient that in June Bethmann Hollweg forced the navy to secretly change its orders to U-boat commanders to forbid attacks on passenger liners.[233] An exchange of notes followed over the course of the summer until the sinking of the *Arabic* on 19 August. Bethmann Hollweg became very fearful of an American entry, in part because he thought other neutrals, including Romania, might join the Entente if the US entered the war.[234] He quickly apologized for the incident, said it would never happen again, and published the previously secret

226 Seymour 1967, 35.

227 Ibid, 7.

228 Ibid, 9–10.

229 May 1959, 329.

230 Cooper 2003, 421.

231 Seymour 1967, 15. Wilson certainly was comfortable with the use of force. He had dispatched troops to occupy Veracruz in 1914 as a response to what he saw as insults by the Mexican government to the US flag and was later to dispatch a punitive expedition to capture Poncho Villa on Mexican soil (Shirkey 1999, 24).

232 Gregory 1971, 63–4; May 1963, 10.

233 Gregory 1971, 68.

234 May 1959, 123–9, 166–7, 210, and 219.

injunction against attacking liners.[235] The German navy also secretly withdrew its submarines from the Atlantic.

This stabilized relations between Germany and the US until the following spring. In the meantime the US initiated an abortive mediation effort. It failed to lead to anything substantive, but during the negotiations with Britain over the blockade, the US had sent mixed signals on the issue of arming merchantmen. This convinced Bethmann Hollweg that the US was also irresolute in its opposition to submarine warfare.[236] Bethmann Hollweg acquiesced to the navy's pressure to resume the submarine campaign in February. The new campaign resulted in the attack on the *Sussex*, an unarmed merchantman, on 24 March 1916. The attack resulted in deaths, though the Americans on board either escaped harm or were only wounded. Still, it seemed that the Germans were reneging on their earlier promises and in April Wilson threatened to break relations unless the attacks stopped altogether. On 4 May the Germans again acquiesced and agreed to halt the attacks provided the US put pressure on Britain to bring the blockade back within the confines of international law.[237]

Wilson duly threatened the British, withdrew Page for consultation, and got Congress to authorize retaliation against the British. Lansing and House, however, undermined the threat. They reassured the British that the threat was not serious and the British essentially called the bluff.[238] Additionally, Wilson wanted to press the British only so far, as a rupture with the British would reduce the amount of pressure Wilson could bring to bear on the Germans.[239] Had the British been convinced the threat was serious, they may well have relented.[240] Though Anglo-American relations remained strained throughout late 1916 and early 1917, they never approached a breach.

Meanwhile, internal events in Germany were increasing the odds that the U-boat campaign would be renewed. After the failure at Verdun, Falkenhayn had fallen from power and been replaced by Generals Paul von Hindenberg and Erich von Ludendorff. Their rise greatly increased the military's control over the government. Though they did not favor immediately resuming the U-boat campaign, as the German army had been stretched thin by Romania's entry and a new U-boat campaign might result in a Dutch or Danish declaration of war, they were convinced it would eventually be necessary.[241] The military was divided as

235 Gregory 1971, 69–70; Seymour 1967, 38.

236 Gregory 1971, 86; May 1963, 21.

237 Cooper 2003, 425; Gregory 1971, 91–2; Knock 1992, 74; May 1963, 27; Seymour 1967, 41–2.

238 Gregory 1971, 100 and 114.

239 May 1959, 335.

240 Gregory 1971, 108–109.

241 May 1959, 404; Seymour 1967, 67–8; Tuchman 1966, 137–42. The previous entries of Bulgaria and Italy had lowered German concerns about how a resumption of the U-boat campaign would affect neutrals (May 1963, 11–12).

to whether resuming submarine warfare would result in the US' entry, but even those who believed the US would enter thought the benefits of disrupting the British economy and possibly forcing the British to lift the blockade outweighed the negatives of potential American belligerency.[242] The US Army was generally looked down upon as it was small and its 1916 campaign in Mexico to capture Villa had been less than impressive. The German military believed the U-boats would end the war before America could make a difference. The civilian bureaucracy, however, generally felt the U-boats were not worth the risk of an American entry.[243] On 7 October 1916, the Reichstag main committee sanctioned the resumption of U-boat activity. In November, Gottlieb von Jagow, the foreign minister and main opponent of the U-boat campaign, was forced out of office and replaced with the more belligerent Arthur Zimmerman. These changes in the German government left Bethmann Hollweg hopelessly outnumbered and powerless to prevent the resumption of submarine warfare. He was allowed to undertake one last peace initiative in December while the navy prepared to resume the U-boat campaign. Though Wilson responded favorably to Bethmann Hollweg's initiative, Lansing urged Britain and France to demand terms the Germans would be certain to reject.[244] This undermined the peace initiative and the Kaiser, convinced the Entente would not agree to peace, duly decided upon the resumption of unrestricted submarine warfare on 9 January 1917.[245] On 31 January, the Americans learned of this decision and also of the Kaiser's refusal to participate in any peace conference at which Wilson was present even if Wilson brought the conference into being. Wilson and Lansing were surprised by the resumption of submarine warfare and Wilson was disturbed by the Kaiser's desire to exclude him from any peace conference.[246] Worse, the orders authorizing the new submarine campaign explicitly stated that neutrals should be attacked and ruled out any possibility of compensation. This differed sharply from the 1915 instructions which said neutrals should be avoided if possible and which at least in theory allowed for compensation.[247] Wilson promptly severed relations with Germany on 3 February, though he did not declare war.[248] He wanted to wait to see if the Germans would actually attack US ships, which did not occur until 18 March.

In the interim, several events further pushed the US toward war. First on 24 February, the US government learned about the existence of the Zimmerman telegram which encouraged Mexico and Japan to attack the US with German aid. The telegram electrified American opinion, weakened neutralist opposition in

---

242 May 1963, 13–14; Seymour 1967, 44, 49, and 55.

243 Carnegie Endowment for International Peace 1923, 1130–9; Tuchman 1966, 140–2.

244 Knock 1992, 108–10.

245 Ibid, 115–16; Gregory 1971, 120; May 1959, 41; May 1963, 41.

246 Knock 1992, 116; Lansing 1970, 210–11; Tuchman 1966, 149.

247 Buehrig 1955, 20-21 and 55.

248 May 1963, 41; Seymour 1967, 50–1.

Congress, and significantly affected the President's thinking.[249] Wilson received the news with "much indignation" according to Under-Secretary of State Frank Polk and was particularly upset that the telegram was sent over US lines which the Germans had been allowed to use to further US attempts to bring about peace negotiations.[250] The telegram shattered Wilson's belief that the Germans had good intentions.[251] Wilson's official biographer, Ray Baker, felt that no event was more important in pushing Wilson to war.[252] Second, the abdication of Tsar Nicholas II of Russia on 15 March eased Wilson's conscience, though it affected his thinking far less than either the telegram or the submarine issue.[253] Two days after the Germans finally attacked US shipping on 18 March, Wilson requested a special session of Congress to meet on 2 April at which he delivered his war message. Congress duly declared war on 6 April 1917 ensuring victory for the Entente. The twin shocks of the Zimmerman telegram and the resumption of unrestricted submarine warfare had finally pushed Wilson and the US into war.

Equally important, Wilson did not decide to join in order to bail out the Entente or out of commercial motivations.[254] Indeed, the Entente was not yet hard pressed in April of 1917.[255] American opinion held that the February Revolution should actually improve the efficiency of the Russian government, thereby strengthening, not weakening, Russia.[256] Both General Haig, head of the British army, and General Brusilov, head of the Russian army, had suggested victory could be had in 1917 without the aid of US troops.[257] If Wilson feared the resumption of submarine warfare would alter the military balance between the belligerents, he would have brought the US into the war in February rather than having waited until US ships were attacked. While a number of Wilson's advisors like Lansing and Polk were concerned about a German victory, they were constantly frustrated by Wilson's refusal to think in these terms. Additionally, while these advisors might have seen Germany as inimical to the US's interests, they were not arguing in the spring of 1917 that the Entente was on the verge of defeat. In telegrams leading up to the break in relations and declaration of war, Lansing and US ambassadors in Europe mention the submarine issue and the Zimmermann telegram, but never the relative balance of forces between the Entente and Central Powers.[258] Finally, Wilson did not believe the US held the balance between the Entente and the Central Powers

249 Gregory 1971, 124; May 1959, 429; Seymour 1967, 50; Tuchman 1966, 174–6 and 184–7.

250 Tuchman 1966, 168 and 172–3. Lansing also noted that Wilson was particularly upset by the mode of transmission (Lansing 1970, 228).

251 Knock 1992, 116.

252 Tuchman 1966, 198–9.

253 Gregory 1971, 126.

254 Ibid, 139; Cooper 2003, 441.

255 Gregory 1971, 139; May 1959, 427.

256 May 1959, 431.

257 Ibid.

258 United States Department of State 1917, 109–14 and 195–200.

nor, given the US's lack of preparation, did he think US aid would arrive in time if the Entente found itself in trouble.[259] The US entered because it saw Germany as a threat to its ideals and by 1917 Wilson believed this threat could only be countered by US belligerency. As Wilson himself put it, "The right is more precious than peace."[260]

Like the previous case the revealed information hypothesis receives very strong support. Without the Zimmerman telegram and the surprising resumption of submarine warfare in 1917, the US would never have gone to war. The US may well have gone to war in 1915 over the U-boat issue but for the Germans' willingness to appease the Americans. The Germans' plan to deny Wilson any role in the shaping of the peace also came as a surprise and played a role. All of this is consistent with the revealed information hypothesis, as is any role played by the February Revolution. Even the opposing view, that the US entered in order to balance, rests squarely on information being revealed about German capabilities and intentions by the Zimmerman telegram and renewed U-boat campaign. Thus, the revealed information hypothesis receives strong support.

Ottoman Empire

The Ottoman Empire entered 1914 undergoing major changes. Since the 1908 coup by the Young Turks, the Sultan, Mehmet V, had only a minor role in the governing of the empire, though he officially remained the commander in chief.[261] The Committee of Union and Progress (CUP), the political party of the Young Turks, controlled the affairs of state. The *Meclis-i Umumî*, which functioned essentially as the Central Committee of the CUP, was the main policy making body in the Ottoman Empire. For any policy to succeed it needed strong backing in the *Meclis-i Umumî* and the support of a majority of the cabinet members.[262] The CUP was composed of rival factions and there had been several assassinations and coups within the Turkish government after the Young Turks' seizure of power in 1908. In 1914, the most powerful members of the cabinet were Enver Pasha, the Minister of War, and Talaat Bey, the Minister of the Interior, though the Grand Vizier, Said Halim Pasha, was still an important figure.

The CUP's foreign policy had not been a success prior to 1914. In the proceeding three years, the Ottomans had been defeated by Italy in the Italo-Turkish War and by a coalition of Balkan states in the First Balkan War. True, they had regained Adrianople in the Second Balkan War, but they had lost Libya and the Dodecanese to Italy, the Aegean islands to Greece and all of their European possessions other than a part of eastern Thrace to Bulgaria, Greece, Serbia, and Montenegro. These

259 May 1959, 169 and 176–7.
260 Cooper 2003, 440.
261 Trumpener 2003, 338; Weber 1970, 6–9.
262 Trumpener 2003, 342.

losses had led to the rise of strong irredentist feelings and ambitions that melded with emerging nationalist and Islamist strains within the CUP's program.[263] The domestic situation was not much better. Unrest was endemic in much of the remaining empire, especially Arabia. The CUP's modernization and reform movements were slow to produce results. These difficulties and the impatience of some within the CUP for results further fueled some Young Turks' desire for a radical foreign policy.

The Ottoman Empire's foreign policy had not been radical at all prior to the Young Turk's coup. Turkey had maintained a close relationship with Germany since 1889 in the 19th century tradition of European powers having special privileges within the Empire. The Germans had courted Sultan Abdulhamid II with great success. During his reign, the Germans had established a military mission in Constantinople to train the Turkish army and were heavily involved in the Baghdad railroad project. Germany also accepted numerous promising Turkish officers to train in German military academies, Enver Pasha among them.[264] The Young Turks' rise to power and the overthrow of Abdulhamid, however, hurt Turko-German relations. Not only had the coup removed a friend of Germany from power, but also the CUP originally had liberal leanings. The Young Turks had initially looked to Britain for help with reforms but Britain's inability to help the Ottomans reform fast enough and British intervention in Persia in 1910 cooled the relationship.[265] Still, in the long run it seemed likely that the CUP would come around to British aid and abandon the German connection. The German foreign office concluded that the CUP's rise to power had placed a time limit on German influence in Turkey.[266]

Surprisingly, Germany began to move away from the Ottoman Empire before being pushed by the Turks. By 1913, disappointment with Turkish failures in the Balkans and fears that its proto-alliance with the Ottoman Empire was hurting its relationship with Russia, led Germany to begin distancing itself from the Turks.[267] Germany's backing of Greek aims in southern Albania after the Balkan wars also significantly hurt relations, as Turkey had hopes of retaining influence in Albania.[268] Thus, prior to Franz Ferdinand's assassination, Turko-German relations, though still cordial, were cooling.

By 1914, the empire's defeats and the slow decline of the German alliance meant that new allies were needed. Fortunately, relations with some of the Balkan powers were improving, specifically those with Romania and Bulgaria.[269]

263 Emin 1930, 64; Toynbee 1991, 15. The CUP was not originally a nationalist organization, but became one over time.

264 Jairazbhoy 1914, 6.

265 Ibid, 2–3.

266 Weber 1970, 6–10.

267 Ibid, 5 and 11.

268 Ibid, 51–2.

269 Ibid, 47.

Romania had fought on the same side as the Ottomans in the Second Balkan War and was the only Balkan state not to attack the Turks in the first war. Geography, however, made cooperation with Romania difficult. Bulgaria was more promising. The Ottoman Empire and Bulgaria shared Greece as an enemy, both having lost territory to the Greeks in the recent wars. But while Bulgaria might be a useful ally in a war with Greece, the aid of a great power would be needed to fulfill any of Turkey's larger irredentist ambitions and to protect the territorial integrity of the empire from the other great powers. Further, it had proven impossible to obtain a formal alliance between Constantinople and Sofia. The Turkish cabinet, therefore, resolved upon an alliance with one of the great powers.

The cabinet was split on which great powers should be approached. Those cabinet members with generally more moderate foreign policy aims favored an alliance with Russia, France, or Britain, while those with more ambitious aims favored renewing good relations with Germany and Austria-Hungary.[270] In May 1914, Talaat proposed an alliance with Russia but Sazonov suspected the offer was insincere and demurred.[271] In July, Djemal Pasha, the Minister of the Marine, sought the help of France in pressuring Greece to relinquish some of the Aegean islands captured in the First Balkan War, but this too proved of no avail.[272] Thus, prior to the crisis caused by Franz Ferdinand's assassination, though the Turks were not firmly in the German camp, Germany remained their closest friend.[273]

Unlike Talaat and Djemal, Enver was an unflinching Germanophile who preferred strengthening the alliance with the Second Reich over new alliances with members of the Entente.[274] He was convinced of the Germans' military superiority and the Entente's rebuffs in early 1914 only served to spur his desire for an alliance with Germany.[275] Both he and Talaat feared the Russians wanted to make the Turks their vassal or dismember the empire completely.[276] Talaat had tried to minimize this danger by making Russia a partner. Enver preferred to balance against this threat and opened negotiations for an alliance with Germany on 22 July 1914.[277] Germany saw increased value in its relationship with the Ottoman Empire given the European crisis. In the event of war, the Turks could close the Straits to Entente shipping and cut Russia off from much needed war supplies.[278] From 28–31 July, Talaat and Enver secretly worked out the final details of a defensive pact with

270 Emin 1930, 65–7.

271 Trumpener 2003, 344; Weber 1970, 54.

272 Trumpener 2003, 344.

273 The Ottomans also had formal arrangements with the British, most important of which was that a British admiral commanded the Turkish fleet.

274 Jairazbhoy 1914, 9.

275 Trumpener 2003, 345.

276 Ibid, 345; Lowry 1990, 36.

277 Howard 1931, 84.

278 Weber 1970, 1.

Germany, which was in fact a treaty directed at Russia.[279] Initially, the treaty was to run for the duration of the Austro-Serbian conflict, but it was changed to last for the duration of the German military mission in Constantinople—in other words until 1918—and was to become active in the event of a Russo-Turkish, Russo-German, or Russo-Triple Alliance war.[280]

It is remarkable that this treaty was to result in the Ottoman Empire's entry into the war, because at the time of its signing, it had very little support in the cabinet and most cabinet members had been totally unaware of the negotiations. Only Talaat and Enver knew the full text of the treaty and only Enver fully backed its provisions.[281] Only three other cabinet members even knew of the treaty's existence.[282] Mehmet Djavid Bey, the minister of finance, thought it was a draft and opposed it.[283] Djemal Pasha favored it, but seemed to misunderstand its implications. He felt even with the treaty, war could be avoided for five years.[284] Said Halim, who as Grand Vizier was also aware of the negotiations, also seemed to think war could be avoided.[285] Talaat knew it meant war and reluctantly supported it, feeling that war was a great gamble.[286] Thus, only Enver and Talaat had decided on war. The question became whether the two of them could take their country to war.

On 3 August, one day after the treaty of alliance was formally signed, the Ottoman Empire declared neutrality but mobilized its armed forces. While officially declared only a defensive precaution, and though some members of the cabinet may have seen the treaty as such, it is doubtful Enver did. Adding to the uncertain situation on 5 August, Enver tried to reopen negotiations with Russia; specifically Enver sought to neutralize the Armenian frontier.[287] This was not a case of Enver getting cold feet, but an attempt to gain a military advantage over the Russians. Enver originally planned to have the Turkish army attack Russia from Thrace through Bulgaria and Romania, both of which he expected to be on the side of the Central Powers.[288] If Russia agreed to the neutralization of Armenia, it would provide cover for moving troops from Armenia into Thrace.[289] Just as important, if Russia refused to negotiate, it gave Enver ammunition with which to outmaneuver pro-Entente members of the cabinet.[290] Just as he did earlier in the year, Sazonov refused to enter serious negotiations believing, correctly this

279 Emin 1930, 67; Howard 1931, 85. The treaty was formally signed on 2 August.

280 Howard 1931, 85–6.

281 Ibid, 87.

282 Ibid.

283 Emin 1930, 68.

284 Ibid.

285 Ibid.

286 Ibid.

287 Howard 1931, 92 and 98.

288 This belief was not entirely foolish given Bulgaria's warm relations with Austria-Hungary and that Romania was a formal, if secret, member of the Triple Alliance.

289 Trumpener 2003, 346–7.

290 Ibid.

time, that they were simply a means for the Turks to gain an advantage rather than a serious attempt at reconciliation. Indeed, Entente states did little to woo the Turks outside of promising to uphold the empire's territorial integrity in return for neutrality and the Entente's efforts were poorly coordinated.[291] This meant that the Turkish moderates had little with which to counter Enver and his fellow interventionists.[292]

British policy in particular helped to strengthen Enver's hand. Britain was building two warships for the Turks and they were nearing completion in late 1914. Britain announced on 3 August that the ships would not be allowed to leave Britain. Britain did not want the ships to fall into the hands of its enemies and as Britain feared the Ottoman Empire might join the Central Powers, Britain was unwilling to release the ships. If the Turks eventually went to war with Britain, the ships could be added to the British fleet. Though such seizures were permitted by international law, they infuriated Turkish public opinion.[293] No legal framework could cover the fact that Britain had effectively, if not legally, stolen two Turkish warships constructed at Turkish expense. The outrage was all the greater as the ships had been paid for in part by public donations that had been collected in a major statewide fund-raising campaign. The seizures also greatly angered Djemal Pasha, the Minister of the Marine, who had previously been interested in closer ties with the Entente.[294] Though the Grand Vizier, Said Halim, told the British ambassador on 9 August he would do his best to keep the incident from leading to war, the situation was obviously becoming difficult for Said Halim to control.[295] The situation became even more tenuous the next day when two German warships, the *Breslau* and *Goeben*, entered the Dardanelles in violation of the Straits Convention. The arrival of the ships was most unexpected as their arrival had only proven possible through the incompetence of the British naval commander in charge of preventing them from entering the Straits. The Turks made a show of buying the ships as replacements for those seized in Britain, but

291 Howard 1931, 95; Jairazbhoy 1914, 8; Weber 1970, 80. Grey and Sazonov favored offering certain territories to the Turks, but Kitchener opposed this. In the end, little of actual substance was offered to the Turks.

292 Emin 1930, 70–1.

293 Ibid, 69.

294 Weber 1970, 79.

295 Jairazbhoy 1914, 11–12. Whether this offer was sincere is difficult to tell. Weber (1970, 66–72) claims Said Halim was willing to support joining the Central Powers at this time, provided the Austro-Hungarian fleet was sent to Constantinople. Austro-Hungarian plans for expansion in the Balkans, including the annexation of Salonika, were supposedly discovered by Said Halim shortly after the sale of the *Breslau* and *Goeben*. This revelation, according to Weber, caused Said Halim to become opposed to Enver's activist policy. Whatever is to be made of this, it is clear that by late August Said Halim was opposed to entering the war on the side of the Central Powers.

no one doubted that the ships remained under German control.[296] Command of the Turkish fleet was transferred from Admiral Arthur Limpus, a British officer, to a German admiral, Wilhelm Souchon. He was made a Turkish admiral to maintain the charade of Turkish control.[297] These ships greatly strengthened the Turkish fleet, which was now stronger than the Russian Black Sea Fleet.[298] These ships were of critical importance for two reasons. First, they effectively gave the Germans control of Constantinople. Given that the Germans also had a large military mission in Constantinople headed by General Otto Liman von Sanders, their local military presence was significant. Second, the ships made it impossible for the Russians to successfully attack Constantinople from the Black Sea. Prior to the ships' arrival, such an attack had been a distinct possibility as the Turks had yet to ready the Bosporus defenses out of fear of provoking Russia.[299]

Still, the Turks had reasons to be cautious. Britain's entry on the side of the Entente combined with Bulgarian and Romanian neutrality, gave the Entente a very strong position in both the Mediterranean and the Balkans.[300] Turkish leaders were particularly worried about Bulgaria. Moreover, the Dardanelles' defenses were in poor shape.[301] The Turks developed a policy of waiting on events, watching for any opportunity to retake lost territory.[302]

Meanwhile, the Turkish cabinet was steadily becoming divided into two camps: one interventionist headed by Enver and one neutralist headed by Said Halim and Djavid. A compromise was reached on 9 August to seek alliances with the Balkan states and to wait on events.[303] This simply bought the neutralists a little time. By mid August, it was clear to the Russian ambassador in Constantinople that Enver's faction was steadily gaining more power.[304] The only reinforcement for the neutralist camp came in the form of a warning from Rifat Pasha, the Turkish ambassador to France. He warned that the Entente was having significant military success—the Russians had just captured Lviv in Galicia—and that this might induce Romania to join the Entente.[305] The attitude of the Balkan states

296 Morgenthau 1918, 78. The Germans even told the Greeks that the ships remained under German control. The Greeks feared a strong Turkish fleet and if the Germans had helped Turkey acquire a strong, independent fleet, Greco-German relations would have certainly suffered greatly (Theodoulou 1971, 27). As it was, the incident still hurt Greco-German relations to a lesser degree.

297 Howard 1931, 95.

298 Morgenthau 1918, 80.

299 Weber 1970, 65.

300 Trumpener 2003, 349

301 Ibid, 350.

302 Howard 1931, 93.

303 Emin 1930, 72.

304 Howard 1931, 99.

305 Emin 1930, 74. Lviv is also known as Lwów or Lemberg.

concerned the interventionists; indeed it was all that seemed to dissuade them from advocating joining the war immediately.[306]

Despite this, the interventionists, led by Enver, took a series of small steps that steadily moved the Ottoman Empire closer to war with the Entente. First, on the 9 September, the Capitulations, laws that granted Europeans special legal and commercial privileges within the Empire, were renounced.[307] Hoping he could cause a rupture, on 15 September Enver advocated to the cabinet an immediate attack on Russian shipping in the Black Sea. Though the proposal had wide support in the CUP at large, it was blocked in the cabinet, as Said Halim was able to enlist the aid of Talaat, who still held out some hope for a negotiated settlement with Russia.[308] Though temporarily defeated, Enver did not give up. Five days later he was able to get the cabinet to approve sending the navy into the Black Sea by removing the instructions to attack Russian shipping.[309] Enver hoped the naval maneuvers would provoke the Russians. Four days after that, irregular Arab forces violated the frontier of British controlled Egypt.[310] No doubt Enver hoped this would provoke the British much as he hoped sending the fleet into the Black Sea would provoke the Russians. The British rose to the bait. Partly in response to the frontier violations and also to prevent a repeat of the *Goeben* and *Breslau* incident, Britain blockaded the Dardanelles on 26 September, allowing only commercial ships to pass.[311] The Germans assigned to improve the defenses of the Dardanelles promptly responded by closing the Straits to all shipping, military or commercial.[312] The Ottoman government did nothing to contravene the Germans' decision to close the Straits. Enver's maneuvering had succeeded in moving his country closer to war.

This slow move toward the German camp had been made possible by shifts within the Turkish cabinet. Around the time the Straits were closed, Enver Pasha won Djemal Pasha, the Minister of the Marine, over to the pro-war faction.[313] As mentioned above, the British seizure of the Turkish ships under construction in Britain greatly contributed to the change in Djemal's position. The British blockade no doubt reinforced his growing belief Britain was hostile to Ottoman interests in general and those of the Turkish navy in particular. By early October, there was a clear struggle within the cabinet over the question of war.[314] As of 4 or 5 October, Enver Pasha had won the definite support of Talaat Bey and of

306 Ibid, 74–5; Howard 1931, 106.
307 Emin 1930, 73; Howard 1931, 106.
308 Trumpener 2003, 351; Weber 1970, 74.
309 Weber 1970,75.
310 Jairazbhoy 1914, 14.
311 Howard 1931, 107–108; Trumpener 2003, 351.
312 Howard 1931, 107–108.
313 Weber 1970, 78–9.
314 Howard 1931, 109.

Halim Bey, the President of the Chamber of Deputies.[315] Combined with the prior defection of Djemal Pasha to the war party, this left Said Halim Pasha and the Minister of Finance, Mehmet Djavid Bey, as the only powerful members in the shrinking neutralist faction. Even given Said Halim's position as Grand Vizier, he was in grave danger of being overruled by the majority in the cabinet. Only the want of sufficient specie prevented Enver from being able to force war on the Grand Vizier and the finance minister.[316] The Germans were more than willing to remove this obstacle. On the 11 October, they agreed to provide the necessary hard currency in exchange for Enver's promise that he would send the fleet, including the German ships, into the Black Sea after the gold arrived.[317] The specie duly arrived in two shipments five and ten days later.

Enver's problems, however, were not wholly solved. Halim Bey had once again joined the neutralist camp and even Talaat was wavering, in large part because of difficulties in carrying out the Ottoman military plans.[318] It was now clear that Romania was unlikely to join the Central Powers, which derailed Enver's plan to launch an attack on Russia through the Balkans. On top of this, Turkish forces would not be ready for an assault on the Suez Canal for six weeks. Enver's plan for war was in serious danger, but he had one card left to play.

On 21 October, the same day the final gold shipment arrived, Enver managed to get himself appointed deputy-commander in chief of the Ottoman armed forces, which gave him *de facto* control over the army.[319] He and Djemal, without the knowledge of the rest of the Turkish government, conspired with Admiral Souchon to send the Turko-German fleet into the Black Sea and force a naval encounter.[320] The fleet entered the Black Sea on 27 October and finding no Russian fleet to provoke, it proceeded to bombard several Russian ports before retiring to Constantinople. This presented the cabinet with a *fait accompli*. The Russians were willing to remain at peace provided the German fleet was dismissed. The Turkish cabinet was amenable to the idea, but Talaat persuaded a majority of the ministers that the German ships and to a lesser extent the German military legation were too great of an imminent threat to Constantinople to dismiss.[321] The German military preponderance at Constantinople, combined with the *fait accompli* of having attacked Russia, forced the Turkish cabinet to accept war with Russia.[322]

---

315 Trumpener 2003, 351; Weber 1970, 81.

316 Trumpener 2003, 351.

317 Ibid, 352.

318 Ibid.

319 Ibid, 353. The Sultan was the *de jure* commander in chief, but the CUP had long since relegated the Sultan to position of minor political importance.

320 Emin 1930, 75; Howard 1931, 110–11; Trumpener 2003, 353; Weber 1970, 85.

321 Emin 1930, 75; Howard 1931, 111–12.

322 Trumpener 2003, 354. Djavid Bey and several lesser ministers resigned rather than endorse war. Several meaningless concessions, such as sending a letter to Russia promising an investigation, were decided upon in order to convince Said Halim to remain

Russia broke relations on 31 October and declared war on 4 November.[323] The next day Britain and France did the same. The Ottoman Empire was now fixed on a course that would result in its dismemberment.

The Turkish decision to intervene depended greatly on Enver's rise to supremacy over the neutralists in the Turkish cabinet. As such, the case does not support the work's hypothesis as clearly as the earlier cases. Looking slightly deeper, however, there is indeed support for the hypothesis in the Turkish case. The actual declaration of war depended on Enver and Djemal being able to present a *fait accompli* to the rest of the cabinet. Enver would never have been in the position to orchestrate the *fait accompli* without Djemal's support. Djemal had originally been in favor of neutrality, but the British seizure of the Turkish ships under construction in Britain and Britain's closure of the Dardanelles caused Djemal to change his position. The seizure of the ships was certainly unexpected. Whether the chain of events that followed, including the arrival of the *Goeben* and *Breslau* and the British blockade, can be called unexpected is more difficult to say.

The hypothesis is not without its difficulties in this case. The Turkish leadership seems not to have based its decisions on the course of the war as a whole. The interventionists, who had actually signed a treaty of alliance with Germany before the war and wanted to join immediately, never wavered in the desire for intervention regardless of battlefield results. Most of the neutralists also did not take battlefield results into consideration with the exception of the attack on the Russian ports. Thus, on the whole, the Turkish case provides incomplete support for the hypothesis that revealed information lead states to join ongoing wars.

Greece

On the eve of the First World War Greece was triumphant, yet vulnerable. The Treaty of Bucharest, which terminated the two Balkan Wars, had enlarged Greece in both population and territory by roughly 50%. Yet Greece's military and economy were weaker than that of the Ottoman Empire, Bulgaria, Serbia, or Romania. Moreover, both the Ottoman Empire and Bulgaria wanted to dispossess Greece of many of its gains in Thrace and the Aegean that had been made at their expense. Greece's only protection against this threat was a defensive treaty with Serbia against Bulgaria.[324] Thus, Serbia's involvement in a conflict with Austria-Hungary left Greece dangerously exposed.

---

in the cabinet. It was clear that these concessions would not be sufficient to prevent Russia from breaking relations.

323 Emin 1930, 76–7. COW dates the Ottoman Empire's entry from the attack on the Russian ports.

324 Leontaritis 1970, 89–90; Seligman 1920, 28. Literally, it was a general defense treaty, but the Serbs agreed that in spirit it did not require the Greeks to aid them against Austria-Hungary initially. Serbia took this stance largely because Greek neutrality served

Greek decisions about involvement in the First World War were not made by a unified government. There were significant internal divisions in Greece and these divisions were magnified by the war. Power was divided between the liberal prime minister, Eleftherios Venizelos, and the conservative King Constantine I. Both had gained popularity through the successful prosecution of the Balkan Wars. Venizelos had wide support, especially in the newly conquered territories and in the newly rising bourgeoisie, and a majority in parliament.[325] Constantine had the support of much of the military, the traditionally ruling elite, and a strong following in "Old Greece," the regions that had been part of the country prior to the Balkan wars. Many of Constantine's conservative supporters were irritated at Venizelos' power and longed for an opportunity to force him from office.[326] Venizelos, along with most of the population, was pro-Entente and believed that the Entente would win the war.[327] Even if the Entente lost on land, Venizelos believed that the Entente's naval prowess would protect Greece.[328] Venizelos, therefore, favored joining the Entente if conditions allowed. Venizelos, as revealed by a letter he sent to Constantine at the beginning of the war, was also motivated by the persecution of Greeks in the Ottoman Empire.[329] Constantine, whose wife was Kaiser Wilhelm II's sister, was convinced the Central Powers were the stronger military alliance and would win the war.[330] Constantine, however, did not want to bring Greece into the war, as Greece's long coast was indefensible given the Entente's naval dominance in the Mediterranean.[331] Rather, he hoped to keep Greece out of the war, and was staunchly anti-Bulgarian antebellum and in the war's early stages.[332] Even the Germans, other than the Kaiser, saw the impossibility of Greece joining their side and their diplomatic efforts were aimed at maintaining Greek neutrality.[333]

Venizelos opened negotiations with the Entente in August 1914, in hopes of signing a treaty that would add to Greek territory in exchange for Greek participation

---

as a deterrent to Bulgaria's entry. Additionally, if Greece entered, Bulgaria was likely to enter and Serbia's military position was better with both states out of the war than with both states in the war. Serbia did request Greek aid in December 1914 in response to an Austro-Hungarian offensive.

325 Leontaritis 1970, 60; Theodoulou 1971, 47.

326 Leontaritis 1990, 4; Theodoulou 1971, 47. Constantine and his supporters tended to favor more autocratic means of governing than did the Venizelists (Mélas 1920, 25–7 and 55–6).

327 Dewing 1924, 38; Leontaritis 1970, 14 and 30; Mélas 1920, 87; Seligman 1920, 32.

328 Leontaritis 1970, 63.

329 Ministry of Foreign Affairs of the Greek Government 1919, 8–10.

330 Leontaritis 1970, 14, 32 and 67–70; Mélas 1920, 127.

331 Leontaritis 1970, 29; Leontaritis 1990, 3; Nicholas 1928, 25 and 42–3; Seligman 1920, 31–32.

332 Mélas 1920, 19–21.

333 Leontaritis 1970, 24.

in the war.[334] The Entente, however, was not interested. Russia did not want Greece to acquire any territory near Constantinople as Russia hoped to obtain the city for itself. All the major powers in the Entente opposed wooing Greece on the grounds that it would hurt their chance to attract Bulgaria, the Ottoman Empire, and even Italy, all of which were of significantly greater military value than Greece.[335] Sir Edward Grey, the British foreign secretary, also felt territorial promises to the Balkan states were of "secondary value and are entirely subordinated to military events."[336] Because of this, Grey felt that the appropriate Entente policy was to suspend diplomacy until the military situation took a decisive turn in favor of the allies.

Venizelos was also concerned about an attack by Bulgaria. He tried to interest Romania in concerted action to offset the threat from Bulgaria—Venizelos was very reluctant to join without a Romanian alliance—but the Romanians were not interested.[337] The lack of interest in Venizelos' offers and his lingering concern about Bulgaria led him to withdraw the offers. Of equal importance were the military results at Tannenberg, the Marne, in Galicia, and around the Masurian lakes. In *toto*, these battles convinced Venizelos the war would last a long time.[338] Accordingly in mid September, Venizelos became more hesitant in his diplomacy.

In early 1915, Venizelos decided to reinvigorate the negotiations with the Entente as word of the planned Gallipoli Offensive spread. Initially, Venizelos was only interested if Bulgaria also joined the Entente or if Romania joined to offset the threat posed to Greece by Bulgaria. The British ambassador to Greece, Sire Francis Elliot, reported Venizelos' thinking to Grey:

> Greece could not help … without a guarantee of at least neutrality on the part of Bulgaria. No Bulgarian assurances would suffice; best of all would be Bulgarian co-operation; next best, an engagement on the part of Roumania to Triple *Entente* to keep Bulgaria quiet, if necessary.[339]

Venizelos repeated these requirements regarding Bulgaria and Romania to the Russian ambassador and the inability of the Entente to get Bulgaria to join or be

---

334 Theodoulou 1971, 24.

335 Churchiill 1928, vol. 1, 486 and 493; Dewing 1924, 42; Leontaritis 1970, 37 and 43; Mitrakos 1982, 5; Theodoulou 1971, 29–34. Both Greece and Italy desired territory in Albania and had territorial ambitions in Asia Minor, specifically around the city of Smyrna, while Bulgaria and the Ottoman Empire wanted the territory Greece had taken from them in the late Balkan wars.

336 Leontaritis 1970, 58.

337 Ibid, 19 and 92; Nicholas 1928, 30–2; Seligman 1920, 36–7; Theodoulou 1971, 17–19.

338 Leontaritis 1970, 59.

339 Theodoulou 1971, 81–2.

offset by Romania led Venizelos to refuse a definitive Entente offer of alliance on 15 February 1915.[340] The early success of the Gallipoli campaign, however, made war with the Turks attractive even without Romanian assistance and offered prospects of significant Greek gains at Turkish expense. Venizelos now actively sought an alliance regardless of Bulgaria's position.[341] Additionally, in order to obtain Greek aid for the Gallipoli Campaign, the Entente was now willing to offer Greece some Turkish territory.[342] On 5 March Venizelos won over the opposition Greek politicians to a pro-war position, but the King rejected the plan the next day.[343] Faced with the possibility of a constitutional crisis, Venizelos resigned to avoid an open fight with Constantine. Dimitrios Gounaris, a conservative who was in favor of neutrality, replaced Venizelos. He continued negotiations with the Entente for domestic consumption, but made sure they failed by insisting on unreasonable concessions.[344] The hand of the neutralists was further strengthened by the Central Powers' successful Gorlice-Tarnow offensive beginning in March.[345]

In June, the Venezelists won the parliamentary election that had been necessitated by Venizelos' resignation in March. By August, Venizelos was back in as prime minister. He too, was now in favor of neutrality due to the continued Russian defeats in Poland and Galicia.[346] In September, however, a new crisis emerged. On 21 September Bulgaria mobilized with the clear intention of attacking Serbia in conjunction with the Central Powers. This would mean the certain defeat of Serbia, unless the Serbs received timely military aid—aid that the Greeks were legally obligated to deliver. No one in Greece wanted to see Serbia crushed and Venizelos was able to convince Constantine, though not without difficulty, to authorize a defensive mobilization both to protect Greece from Bulgaria and hopefully, though less realistically, deter Bulgaria from attacking Serbia.[347]

Venizelos also wanted to allow allied forces to move through Greece and march in conjunction with Greek forces to Serbia's aid. Constantine refused, still convinced the Central Powers would eventually win and that it was best not to

340 Ibid, 96–7 and 106–107.

341 Leontaritis 1970, 120–24; Nicholas 1928, 34–8; Theodoulou 1971, 112–17. Interestingly, Venizelos was convinced of the likely success of the Gallipoli campaign despite grave doubts on the part of the Greek General Staff (Mélas 1920, 151).

342 Nicholas 1928, 31–2.

343 Leontaritis 1970, 131–9; Theodoulou 1971, 119. Additionally, Russia and France had become lukewarm about Greek involvement out of concern that it might lead to Anglo-Greek control of the Straits.

344 Leontaritis 1970, 155–60 and 178–79. Gounaris revived concerns about the Bulgarians. Additionally, Entente efforts began to focus on getting Bulgaria, rather than Greece to join (Theodoulou 1971, 142–50).

345 Leontaritis 1970, 184.

346 Ibid, 209.

347 Ibid, 218–21; Theodoulou 1971, 171–2. Constantine remained against actually sending troops to aid Serbia, while Venizelos was consistently in favor of aiding Serbia (Mélas 1920, 70).

irritate them.[348] Despite this, Venizelos told Britain and France they could land troops at Salonika. They landed on 30 September, though the operation was begun too late to save the Serbs.[349] This led to a vote of no confidence being conducted against Venizelos in parliament the night of 4 October. Though Venizelos narrowly survived the vote, the King dismissed him anyway replacing him first with Alexander Zaimis followed by Stephanos Skouloudis a month later. Venizelos consented to being removed from office to avoid civil war.[350]

The Zaimis ministry was formed with the express purpose of not carrying out the Greco-Serbian treaty. Zaimis made this quite clear. In response to government bureaucrats who were trying to inform him of the details of the treaty he said, "I do not want to waste my time in the study of such details. For what is the use, when I have taken office with the express purpose of not carrying out the treaty?"[351] The government came up with the convenient excuse that Serbia could not deploy the 150,000 troops against Bulgaria as was required by the treaty—they were fully occupied fighting Austria-Hungary—though the real reason for the government renouncing the treaty was its fear of the upcoming Central Powers' offensive in the Balkans.[352] Zaimis, when promised Cyprus in exchange for Greek aid for Serbia, told the Russian ambassador that opposing the upcoming Central Power offensive against Serbia would be a military disaster, especially as it was not clear Britain was committed to the Salonikan force.[353] The new government informed the allies that not only would Greece not join the Entente, but that they were going to intern the allied forces at Salonika as well as the retreating Serbs and Montenegrans as was required by international law. The allied threat of a blockade, however, convinced the conservative government to relent.[354] The government even allowed the Serbs to be transferred from the Adriatic coast to Salonika, though they had to go by sea rather than overland. The illegal Entente landings at Salonika and the threat of a blockade led to a significant erosion of pro-allied and Venizelist popular support. The events also further polarized Greek public opinion between the Venizelist and monarchist camps.[355]

Thus began the odd situation of having a large, but ineffective, Entente army camped on officially neutral territory and in danger of being attacked by German and Bulgarian forces. The French, who commanded and contributed the most forces to the Salonikan army, took the undisputed lead in determining Entente policy toward Greece. In many ways, they gave up on obtaining a Greek alliance, seeing

348 Nicholas 1928, 62.
349 Leontaritis 1970, 220–38.
350 Seligman 1920, 64.
351 Ibid, 65.
352 Mitrakos 1982, 9.
353 Theodoulou 1971, 201 and 205.
354 Leontaritis 1970, 253 and 278–83.
355 Ibid, 286–7 and 318.

it as unhelpful, and instead began looking for ways to establish a protectorate over Greece.[356]

Little happened from late 1915 through early 1916. The German and Bulgarian militaries wanted to advance slightly into Greece to improve their defensive positions, but the German foreign ministry, fearful of provoking a Greek reaction, restrained them.[357] Constantine and his government would have supported a large advance that would have driven the allies from Greek territory, but opposed a limited advance that would further violate Greece's territorial integrity without disposing of the Entente forces.[358] The generals of the Central Powers eventually got their way and advanced a short distance into Greek territory taking Fort Roupel in late May 1916.

This action convinced Britain and France that the Greek government was hostile to their cause and in response they imposed a partial blockade on Greece. This was sufficient to cause Skoloudis' government to fall on 19 June and Zaimis was returned to power four days later.[359] The surrender of Fort Roupel also caused Constantine's public support within Greece to plummet, though the allied counteractions were just as damaging to Venizelos' image.[360] This drop in support for Constantine was reinforced by the Central Power's failures in 1916—Verdun, the Brusilov offensive, and the failure to attack the allies at Salonika—which convinced the Greek public that the German military was not as strong as Constantine suggested.[361]

In August, major fighting occurred between the Central Powers and Entente forces as the Entente attacked in a failed attempt to draw Bulgarian forces away from the frontier of Romania, which had just entered the war on the Entente's side. There were also hints that Constantine might have been willing to take Greece into the war on the Entente side due to the Bulgarian incursions and the Romanian entry.[362] A Venizelist revolt in Salonika—interestingly without Venizelos' approval—and Romania's crushing defeat, however, ended the King's brief flirtation with the allies.[363] The Venizelists set up a provisional government in Salonika without Venizelos who remained in Athens. Open rupture was becoming unavoidable and Zaimis, unable to satisfy both the King and the allies, fell from power on 11 September. He was replaced by pro-monarchist, pro-German governments, led

356 Mitrakos 1982, viii, 13 and 71–2.

357 Leontaritis 1970, 335 and 340.

358 Ibid, 355. After the war, royalists claimed Constantine opposed any attack against the Salonika forces (Nicholas 1928, 108–10), but this is self-serving and suspect.

359 Ibid, 367–71. The fall of Skoloudis was not announced until 23 June. In the interim, the British and French had threatened military action unless Skoloudis was replaced. This threat, however, came after the decision to remove Skoloudis had already been made.

360 Dewing 1924, 50; Leontaritis 1970, 361–2 and 373.

361 Leontaritis 1970, 330.

362 Mitrakos 1982, 88–9.

363 Leontaritis 1970, 387; Mitrakos 1982, 97.

first by Nicholas Kalogeropoulos and later by Spiridon Lambros. This prompted Venizelos to leave the capital and join the provisional government being set up in Salonika. Though the Entente powers did not recognize the provisional government as the *de jure* government, it nevertheless began operations against the Central Powers on 26 September and formally declared war in November.[364] By mid October, the British and French effectively forced the King's government, which they still recognized as the *de jure* government, to act under allied protection and to allow the allies substantial control of Greek affairs, though they did not force the government to enter the war.[365] They did, however, force the army to demobilize and seized much of Greece's war material.[366]

This arrangement worked poorly as both sides often tested to see how far they could push the other side. The Greek economy and army slid into steadily worse shape. Organized violence even broke out in the streets of Athens between royalist and French troops.[367] The main reasons the allies did not execute a coup in 1916 or early 1917 were opposition from Nicholas II, who was against overthrowing monarchs, and fear of offending the United States, the champion of neutral rights.[368] Also, Britain was reluctant to appear as an oppressor.[369] By May 1917, Nicholas had been overthrown, the US was no longer neutral, and Britain's patience was exhausted. Constantine tried changing the government again as a conciliation measure—he made Zaimis prime minister yet again—but it was not enough. On 29 May, the British and French decided to overthrow Constantine.[370] They occupied Thessaly, the country's main agricultural region on 10 June. Constantine knew the game was up and abdicated the next day in favor of his son Alexander and the allies occupied Athens. Alexander asked Venizelos to form a government on 24 June. Venizelos took office four days later and promptly declared war on the Central Powers, though by this time the Greek army and economy were in such poor shape the declaration had little effect other than making the allied occupation of Salonika legal.[371]

The Greek case provides the weakest support for the revealed information hypothesis. Greek intervention was determined primarily by the struggle between Venizelos and Constantine. Venizelos ultimately won with allied support and this is what led to intervention. Unlike the Turkish case, revealed information did not lead to one faction being able to defeat the other. This is not to say revealed

364 Leontaritis 1970, 409 and 423; Mitrakos 1982, 179.

365 Leontaritis 1970, 414; Mitrakos 1982, 111. The Venizelists had extended their control to the Aegean islands by this point. Constantine had done nothing to resist this (Mitrakos 1982, 102).

366 Mitrakos 1982, 116–17 and 128–9.

367 Theodoulou 1971, 298.

368 Leontaritis 1970, 469–83; Leontaritis 1990, 5; Mitrakos 1982, 162.

369 Mitrakos 1982, 85.

370 Leontaritis 1970, 483–4.

371 Ibid, 489.

information played no role in the case. Venizelos was clearly influenced by the astonishing initial success of the Schiefflen plan. At the onset of war, he wanted to join the Entente, but the German's initial successes caused him to rethink his position. After the Battle of the Marne, Venizelos returned to his initial desire to join the Entente. Likewise, when it looked as though the Gallipoli campaign would be successful, Venizelos increased his efforts to bring Greece into the allied camp. Constantine was less influenced by events, though even he briefly considered joining when it became clear Serbia was in danger in the autumn of 1915. He also considered revealed information in 1916 after the Bulgarian infringements on Greek territory and the apparent vulnerability of the Central Powers that the Brusilov offensive had exposed but was dissuaded by Romania's rapid defeat. Entente strategies toward Greece also changed as the course of war changed. This is less true for the Central Powers. Britain became disinterested after Gallipoli failed and both France and Britain became more willing to pressure the Greek government after the US entered and the need to worry about the rights of neutrals declined. The main actors and Greek public opinion did react to surprises and shifts in the course of the war in the manner predicted by the theory, but internal events predominated. Overall, the Greek case does not provide strong support for the work's main hypothesis, though it certainly does not support the counter-hypothesis of states waiting on a chain of anticipated events before joining. Thus, the work's hypothesis fares better than the counter-hypothesis, though the complex domestic situation in Greece meant to the extent that revealed information affected the case, it did so through complex and indirect pathways with domestic events predominating.

Portugal

The case of Portugal is an unusual one. Portugal and Britain had been allies on and off since the 14th century. The alliance had been continuous, at least in name, since the Napoleonic wars. In general, the alliance granted Britain the use of Portuguese ports in time of war, including those in the Azores, in return for Britain's military guarantee of Portuguese independence. It would not have been surprising if Portugal had been unwilling to honor the alliance, as its monarchy had been recently overthrown resulting in deep domestic divisions and its military was in poor shape.[372] Portugal, however, was willing to aid Britain from the outset. Yet, for various reasons the Portuguese did not formally enter the war until 1916.

Part of their willingness to aid the Entente stemmed from the alliance with Britain, but the Portuguese also had grievances against Germany. Germany had taken the Kionga region of Mozambique from Portugal in 1894 and also held a strip of southern Angola.[373] Additionally, the Portuguese blamed the Germans for

372 De Meneses 2004, 2–5.

373 Almeida, et al 1917, 23; Bragança-Cunha 1938, 185 and 205.

fomenting unrest in their African colonies in the years before the war.[374] Portugal feared that it would be unable to hold its African possessions if it opposed the victorious side in the European war.[375] Prior to the war, the British, South Africans, and Germans had all suggested various partition plans. Whichever motive was predominant, it was clear from the beginnings of the First World War that Portugal was willing to aid Britain in whatever way Britain saw fit. The Portuguese announced on 7 August 1914 that, while Portugal would remain out of the war at the moment, it would do all Britain asked, including entering the war.[376] Notably, unlike other countries that later joined or managed to stay neutral throughout the conflict, Portugal never declared neutrality.[377] From September 1914 onwards Portugal allowed British and French ships to refit in Portuguese ports, but interned the German merchant vessels that were in Portuguese ports.[378] Portugal also sent a military mission to Britain to plan joint action in the war and allowed British troops to march through Mozambique to attack German possessions in Africa.[379] Finally, Portugal turned over two-thirds of its modern field artillery to Britain in December of 1914.[380] This resulted from a French request for the artillery in September. Portugal had been willing to send the guns only if they were manned by Portuguese crews and protected by Portuguese infantry.[381] This in turn led Grey to ask Portugal to join the war. In replying to the Portuguese offer he said that,

> The loyal and unhesitating manner in which your Government have acceded to this request, encourages me to invoke the ancient alliance between Portugal and this country, and formally invite the Portuguese Government to depart from their attitude of neutrality and range themselves actively on the side of Great Britain and her allies.[382]

Britain was not really interested in active Portuguese military assistance. Grey had solicited Portuguese belligerency simply as a way to obtain the artillery, so when Portugal proved unable to outfit a division to man and protect the artillery, Britain simply accepted the guns and remained content with a benevolent Portuguese neutrality.[383]

374 Newitt 1981, 41.

375 Ibid, 40–1.

376 Bragança-Cunha 1938, 198; De Meneses 2004, 5.

377 Almeida, et al 1917, 13.

378 Ibid, 12–13. The merchant ships remained in German hands and were not seized for Portuguese use at this point in the war. They were, however, forbidden to leave port.

379 Almeida, et al 1917, 13; De Meneses 2004, 20.

380 Bragança-Cunha 1938, 199.

381 De Meneses 2004, 11.

382 Ibid, 12.

383 Bragança-Cunha 1938, 199; De Meneses 2004, 12.

German forces in Africa certainly did not expect Portugal to remain neutral. Beginning on 24 August 1914, the Germans launched numerous attacks against Angola from South West Africa. They attacked Portuguese forts and troops at Maziua, Naulila, Cuangar, Bunja, Sambio, Dirico, and Mucusso in Angola and engaged in minor border skirmishing in Mozambique.[384] Even after the Germans withdrew in December of 1914, they continued to support a rebellion in Angola until South African troops finally captured South West Africa. These attacks and the rebellion forced Portugal to dispatch much of its available army to Africa.[385] This need to dispatch troops to Africa and the overall disorganization of the Portuguese military made it impossible for Portugal to dispatch forces to Europe in 1914 or 1915.[386] Two bills endorsing Portuguese involvement in the European conflict were introduced into parliament on 23 November 1914 and passed in December, though they did not lead to any actual actions. They, in part, read as follows:

> The Executive Power is hereby authorized to make military intervention in the present international conflict of arms whenever and in whatever manner it may be deemed necessary in our higher interests and duties as a free nation and an ally of Great Britain, and to take such extraordinary measures toward that end as the circumstances of the case may demand.
>
> At the very beginning of the war, Portugal spontaneously announced herself ready, as the ally of Great Britain, to give the latter every assistance. The British Government, heartily grateful for this clear proof of solidarity, invited the Portuguese Government to act conjointly in such a manner as might be stipulated between them, in military co-operation. Thus would the two Governments secure the objects of the alliance for centuries subsisting between their nations, the maintenance of which was matter of common and equal interest to both parties.[387]

Thus, though not officially at war in 1914 or 1915, Portugal's actions suggest that it was willing to join the Entente whenever Britain and France requested aid and in fact was already providing significant aid, both military and non-military. Portuguese forces had already actively fought German forces in Africa, though the Portuguese troops had not coordinated their actions with the British. Portugal had also refused the use of its ports to the Central Powers, while allowing the Entente to use them freely. Portugal had even interned German merchant ships that had been in Lisbon in the fall of 1914. Thus, though Portugal had yet to declare war or dispatch large forces to the conflict, it was clearly in the Entente camp and doing everything that the Entente powers requested. Indeed, Portugal had wanted

384 Almeida, et al 1917, 9–11; De Meneses 2004, 34 and 39–40; Newitt 1981, 40–1.
385 Almeida, et al 1917, 15–16.
386 Ibid, 15; Bragança-Cunha 1938, 199.
387 Almeida, et al 1917, 14; Bragança-Cunha 1938, 179–80.

to dispatch forces to the Western Front on several occasions, but the French and British had demurred. The Germans even sunk a Portuguese merchant vessel in May of 1915 apparently after identifying it to be Portuguese.[388] Evidently, the Germans were willing to treat Portugal as something less than neutral, if not a formal enemy.

The formal break came in early 1916. On 16 February, with merchant shipping losses to submarines mounting, Britain requested that Portugal seize the interned German merchant vessels for Portugal to use to trade with the Entente.[389] Portugal complied on 23 February after ensuring Britain would welcome Portugal into the Entente if Germany declared war as expected.[390] This was one more act than the German government could tolerate. Germany declared war on 9 March. Portuguese troops in Africa quickly coordinated with the British in battling the German troops in German East Africa. This resulted in Portugal regaining the Kionga enclave, but the performance of the Portuguese troops was generally disappointing.[391] Britain and France were still uninterested in Portugal sending troops to the Western Front and refused a formal offer of military aid in the early summer of 1916.[392] Not until August, after the losses in the Verdun campaign had made the need for soldiers acute, did France and Britain send a military commission to inspect the Portuguese army.[393] Portugal again offered to send troops in October and this time the offer was accepted. The first troops arrived in France in January 1917. Portugal's contribution never exceeded two divisions, but Portuguese forces remained in France until the end of the war serving as part of the British Expeditionary Force.

The Portuguese case is unlike any of the other cases. In many respects the Portuguese entered the war shortly after the British. They completely fulfilled their alliance obligations, gave Britain military aid in the form of war material, fought German troops in Africa, and maintained a form of neutrality that was extremely benevolent toward the Entente. Portugal even frequently offered to send troops to Europe. These offers were refused until after Germany declared war on Portugal. Only these refusals kept Portugal from joining sooner. Portugal honored every request from Britain prior to Portuguese intervention. Britain simply did not want Portugal's military assistance. Interestingly, the Portuguese offer to send troops to

388 Almeida, et al 1917, 17. The Germans had also sunk a Portuguese merchant vessel in April of the same year, but without identifying it first. As it was not unusual for the Germans at this time to sink shipping without bothering to identify the vessel, the April sinking is not significant. It should also be mentioned that during this period Portugal was beset with internal violence and the government was controlled by more neutralist factions, though Portugal continued to comply with all Entente requests. The ascension of a pro-interventionist government in August 1915 did not change Portuguese behavior as Entente interest remained minimal (De Meneses 2004, 16–19).

389 Almeida, et al 1917, 19; Bragança-Cunha 1938, 200.

390 De Meneses 2004, 24.

391 Almeida, et al 1917, 23; Bragança-Cunha 1938, 205.

392 Bragança-Cunha 1938, 200.

393 Ibid, 202.

Europe was finally accepted after the unprecedented bloodshed at Verdun changed the allies' calculus. Also, the German's declaration of war was clearly a response to Portugal's seizure of the German ships. While this action may not have been unexpected, it did reveal information that Portugal was not going to let a lack of a declaration of war hinder its efforts to aid the British. Thus, the seizure revealed that the German's had nothing to lose by declaring war. These two events, the response to the losses at Verdun and the German declaration of war after the ships' seizure, lend support to the work's hypothesis that revealed information can lead to changes in states' policies toward both the war and non-belligerents.

On the whole, however, the Portuguese case does not fit into the type of state whose behavior the hypothesis tries to describe. Portugal was not a state that was unsure if or when it should join the war. It was willing and ready to provide all the support Britain required from the outset. Thus, it is not surprising that Portugal fits poorly with the predictions of the theory, as the theory is not designed to predict the behavior of a state in Portugal's position as Portugal essentially joined at the war's outset.

Termination of the War

The first years of the war saw little in terms of peace negotiations. After the Battle of the Marne, neither side was in position to knock its opponents out of the war quickly. True, Austria-Hungary was in a precarious position prior to the Gorlice-Tarnow campaign, but as the Austrians had been able to hold the Carpathian passes, they were not forced to seek peace.[394] 1915 saw further stalemate in the West. The Central Powers, however, had several successes elsewhere, including the highly successful Gorlice-Tarnow campaign, the repulse of the British at Gallipoli, and the successful invasion of Serbia. Even given the Central Powers' success, events 1915 again did little to cause any state to seriously seek peace, as Russia was able to absorb significant territorial losses, and Serbia and Montenegro could keep their forces in the field under the protection of the Anglo-French force at Salonika. Still, the war was beginning to strain all of the combatants' resources.

Several attempts were made in 1916 to bring about peace talks, but all failed.[395] In 1917, Charles I of Austria-Hungary attempted to make a separate peace with the Entente.[396] By this point, the Habsburgs were heavily dependent on their German allies to keep the Russians at bay and had few reserves with which to meet new threats. Also, outside of the campaign against Italy, the war was unpopular among much of the populace, especially the Slavs. Among all of the great power combatants, a defeat for the Habsburgs would likely result in the worst fate as the

394 Of course, as mentioned above, the Habsburgs' difficulties did affect their negotiations with Italy.

395 See the US case.

396 Franz Joseph died in November 1916.

empire was barely holding together antebellum. A serious defeat might be more than the structure could withstand. Thus, the Habsburgs had stronger incentives than the other belligerents to seek peace.

Given this difficult position, the Habsburgs were willing to make concessions, though they knew their German partners were not. Charles, therefore, sent out private peace feelers through his brother-in-law, Prince Sixtus of Bourbon-Parma, to the French without first consulting his allies. Sixtus was an officer in the Belgian army and had contacts in the French government. Charles offered some territorial concessions to Serbia and Italy and promised to leave the war. This would have allowed France and Britain to concentrate on Germany or perhaps pressure Germany into settling. There were several pitfalls that ultimately undermined this opening. First, a separate peace would have left Austria-Hungary diplomatically isolated and vulnerable after the Entente triumphed over, or settled with, Germany.[397] Second, the proposed territorial concessions were far smaller than Italy's minimal demands. France, Russia, and Britain undoubtedly could have forced Italy to settle, but it would have been difficult and, if negotiations with Austria-Hungary fell through, the Entente would have estranged Italy for little or no gain. These various concerns kept the Austrian proposal from developing. The Entente remained interested, but while back-channel discussions went on, Russia and Romania collapsed. This relieved the pressure on Austria-Hungary. This turn of events, combined with the Habsburgs' fear of the wrath German allies and non-committal position of the Entente, led Charles to withdraw the offer. After the collapse of the Austro-Hungarian initiative, no serious attempt was made to end the war until after the collapse of Tsarist Russia.

By the beginning of 1917, the incompetence of the Tsar's government and the worthlessness of the money it issued were clear to all. The economy collapsed and in March, the Tsar was overthrown and replaced by a liberal government. This new government, headed by Aleksandr Kerensky as of July, resolved to continue the struggle. The government was strongly supported at first and initially the Bolsheviks made no headway against it. At this point, both the Entente and Central Powers sent out official peace feelers.[398] Though increasing war-weariness had made peace more attractive to both sides, they remained far apart.[399] Given Russia's willingness to continue the fight, the Entente was not obliged to make peace, especially as the US was now in the war and would eventually make its weight felt. Russia, however, was visibly ailing and no longer able to put the same pressure on the Central Powers as before. By November, it was clear that even in more capable hands than those of the Tsar, Russia simply could not continue. The

397 The worst case scenario for the Habsburgs was angering Germany by seeking a separate peace but failing to obtain one, as the Austro-Hungarian military situation was hopeless without German assistance.

398 Though these peace moves occurred at roughly the same time as Charles' private initiative, they were not related.

399 Stevenson 2005, 110–12.

Bolsheviks instigated the revolution that shook the world and under their leadership Russia immediately sued for peace. Russia left the war on 5 December 1917. In the Treaty of Brest-Litovsk, signed 3 March 1918 and modified to Germany's benefit in August of that year, Russia surrendered the Ukraine, Finland, Russian Poland, the Baltic States, and Georgia. The Germans also occupied Belarus and some additional districts on the Black Sea.

With Russia out of the war, Romania clearly had to surrender. Its small army, now isolated on the eastern front, could not fight on alone. Romanian leaders agreed to an armistice on 9 December 1917 only four days after Russia left the war. Romania accepted the Central Powers' humiliating terms, much as Soviet Russia had. Romania lost the entire Dobrudja and had to make major frontier adjustments in favor of Austria-Hungary. Thus, the unexpected overthrows of both the Tsar and the liberal government headed by Kerensky led directly to the withdrawal of both Russia and Romania from the war.

No other states left the war until the final collapse of the Central Powers in the autumn of 1918.[400] This is not to say nothing happened between Romania's exit and late 1918. When and how the war would end remained unclear until late 1918.[401] The situation in early 1918 was precarious for both sides. The defeat of Russia and Romania had freed up many of the German divisions that had been fighting on the Eastern Front. The transfer to the West gave the Central Powers an opportunity to defeat the Entente forces. Speed, however, would be vital as the growing number of Americans in France would more than offset the new German forces by late 1918. Additionally, the German economy and the morale of the German populace were both weakening, though neither was approaching collapse.[402] The Central Powers needed either to make peace while still in a position of strength or win the war before the American army entered Europe in force. At first, the Central Powers toyed with the idea of seeking peace on the basis of Wilson's fourteen points, but the crushing peace they imposed on Russia and Romania was completely at odds with the principles espoused therein.[403] They could not both sue for peace on the basis of the fourteen points and retain their gains in the east. Additionally, any peace which included self-determination boded ill for both the Habsburgs and continued German control of western Poland.

Having decided against seeking peace, the Central Powers authorized Ludendorff to launch his famous Spring Offensive against the Entente forces in France on 21 March 1918 in an attempt to win the war while Germany still enjoyed a favorable balance of forces on the Western Front. The offensive continued until mid July and, though it made good headway, it never created an exploitable breakthrough.

---

400 Serbia and Montenegro fought until the end of the war, even though their respective countries had been occupied.

401 Stevenson 2005, 109.

402 Ibid, 119.

403 Knock 1992, 145 and 154–5. Wilson made his famous fourteen points speech on 8 January 1918.

The offensive had come close to overwhelming the Entente forces on several occasions; however, it had ruined the German army. The Spring Offensive had reduced the size of the German forces on the Western Front from 5.1 million men to 4.2 million men while at the same time it lengthened the front from 390km to 510km. Additionally, the failure of the offensive demoralized the German soldiers who knew the offensive had been Germany's last, best chance to win. After the offensive was shut down, the German soldiers began to surrender in significantly higher numbers than before.[404] Finally, from August onward the Entente was able to mount a steady, if somewhat slow, offensive against the Germans. Still, the German military leadership remained confident of a favorable military outcome for the war as late as August 1918.[405] Even as late as 14 September, Ludendorff was against an Austro-Hungarian plan to negotiate an armistice with the Entente and given the military's ascendency over the civilian government by this stage in the war, Ludendorff's opinion was the one that mattered. Yet, only two weeks later Ludendorff favored negotiations even if they were on unfavorable terms and he actually sent a request for negotiations to the Americans on 5 October.[406] What caused his remarkable change of heart?

Like the beginning of the war, the roots of the end of the war can be found in the Balkans. The clear faltering of the German army during the summer had caused Radoslavov to fall from power and be replaced by Alexandŭr Malinov.[407] Malinov sought a favorable separate peace for Bulgaria throughout the summer, though without success.[408] In September, Entente forces debouched from Salonika. The offensive was surprisingly successful and, combined with a soldiers' revolt, forced Malinov to throw in the towel and sue for peace on the basis of Wilson's Fourteen Points.[409] Bulgaria asked for an armistice on 28 September 1918 and left the war the following day. This cut the Turks off from their allies and threatened Germany's link to the Romanian oil fields. Plus, Ludendorff had no troops available to plug the hole that now existed on Austria-Hungary's southern flank.

This disaster in the Balkans occurred at exactly the same time the Entente launched four coordinated offensives on the Western Front from 27–29 September. The combined setbacks were simply too much for Ludendorff and led directly to his support for seeking negotiations.[410] The shock of the setbacks was great enough that it actually caused Ludendorff to have a mental breakdown. As the German

---

404 Stevenson 2005, 117.

405 Ibid, 113.

406 Ibid, 113–14.

407 Petkov 1991, 70.

408 Ibid, 72 and 76. Part of Malinov's difficulty was his monarch's opposition to a separate peace. Despite this, Malinov never joined with those who favored overthrowing Ferdinand.

409 Ibid, 77–9 and 83.

410 Stevenson 2005, 113–16.

military had by this point, at a minimum, a veto over foreign policy decisions, Ludendorff's change of position was crucial.

Though the military situation was clearly grim for the remaining three Central Powers, the Entente's armies were a long way from being able to threaten the capitals of the remaining belligerents. Entente forces had yet to completely drive the Germans from French soil nor the Austrians from Italian soil for that matter. The Salonikan army would still have to cross much of the Balkans to bring the Habsburg Empire under attack. Even the faltering Ottomans were a long way from being completely conquered. British forces were just beginning to attack Syria and, though Constantinople could now be attacked from Bulgaria, it was not clear that sufficient forces were available to capture the city, as much of the Salonikan force was earmarked for an offensive against Austria-Hungary. Additionally, the Germans' offer on 5 October to negotiate was not an offer to surrender.[411] Thus, though by October it was clear the Central Powers had lost, they were apparently a long way from being forced to cease military operations.

The German military's request for negotiations, however, had been the last blow the morale of the soldiers and populace could take.[412] The will to fight was gone and the civilians in the Central Powers were not willing to make continued sacrifices for a cause that even the military leadership had now admitted was lost. This was especially true of the Slavic minorities in Austria-Hungary. The request for negotiations led to a series of ethnic revolts in the Habsburg Empire in October and early November. In the past, the government had been able to put down such revolts, but the war had drained the state's resources.[413] The central authorities lost control of Bohemia, Galicia, and the Balkan portions of the empire. Finally, Hungarian and Austrian nationals revolted and opted for separate states. Austria-Hungary was out of the war and out of existence on 3 November. The centuries old family empire was dead.

The German and the Ottoman empires did not last much longer. Bulgaria's surrender left the Ottomans completely isolated. They were unable to halt the British offensive from Egypt, which by October had conquered not only Palestine, but Syria as well. British forces freed by Bulgaria's surrender were attacking Ottoman forces in Thrace. With the war clearly lost, the Turks began to seek an armistice in late October. Still, they grimly hung on and did not leave the war. As long as the Germans remained in the war, so would the Turks.

411 Ibid, 119–20. As late as 15 October, the Germans believed they would be able to keep their gains along the Baltic.

412 Ibid, 114–15 and 128.

413 It is true that the Habsburgs had needed Russian help to suppress the Hungarians in 1848 and 1849, but the government had always been able to put the Slavs down, even if it was often with difficulty. As the Hungarians had been fully co-opted into the state since 1866 and were now a force for stability rather than disruption, the success of the revolts caught the Entente off guard.

The German government had decided to accept the United States' demands on 17 October and Ludendorff resigned to avoid being associated with defeat. On 3 November, there was a naval mutiny in Kiel. This indiscipline quickly spread throughout the military and to the populace. Faced with the specter of revolution and with no power resources to fall back on, Wilhelm II abdicated on 9 November. An armistice was reached two days later working out the exits of both Germany and the Ottoman Empire. The largest war the world had yet seen was over.

Revealed information clearly contributed to the end of the war. The Russian Revolution, the collapse of the Bulgarian army, and the large allied offensives in late September 1918 all led to the exits of Russia, Romania, Bulgaria, the Ottoman Empire, Germany, and Austria-Hungary. The Russian Revolution was more surprising to contemporaries than it is in hindsight. Lenin had been forced to go into hiding only months before his successful rise to power and, though Britain and France knew Russia was in trouble, the October Revolution caught them off guard. Similarly, though in hindsight it seems clear the Central Powers were destined to lose the war after the failure of the Spring Offensive, it was not clear in the early autumn of 1918 how, when, and on what terms the war would end. Only after the twin blows of the Salonikan and late September offensives, did Germany decide it had to end the war. Additionally, the mutinies and revolts that resulted from the Germans' request for negotiations caught contemporaries off-guard. The Germans had already decided to exit the war; the possibility of revolution made accepting the Entente offer imperative.[414] The Germans' decision to exit made it impossible for the Turks to continue. Thus, surprising events led to every state's decision to exit the war.

Conclusions

Overall, the First World War provides good support for the hypothesis that revealed information causes states to reevaluate their decisions about whether or not to join the war. Information generated or revealed by unexpected events clearly triggered the interventions of Bulgaria, Romania, and the United States. The remarkable success of the Central Powers in the Gorlice-Tarnow offensive led directly to Bulgarian intervention. Similarly, the Brusilov Offensive caused Romania to join the war, while the unexpected resumption of unrestricted submarine warfare and the Zimmerman Telegram caused the US to enter the conflict. On top of this, information revealed by various other events discouraged Bulgaria and Romania from entering at earlier points in the war. The Romanian case also provides evidence against the alternate hypothesis that states wait for an expected chain of events to be completed. Romania never made satisfactory progress with securing replacement munitions and improving its army, both of which had discouraged

414 Stevenson 2005, 129.

Romanian intervention in 1914. Yet, despite failing to solve these deficiencies, Romania joined anyway when favorable information was revealed.

The Italian case also provides support for the revealed information hypothesis. Initial Entente defeats in the west deterred Italy, while later Entente successes ultimately led to Italian intervention. The Italian case also provides support for the alternate hypothesis. Italy became an active belligerent shortly after its military buildup was believed to be complete. While the foolish Italian behavior in May 1915 fits poorly with either theory, this is not a crushing blow to either hypothesis, though it does suggest incompetence will cause difficulties for any theory based in rationality.

The Ottoman and Greek cases show internal divisions within a government complicate how states respond to information. In the Ottoman case, much like Britain during the Crimean War, unexpected information allowed the pro-war faction to gain ascendency over the anti-war faction. Unanticipated actions by the belligerents and ultimately the Turkish navy led to the ascendancy of Enver Pasha and caused pivotal ministers to shift from favoring neutrality to advocating belligerency. This ultimately resulted in the Turkish declaration of war. Internal politics were even more important in the Greek case, but the revealed information hypothesis does not fair as well here. Greek politics from 1914 to 1917 were dominated by internal factors and Greece's foreign policy was often incoherent. In reality there were two foreign policies: Constantine's and Venizelos'. Each faction did react to surprising battlefield results, especially Venizelos in 1914 and 1915, but in general the overall course of the war did not affect the likelihood that Greece would join and Greece's actual declaration of war could occur only after allies finally overthrew Constantine. The difference in the Greek case is that there were no pivotal members of the government or the electorate that could resolve the impasse between Constantine and Venizelos. Eventually it became impossible for them to share the reins of government. In the end, their split became total and irreconcilable, with each heading a rival government. By 1917 Greece had two governments: one headed by Constantine committed to neutrality, the other by Venizelos, committed to joining the Entente. Both responded to events, though by this point events within Greece and not in the wider war were foremost in each faction's calculations. Thus, in the Greek case the severity of the internal divisions and the lack of a decisive pivot between the two factions left the Greek government unable to pursue a unified course in response to external events.

Finally, the Portuguese case simply does not belong in this study. Portuguese actions parallel those of states that joined in the first month of the war, rather than later. Given that the Portuguese army was actually involved in military engagements in 1914, it does not seem unreasonable to discard this case. Remarkably, however, even though the Portuguese case does not really belong in the study, it does lend support to the idea that revealed information causes states to change their decisions regarding war and peace. Germany declared war on Portugal only after Portugal seized German ships and Portuguese troops served on the Western Front only after the acute need for troops became apparent after Verdun. Thus, the importance of

Table 5.1 Summary of State Motives for Joining

Country	Event	Reason
Bulgaria	Gorlice-Tarnow Offensive	Revealed Shift in Balance of Forces
Romania	Brusilov Offensive	Revealed Shift in Balance of Forces
United States	Resumption of U-Boat Campaign and the Zimmerman Telegram	Changed Beliefs about German Intentions
Italy	Russian advance in Galicia	Revealed Shift in Balance of Forces
Turkey	British Seizure of Warships	Changed Beliefs about Entente Intentions which Shifted Cabinet Alignments
Greece	None	No Unified Policy Due to Near Civil War
Portugal	None	Already acting as a British Ally

revealed information in relation to intervention is not limited to those states that decided to remain truly neutral in the first months of a war.

On the whole the First World War provides strong support for the hypothesis that revealed information dictates the timing of joining and its corollary that revealed information can sometimes discourage states from joining ongoing wars. The Bulgarian, Romanian, and US cases provide exceptionally strong support and the Italian and Turkish cases provide good, if somewhat qualified support. Only the Greek case did not provide solid support, while the Portuguese case was shown to be inappropriate to the study, though it did actually lend some support. The First World War also lends support to the hypothesis that revealed information causes states to leave wars. Russia, Bulgaria, Germany, and Austria-Hungary all left the war as a direct result of revealed information and these states' exists led to Romania's exit and the termination of the war as a whole—in other words, the exits of Turkey, Britain, France, Serbia, Montenegro, Italy, Portugal, Greece, Belgium, Japan, and the US. Thus, the First World War case strongly supports the hypotheses advanced in Chapter 2.

Chapter 6
The Franco-Prussian War: The War that Refused to Grow

> We cannot enter into alliances until
> we are acquainted with the designs
> of our neighbors. ----Sun Tzu[1]

The negative case is often as informative as the positive. Indeed without a negative example, it may not be at all clear what conclusions should be drawn from positive cases. Competing theories may cite the same exact case as support making it impossible to discern which is the better explanation. It may appear to be fairly clear why states joined the Crimean War and the First World War but perhaps something is being overlooked or misinterpreted. How certain is it that given a similar set of conditions intervention would in fact occur? Is there a variable that may lower the likelihood states will join? For these reasons, a negative example is needed.

The Franco-Prussian War of 1870–71 is just such a negative case. On the surface, it seems a likely candidate for joining. It involved two great powers and several minor ones, lasted many months giving other states time to join, greatly altered the balance of power in Europe, and proceeded along unexpected lines.[2] Why was there no intervention? In order to answer this question, it is first necessary to determine which states were both capable of and interested in joining. In this case, there were five states that plausibly might have entered the war. Three of these, Italy, Austria-Hungary, and Denmark, held grudges against Prussia. Italy was bitter that Prussia had ended the Six Weeks War of 1866 before Italy could capture a significant amount of Austrian territory. Austria-Hungary was still smarting from its defeat at Prussia's hands in the same war. Similarly, the Danes wanted to recover the duchies they lost to Prussia in the Second Schleswig-Holstein War in 1864. All of these states could have conceivably entered the war on behalf of France against Prussia.

Great Britain and Russia were also potential joiners. Both were great powers whose respective interests would be affected by any significant shift in the European balance of power. Russia was allied to Prussia and very unlikely to join except on

---

1 Edwards 2004, 70.

2 Recall Haldi claims that joining is more likely in the post-Napoleonic era if the balance of power is threatened.

Prussia's side. Britain was not allied with either state, but had cooperated militarily with the Second Empire in the past and traditionally was opposed to any one state dominating the continent, an event that could potentially be brought about by a decisive victory by either side. Additionally, Britain wished for the peaceful, liberal unification of Germany and for Napoleon III to remain on the throne of France.[3] Britain also wanted to maintain peace between Prussia and France and had even attempted to mediate disarmament talks between France and Prussia, but these had proved abortive.[4] Obviously the results of the Franco-Prussian War—the destruction of the Second Empire, a less liberal Germany, and the laying of the groundwork for German domination of the continent—were contrary to British desires. These considerations seemingly should have made Britain likely to join. They did not, as will be shown below, in large part because British interests on the continent were primarily confined to Belgium.[5]

No other states were likely to join. They were disinterested in the conflict and, for the most part, weak. Of the other states that were geographically contiguous to the belligerents, Switzerland, Belgium, and the Netherlands were committed to policies of general neutrality and were too weak to affect the issue anyway. Spain was beset by internal problems stemming from the overthrow of Queen Isabella in 1868 and was in no condition to go to war. In fact, it was this unstable internal situation in Spain that provided the spark for the war. After failing to find a suitable monarch in the royal households of Portugal and Italy, the junta ruling Spain offered the crown to Prince Leopold of Prussia, a Hohenzollern. French opposition to the candidacy would prove to be the *casus belli*.[6]

The Build-Up to War

Ever since the Prussian victory in the Six Weeks War, Franco-Prussian relations had been poor. The French government saw Prussia as challenging France's traditional position as the most powerful state in Europe. Napoleon III felt a need to seek compensation for Prussia's growth in power. Specifically, France sought territorial annexations along the Rhine and in Luxembourg, which at that time was dynastically connected to the Netherlands. The diplomatic details of these episodes between 1866 and 1870, though fascinating, are not central to the point at hand. On the whole, they resulted in no gains for France except the neutralization

3 Herkless 1972, 458–9.

4 Ibid.

5 Raymond 1921, 87; Millman 1965, 115.

6 Leopold was from the Sigmaringen branch of the Hohenzollern family and was not in line for the Prussian crown. Thus, there was no chance Prussia and Spain would be dynastically united. His brother previously had been anointed King of Romania.

of Luxembourg.[7] Given the grand French goals of annexations along the Rhine and of Luxembourg itself, this was a terribly small gain.

On top of this failure, the various French demands for compensation made France appear to be an aggressor and cost France the sympathy of Britain and much of continental Europe as well.[8] The British public had been suspicious of French designs ever since the annexations of Nice and Savoy in 1860.[9] Britain in particular had been upset by the French designs on Luxembourg as they were seen as potentially threatening Belgium.[10] Britain's fixation on Belgium may appear odd, but it was both a matter of honor—and honor most definitely mattered in the Victorian Era—and national interests. The Belgian ports along the English Channel were potential launching sites for an invasion of Britain.[11] British fears for Belgium had been recently reawakened by a French attempt to buy a major Belgian railroad. Additionally, Belgium was important because it gave Britain a role on the continent.[12] Without the issue of Belgium, Britain had very limited legitimate reasons for interfering in the affairs of the other great powers, especially in Northwest Europe.[13] While Britain certainly was strong enough to meddle most anywhere on the continent, its concern for Belgium had an air of legitimacy and sincerity that interference elsewhere might lack. Thus, the issue of Belgium served as a device through which Britain could attempt to influence events on the continent. By the time of the crisis over the Hohenzollern candidacy to the Spanish throne, Lord Clarendon was the only pro-French statesman in power in Britain.[14] It was he who had brought up the issue of disarmament with Prussia at France's behest. Clarendon may have even been trying to use the negotiations as means of moving Britain into an entente with France.[15] His death just as the crisis was about to break left Britain without strong leadership in foreign affairs and France without

7 Prior to the neutralization, Prussia had maintained a garrison in Luxembourg. Even though the duchy was dynastically linked to the Netherlands, the Grand Duchy had been part of the old German Confederation prior to its dissolution at the end of the Six Weeks War. The Dutch King, William III, wanted to sell Luxembourg to France and Bismarck had promised to allow it in exchange for France's neutrality during the Six Weeks War. Bismarck, however, engineered protests within Germany, which he claimed prevented him from being able to agree to the sale. Prussia did agree to withdraw its garrison at the behest of Britain and Russia.

8 Raymond 1921, 19.

9 Ibid, 17. The annexations had been compensation from Sardinia for French aid in driving Austria out of Lombardy and for French recognition of the annexation of Tuscany.

10 Millman 1965, 71.

11 Ibid, 115.

12 Ibid, 120–21.

13 Britain had guaranteed Belgium's territorial integrity and independence since Belgium gained independence from the Netherlands in 1838. Britain could also claim a special interest in Portugal and the Bosporus.

14 Millman 1965, 112.

15 Herkless 1972, 466.

a friend in the British government, ending the remote chance of a Franco-British entente.[16]

These diplomatic episodes also had the effect of creating the perception among the French that Prussia and France were engaged in a constant-sum game and that France was losing. Napoleon and his cabinet believed that public opinion would not tolerate any further setbacks. Thus, when news that Prince Leopold of Hohenzollern-Sigmaringen was a candidate for the Spanish throne reached Paris, a full-blown crisis erupted. France simply would not tolerate a member of the Prussian royal household to sit on the throne of Spain or the possibility of a Prussian ally at the backdoor of France.

Many European states worked for peace and urged Prussia to withdraw the candidacy as it was seen as an unnecessary provocation.[17] In the end, the Prussians succumbed to French and international pressure and withdrew the candidacy. King Wilhelm I simply was unwilling to start a war over the candidacy. Europe breathed a sigh of relief. The French, however, wanted assurances that the candidacy would never be resumed and insisted upon them in a most undiplomatic manner.[18] This was too much for the Prussian king. Much to the relief of his ministers, he refused to yield to the French demands and war resulted. The lesser German states, Würtemberg, Baden, Bavaria, and Hesse-Darmstadt, were aligned with Prussia from the war's beginning.[19] Because the French had refused to accept Prussia's withdrawal of the candidacy as sufficient, something almost all of the non-belligerents felt was more than fair, France and not Prussia was perceived as the aggressor.[20]

Opinion outside of Germany expected a French victory as the French army was entirely professional and its rifle, the *chassepôt*, was superior to the Prussian needle-gun. These advantages were seen as more than offsetting the numerical advantage of Prussia and its allies. It was believed the French would mobilize more quickly than the German states and launch an offensive before Prussia's superior numbers would be able to tell on the battlefield. All of Europe expected

---

16 Ibid, 469; Millman 1965, 174.

17 Wetzel 2001, 103. British and especially Italian mediation efforts were notable.

18 Bismarck's clever editing of the Ems telegram, which made it look as though King William and the French ambassador had swapped insults, helped the exchange along but even so the French were unduly brusque and rigid in their diplomacy. Bismarck and the Prussian army wanted war throughout the crisis.

19 There were also quite a few minor states in northern Germany, such as the Mecklenberg duchies and Oldenberg, which also entered the war on Prussia's side at the outset. They were technically independent, but in fact Prussia had controlled their foreign policies and almost all of their internal affairs since the Six Week's War and their militaries had been fully integrated with Prussia's.

20 Wawro 2003, 37–8; Wetzel 2001, 164. This was especially true in Britain, where the whole episode was seen as brought on by French intransigence, though the government was less hostile than the public at large (Millman 1965, 187 and 195–6).

such an offensive.[21] Additionally, Napoleon and his cabinet believed that they would be able to draw Italy, Austria-Hungary, and Denmark into the war on the French side. The French hoped these potential allies, along with a rapid French offensive, would cancel the numerical advantage held by the German states.

The French had attempted to bring about a triple alliance with Italy and Austria-Hungary throughout the late 1860s, but without success. The proposed alliance failed in large part because France did not take into account the goals of Italy and Austria-Hungary. The treaty proposed by the French took into account only the French need for allies against Prussia, and therefore, would have benefitted only France.[22] Though both Italy and Austria-Hungary held grudges against Prussia, neither placed opposition to Prussia at the center of their foreign policy in the late 1860s.

Italy's main goal was the acquisition of the Patrimonium, the area in and around Rome. Two French regiments had held this territory for the Pope since 1849.[23] Italy was highly unlikely to come to any sort of agreement with France, unless the troops were withdrawn.[24] Napoleon felt he could not withdraw the troops without losing the support of the Clerical party in France. Given the shaky state of the Bonaparte dynasty in the 1860s, Napoleon III simply was not willing to risk alienating this important group. Quintino Sella, the Italian minister of finance, and Giovanni Lanza, the prime minister, forced King Victor Emmanuel II to break off negotiations with France out of fear that France was simply using Italy and would never allow Italy to annex the Patrimonium.[25] The furthest concession France gave was the September Convention of 1864, in which it promised to withdraw its regiments on the condition that Italian troops would not march into the Patrimonium.[26] Pro-Italian disturbances within the Patrimonium, however, required the French regiments to remain well past the date of their agreed departure in order to preserve the Pope's temporal rule. This led to the September Convention becoming a dead letter. The Italian cabinet, therefore, remained steadfast against any alliance with France without an explicit guarantee that Italy could annex

---

21 Wawro 2003, 73. Much of Prussia's conscript army was in the form of reserves, which were not under arms during peacetime. It took some time to put these men in the ranks. Prussia's ability to mobilize its reserves as quickly as France could mobilize its regular army was one of the keys to the Prussian victory.

22 Wetzel 2001, 44.

23 The Papacy did not possess sufficient forces to hold the Patrimonium on its own. The Papal army had been crushed by the Sardinians at Castelfidardo in 1860, which in conjunction with other events led to the unification of Italy, bar the Patrimonium, under Sardinian rule.

24 Edelston 1915, 28–32; Decsy 1979, 69.

25 Wetzel 2001, 59. Sella and Lanza also convinced the King to withdraw his son from consideration for the Spanish throne out of fear this would just entangle Italy with France. The candidacy had been encouraged by the French government.

26 Halperin 1963, 28.

Rome. Though Victor Emmanuel remained interested in an alliance with France, negotiations collapsed.

Antebellum negotiations between France and Austria-Hungary proved equally sterile. This was largely due to the new internal political arrangement of the Habsburg Empire. The Dual Monarchy, created after Austria's defeat in the Six Weeks War, gave the Hungarians a parliament of their own and a great deal of influence over the making of both foreign and domestic policy. After 1868, Count Gyula Andrássy, the Hungarian prime minister, was the most powerful political figure within the Austro-Hungarian Empire.[27] Andrássy's influence essentially gave the Hungarians a veto over foreign policy decisions. The Hungarians saw the Russians and not the Prussians as the greatest threat and were eager to mend the empire's relationship with Prussia to the extent that Prussia would help contain Russia.[28] Beyond this, the Hungarians were not pro-Prussian, but rather saw enmity toward Prussia as a distraction from the real threat of Russia. Andrássy and his fellow Hungarians certainly did not support Prussia's alliance with Russia, nor did they want Prussia to annex the German-speaking portion of the empire. Additionally, Andrássy was not opposed to an alliance with France, provided it was confined to the Near East and the containment of Russia.[29] This set of priorities would cause Andrássy to vigorously oppose joining the Franco-Prussian War.[30]

The liberal Germans in the Habsburg Empire were also against pursuing an anti-Prussian policy. They supported the unification of Germany under the rule of the relatively liberal Prussian constitution. The Emperor Franz Joseph was also skittish at the idea of allying with France, the traditional enemy of Austria, against a fellow German power.[31] Even the foreign minister, Count Ferdinand von Beust, a Saxon by birth and dogged opponent of Bismarck, was opposed to war with Prussia in the late 1860s. He wanted an alliance with France, but he knew Austria-Hungary was in no condition to fight a war.[32] He also believed every attempt should be made to win the support of the minor German states in a contest with Prussia. Still, Beust pressed ahead with the negotiations. In the immediate aftermath of the Six Weeks War, France was uninterested as the Habsburgs seemed hopelessly weak, but by 1867 negotiations were underway.[33] Beust, however, had to reject the treaty due to the above-mentioned domestic constraints. He could not back any plan that risked war with Russia or involved the French annexation of German territory. The Hungarian and the liberal German factions would not

27 Decsy 1979, 66.

28 Ibid, 29 and 33; Wawro 2003, 67.

29 Wetzel 2001, 44. Count Ferdinand von Beust, the Austro-Hungarian foreign minister, initially also wanted any alliance with France confined to the Near East.

30 Edelston 1915, 14.

31 Decsy1979, 43–46.

32 Ibid, 25.

33 Ibid, 38.

allow it.[34] An alliance with France against Prussia might also alienate the lesser German states. This was unappealing to Beust as it would make it impossible for Austria-Hungary to regain its traditional role as the leader of the German states. On top of this, the French conducted the negotiations in a very highhanded manner. They ignored Beust's advice to try to isolate Prussia within Germany and refused to show Beust their plans for joint military action.[35] Given the potential drawbacks and the condescending attitude of the French it is not surprising that even Beust, anti-Prussian though he was, refused to sign a treaty of alliance. Thus, as with Italy, France failed to cement an alliance with Austria-Hungary prior to the Hohenzollern candidacy.

France also failed to reach an understanding with Denmark, though some conversations had taken place. As the Danes likely could not make much of a difference by themselves, this was not a great failing. Still, France spent the late 1860s alienating much of Europe by posturing aggressively along the Rhine, while at the same time failing to establish any alliances with which to meet the coming Prussian threat.

Prussia never sought allies for a war with France outside of the lesser German states. Otto von Bismarck, the Prussian Chancellor, and General Helmuth von Moltke, the head of the Prussian General Staff, were confident of a Prussian victory provided France remained isolated. Bringing Russia into the war on Prussia's side would have been difficult and possibly counterproductive as it risked making the war general. Given a Russian entry, the Hungarians would likely force the Habsburgs into war in order to prevent Russian gains and the British might join in order to contain the Russians in the Near East. Also, it would prevent the war from being fought for exclusively Prussian aims. Russia was far more valuable on the sidelines as an implicit threat to Austria-Hungary. Were that power to enter the war, Russia was certain to come to Prussia's aid.[36] Thus, Russia was much more effective as a deterrent to Austria-Hungary, than as an active belligerent.

This appears to beg the question of why Russia was an effective deterrent to Austria-Hungary as the Austro-Hungarians should have been able to see that Prussia wanted Russia to remain on the sidelines and thus, should not have seen Russia as likely to enter. This, however, is not the case. While the Austro-Hungarians certainly could surmise Prussia would prefer to have both Austria-Hungary and Russia stay out of the war, it was just as clear that if Austria-Hungary entered, Prussia would want Russia to join the war and that Russia was likely to do just that. Austria-Hungary would be in a very difficult spot having to fight Russia and Prussia simultaneously and any benefit derived from hurting Prussia would be more than offset by a Russian attack on Galicia. Thus, while Austria-Hungary could make life worse for Prussia by joining the war, it would also weaken its

34 Ibid, 45.
35 Wetzel 2001, 177.
36 Edelston 1915, 61–2.

own position by inducing a Russian entry. For this reason, Russia was an effective deterrent even though Prussia hoped Russia would not have to join the war.

The Antebellum Crisis and Early Stages of the War

During the crisis leading up to the war and the period just after war was declared, France found itself trying to obtain the alliances it had failed to create during the 1860s. French diplomats tried unsuccessfully to enlist Austria-Hungary, though the attempt was not without reason for hope. Within the Habsburg empire, the military, the central bureaucracy, the Court party, and Franz Joseph himself were all pro-war.[37] Beust especially wanted to aid France.[38] France also made extravagant promises to Austria-Hungary. France offered Silesia, lost by the Habsburgs to Prussia in the 1740s during the war of the Austrian Succession, and perhaps part of Bavaria as spoils.[39] With such powerful figures and factions favoring war and France promising such large territorial gains, why did Austria-Hungary fail to join the war?

First, the spoils would exist only if France won. This was not a huge obstacle as a French victory was anticipated by many of the major players in Austria-Hungary, even those, such as Andrássy, who opposed joining the war.[40] Still, the Habsburg army could not contribute greatly to victory as it was in poor shape and the country was strapped for cash.[41] Given the slow mobilization time of the army, it made sense to sit back, observe the initial battles, and make sure that France was indeed going to win the war.[42] This way, any available spoils could be picked up cheaply without risking another major defeat that might threaten the existence of the empire.

Second, there were very strong forces and figures opposing the war. After the retraction of the Hohenzollern candidate for the Spanish throne, the lesser German states began to back Prussia.[43] This meant that if Austria-Hungary attacked Prussia it risked alienating those very states it hoped to win back as allies. Additionally, there were significant domestic constraints. The Poles in Galicia favored neutrality and it was feared that the Croats might use a war as an opportunity to rebel.[44] Far

37 Decsy 1979, 83 and 89. Franz Joseph evidently was no longer bothered by aiding France against a fellow German state.

38 Ibid, 74.

39 Oncken 1928, 185.

40 Decsy 1979, 90–3 and 100; Halperin 1963, 79. Some in the army and most of the Court party thought the French army was suspect, but even most of these expected an eventual French victory, though only after a long war.

41 Decsy 1979, 90.

42 Oncken 1928, 158.

43 Halperin 1963, 135.

44 Decsy 1979, 85.

more important than these groups were the German liberals and the Hungarians. Both groups were very much against the war.[45] The former opposed war because they did not want to aid France in the defeat of their fellow Germans. The latter opposed it because if the war were successful, the Habsburgs would be back in the competition for dominance in Germany and would be greatly strengthened. They might then feel it possible to again ignore the Hungarians and focus on German affairs rather than the eastern issues facing the empire. In essence, the Hungarians' current favorable position within the Habsburg Empire depended on the continued exclusion of Austria-Hungary from Germany.[46] Also, Bismarck had been consistently friendly and supportive of the Hungarians.[47] Thus, the Hungarians felt no animosity toward the Prussians, nor did they feel the need for revenge that was felt throughout much of the Austrian dominated army and central bureaucracy. The Hungarians also feared that entering the war would cause the Russians to enter. The Russian army easily outclassed the Austro-Hungarian army and the Hungarians greatly feared a repeat of the Russian invasion during their unsuccessful revolution of 1848–49. If Russia were to join, the Hungarians would then support entering the war in order to prevent Russia from being strengthened by the spoils of war.[48] Such a war would bring great risks and was certainly not guaranteed to meet with success, but would be favorable to seeing Russia strengthened. Thus, it was preferable to not have to fight Russia; if Russia stayed out of the conflict, there was no reason to provoke a war. Franz Joseph was committed to the new Duel Monarchy and this commitment effectively gave Andrássy a veto over Austro-Hungarian foreign policy decisions. The military also feared Russia and thus, though they were pro-war, they could be convinced to take a less aggressive line.[49] Austria-Hungary officially declared neutrality on 20 July.[50] Still, Beust and others hoped to enter the war once it became politically feasible, but they needed a reason, preferably a convincing French victory or possibly the entry of Italy into the war.[51] Beust had always felt that the entry of Italy would give him greater leverage over Andrássy and the Hungarians.[52] He worked hard to get Italy to join, encouraging France to withdraw from the Patrimonium and hinted

45 Wetzel 2001, 81 and 87.

46 Decsy 1979, 32.

47 Ibid, 67–8.

48 Ibid, 76. Obviously, in this scenario the Hungarians would try to obtain an alliance with Britain to help contain Russia in the Black Sea. Such an alliance was possible, if far from guaranteed, as Britain was still committed to enforcing the provision of the Treaty of Paris that ended the Crimean War.

49 Edelston 1915, 28.

50 Decsy 1979, 108. The decision to remain neutral had been reached in a cabinet meeting on 18 July.

51 Ibid, 74, 97–8; Wetzel 2001, 177.

52 Halperin 1961, 39. This was in part because going to war without Italy risked Italian attacks against Austria-Hungary in order to seize the Trentino (Edelston 1915, 28).

at border rectifications favorable to Italy.[53] Thus, the combination of Hungarian opposition and fear of Russian intervention initially kept Austria-Hungary neutral and waiting on events.[54] As will be seen below, Italy never joined and the French victories never materialized, which in turn meant Austria-Hungary remained on the sidelines.

France's other great hope, Italy, proved as disappointing as Austria-Hungary. France had reasons for hope of an alliance. In addition to Italy's anger at the quick peace Bismarck had signed in 1866, the king and the Italian right wing favored France.[55] Italy's king, Victor Emmanuel was a staunch hawk. War was his favorite activity, so much so that he once told Prussian Crown Prince Frederick that he planned to make war "as often as the opportunity presents itself."[56] This attitude had much to do with Sardinia's entry into the Crimean War fifteen years earlier. Victor Emmanuel hoped to lead his country into war once again.

The forces opposed to an Italian entry, however, were daunting. The Six Weeks War in 1866 had left Italian finances in even worse shape than Austria-Hungary's.[57] The army was a disaster as well.[58] Emilio Marchese di Visconti-Venosta, the foreign minister, sincerely wanted peace, as did both Lanza and Sella.[59] Unlike Lanza and Sella, however, Visconti-Venosta was not entirely against belligerency if war did in fact occur. He considered intervention a possibility if it could be used to obtain Rome or if Austria-Hungary entered on France's side.[60]

The Italian public, especially the Left, however, was strongly for neutrality.[61] Public reaction to any treaty with France, unless it resulted in Italy acquiring the Patrimonium, was likely to be violent. There were even threats of insurrection.[62] Yet, Napoleon's government found itself unable to withdraw from Rome, due to its dependence on the Catholic faction.[63] At first, it offered only the southern Tyrol to Italy in exchange for Italy's entry into the war. This was clearly insufficient and Italy's government remained committed to a course of neutrality.

Despite this, King Victor Emmanuel tried to negotiate a pact with France over the head of his government and these negotiations nearly proved successful.[64] This

53 Halperin 1963, 80 and 129.

54 Oncken 1928, 181.

55 Halperin 1963, 74 and 148; Wetzel 2001, 122. The Italians wanted to obtain the Trentino in 1866 and felt that the quick peace had prevented them from being able to force Austria into relinquishing it at the bargaining table.

56 Halperin 1963, 60. During his reign, Italy/Sardinia had already been involved in five wars in 21 years.

57 Ibid, 3; Wetzel 2001, 122.

58 Wetzel 2001, 125.

59 Edleston 1915, 22–3; Halperin 1963, 2.

60 Edelston 1915, 22–3; Halperin 1961, 38.

61 Halperin 1963, 94 and 149.

62 Ibid, 178.

63 Ibid, 24.

64 Ibid, 76–7 and 93.

was in large part because Napoleon came around on the evacuation of Rome and the renewal of the September Convention provided Italy promised not to occupy Rome.[65] Napoleon was still unwilling to accept the annexation of the Patrimonium. The Italian government became aware of these negotiations and worked to stop them, though the king still pressed an alliance with France. The government argued that simply renewing the September Convention was not enough; France must consent to the Italian annexation of Rome.[66] This did not sway Victor Emmanuel. He remained committed to entering the war on the French side. His only concern was the position of Austria-Hungary, as the plan he and Napoleon had drawn up required the Italian army to march through the Austrian Tyrol and attack Bavaria.[67] It looked as though Italy's decision hinged on that of Austria-Hungary.[68] The government was forced to call up 70,000 reservists in case it did come to war.[69] After Austria-Hungary's declaration of neutrality on 18 July, the government had the means to temporarily outmaneuver the king. It declared that Italy would join France only after Austria-Hungary did and only if the Roman question was satisfactorily resolved.[70] This preserved neutrality for the moment, but the king still wanted war and continued to work for an alliance with France. The success of his endeavors would depend in part on events within the course of the war.

Denmark also remained neutral despite French promises of recapturing Schleswig.[71] France had good reasons for wanting to secure Danish aid even given the small size of the Danish army. Danish ports and the Danish fleet would be useful in harassing the Prussians with raids on the Baltic and North Sea coasts. Still, Danish aid was not crucial. Such raids could not win the war and France might be able to conduct them without Danish help.[72] Given the small size of the Danish army, the Danes could hardly affect the course of the war on land. The Danes saw this just as clearly as the French, and therefore, when the French sent an emissary to bring about an alliance, the Danes insisted on some sign that France was winning the war before they would commit to an alliance.[73] On top of this, both Russia and Britain strongly encouraged Denmark to remain neutral and warned the Danes about cooperating with the French fleet in the Baltic or in the North Sea.[74] The Danes could not afford to provoke either of these powers.

65 Ibid, 161–2.

66 Ibid, 175; Edelston 1915, 28–32. The government also remained concerned about Italy's ability to bear the costs of another war.

67 Edelston 1915, 28; Halperin 1963, 166–7.

68 Halperin 1963, 145

69 Ibid, 168.

70 Ibid, 182.

71 Oncken 1928, 185.

72 As it turned out, the French fleet was badly led and played almost no role in the war. It sailed aimlessly about the North Sea at the war's beginning and then returned permanently to port.

73 Jones 1986, 61.

74 Wawro 2003, 189.

The Danes did attempt to get Prussia to hold a plebiscite in Schleswig on pro-Danish terms in exchange for neutrality, but Bismarck declined.[75] Still, Bismarck remained uncertain about Denmark's intentions longer than any other potential joiner.[76] In the end, early French defeats convinced the Danes to remain neutral.

Britain was another state that conceivably could have joined the war. Unlike Austria-Hungary, Italy, and Denmark, Britain was not interested in picking up spoils, but rather would have joined to preserve the balance of power in Europe. In actuality, Britain never came close to entering the war. Its army was in a terrible state. This had become clear for all to see after Britain had been unable to come to Denmark's aid in 1864 during the Second Schleswig-Holstein War. Also, initially Britain believed France was stronger than Prussia. Because the British overrated the French army, they simply did not see the war as threatening the balance of power.[77] On top of this, outside of Ireland there was little public sympathy for France.[78] When war was declared the *Times* stated:

> The greatest national crime that we have had the pain of recording in these columns since the days of the First French Empire has been consummated. War is declared–an unjust but premeditated war. This dire calamity, which overwhelms Europe with dismay, is, it is not too clear, the act of one man in France.[79]

The hostility of the British press and public was in part, the result of the publication by Bismarck of an old French plan for the annexation of Belgium by France and Prussia.[80] Though the British government correctly smelled a rat, France did not gain any friends among the British public due to the publication. Even without this Prussian ruse, public opinion would have been against France because of its refusal to accept the withdrawal of the Hohenzollern candidacy as sufficient and because of the aggressive nature of French policy since the Six Weeks War. Given the belief in the strength of France and the general public displeasure with current French policies, there was little reason to intervene as Britain's main concern was the independence of Belgium, which was not threatened by the war.[81] Both sides agreed to honor Belgian neutrality, so Britain had little cause for fear. After Belgium, Britain's secondary concern was to prevent the war from becoming general. The British foreign office was opposed to Italy, Denmark, or Austria-Hungary entering the war and attempted to discourage their joining, though only

75 Holbraad 1991, 45.
76 Lord 1966, 115.
77 Wetzel 2001, 128.
78 Raymond 1921, 79; Wetzel 2001, 180.
79 Raymond 1921, 73–4.
80 Ibid, 88.
81 Millman 1965, 198.

Denmark was actually threatened.[82] Thus, prior to Prussia's victories the British saw little reason to enter the war.

Russia was the only power that might have joined on the German side. Russia had consistently disapproved of French conduct throughout the crisis and especially after Prince Leopold's candidacy had been withdrawn.[83] Though the Russians favored Prussia, they very much wanted the war to remain localized. A Russian entry into the war would run the risk of conflict in the Black Sea, where Russia had no fleet due to the provisions of the Treaty of Paris of 1856. Britain and Austria-Hungary shared France's interest in limiting Russian influence in the Near East. If Russia joined, these two powers might enter the war on France's side in order to contain Russia. If Russia entered a replay of the Crimean War was possible, while if Russia remained neutral the war with Prussia would distract France and it might be possible for Russia to rebuild the Black Sea fleet without having to fight a war.[84] Also if Russia were to join, the war would likely become general, something neither Russia nor Prussia wanted. In addition to its concerns in the Near East, Russia feared a general war might open up the question of Poland.[85] Prussia opposed a general war because, in addition to making the war bloodier and slower, it would link Franco-Prussian issues to other issues thereby potentially reducing Prussia's leverage. Finally, Russian neutrality served Prussia very well by acting as an implicit threat to both Austria-Hungary and Denmark. There can be no doubt that Austria-Hungary was frightened by the Prussia-Russian alliance.[86] Clearly, Russia had many strong reasons for remaining a non-belligerent and Prussia had no desire to have Russia join the war.

Thus at the beginning of the Franco-Prussian war there were three states, Austria-Hungary, Italy, and Denmark, which though inclined toward neutrality might join if it looked as though France were headed toward an easy victory. These three states were more likely to enter jointly, rather than independently. A fourth state, Russia, might enter if either Denmark or Austria-Hungary entered. Additionally, all of Europe outside of Germany, including the above states, expected an early French offensive and a French victory.[87] Only the magnitude and speed of the French triumph were in question. These expectations were to prove very wrong with important consequences for the likelihood of intervention.

---

82 Ibid, 207.

83 Lord 1966, 76; Wetzel 2001, 108–10.

84 Decsy 1979, 112. As it turned out, Russia did not significantly rebuild its fleet until years later, though it did obtain permission to due so at an international conference in London in 1871.

85 Ibid, 87. Palmerston had wanted to open up the Polish question during the Crimean War.

86 Ibid, 53.

87 Ibid, 90 and 100; Halperin 1963, 79; Millman 1965, 198; Wawro 2003; 73; Wetzel 2001, 177–9.

Prussia Triumphant

The expectation of an early French offensive was soon proved wrong. The French mobilized slowly and limited themselves to a small offensive in the direction of the Saar. Though it was successful, it achieved nothing useful. It did, however, put the French army in an awkward position tactically. This lack of a meaningful, early offensive was discouraging to France's potential allies.[88] The crushing defeats in early August would scare off any potential pro-French bandwagoners for good.

The twin battles of Rezonville and Wörth shattered the illusion of French superiority. The French were badly beaten and were forced to retire all along the front. The defeats cooled the ardor of the Danish public for war and convinced Victor Emmanuel of Italy to give up his project of an alliance with France, much to the relief of his government.[89] All chance of a triple alliance between France, Italy, and Austria-Hungary evaporated.[90] British fears of intervention by Denmark, Italy, and Austria-Hungary also greatly lessened.[91] The battles dissuaded not only France's potential allies—Italy, Austria-Hungary, and Denmark—but worried Russia as well.[92] The following month the battle of Sedan and Napoleon's capture made it clear France was going to lose the war and lose it badly. This ended all chance of intervention by Austria-Hungary or any other power looking to pick up spoils at Prussia's expense.[93]

Even though the opportunity to pick up spoils had vanished, the possibility that a state might join had not completely disappeared. The prospect of Prussia completely crushing and dismembering France was unattractive to the other European powers. Immediately after Sedan, foreign powers, especially Austria-Hungary, pressured Prussia to end the war.[94] British sympathy for France also grew considerably.[95] Italy asked Britain and Austria-Hungary to form a league of neutrals, with the object that without becoming active belligerents, they could prevent France from being treated too severely.[96] The league came into being in September.[97] In October, Britain tried to use the league to force neutral mediation on the belligerents, but Russia was not interested and the idea collapsed.[98] Unilateral British intervention remained unattractive, in no small part because it would

88 Wawro 2003, 73.

89 Edelston 1915, 39; Halperin 1963, 186; Raymond 1921, 123.

90 Edelston 1915, 43–4; Decsy 1979, 111; Oncken 1928, 182.

91 Millman 1965, 207

92 Decsy 1979, 110–11.

93 Edelston 1915, 67; Halperin 1963, 189.

94 Wawro 2001, 187–8.

95 Millman 1965, 208 and 217.

96 Wetzel 2001, 187–8.

97 Halperin 1963, 189. The Italian government had wanted to form a league of neutrals even before Sedan and at first saw the league primarily as a way to keep Italy out of the war and out of danger.

98 Millman 1965, 214.

have created difficulties in Britain's relationship with the Belgians, who greatly feared the French, and because it would have created an even greater window of opportunity than already existed for Russia to act aggressively in the Near East.[99] In the end, Britain simply lacked both the might and the will to join the war.[100]

Seeing the growing sympathy for France, Bismarck strove to end the war, but the new Third Republic proved unwilling to negotiate. His fear of foreign involvement became particularly acute as the siege of Paris dragged on into the early winter and he forced Moltke to open up the guns on Paris, rather than simply waiting for the garrison to starve. Outside of Paris, the war slowly began to devolve into something close to guerilla warfare. The French regularly attempted to attack German supply lines and also the main German formations, but the raw French recruits were defeated regularly. Only the French effort to relieve Belfort offered any chance of success. Though this sort of warfare drained German resources, it also extracted a heavy toll on the French citizenry. With Paris in German hands and the rest of the war going badly, the French government finally agreed to negotiate.[101] Bismarck was able to resist Russian and British pressure to have the negotiations become part of an overall European conference, in part by buying time with a preliminary conference in early January.[102] In the end, intervention to preserve the balance of power did not occur because Britain was not opposed to the unification of Germany and German annexations of French territory were limited to Alsace-Lorraine. While this was a significant amount of territory, all the powers knew that France had planned to annex at least as much territory along the Rhine if the German states had lost, not to mention what France had promised to Denmark and Austria-Hungary. In the end, the non-belligerents felt Prussia's treatment of France was not unduly harsh. The threat a united Germany posed to the European balance of power was not entirely foreseen, perhaps in large part because much of Germany, including the Ruhr, had yet to industrialize.[103]

The war ended in large part because of the exhaustion of the French populace and the clearly hopeless military situation that had developed by mid January 1871. The French public was willing to accept peace even at very high costs.[104] Many of the civilian leaders of the new Third Republic were in favor of continuing the

---

99 Ibid, 210. The Belgians were very fearful of France and likely would have been suspicious if their protector, Britain, cooperated with France.

100 Millman 1965, 218.

101 The French insisted that the campaign around Belfort be fought to its conclusion in hopes of attaining a victory to offset their defeats elsewhere. In the end, the French relief force was defeated and forced to retreat into neutral Switzerland where it was interned (McEvedy 1982, 28).

102 Wawro 2003, 290. The general conference was to discuss Russia's renunciation of the clauses of the 1856 Treaty of Paris limiting the size of the Russian Black Sea Fleet.

103 The Second Reich was far less powerful economically in 1871 than it was twenty years later (McEvedy 1982, 30 and 40).

104 Howard 1962, 432.

war, but the need for elective support forced them to accept peace.[105] The Germans also were under great strain trying to supply their army and occupy the French countryside. On 25 January, a three-week armistice was signed which ultimately led to the permanent cessation of hostilities. The French had been clearly and decisively defeated. Though further resistance was possible, it was pointless unless the Germans aimed at greatly reducing the French state. As annexation was limited to Alsace-Lorraine, peace was preferable to continuing a war that was slowly devolving into a guerilla conflict as regular French formations were almost always beaten by their German opponents.

Conclusions

The Franco-Prussian War failed to expand for six main reasons. First, France failed to establish alliances in the antebellum period. Second, the unexpected Prussian victories in the early stage of the war scared off many of the non-belligerents that had considered bandwagoning with a victorious France. Third, warnings and the threat of hostile action from other non-belligerents such as Russia deterred some potential joiners. Fourth, the threat that a Prussian victory presented to the balance of power was not apparent to the non-belligerent great powers. Fifth, Prussia took steps to avoid angering the non-belligerents. Finally, domestic constraints in the non-belligerents reduced the likelihood of intervention.

Siverson and Starr's research, combined with the findings in Chapter 3, strongly suggests that allies do get drawn into wars, but that alliances are not correlated with joining after the first month of a war. Thus, alliances are useful for procuring military help at the onset of a war, but not thereafter. The First World War, in which states quickly came to the aid of their allies, lends support to this hypothesis. At the outbreak of the Franco-Prussian war, France had no formal alliances and had only begun to feel out potential allies. This lack of alliances deprived France of immediate aid. This left France in the position of being able to obtain aid only if non-belligerents believed the course of the war indicated it would be in their interest to join the French side. Thus, the lack of antebellum alliances meant that whether France would receive military assistance depended upon events within the war.

These events took the form of stunning Prussian victories. Rather than leading to intervention, however, they played a crucial role in deterring intervention. Recall that in Chapter 2, it was argued that revealed information can make joining a war more attractive, but it also can make joining less attractive. Chapters Three through Five offered clear statistical and historical support for the argument that surprises lead to joining. The notion that such events could also reduce the appeal of joining received solid support in the First World War case, but not until this case had it been systematically examined. The Franco-Prussian War case strongly

105 Ibid, 443.

supports this secondary hypothesis. The Prussian victories at Rezonville, Wörth, and Sedan were unexpected events that reduced the attractiveness of intervention for Italy, Austria-Hungary, and Denmark. King Victor Emmanuel of Italy and Beust, the foreign minister of Austria-Hungary, did not give up on joining the war until after these crushing French defeats. Denmark, too, became less interested in joining though it is likely the Danish government, if not the populace, had already decided against intervention. True, Italy and Austria-Hungary might still have failed to join even if France's military had fared better, but there can be no doubt that the unexpected military defeats greatly reduced the likelihood of intervention. This finding helps to confirm that this work's theory is consistent with prior work on private information and the likelihood of conflict.

Still, it is somewhat striking that no one bandwagoned with Prussia and its German allies to pick up spoils from a defeated France. The mystery is easily resolved, however, when it becomes apparent that France's neighbors were neither desirous of acquiring French territory nor in a position to do so. Britain had no desire to make France's defeat any worse than it already was. Aiding Prussia would simply further unbalance the power alignments on the Continent. Belgium, though no friend of France at this stage in history, certainly was not going to seek spoils at the risk of antagonizing its British protector. Spain was in no position to do anything as it was still disorganized from the overthrow of Isabel II in 1868. Remember Spain's internal problems had been instrumental in causing the war in the first place. The Swiss were committed to their policy of neutrality. Only the Italians really were in a position to bandwagon with Prussia. France held both Nice and Savoy, territories that had been Italian only a decade before. Yet, Italy never considered aiding Prussia as the Italian government was still smarting over Bismarck's ending the Six Week's War before Italy could pick up all of the spoils it wanted to acquire from Austria. Additionally, during the war Italy was busy occupying the Patrimonium as it was now defenseless. Necessity had caused the French had pulled their troops out to aid in the war against Prussia. If this was not enough, Prussia did not want allies—other than the minor German states—as active belligerents. Bismarck had made sure to keep Russia on the sidelines so that the war remained as controllable as possible. If states entered to pick up spoils from France, other states might come to France's aid. Even barring that, Bismarck would have a harder time creating a peace that served exclusively German interests. Thus, the German states never sought additional aid and no states were both capable and eager to help the German cause. For these reasons, the unexpected events discouraged rather than encouraged bandwagoning.

The actions of other non-belligerents also played an important role in lowering the likelihood of intervention. Fear of Russia clearly played a major role in deterring Habsburg intervention. This was the main reason Andrássy and his fellow Hungarians opposed joining the war. The Austro-Hungarian army was outclassed by the Russian army in both size and quality. This was a significant deterrent. Denmark, too, was deterred by the Russians. Russia, as well as Britain, had warned Denmark against entering the war. A small nation such as Denmark could ill afford to risk a war with either power while it was simultaneously engaged with Prussia. Britain also tried to discourage the entry of Italy and Austria-Hungary, but it is not clear that this had much effect as British military action against either country was not plausible, nor was it actually threatened. The threat of Russia, however, clearly played a major role in keeping Denmark and Austria-Hungary out of the Franco-Prussian war.

This ability of non-belligerents to deter other states from joining is consistent with the logic that underpins the theory advanced herein. Just as non-belligerents have tacit agreements with the belligerents to remain out of the fighting, non-belligerents have tacit agreements with each other. On the same line, just as the actions of a belligerent can affect and even destroy its tacit agreement to remain at peace with another non-belligerent, the decision of a non-belligerent to join can destroy its tacit agreement with another non-belligerent. Because of this, non-belligerents may refrain from taking certain actions that would cause their agreements with other non-belligerents to break down, just as a belligerent may refrain from certain actions in order to avoid intervention. Thus, other non-belligerents may deter non-belligerents from joining a war.

The fourth reason the Franco-Prussian War did not expand is that the long-run Prussian threat to the balance of power was not yet evident. Looking back, it seems clear that Britain, Russia, or some other non-belligerent should have intervened and prevented the creation of the Second Reich. This would have prevented a united Germany from becoming the threat it was on the eve of the First World War. This is clear, however, only in hindsight. In 1870, much of Germany had yet to industrialize. It was not close to being the equal of the combined forces of Russia and France. It had no navy and its army was smaller than Russia's. Prussia was allied with Russia and had reasonably good relations with Britain. Also, Britain had favored the unification of Germany, though preferably by peaceful means. Moreover, at the beginning of the war, both Russia and Britain expected France to win. Thus, there seemed little to fear from Prussia.

Fifth, even after Prussia's military might became apparent, Bismarck took steps to make sure Prussia did not overly alarm Russia or Britain. As these states had expected a French victory, it certainly was possible that they would be alarmed by a crushing French defeat and come to France's aid to balance against Prussia. This seemed especially likely of Britain, as Russia was Prussia's ally and unlikely to be troubled by the German triumph. In light of this danger, Bismarck pressed Moltke to finish the war as quickly as possible and tried to negotiate with the French. He even agreed to a preliminary conference sponsored by the league of neutrals. Most importantly, Bismarck did his best to limit Prussian war aims. Though he did seek the annexation of Alsace-Lorraine—in large part at the military's behest—Prussian territorial demands were in line with and perhaps even smaller than the scale of territorial demands that Napoleon would have presented to Bismarck had France triumphed. The European powers knew Napoleon would have sought large annexations along the Rhine in the event of a French victory. Thus, the Prussian demands appeared limited and appealed to a sense of fairness among some of the British statesmen and portions of the British public. Also, the territories Bismarck asked for had at least a partial German ethnic makeup. Seen in light of the likely French demands of predominantly ethnic German territories had the situation been reversed, the Prussian annexation of only Alsace-Lorraine, which though traumatic to the French, was considered reasonable by the non-belligerent powers. This, combined with the fact Prussia had not annexed any of Austria's territory after the Six Week War, made Prussia appear less threatening. On the whole, Prussia's territorial acquisitions after winning two major wars against great powers appeared quite restrained in an era where important territorial adjustments after a war were still the norm. Bismarck never would have taken these steps to limit annexations and press Moltke to conclude the war as speedily as possible if not for the danger of intervention. The potential of intervention caused Bismarck to make sure Prussia did not appear threatening, thereby reducing the likelihood states would enter on France's side.

Additionally, much of the French defeat could be blamed on poor generalship and French reliance upon a relatively small professional army rather than upon a large conscript army. These were weaknesses the French would be sure to correct, and in fact did correct, in the coming years. Finally, the new German Empire could at that point credibly commit to not using its new found dominance on the continent against either Britain or Russia. Bismarck had no quarrel with either power and sought to maintain relations with both states. The empire of Wilhelm I was not the empire of Wilhelm II in intentions or capabilities. Thus, on the whole Prussia did not appear to be the threat to the balance of power that it in fact was because much of its growth was in the future. It appeared to be a status quo power—and was one until Bismarck's dismissal in 1890—and France appeared capable of considerable internal balancing.

The sixth and final reason intervention did not occur was that Austria-Hungary, Italy, and to a lesser degree Denmark faced considerable internal constraints. Both Austria-Hungary and Italy were in financial difficulty and had weak, disorganized armies. All three states' militaries had been defeated within the last six years. Austria had been crushed by Prussia in the Six Weeks' War. Denmark's army had been beaten six years previously by the combined forces of Prussia and Austria in the Second Schleswig-Holstein War. Though Italy had been on the victorious side in the Six Weeks War, its forces had been beaten on the field and the sea by Austria's army and navy. Additionally, the Italian public was strongly against joining, especially if the annexation of the Patrimonium was not guaranteed. Even internal civilian armed insurrection was not out of the question. For Italy, war was a great risk domestically without any clear reward. Austria-Hungary, too, faced significant domestic opposition to joining. The Hungarians, German liberals, and many of the Slavs were against the war. The Habsburgs had barely survived the combined uprisings of these groups twenty years before and then only with the help of the Tsar. No such help would be forthcoming this time. The Tsar was allied with Prussia, clearly unfriendly as a result of the Crimean War, and a threat to become an active, hostile belligerent. The Habsburgs could still suppress the

Slavs on their own and it might be possible to ignore the German liberals, though at considerable risk, but the empire could not survive if the partnership with the Hungarians was dissolved. As the Hungarians opposed intervention, the Habsburgs had little choice but to concur. Clearly, domestic constraints significantly lowered the likelihood of both Italian and Austro-Hungarian intervention, while Denmark's military weakness meant it would join only if a French victory appeared likely.

The lack of intervention in the Franco-Prussian war is consistent with the theory advanced in this work. The case shows that revealed information does indeed change states' expected utility for joining, in this case making it less attractive. It also shows that states must and do take into the account the likely actions of third parties. The Prussians tried to avoid angering Britain in order to discourage British interference, while Denmark and Austria-Hungary failed to enter the war, in large part, because they feared Russia's reaction. Finally, the case also shows that domestic constraints can play an important role in determining whether or not intervention occurs. Thus, this case both helps confirm the work's main theoretical arguments and fleshes out the lesser hypotheses as well.

Chapter 7
Joining Since 1945: Balancing, Bandwagoning, and the Changing Nature of Spoils

> The Allies gave us help neither out of compassion for our people, nor out of respect for our political system … the Allies helped us out of a sober assessment of the situation—Nikita Khrushchev[1]

Since 1945, territory has changed hands far less frequently as a result of interstate wars than in preceding periods (Fazal 2007; Zacher 2001). This has implications for states' decisions about whether or not to join ongoing wars. In general, states join ongoing wars to prevent friendly states from losing territory—in other words balancing—or bandwagoning with the hope of being rewarded by the victorious coalition. As was shown in the earlier cases, prior to 1945, such rewards usually came in the form of territorial spoils. However since territory now rarely changes hands, something else must have motivated the late joiners in the three interstate wars in the post 1945 period that experienced intervention: the Korean War, the Vietnam War, and the 1990–91 Gulf War. Interestingly, each war began as an attempt to change the territorial status quo. In each case the aggressor was hoping to annex its opponent and would have succeeded if the target state had not received outside aid—and in the case of Vietnam, succeeded despite outside aid.[2] Thus, states may still seek territorial gains and attempt to prevent others from obtaining such gains. Certainly, the states which engaged in balancing in these three wars—the US and several of its allies—wanted to stop states from altering the territorial status quo. Thus, territory still plays a role in balancing, as states often act to uphold the territorial status quo.

Balancing, however, seem unlikely to have motivated the smaller states which joined the US and its larger allies in these wars. These states often sent very small

1 Starr 1972, 53.

2 The aggressors used the notion of reunification to attempt to get around the norm of territorial integrity. Saddam Hussein's claim that Kuwait was historically the 19th province of Iraq was by far the least compelling of these claims. This may help explain the widespread condemnation of his invasion. Certainly, his formal annexation of Kuwait based on appeals for such a move by transparent Kuwaiti puppet groups led to an immediate strong condemnation of the action in UN Security Council Resolution 662, which was backed fifteen to zero, and thus included rare yes votes by both Cuba and Yemen (Time Books 1992, 102).

contingents which could not really alter the course of the war. While it is possible that such states were still motivated by balancing concerns and felt that even limited contributions were better than none, likely many had other motivations. In the previous cases, though some small states engaged in balancing, most joined wars in an attempt to bandwagon with the winning side and pick up territorial spoils.[3] As mentioned above, such spoils have been generally unavailable in the post-1945 system. Even though the growing norm of territorial integrity is certainly not absolute, territorial spoils have generally been unavailable in the wars with late joining for two reasons beyond the norm. First, all of the small bandwagoning states in the post-1945 era have joined the side that was attempting to preserve the territorial status quo. Second, many of the bandwagoners were geographically removed from the conflict, making it impossible for them acquire territory even if it had been available. What sort of rewards are such states pursuing in the post-1945 era?

They are still pursuing spoils, but not territory. Bandwagoners may seek increased development aid, military aid, or a better relationship with a powerful state. Such an improved relationship could take the form of a new or strengthened military alliance or other diplomatic help. Additionally, states may bandwagon with a powerful state simply to avoid becoming a target of that state.[4] What is distinct about these benefits is they are not directly tied to the outcome of the war itself. A state which is rewarded financially receives that benefit regardless of the military outcome of the war. Additionally, states seeking better relations with a great power will likely retain the great power's good will regardless of who wins the war. The only concern for such bandwagoners, beyond the direct costs of the war, would be a severe defeat that would prevent their ally from providing significant aid—financial, diplomatic, or military—to the bandwagoning state. This was not a concern in the three interstate wars that experienced late joining in the post-1945 period. None of these wars threatened to significantly reduce the US's ability to provide aid.[5] Even in Vietnam, where the US experienced a clear defeat, the US's power potential was not seriously affected, though the US public's tolerance of military action was certainly reduced. Thus, as long as the minor

3 Sardinian participation in the Crimean War was an exception. Sardinia sought a seat at the peace conference so that it could raise the issue of Italian unity. Of course, this could be seen as seeking territorial spoils, albeit ones not directly connected to the outcome of the war at hand.

4 Walt 1985.

5 In large part, this is because the likelihood the Gulf or Vietnam War would become general was low. While Korea could have expanded into a full scale East / West conflict, such a war would have directly threatened the US's small allies regardless of their participation in the Korean War.

states allied with the US were not seeking direct combat assistance from the US, they had little reason to worry about the US's ability to aid them.[6]

This is significant because it means such bandwagoners need to be far less concerned about the course of the war they are considering joining than bandwagoners seeking territorial spoils. The latter have to closely monitor battlefield events to ensure that they are joining the winning side and are joining early enough for their contributions to be valuable enough to be rewarded. This is why traditional bandwagoners, as well as balancers, are very sensitive to revealed information about the course of the war they are considering joining. Bandwagoners not seeking territory, however, need not have such concerns as the rewards they are seeking are not tied to the war's outcome. Certainly, bandwagoners will still be concerned about their costs, such as casualties, which are of course related to the war, but otherwise such joiners only need to ensure their contributions will be rewarded. Indeed, potential joiners can limit their costs by specifying a limit to their troop deployments in size, geographic scope, and time duration. Such methods of cost control and ensuring rewards require close attention to the negotiations with their prospective allies, but not to the war itself. For this reason, their decisions to join are much less likely to be driven by unexpected battlefield events. The decisions of balancers, and of bandwagoners seeking territorial spoils, should still be driven by concerns about the relative balance of forces and battlefield surprises.

This chapter will look at two of the post-1945 wars which experienced joining: Vietnam and the Gulf War. The former was fought during the Cold War for the purposes of national unification, while the latter was fought in a period of unipolarity, under the auspices of a UN mandate, and in response to naked aggression. The two wars are fairly different from each other in nature; therefore, if patterns of joining emerge they should be indicative of the post-1945 era rather than due to something specific to these wars.

The Vietnam War

Vietnam is somewhat of an awkward case for looking at the spread of interstate war as it is not considered an interstate war by COW until after the US escalated its involvement in February of 1965. Thus, technically the US is not a late joiner. Even disregarding COW's point of view, it is difficult to determine if Vietnam should be seen as a civil war with outside participants or a multilateral interstate war. These concerns noted, it seems worthwhile to examine how outside powers became involved in Vietnam, especially those that joined after the war became

6 And even in the immediate post-Vietnam period, it is likely the US would have come to the military aid of many of its allies in the event they were attacked by allies of the Soviet Union. For example, it is extremely difficult to believe that the US would have allowed the Korean peninsula to be overrun unopposed.

internationalized, and if the process differs from that which led to involvement in earlier wars.

Outside powers took one of two paths to involvement in Vietnam. First, the US, as well as Australia,[7] became engaged because of concerns about the stability of the South Vietnamese regime and entered out of traditional balancing reasons. For the most part, the US' entry was dictated by events within South Vietnam. Second, Thailand, the Philippines, and South Korea all saw the war as an opportunity to extract concessions from the US in return for providing military support. They were bandwagoning for non-territorial spoils, and thus their decisions to join were largely independent of events in South Vietnam.

The Balancers

While the story of the US's involvement in Vietnam is well known, it is worth reviewing here in light of its relationship to revealed information. The US slowly became more involved in Vietnam in the 1950s and early 1960s. Thus, unlike joiners in earlier wars, it is difficult to point to one event which triggered their involvement. An in depth case on US involvement in the war might be able to show that each move deeper into the conflict occurred as a result of setbacks to the South Vietnamese government. Such a full examination is not possible here. Instead the section will focus on the decision to internationalize the war and attack targets inside North Vietnam using land based air power beginning on 7 February 1965.[8]

US concern about the spread of communism in Southeast Asia grew steadily over the course of 1964 due to increasing governmental instability in South Vietnam and higher levels of communist infiltration. By autumn, South Vietnam's military losses for 1964 were already more than double their 1963 totals, mutiny had broken out in small sections of the army, and the Vietnamese government was rocked by a series of leadership changes, coups, and failed counter-coups all instigated by or aimed at removing from power General Nguyen Khanh.[9] Eventually, the US came to the conclusion that without the introduction of US forces, South Vietnam would collapse. This conclusion was strongly influenced by three events in late 1964 and early 1965 which caught the US off-guard: yet another and further reaching coup by Khanh on 20 December; the South's defeat at Binh Gia from 28 December to 4 January; and the attack on South Vietnamese and US bases by the Viet Cong, especially Pleiku, on 6 February.

---

7 Australia joined for largely the same reason as the US: concern about the spread of communism in SE Asia. The Australians actually wanted to intervene before the US did but, due to a lack of capabilities, could not until the US joined. Thus, the same events which triggered US intervention triggered Australia's intervention.

8 COW uses this date as the starting date for the interstate war.

9 Barclay 1988, 62–3.

It is clear that the first of these events surprised the US. While Ambassador Maxwell Taylor had been warning Washington in regular cables about the growing Buddhist opposition to Prime Minister Tran Van Huong, he did not expect the military to anticipate the Buddhists by preemptively getting rid of much of the civilian government. On 20 December, the military, backed by Khanh, dissolved the civilian run High National Council, essentially terminating civil control of the government. While Huong lingered on until late January, he was essentially powerless, and though Khanh did not officially assume power, over the next month he solidified himself as the power behind the military dominated government. Meanwhile Saigon was plunged into what Taylor called, "another first-class governmental crisis."[10] The coup was troublesome for several reasons. First, Khanh had displayed anti-US and neutralist tendencies in the past raising concerns that he might seek accommodation with the North. Second, the coup caused the already dismal morale in the South to sink even lower. Third, the conflict between Khanh and the civilians paralyzed the government and anti-guerilla operations, resulting in communist successes.

One such success was particularly notable. Staring on 28 December, South Vietnamese forces were heavily beaten at Binh Gia over the course of eight days. The US had not expected such a severe military defeat. As recently as 3 December, Assistant Secretary of State William Bundy, while acknowledging the deteriorating situation in South Vietnam, had told the British Foreign Minister and New Zealand Ambassador that there was "little likelihood [of] really major VC military successes at least in [the] next two months or so."[11] Chairman of the Joint Chiefs, General Earl Wheeler, and Bundy, along with other high ranking Defense, State, CIA, and NSC officials, felt Binh Gia might signal an escalation on the part of the Viet Cong.[12] General Westmoreland saw it as "the beginning of an intensive military challenge which the Vietnamese government could not meet within its own resources" and even Bundy conceded that "the situation in Vietnam is now likely to come apart more rapidly than we had anticipated in November."[13] This, combined with the political crisis and the sinking morale in Saigon, brought into doubt whether Saigon could win without far more help. President Lyndon Johnson apparently was beginning to be open to the idea of introducing significantly more US forces to Vietnam, though he tended to favor ground forces over air power. In a 30 December telegram to Taylor, he wrote:

10 United States Department of State 1964, 1031.

11 Barclay 1988, 70.

12 United States Department of State 1965, 9. In their discussion, they cited the new equipment, such as steel helmets, that Viet Cong troops were using.

13 Barclay 1988, 78–9.

> Every time I get a military recommendation it seems to me that it calls for large-scale bombing. I have never felt that this war will be won from the air, and it seems to me that what is much more needed and would be more effective is a larger and stronger use of Rangers and Special Forces and Marines, or other appropriate military strength on the ground and on the scene. I am ready to look with great favor on that kind of increased American effort.

He added,

> I am not saying that all this has to be done before there can be any [air] reprisals.[14]

With the president in this state of mind, all that was required was a united push by his top advisors in favor of the robust use of American military might. As the situation continued to deteriorate in early 1965, this began to happen. In a series of telegrams on 6 January 1965 Taylor made the case for greater US involvement in Vietnam. Taylor laid out the situation as follows:

> We are faced here with a seriously deteriorating situation characterized by continued political turmoil, irresponsibility and division within the armed forces, lethargy in the pacification program, some anti-US feeling which could grow, signs of mounting terrorism by VC directly at US personnel and deepening discouragement and loss of morale throughout SVN. Unless these conditions are changed and trends reversed, we are likely soon to face a number of unpleasant developments … [leading to the] installation of a hostile govt which will ask us to leave while it seeks accommodation with the National Liberation Front and Hanoi.[15]

Taylor went on to speak about the increases in Viet Cong infiltrations and the inability of the South Vietnamese government to provide the necessary manpower to win the guerilla war. While Taylor did not favor the immediate introduction of ground troops, he did present some scenarios for the introduction of 20,000 to 75,000 US troops. Mainly, he argued that limited steps such as adding additional advisors would be of little help and that the best step that the US could take at this time were retaliatory airstrikes into North Vietnam.[16]

These telegrams formed the basis for a serious discussion that day at the White House which determined that air reprisals were likely necessary.[17] While the decision was not immediately acted on, the reasons Taylor listed were to form the

14 United States Department of State 1964, 1058–9.
15 United States Department of State 1965, 13.
16 Ibid, 14–30.
17 Ibid, 39.

basis for US action a month later. William Bundy's response upon reading Taylor's telegrams was typical:

> I think we must accept that Saigon morale in all quarters is now very shaky indeed, and this relates directly to a widespread feeling that the US is not ready for stronger action and indeed is possibly looking for a way out ... We have not been able to assess the overall impact of the continuing political crises and of the Bihn [sic] Gia military defeat, but there are already ample indications that they have had a sharp discouraging effect in the last two weeks.[18]

Thus, American officials felt that without US military action, the South was likely to concede to the North or be overwhelmed. If nothing else, it was obvious the war effort lacked clear, strong direction and that events on the ground were trending strongly toward the communists.

These concerns only increased when in late January Khanh completed his creeping bloodless coup and ousted Huong. McGeorge Bundy, the National Security Advisor, was now convinced South Vietnam would lose without a major increase in US aid. In speaking for himself and McNamara, On 27 January, Bundy advised Johnson to take military action to shore up the situation in Vietnam. He said,

> [B]oth of us are pretty well convinced that our current policy can lead only to disastrous defeat ... Bob and I are persuaded that there is no real hope of success in this area unless and until our policy and priorities change.[19]

Bundy went on to say that unless the US used its military assets to "force a change of Communist policy", that the situation in Vietnam would "lead to defeat and an invitation to get out in humiliating circumstances."[20] In this environment Taylor, Bundy, McNamara all weighed various options for increased US aid. Little was decided, but the ground work for a response was laid. While ground troops were discussed, air strikes were the quickest way to give aid and respond to communist actions. In fact, formal options for greater military involvement in Vietnam had been available since late December. They had been drawn up in response to an attack at Bien Hoa in September.[21] When US and South Vietnamese bases were attacked at Pleiku on 6 February, attacks which Wheeler described as "a surprise",

18 Burstall 1993, 22.

19 United States Department of State 1965, 95.

20 Ibid, 96. Bundy argued that the only other course of action was the removal of US military assets, combined with negotiations and essentially capitulation to the communists in Vietnam. He did point out that Rusk, who agreed with the grim assessment of the situation in Vietnam, believed that continuing the current policy was the best option.

21 Pemberton 1987, 249. These options were not formalized until late November.

Johnson decided in was time to act.[22] Johnson told his advisors "I want three things. I want a joint attack. I want it to be prompt. I want it to be appropriate."[23] He forthwith authorized the launching airstrikes into North Vietnam for the next day which internationalized the war. Thus, the US joined out of traditional balancing motives and made its decision based on information about the South's capacity as revealed by military and political events.

The Bandwagoners

Thailand, the Philippines, and South Korea all choose to bandwagon with the US in return for non-territorial spoils as a result of Johnson's More Flags policy.[24] The policy aimed to make US efforts in Vietnam appear less Western or imperialist by obtaining the support of Asian states.[25] Enhancing the combat ability of the forces in Vietnam and reducing direct US costs were always secondary concerns. This focus by the US on getting foreign forces deployed to South Vietnam, rather than enhancing the military capabilities of the non-communist forces, shaped the negotiations with its potential allies. Additionally, while all three of the states were staunchly anti-communist, none went to war mainly for fighting communism as all had serious communist threats closer to home. Thailand and the Philippines faced communist guerilla insurgencies of their own and South Korea had North Korea sitting just across its border.

Thailand's main motive for intervening in Vietnam was acquiring US aid to modernize the Thai military. The Thai government was worried about domestic insurgents, not the communist threat from North Vietnam. US aid would strengthen the Thai government at home. This focus on domestic threats was in part a result of the government's instability in the 1960s and early 1970s.[26] Even in the realm of external threats, North Vietnam was not the top concern. Though the Thai government was staunchly anti-communist, it saw China as a much larger external threat than communist Vietnam.[27]

In late 1966, the Thai government decided to become far more involved in Vietnam. Despite government proclamations that Thailand was joining for the purposes of containing the spread of communism, the record of the negotiations

22 United States Department of State 1965, 153–6.

23 Barclay 1988, 85.

24 Cambodia also joined the war, though as the result of a right wing coup. The new government needed US support for domestic reasons and the easiest way to secure this support was joining the war. Thus, Cambodia bandwagoned for spoils not connected to the war.

25 Larsen and Collins 1975, 7 and 25. Taiwan was also interested in sending troops, but concern that Taiwanese involvement would cause China to join led to Taiwan's offer being turned down. South Vietnamese xenophobia towards ethnic Chinese also played a role.

26 Blackburn 1994, 103.

27 Ibid, 115.

suggests the Thais saw their contributions primarily as a way to strengthen their own military, rather than as a way to help South Vietnam win its war. Beyond soldiers, Thailand wanted to minimize its contributions to the conflict in terms of money and equipment. The idea was to profit from the involvement and exit the war with a better equipped military than it entered with. Essentially, the Thai government wanted to exploit the US's desire to obtain foreign contributions to greatly increase US military aid to Thailand. The list of concessions the Thais were able to extract was significant. In February 1967, the US ambassador summarized them as follows:

> Fully equip and provide logistical support for the forces going to South Vietnam. The equipment would be retained by the Royal Thai government upon final withdrawal of Thai forces from South Vietnam.
>
> Assume the cost of overseas allowance at the rates now paid by the US government to the Royal Thai Army volunteer Regiment in South Vietnam.
>
> Provide equipment and consumables for rotational training in an amount sufficient to meet the agreed requirements of forces in training for deployment; and undertake the repair and rehabilitation of facilities required for such rotational training. The equipment would be retained by the Royal Thai government following the final withdrawal of Thai forces from South Vietnam.
>
> Assume additional costs associated with the preparation, training, maintenance, equipment transportation, supply and mustering out of the additional forces to be sent to South Vietnam.
>
> Assist in maintaining the capability and in accelerating the modernization of the Royal Thai armed forces—including the additional helicopters and other key items—as well as increase to $75 million both the Military Assistance Program for fiscal year 1968 and the program planning for 1969.
>
> Deploy *to Thailand* a Hawk battery manned by US personnel to participate in the training of Thai troops to man the battery. Provide the Thai government with equipment for the battery and assume certain costs associated with the battery's deployment.[28]

In essence the US paid the full economic cost of the Thai deployment including doubling the salaries of the deployed soldiers, increased the already large Military Assistance Program (MAP) by $30 million to a total of $115 million a year for both 1968 and 1969, and sent equipment including antiaircraft artillery to Thailand

28 Larsen and Collins 1975, 37. Emphasis added.

which was not even intended to be used in Vietnam.[29] US material support for the Thai contribution went as far as providing the rifles the Thais would use and contributing ships for a small Thai naval contingent.

It might be argued that such US support was simply necessary to allow the Thais to participate effectively in fighting the Viet Cong and North Vietnamese forces; however, the way in which the Thai government wanted to use these resources dispels this notion. The Thais proposed the naval mission simply so that they could obtain ships from the US which could be later used to counter a domestic sea-born insurgency threat.[30] Even more telling is that the Thais wanted to use these newly equipped forces to fight insurgents in northeastern Thailand rather than in Vietnam, though the US overruled this plan in the summer of 1967.[31] When in the fall of 1967 the Thai government agreed to supply an additional 10,000 troops by the next summer, the motive was mainly to expand the Thai military as cheaply as possible, rather than any concern with events in Vietnam.[32] The US clearly understood that that Thais were simply after aid and made it clear the US expected a quid pro quo of troop deployments in return for US aid. The US felt that the lower level of US casualties and the improved international image this brought was worth the cost and the Thais felt the increased internal security the aid allowed them to achieve was worth the costs in lives.

Philippine involvement in Vietnam was driven by similar motives. The Philippine government, under Presidents Diosdado Macapagal and Ferdinand Marcos, hoped to get increased aid from the US in return for sending troops to Vietnam. Much like Thailand, the Philippine government succeeded in extracting aid from the US in return for troop contributions. The level of contributions, however, was always much smaller, in large part because of weak domestic support for such deployments.

The Philippine government initiated the talks over increased involvement in Vietnam out of hopes of obtaining additional US aid. In late 1964, Macapagal broached the idea of increasing Philippine aid to US forces in Vietnam above its current level of 16 advisors. In return, Macapagal hoped to get an increase in its MAP so that the Philippines could counter the then perceived threat from Indonesia.[33] From the start, US negotiators realized the main Philippine concern was not the situation in Vietnam, but rather how much aid they would receive. The US ambassador cabled Washington during the early stages of negotiations:

29 Blackburn 1994, 111.

30 Larsen and Collins 1975, 30.

31 Ibid, 32.

32 Ibid, 36–42.

33 Ibid, 53.

> Inevitable question which US would have to face in raising question with [the government of the Philippines] is whether US would be willing to finance all or part of such effort. GOP has capacity to finance the effort. Believe we should initially indicate that we expect them to do so. Further insistence on this point would depend upon degree of importance US attaches to Phil presence in RVN.[34]

Despite the ambassador's preference, the US was most willing to pay for Philippine aid. The US State Department telegrammed its embassy in Manila that, "In order to enhance possibility of maximum Philippine contributions … be prepared to add supplemental inducements."[35] Additionally, in November of 1964 General Wheeler, telegrammed, "[I]f necessary in order to secure meaningful and substantial third country aid to Viet Nam, we are prepared to pay entire bill."[36] The main sticking point in the negotiations was how large the per diems the US would pay to Philippine personnel serving in Vietnam.[37] Whether and how the Philippine forces would make a significant contribution to the war effort was not a point of concern.

In the end, the initiative failed to result in significant action during the Macapagal administration not because of unwillingness on the part of the US to pay, but rather for reasons of Philippine domestic politics. First, the US was unwilling to increase aid unless the Philippine government increased its own military spending, which was not popular in the Philippine Congress. Second, the Philippine government did not want to contribute troops until other Asian nations did. Third, and perhaps most significant, the deployment of troops to Vietnam was unpopular in both the Philippine Congress and among the public at large.[38] Because of this, even though Macapagal and the US negotiators were able to agree on the Philippines sending rough 2,000 engineers to Vietnam in return for \$9.13 million in US aid a year, Macapagal declined to submit the proposal to the Philippine Congress until after the elections.[39] Marcos took advantage of this sentiment to defeat Macapagal in the 1965 presidential elections.

Once president, however, Marcos' position shifted. Like Macapagal, Marcos wanted to acquire US aid. Additionally, he was staunchly anticommunist. Like the Thai government, Marcos wanted to extract the maximum amount of aid from the US. Due to concerns about public opinion, however, he did not want to appear to be bought. On negotiations with Marcos regarding the sending of troops to Vietnam, the US ambassador to the Philippines reported to the State Department:

---

34 Blackburn 1994, 69.

35 Ibid, 71.

36 Ibid, 77–8.

37 Ibid, 77–8.

38 Larsen and Collins 1975, 53–4.

39 Blackburn 1994, 80–3.

> Marcos takes the position that he does not RPT not want the terms of our delivery with him to be revealed. … As usual, we have the ambivalent Phil attitude of not wanting to appear to be bought, but at the same time wanting something they can show their people.[40]

These negotiations proved successful and in mid 1966 an armed engineering task force was sent to work on development and engineering projects in South Vietnam. In return, the Philippines got M14s, river patrol boats, and engineering equipment on top of larger naval vessels which had been previously promised to the Philippines. The US also paid $36 million to directly support the deployment of the action force as well as providing the necessary logistical support. Additionally, US donations to the Philippines of F-5s and helicopters for use *in the Philippines* was discussed at various points, but never actually implemented.[41] Marcos was also able to obtain additional economic concessions later in the summer of 1966, including a $45 million cash grant, as a direct result of the deployment.[42]

Thus, like Thailand, the Philippines were able to extract significant financial and military aid concessions from the US in return for sending troops to Vietnam. Additionally, Philippine involvement was not triggered by events within the war, but rather by the fact the Philippine government saw an opening to approach the US about more aid in return for the diplomatic cover a Philippine deployment to Vietnam would provide US policy. Similar motives drove the South Korean government to become involved in Vietnam.

Outside of the US, South Korea provided one of the largest and most effective allied contributions to the South Vietnamese war effort. South Korea had expressed interest in sending aid as early as 1954, but did not act until the mid 1960s. It was the Korean government, rather than the US, that broached the idea of deploying a division to Vietnam. Korean interest was not triggered by the situation in Vietnam, but rather by the possibility that the US would be willing to pay for the deployment and provide logistics.[43] By early 1965, South Korea had 2,000 plus non-combat engineers and medical personnel in the country as part of a "Dove Unit" which was paid for indirectly by US increases in Korea's MAP and the Food for Peace program.[44] In May 1965, the Korean government began considering sending a division of combat troops to South Vietnam. Publically, balancing motives were given. As President Park Chung-hee later said,

40 Ibid, 92.

41 Larsen and Collins 1975, 55–7 and 65–6.

42 Blackburn 1994, 87–8.

43 Ibid, 33–4; Park 1981,101.

44 Blackburn 1994, 40–1; Larsen and Collins 1975, 120–2

> We felt that keeping Vietnam secure from Communism was closely related to Korea's security. This dispatch of out troops would encourage the people of Vietnam in their struggle against Communism. It was a way of repaying those 16 free nations which came to our military aid during the Korean War.[45]

There can be no doubt that South Korea was staunchly anti-communist and favored a South Vietnamese victory. Additionally such a deployment, South Korea's first outside of the Korean peninsula, would be a source of pride for South Korea showing that South Korea had been successfully rebuilt following the Korean War.[46] In part because of prestige concerns, the balancing and repaying of moral debts arguments were advanced to hide more immediate motives. Much like Thailand and the Philippines, South Korea hoped to use the deployment as a way to obtain military aid.

This is evident from the initial demands the Korean government made on the US. General Dwight Beach who was involved in the negotiations with the Korean government six years later described their initial demands as follows:

> The initial Korean bill (wish-list) was fantastic. Basically, the ROK wanted their troops to receive the same pay as the Americans, all new US equipment for deploying troops and modernization of the entire ROK Army, Navy and Air Force. I told them with the Ambassador's concurrence that their bill was completely unreasonable and there was no chance whatever of the US agreeing to it. The final compromise included a very substantial increase in pay for the troops deployed, as much good equipment as we could then furnish and a US commitment that no US troops would be withdrawn from Korea without prior consultation with the ROK.[47]

Of particular concern to the Koreans was that the US not suspended its MAP and that the Vietnam War would not result in the US weakening its commitment to defending the Korean peninsula.[48] These conditions were essentially met. Including the $7 million increase to MAP and overseas allowances to Korean troops, the US spent roughly $43 million to keep the Korean division in Vietnam, plus $150 million in development loans, offered technical and development assistance, and guaranteed that it would not withdraw troops from South Korea without prior consultation.[49] Much of this expense was in the form of providing logistical support, replacing Korean equipment lost in combat, and modernizing Korean forces *in Korea*.

45 Blackburn 1994, 46.
46 Larsen and Collins 1975, 133–5 and 141.
47 Ibid, 125.
48 Ibid, 124.
49 Blackburn 1994, 43–5 and 50–1; Larsen and Collins 1975, 127–9; Park 1981, 90.

The Korean government also believed the deployment would strengthen the US-Korean alliance. President Park argued directly in the National Assembly that deploying troops was important to maintaining US goodwill.[50] The South Koreans were particularly concerned that the US might weaken the defense of the Korean peninsula to prosecute the war in Vietnam as the US had suggested it might redeploy two divisions to Vietnam.[51] Given that the US alliance was at the core of Korean defense calculations, maintaining the US alliance was a major concern. If the alliance could be maintained by deploying Korean troops, it was worth the cost. Concerns about events in Vietnam were never central and South Vietnamese officials opposed the deployment of the Korean troops.[52]

Over the course of 1966, the US attempted to get Korea to send a second division to Vietnam, but without success. The Koreans were no longer worried about further strengthening their relationship with the US and economic concerns became the entire sticking point.[53] The US offered significant concessions including equipping and financing units to replace those sent to Vietnam, completely equipping and paying for the division to be deployed, modernizing 18 additional divisions which were to remain *in Korea*, suspending scheduled MAP reductions, and providing $165 million in economic loans.[54] These offers and similar ones through the summer of 1967 were enough to sway President Park in favor of sending a second division, but they could not overcome opposition in the National Assembly.[55]

Over the course of the war, the US spent roughly $927 million to maintain Korean troops in Vietnam, plus $750 million in development loans and military procurement.[56] Lest it be thought that South Korea simply sought compensation to offset its costs, it should be noted that a Korean soldier in Vietnam was paid nearly as much per day as the same soldier received in an entire month when stationed at home.[57] Vietnam associated earnings accounted for 16% of all of South Korea's foreign receipts from 1965 to 1969 and from 1965 to 1973 added a $1 billion boost to the South Korean economy.[58] These revenues significantly aided Korean economic development, especially since at the time South Korea was faced with a capital shortage.[59] Thus, like Thailand and the Philippines, the Korean government was motivated by the possibility of receiving aid from the US, rather than out of concern for the situation in South Vietnam. This is not to say any of these governments were opposed to the US actions in Vietnam. They were not. All were

50 Park 1981, 89.
51 Ibid, 92 and 102.
52 Blackburn 1994, 38 and 53.
53 Ibid, 54.
54 Ibid, 56–7.
55 Ibid, 59–63.
56 Ibid, 64.
57 Ibid, 64–5.
58 Park 1981, 113.
59 Ibid, 113.

staunchly anti-communist, but faced communist threats far closer to home. All three governments saw the war in Vietnam as a way to obtain significant aid which would allow them to face those threats at home rather than as a way to defeat communism abroad. Additionally, the rewards they sought for bandwagoning with the US were not dependent on the outcome of the war in Vietnam. They would receive the aid regardless of whether or not South Vietnam survived. Thus, events on the battlefield in Vietnam played little or no role in their decisions to deploy troops.

The Gulf War (1990–91)

The Gulf War spread from a bilateral conflict between Iraq and Kuwait into a much broader war for a variety of reasons. It arose out of a series of long running disputes over Iraqi debts, the possession of several islands in the Gulf, and Kuwaiti over production and alleged slant drilling of oil.[60] Saddam saw the combination of these actions as crippling Iraq's economy and dignity. Over the course of the summer of 1990, Iraq and Kuwait engaged in a series of negotiations in an attempt to resolve their differences, but made little progress. However, expectations in Kuwait and throughout the region were that the dispute would eventually be resolved diplomatically—perhaps through mediation.

In this frame of mind, reactions to the Iraqi mobilization in late July were subdued. Even though Iraq had mobilized much of its army near the Kuwaiti border, no one seemed to expect war. Instead, the assumption was that Iraq was simply using the mobilization as a way to obtain leverage in the ongoing negotiations, the most recent round of which was being held in Jeddah from 30 July to 1 August. Iraqi officials had directly reassured Hosni Mubarak, King Hussein, and Yasser Arafat that Iraq would not attack Kuwait despite the tensions. These reassurances were passed on to the US.[61] Though the Jeddah conference broke up with little progress having been made, talks were due to resume on 3 August in Baghdad. When, instead, Iraq overran and occupied Kuwait on 2 August, Egypt, Saudi Arabia, the US, and much of the Arab world were shocked.

States joined the war for reasons ranging from pure balancing motives, to hopes to pick up diplomatic rewards, to institutional motives. These wide ranging motives make the war particularly useful for examining the changing nature of spoils and motives for late joining in the post WWII era. While it is impossible to examine the motives of every state which participated in the conflict, especially if very minor or non-military participants are considered, states which typify the various motives behind joining the war can be examined.[62]

---

60 Kaur 1994, 47–8; Time Books 1992, 20–1.

61 Goodman 1992, 2.

62 Two COW-listed participants, Morocco and Italy, are not covered in detail. Morocco shared similar motives to those of Egypt, while Italy shared similar motives to

The Balancers

The shock at the Iraqi invasion led quickly to its condemnation, by countries individually and by institutions such as the UN, Arab League, and the European Community (EC). In the first two days after the invasion, the US froze Iraqi and Kuwait assets, Turkey closed the oil pipeline running through it from Iraq, the USSR proposed a worldwide arms embargo on Iraq, while Japan and the EC states froze assets and began working on sanctions.[63] Action at the UN was equally swift. The Security Council promptly passed Resolution 660 condemning the invasion by a fourteen to zero vote and three days later imposed an economic and military embargo on Iraq thirteen to zero.

In these actions, the US often took the lead in coordinating a response to the Iraqi invasion. Like most states, the US had not expected Iraqi aggression; most US intelligence officials believed the Iraqi mobilization to be a bluff aimed at influencing the ongoing Kuwaiti-Iraqi negotiations.[64] In May, US Central Command (CENTCOM) had determined that, "Iraq is not expected to use military force to attack Kuwait or Saudi Arabia to seize disputed territory or resolve a dispute over oil policy."[65] This view was shared by core Bush administration officials to such an extent that Secretary of Defense Dick Cheney, CIA Director William Webster, and CENTCOM's staff never even discussed the possibility of an Iraqi invasion.[66] The US's main diplomatic energies in the summer of 1990 had been focused on European issues such as German reunification.[67] The State Department's lack of concern over the Iraq-Kuwaiti negotiation was exhibited by its failure to give more forceful instructions to Ambassador April Glaspie, who famously told Saddam in their 25 July meeting that though the US desired a peaceful resolution, the US had "no opinion on Arab-Arab conflict, like your border disagreement with Kuwait."[68] While whether Saddam interpreted this as a green light has been much debated, there is little doubt that if the US had expected Iraq to invade, Glaspie would have issued sterner warnings. As the Iraqi mobilization became more ominous on 1 August, even those few US officials that thought an invasion was now probable

---

those of France. Additionally, members of the Gulf Cooperation Council other than Saudi Arabia are covered as a group rather than individually.

63 Time Books 1992, 38, 55, 58, and 68. For its willingness to impose sanctions on Iraq and allow the US to use its NATO airbases to attack Iraq, Turkey received $1 billion in US aid, $1 billion in World Bank aid, an increase in the number of textiles it could export to the US, and the US endorsed the Turkish application for EC membership. Additionally, Turkey's military was further integrated into NATO's command structure and promised NATO military aid in case of Iraqi retaliation (Brown 1991, 44–5; Khadduri and Ghareeb 1997, 125).

64 Khadduri and Ghareeb 1997, 123–4; Nyang and Hendricks 1995, 79.

65 Gordon and Trainor 1995, 14.

66 Ibid, 4-5 and 14; Swartz 2004, 46.

67 Time Books 1992, 16.

68 Nyang and Hendricks 1995, 63; Time Books 1992, 24–5.

thought it would be limited. General Norman Schwarzkopf, head of CENTCOM, believed the attack would be limited to seizing Bubiyan Island and the Rumaila oil field.[69]

The Saudis shared the Americans' surprise. King Fahd had thought the Jeddah talks were making progress, especially since they were scheduled to resume in Baghdad in just two days.[70] Even after CENTCOM warned that a limited invasion was probable, the Saudis dismissed the US military's warnings and after the invasion occurred, Prince Bandar, the Saudi ambassador to the US, expressed his surprise at the turn of events to his American hosts.[71]

While many states shared their surprise at the Iraqi invasion, the motives that drove them to join this vast coalition varied greatly. The core of the coalition was driven by balancing motives.[72] The US, UK, and the members of the Gulf Cooperation Council (GCC),[73] including Saudi Arabia, all joined to prevent Iraq from dominating the Gulf region and its oil resources. The US was concerned Iraq would continue its offensive into Saudi Arabia or elsewhere in the Gulf. This concern was reinforced by US satellite intelligence showing Iraqi forces continuing to move south toward the Saudi border even though Kuwaiti resistance had collapsed.[74] Additionally, it was clear to US officials that Iraq intended to stay in Kuwait long-term, in part due to inopportune comments made by Saddam to the US *charge d'affaires* that the Sabah family would not be restored to the Kuwaiti throne.[75] Finally, Iraq's naked aggression repulsed President George Bush, a view which his meeting with British Prime Minister Margaret Thatcher, who happened to be with Bush at a conference in Colorado, only reinforced.[76] Within days, the US position had crystallized into one of armed resistance—at least to protect Saudi Arabia. On 5 August, Bush issued his famous "line in the sand" and that the invasion "will not stand" statements and dispatched Cheney to the Gulf to brief the

---

69 Gordon and Trainor 1995, 16–17 and 26. Defense Intelligence Agency and National Intelligence Council officials believed an invasion was likely, but their views were generally dismissed by higher officials, such as Richard Haass, in favor of more plentiful intelligence estimates that suggested an invasion was unlikely.

70 Gordon and Trainor 1995, 19; Nyang and Hendricks 1995, 75.

71 Gordon and Trainor 1995, 28 and 38.

72 Perhaps "balancing" is not quite the right word since the coalition was clearly far stronger than Iraq. For better or worse, however, "balancing" is still the preferred term for the arraying of military power for the purpose of rolling back or containing aggression and that is the sense in which it is used here.

73 The GCC consisted of Saudi Arabia, Kuwait, Bahrain, Qatar, the United Arab Emirates, and Oman.

74 Swartz 2004, 51.

75 Nyang and Hendricks 1995, 92.

76 Gibbons 1992, 2–3. Thatcher also reassured Bush that the French would support actions against Iraq. Throughout the crisis, the US and UK worked very closely and generally presented a unified front.

Saudis on the proposed US military response.[77] It was clear from public comments then and after the war that the US was concerned about the Iraqi threat to the world's oil supply and the precedent the aggression set. Bush and his staff had concluded that military confrontation was the best way to address these concerns. On 12 August, Bush publically expressed his concern about Iraq's "potential domination of the energy resources that are crucial to the entire world."[78] After the war was over, President Bush related his early reactions to the invasion:

> I did feel early on that the aggression by Iraq could not—must not—go unchallenged. The overriding reason for this was the fact that bold and naked aggression could not be permitted to stand. I worried that Saddam's intentions went far beyond taking over Kuwait. With an attack on Saudi Arabia, he would have gained control over a tremendous amount of the world's oil supply. But the bottom line was that aggression could not stand. If permitted to get away with that, heaven knows where the world would have gone and what forces would have been unleashed.[79]

Brent Scowcroft, the US National Security Advisor, mentioned similar concerns after the war. He indicated that the decision to risk war with Iraq was based on, "our key interests in the Persian Gulf which required that under no circumstances could Saddam get control of oil, and on top of that the horror of what Saddam was doing in Kuwait."[80] Additionally, he felt that it would be "far more costly to fight another day. Someone would have to pay the price if Saddam were allowed out of this."[81]

Thatcher was initially even more bellicose than Bush and urged him to take a strong stand. She was outraged by what she saw as Saddam's deception and saw Iraq's aggression as reminiscent of German aggression in the 1930s. Thatcher felt it was important to oppose aggression on principle, though she also saw opposition to Iraq as a way to renew Britain's special relationship with the US which she feared was becoming very close with Germany.[82]

The Saudis also saw Iraq as a threat for many of the same reasons as the US and UK. Among other things, the invasion had broken a forty year Arab tradition of resolving intra-Arab disputes within the existing territorial framework.[83] Letting Iraq erode this tradition was dangerous for the Saudis and all of the GCC states.

---

77 Yetiv 2004, 43.

78 Ibid, 34. Bush made the comment on *This Week with David Brinkley*.

79 Time Books 1992, 48 and 143. Bush also had as a secondary motive making the UN work as he believed it was intended to function—as a collective security body free of great power rivalries.

80 Yetiv 2004, 34.

81 Ibid, 165.

82 Time Books 1992, 61–2; Khadduri and Ghareeb 1997, 124.

83 Brown 1991, 6.

Very little in the way of reassurance was coming out of Baghdad, though given Saddam's previous perfidy any reassurances would have fallen on deaf ears. Within a day of the invasion, Fahd told Bush "[Saddam] seems to think only of himself. He is following Hitler in creating world problems … I believe nothing will work with Saddam but the use of force."[84] Iraqi actions post invasion reinforced Fahd's thinking. On 4 August, an Iraqi envoy hinted at the future annexation of Kuwait saying "[the] branch has been returned to the root."[85] Additionally, right after the occupation of Kuwait, there had been three Iraqi military incursions into Saudi Arabia. The concerned Saudis contacted the Iraqis via a secure military hotline after each incursion. The Iraqi replies were not promising. The first was dismissed as a mistake, the second was being looked into, and after the third incursion the Iraqis did not even bother to answer the hotline.[86] This convinced the Saudis that Iraq was a serious and immediate threat. As King Fahd told the Saudi papers, "We never thought of an Arab state invading another Arab state. Then I realized after Kuwait, it would be the turn of the eastern part of the Kingdom".[87] The Saudis were faced with a basic choice: either attempt to appease Iraq or prepare to resist militarily. Given their lack of sufficient ground forces, Saudi military planning having focused on repelling an Israeli air strike, resistance was not possible without help.

The Saudis' decision to confront Iraq was greatly strengthened by the trip of a US military delegation led by Cheney on 5 August which showed the massive response the US had planned. The Saudis were far more willing to allow US troops on their soil and risk confronting Saddam if the US was fully committed to stopping Iraq. The US offer to send large scale forces fulfilled this requirement and helped swing the Saudis in favor of a strong military response.[88] Interestingly, the US offer to make the coalition a broad based one involving many Arab states did not seem to influence the Saudis. They were far more concerned with whether Iraq actually posed a threat and the degree of US commitment.[89] The Saudis' lack of trust in Saddam and their perception of him as a direct threat were illustrated by the Saudi Minister of Foreign Affairs, Prince Saud-al-Faisal, in a speech to the UN on 17 August:

---

84 Yetiv 2004, 65.

85 Nyang and Hendricks 1995, 79.

86 Ibid, 86–7.

87 Ibid, 108.

88 Fahd was more hawkish than some of his ministers who considered bribing the Iraqis to get them to leave (Yetiv 2004, 35). Fahd may have had made his mind up prior to Cheney's trip, but this is not agreed upon (Khadduri and Ghareeb 1997, 134–5). Likely, Fahd had made his mind up, but Cheney's trip helped him sway the rest of the royal family.

89 Yetiv 2004, 35.

> [M]y government would like to draw the Security Council's attention to the Iraqi President's proposal to the Arab States in February 1981, whereby he undertook not to interfere in internal affairs or to use force for the settlement of disputes. He also assured a number of Arab Heads of State and Ministers for Foreign Affairs ... that he had no intention of using force to solve his dispute with Kuwait. Nevertheless, he neither kept his promises nor honored his vows. At dawn on Thursday, 2 August 1990, he invaded Kuwait and overthrew its legitimate Government ... Not content with this act of defiance, the Iraqi Government proceeded to concentrate large military forces in combat formation near the border between Kuwait and Saudi Arabia, thus demonstrating and proving the Iraqi regime's aggressive intentions towards Saudi Arabia.[90]

Thus, the consistent deceit, threatening military dispositions, and hostile rhetoric of the Iraqis, combined with US offers of help, convinced the Saudis to balance against the Iraqi threat for their own protection.

With the Saudis on board, the rest of the GCC, whose members had few military resources but shared the Saudis' concerns, also lined up behind the coalition. Before the war, Saddam had directly threatened the United Arab Emirates (UAE) along with fellow GCC member, Kuwait.[91] Additionally, Iraq had "accidentally" attacked an UAE oil platform in the Gulf during the Iran-Iraq War. The UAE took Iraqi threats seriously and had requested US military aid to beef up the UAE's air defenses as early as July 1990.[92] Given the similar geographic and military vulnerability of the other GCC states, after the invasion of Kuwait the danger they faced was apparent. Between 3 and 7 August, the GCC states condemned the invasion, pledged military contributions, and demanded an Iraqi withdrawal from Kuwait.[93] Other Arab states offered support, but their motives were more complex.

Mixed Motives: The Role of Spoils and Institutions

In addition to the balancers, two other types of states sent troops to support the coalition. These states shared the desire to oppose Iraqi aggression, but this was not enough by itself to cause them to join. Instead they were also motivated by either spoils—usually, though not always monetary—or driven to join in order to uphold the strength of international institutions. Egypt and Syria typify those driven by spoils and balancing motives, while France and Canada typify the second type. These states were sought by the coalition, not necessarily for their military contributions though those were appreciated and in some cases significant, but instead to make international support for the coalition as broad as possible. The

90 Kaur 1994, 57.

91 Gordon and Trainor 1995, 14 and 18; Kaur 1994, 58.

92 Gordon and Trainor 1995, 18.

93 Kaur 1994, 58; Time Books 1992, 85–6.

involvement of Arab states was very important diplomatically from the US's point of view. Syria's participation was especially sought, as Syria was a traditional proponent of radical, anti-Western Arab nationalism, and therefore, could not be credibly dismissed as a US puppet, while Egypt was a traditional leader of the Arab states.[94]

The Egyptian president, Hosni Mubarak, was as shocked as anyone by the Iraqi invasion. Along with the Saudis, Egypt had protested the UAE's mid summer request for US military aid to counter the perceived Iraqi threat. Both Egypt and Saudi Arabia did not see an immediate threat and felt the deliverance of US equipment would only irritate the Iraqis.[95] Also, Mubarak had invested his personal reputation in the pre-war mediation process by personally helping set up the Jeddah conference. It is unlikely that Mubarak would have put his reputation on the line if he had suspected the Iraqis' intentions. Mubarak had gone so far as to get Saddam's personal assurance that no military action would be taken while negotiations were under way, yet to Mubarak's extreme displeasure and surprise the Iraqis invaded just hours after the Jeddah conference broke up and only a day before talks were scheduled to resume in Baghdad.[96]

Egypt had strong motives to react vigorously to the attempted Iraqi *fait accompli*. Iraq was a long running Egyptian rival, posed a challenge to Egypt's mantle of secular Arab leadership, and threatened regional stability. Prior to the invasion, Egypt had been trying with some success to form a Saudi-Syrian-Egyptian axis to balance against Iraq.[97] The invasion of Kuwait showed the Iraqi threat to be real and far graver than the Egyptians' had suspected. Mubarak no longer trusted Iraqi promises, especially those to not push beyond Kuwait. Defending the growing military response to Iraq's invasion he said, "Should [King Faud] wait until a catastrophe takes place there too?"[98] Finally, Egypt had been receiving significant sums of economic aid from Kuwait and other GCC states. If Kuwait and possibly other GCC states ceased to exist, this aid would dry up.[99]

Even with these strong motives to balance against the Iraqi threat, it was not a given that Egypt would move from words to military action. Indeed, immediately after the invasion, Mubarak participated in a Jordanian mediation effort. Deploying military forces against another Arab state would be a major break with tradition, though this was somewhat offset by the fact Iraq had been the first to break the taboo. Additionally, an Arab League vote in favor of a military response might give Mubarak some cover; however, Egypt would have to press hard to get such a vote and would clearly be seen as having sought the military response. When

94 Khadduri and Ghareeb 1997, 131

95 Gordon and Trainor 1995, 19.

96 Brown 1991, 44–5; Kaur 1994, 39; Time Books 1992, 62.

97 Kaur 1994, 38.

98 Ibid, 42.

99 Ibid, 44; Nyang and Hendricks 1995, 137. Morocco was also a major recipient of GCC economic aid.

Egyptian and GCC pressure did get the Arab League to endorse sending troops to Saudi Arabia on 10 August, the vote was only twelve for with six against and two abstentions. [100] The conference broke up deeply divided shortly thereafter. The danger was less a hostile reaction at home—both the Egyptian left and Muslim Brotherhood supported taking action against Iraq[101]—but rather animus within the Arab and Muslim world. Given that Egypt was not directly threatened, Mubarak needed additional incentives to risk the potential regional backlash and join the military coalition.

These incentives were quickly offered. Egypt received a significant share of the $12 billion in aid distributed by Gulf Crisis Financial Coordination Group (GCFCG) to the so called "frontline" states—Egypt, Jordan, and Turkey.[102] The Saudis picked up the entire bill for the Egyptians' deployment and the US forgave $7 billion in debt.[103] Less tangible, but perhaps equally important, working with the US would help cement the US-Egyptian alliance, which had become central to Mubarak's foreign policy and would help Egypt continue to improve relations with Syria and Saudi Arabia.[104] Conversely, if Egypt failed to support the US, Egypt ran the risk of losing one of its main foreign policy gains of the previous decade and a half—the friendship of the US. Given the rapidly fading strength of the USSR, Egypt could not replace the US alliance with a comparable one. Thus, Egypt was driven both by considerations directly linked to the events in Kuwait and by less direct incentives as well.

Like Egypt, Syria also had direct and indirect motives to oppose Iraq. Syria and Iraq had been rivals for decades for the leadership of the Baath party and radical Arab nationalism in general. Syria had even backed Iran against its fellow Arab state in the recent Iran-Iraq War and Iraq had recently called on Syria to leave Lebanon.[105] Since the Syrians shared a border with Iraq, a strengthened Iraq would pose a direct threat. Thus, the Syrians had little to gain from Iraqi successes. President Hafez al-Assad wanted to see Saddam stopped and humiliated, however, he saw no need for Syria to contribute militarily to that humiliation. Syria could not add significantly to the military strength of the coalition and of course war

100 Kaur 1994, 41; Khadduri and Ghareeb 1997, 129 and 161–4; Time Books 1992,100; Yetiv 2004, 40. The League had voted on 3 August fourteen to zero with five abstentions to condemn the invasion. The twelve votes supporting military action were the six members of the GCC—Bahrain, Kuwait, Oman, Qatar, Saudi Arabia, and the UAE—the three other Arab states that ended up sending large scale forces—Egypt, Morocco, and Syria—plus Lebanon, Djibouti, and Somalia.

101 Kaur 1994, 42.

102 Brown 1991, 54. Another $4 billion went to other states to ensure their cooperation with the US led coalition.

103 Ibid, 55; Kaur 1994, 44.

104 Kaur 1994, 44; Nyang and Hendricks 1995, 137. Egypt was heavily dependent on US military aid. This was true of Morocco as well, albeit to a lesser extent.

105 Miller 1994, 62; Time Books 1992, 104.

would be costly and perhaps risky.[106] Syria, therefore, would be pleased by Iraq's defeat, but not compelled by such balancing concerns alone to help bring it about. As with Egypt, the Arab League provided some diplomatic cover to Syria, but this hardly compelled Syria to join. Why then did Syria join the coalition?

Syrian intervention was driven by its ability to obtain significant spoils not directly related to the conflict. First, Syria received roughly $1 billion in economic aid from Saudi Arabia and the rest of the GCC.[107] Second, the US and UK essentially turned a blind eye to Syria's crackdown in Lebanon during the Gulf War which lead to the ouster of Michael Auon and the killing of thousands of his supporters.[108] Similarly, the US and UK ignored or forgave Syria for its role in the Pan-Am 103 bombing. Finally, Syria used the crisis to escape its diplomatic isolation which had become acute. Syria's former patron, the USSR was in decline and had cut off aid. Additionally, Syria had become more isolated within the Middle East. By joining the coalition, Syria was able to appear to be a responsible member of the newly emerging regional order at a fairly low cost since its forces would not bear the brunt of the assault into Kuwait. Additionally, US diplomatic visits to Damascus during and after the war helped end Syria's isolation and raised hopes Syria might get off the US State Department's list of sponsors of terrorism.[109] The most important of these trips was Secretary of State Baker's on 13 September. Syria's reaction to the trip highlighted how important ending its isolation was. Immediately after the trip, which effectively ended Syria's status as a pariah, Syria hosted the exiled Kuwaiti emir and tripled its troop contribution. Thus, Syria was able to replace some of the financial aid lost due to the Soviets' decline, escape diplomatic isolation, improve its relations with the more pro-Western Arab states—notably Egypt and Saudi Arabia—humiliate its old foe, and avoid punishment from the now relatively more powerful West without really altering behavior in Lebanon or support for radical terrorist movements.

A number of western states also contributed to the coalition out of mixed motives. Like the above states, they were concerned by Iraq's aggressive actions and had quickly condemned them. As with Egypt and Syria, these balancing concerns by themselves likely were not enough to get them to actively intervene. Unlike, Egypt and Syria, however, they were not driven by potential non-military spoils. Rather they were driven to join by the role international institutions played in the organizing the conflict. In many ways, the Gulf War was an institutional war. As mentioned above, the Arab League helped provide diplomatic cover for Arab

---

106 The conditions which Syria imposed on the use of its military in the Gulf War shows quite clearly they did not intend to contribute greatly to Iraq's military defeat. Syrian forces could be used only in Kuwait and were hardly relied on at all in the Desert Storm plan. Part of the reason for this is that the Syrians used the same equipment as the Iraqis which raised friendly fire concerns (Brown 1991, 44–5).

107 Brown 1991, 44–5 and 54; Kaur 1994, 3 and 45; Time Books 1992, 94.

108 Kaur 1994, 1–2.

109 Ibid, 3 and 8.

states to join the war, while the GCC helped coordinate the Gulf states' response to the Iraqi invasion and helped induce additional Arab states to join. Likewise, non-Arab institutions paved the path toward intervention for a number of western members of the coalition. Notable among these were France and Canada.

France joined the anti-Iraq coalition with less enthusiasm than most. France had extensive financial ties to Iraq and a history of an independent Middle Eastern policy.[110] Thus, even though President Francois Mitterrand's government opposed the Iraqi invasion, it was hopeful that the resulting crisis could be resolved peacefully through multilateral mediation. Thus, Mitterrand was willing to go along with EC and UN votes condemning and placing sanctions on Iraq, but it was not clear France would back more robust measures. Multilateral, non-military pressure was France's preferred policy. In the end, however, France was willing to support UN sanctioned military measures and dispatched ships to the Gulf as early as 8 August to enforce the UN embargo.[111] As deadlines for the Iraqi withdrawal neared, France appeared to waiver in its commitment to the coalition. Mitterrand's government sent out peace feelers well after the Americans were convinced peace was impossible. The US agreed to the last minute Baker-Aziz summit in large part to appease France and like minded countries.[112] In the end, France agreed to the use of force when the 15 January deadline expired and participated fully in the battle to oust the Iraqis from Kuwait.

France acquiesced to the use of force despite its apparent reticence for two reasons. First, France was never that reluctant to use force. While Mitterrand certainly preferred diplomacy over force, he also preferred an Iraqi defeat over the continued occupation of Kuwait. Thus, while the French wanted to ensure that all diplomatic possibilities were exhausted and took longer to be convinced of this than the Americans, once they were convinced, force became acceptable. In practice this did not even delay the military campaign, though it did lead to a series of failed mediation efforts by the UN Secretary General, French diplomats, Secretary of State Baker, and various heads of state not associated with the US coalition. Second, France saw participation in the coalition as a way to blunt US unilateralism. The US was likely to use force to attempt to expel Iraq regardless of French policy. French participation could channel US actions through the UN, thereby making them multilateral and more palatable. The Bush administration was generally willing, though at times the US and UK did get ahead of the UN, notably by imposing a blockade in the Persian Gulf in August. The rest of the EC and Canada balked at this unilateralism and the UN, largely at the behest of these states, quickly passed Resolution 665 authorizing the blockade to keep the US

110 Brown 1991, 41.

111 Time Books 1992, 94. Spain dispatched ships at the same time to join the US-UK blockade already in place.

112 Mollifying domestic opposition was another major factor.

and UK from acting unilaterally.[113] European concerns that actions in the Gulf be multilateral rather than unilateral were again raised at the Western European Union (WEU) conference in late August.[114] The Americans and British continually expressed a willingness to work through international organs which reassured the French and other EC states. Mitterrand, thus was reassured that he would have a significant say through France's Security Council veto in how the coalition would proceed. The French also saw the coalition as a way to strengthen the UN, the EC, and international multilateralism and institutionalism in general. Given the end of the Cold War and the apparent emergence of a new world order, the French saw these tools as vital to maintaining France's lofty place on the international stage and as important means to check US power in the future without seriously endangering the NATO alliance. Thus, it seems unlikely that joining would have been as nearly attractive for the French if either the balancing or institutional motives had been removed.

Canada's behavior mirrored France's mix of institutional and balancing motives. Like so many others, the Canadians were upset by the Iraqi occupation of Kuwait. Canada immediately placed sanctions on Iraq and Joe Clark, the Canadian Secretary of State, called the invasion a "totally unacceptable action".[115] These initial reactions showed that there was no question that Canada was willing to work diplomatically for an Iraqi withdrawal and generally supported the US's tough stance on the issue. Still, it was far less clear that Canada would send troops to the region.

Since 1945 Canadian foreign policy had consisted of two main pillars: maintaining the US alliance and managing international problems through multilateral institutions. Those pillars remained in place in 1990. Given that the Mulroney cabinet agreed in principle with the Bush administration that Iraqi aggression should be resisted, upholding the first principle was easy enough. There was no major policy tension between the US and Canada. Indeed, even when the US and UK got ahead of the UN and began blockading Iraq, Prime Minister Brian Mulroney indicated he supported the action. Tellingly, however, Canada did not send ships to support the blockade until after the UN approved the action and NATO agreed to coordinate with the blockade.[116]

Though Canada had reliably supported US policy in the post-1945 era, Canada had only deployed troops under the auspices of multilateral organizations like NATO and preferably the UN. Between 1945 and 1990, Canada sent troops abroad

---

113 Brown 1991, 28–9; Gibbons 1992, 6; Khadduri and Ghareeb 1997, 193. The US and UK agreed to not take further actions to enforce the blockade prior to UN authorization.

114 Gibbons 1992, 8–10. The WEU is a military alliance and should not be confused with the European Union. While it has partially merged with the EU, it was clearly distinct from the EC at the time of the Gulf War.

115 Miller 1994, 72–3.

116 Ibid, 122.

into potential combat situations only in support of UN missions. Canada had done this consistently and had even participated in the UN's only other previous war-fighting mission, the Korea War. Thus, while Canada might agree with US and Saudi aims in the Gulf, it was unlikely that Canada would have lent anything more than the weight of diplomacy to support those convictions had the UN not played a central role. However, as the US led coalition was working through the UN, Canada had strong incentives to contribute to that effort military—as it turned out in the form of a naval patrol. The important role the UN played in Canada's decision making can be seen from Mulroney's justification of his policy to the Canadian parliament.

> Canada welcomes the crucial and skilled role played by President Bush of the US in building this international consensus. … Some have suggested that the enforcement by armed force of international law and of UN resolutions is somehow contrary to the spirit of multilateralism … and Canada's tradition. Nothing can be further from the truth. The willingness of the UN to authorize military means to enforce the resolutions it has passed may well presage an important new area of multilateralism—a goal for which generations of Canadians have worked …
>
> Our military response to Iraqi aggression is fully compatible with our tradition as international peacekeepers. … [O]ur peacekeeping role neither excludes nor excuses us from the call to resist aggression. The roles are complementary, as both serve the larger political purpose of preserving international order and both are very much in Canada's interest.[117]

Secretary Clark reiterated this point at the UN on 29 November during the debate on the authorization of the use of force to expel Iraq from Kuwait. He said,

> The presence of Canadian forces in the Gulf is fully in keeping with our traditional role as a peacekeeper under the auspices of the United Nations. … Our position is one of integrity and dedication to the upholding of international law and the universally recognized norms of conduct in the relations between states.[118]

Thus, the Canadian government saw the war as an opportunity to strengthen multilateralism, international institutions, and international norms—all of which were major Canadian policy goals.

There was also a sense that if Canada did not participate, its interests would be severely hurt. First, a Canadian abstention would hurt its relations with the US.

117 Ibid, 146–8. The speech was delivered on 24 September 1990.

118 Ibid, 150.

If Canada would not support its most important ally when the US was working so hard to act multilaterally through the UN, when would Canada back the US? Second, at the time there was a sense that a "new world order" was being created—an order that would emphasize the very institutions and multilateral decision-making processes that had been at the heart of Canada's self-image and foreign policy goals for decades.[119] To not act would be to miss the boat. Thus, UN involvement essentially ensured Canada would contribute troops, while without UN involvement Canadian efforts would have likely been limited to diplomatic activity.

The Enablers

A quick word about the roles of China, the Soviet Union, and Israel is also required. While none sent troops to the Gulf, all could have derailed the UN coalition. China and the USSR could have vetoed the Security Council measures which were so crucial to building the coalition, while Israeli involvement would have complicated Arab participation. Much like Egypt and Syria, all of these states obtained indirect rewards.

Neither China nor the USSR had a particularly strong desire to see Iraq humiliated—Iraq was a traditional Soviet ally and China has historically opposed intervention—yet both voted for or at least refused to veto the anti-Iraq UN resolutions. While initially puzzling, this behavior is easily explained by indirect spoils. Chinese cooperation was rewarded by the US and the West by forgiving the Chinese for the Tiananmen Square massacre and ending China's diplomatic isolation that had gone on for over a year. The US agreed to resume high level contacts as a direct quid pro quo for the Chinese abstention on the UN authorization of the use of force.[120] The Soviets likewise avoided strong condemnation for their crackdown in the Baltic republics in early 1991. Additionally, and far more important for Soviet compliance in the early stages of the crisis, was that the Soviets continued to receive large injections of western capital to shore up and help reform their crumbling state-planned economy. Thus, while the Soviets hoped to avoid a war and the destruction of their erstwhile Iraqi ally, in the end they were more interested in continuing to improve East-West relations.[121] Also, the crisis created an opportunity for the Soviets to reestablish relations with the Saudis and gain

119 Ibid, 136–7.

120 Ibid, 42–3. Overcoming Chinese objections was fairly easy (Khadduri and Ghareeb 1997, 125).

121 Brown 1991, 28–9; Khadduri and Ghareeb 1997, 125 and 245; Time Books 1992, 107–108, 130, 177, 180, and 189. The decision to abandon Iraq was by no means universally supported by the Soviet leadership. These divisions led to Soviet mediation efforts, such as the sending of Yevgeny Primakov to Iraq, and contributed to the fall of foreign minister Eduard Shevardnadze.

access to Saudi credit.[122] Simply put, neither state wanted to pay the high costs that would have been required to oppose the newly emerging world order with the US at its head. While neither state was hostile to Iraq, neither had sufficiently strong interests in aiding Iraq to incur the displeasure of the coalition, especially when such tangible rewards for cooperation where available.[123]

Israeli behavior was also crucial. By declining to become involved in the conflict even though it was attacked by Iraq, Israel allowed the unusual coalition to form. If Israel had attacked Iraq, the retention of the Arab coalition partners, especially Syria, would have been far more difficult. The Israelis were very happy to see Iraq defeated and would have been willing, even enthusiastic, about contributing to Saddam's defeat. Their involvement in the coalition, however, would have been diplomatically challenging to say the least; therefore, Iraq tried to draw Israel into the war via Scud missile attacks. Israel naturally wanted to respond to such an attack, but US insistence and aid kept the Israelis out. The US not only sent Patriot missile batteries and personnel to help Israel to counter the Scud threat, but the US and its allies offered Israel over $1.1 billion in compensation provided that Israel did not respond to the attacks.[124] The minimal damage done by the Scuds and the knowledge that the coalition would likely seriously damage Iraq's military made Israel's decision to not respond a far easier one.

Conclusions

The above cases show that the growth of the norm of territorial integrity in the post-1945 era has changed the behavior of third parties in relation to ongoing wars. Potential joiners are nor longer likely to be enticed by the prospect of territorial rewards as such spoils are not generally available. This in turn changes the behavior of certain types of late joiners. While balancers behave as before, bandwagoners behave fundamentally differently. Prior to 1945, late joining bandwagoners hoped to enter the war on the winning side in time to contribute enough to be rewarded territorially, but late enough to not pay more costs than necessary.[125] While bandwagoners often erred in their calculations and either joined

122 Brown 1991, 39.

123 Similarly, Germany and Japan provided financial support for the coalition in order to maintain good relations with the US and also, like France and Canada, to support the apparently emerging new focus on the use of international institutions. Additionally, threats had been made in the US Congress that Japan would have to cover the cost for basing US soldiers on Japanese soil if Japan did not contribute financially to the coalition.

124 Khadduri and Ghareeb 1997, 172. The sources of the aid were: the US $1 billion; the EC $100 million; and Germany $3.2 million. Egypt clearly stated it would fight Iraq regardless of Israeli actions and the Syrians made vague reassurances of the same (Brown 1991, 73).

125 In practice, bandwagoners often do not have a choice of which side to join, but rather a choice of joining a given side or remaining neutral. This is because the territory

prematurely or joined the losing side, all of them closely watched the wars they were considering joining. The course of those wars and the information revealed by events in those wars were crucial to their decision-making processes and dictated the timing of their entries. This is because the spoils sought by bandwagoners in the pre-1945 era were dependent on the outcome of the war. With the decline in the availability of territorial spoils, bandwagoning has not disappeared, but the type of spoils sought has changed. Rather than seeking territory, bandwagoners now seek benefits such as military and economic aid, strengthened alliances, and diplomatic support. While these benefits existed prior to 1945, they became paramount after the Second World War. Importantly, unlike territorial spoils, such benefits are not coupled to the outcome of the war. Thus, bandwagoners are no longer motivated primarily by the outcome of the war—they of course do have a preferred outcome—but rather by the spoils they can derive from participation. This means post-1945 bandwagoners have far less reason to care about the course of the war and that the timing of their entry is unlikely to be directly determined by events in the war.[126] Instead, their entry is dictated by their negotiations with states seeking their aid. Additionally, as exhibited by Vietnam and the Gulf War, the aid of bandwagoners is often sought not for military reasons, but rather as diplomatic cover.[127] Because of this, events within a war are not as likely to be what causes belligerents to seek the aid of bandwagoners as they were before 1945. Thus, bandwagoners' entries are unlikely to be even indirectly tied to events within the war. This is a major departure from the pre-1945 era.

There are two potential objections to this conclusion. First, it could be argued that the bandwagoning states were simply too weak to merit territorial rewards. Had this been why no territorial spoils were awarded, the bandwagoners should have sought territorial spoils only to be rebuffed for being too weak, but the states never sought such rewards. Remember that in both Vietnam and the Gulf War the US was actively seeking allies, thus the potential bandwagoners had sufficient leverage to at least ask for their preferred form of compensation. Additionally, the bandwagoners in Vietnam and the Gulf War were really no weaker, relative to the size of forces contributed, than some of the bandwagoners covered in previous chapters. For example, Bulgaria and especially Romania were promised very large rewards during the First World War, despite their limited military abilities. It is not at all clear that the post-1945 bandwagoners were significantly weaker than these

---

they seek is likely to be offered by only one side.

126 It also means that these bandwagoners can potentially keep the rewards they received secret or at least below the radar even post-bellum. This is in stark contrast to the acquisition of territory which is obvious to all.

127 This is undoubtedly related to the US's position as a superpower, especially in the military sphere. In most military confrontations, allies will not be able to significantly increase the military striking power available to the US. For conflicts not involving the US, or if the US is in a conflict with another great power, the amount of force a potential ally could contribute to the conflict would certainly increase in importance.

states. Second, it might be argued that the lack of territorial spoils was a product of the Cold War. Specifically, the bipolar aspects of the conflict made any shifts in territory provocative and therefore unlikely to occur. However, it is not at all clear why the US would not be willing to offer spoils to its allies as this would shift the distribution of power in the US's favor and, as the negotiations were not public, concerns about Soviet reactions should not have kept issues like territory from at least being discussed, yet they never were. Thus, it seems likely that the departure from seeking territorial spoils is a result of the norm of territorial integrity.

To the extent that this means potential allies of belligerents will now more readily accept non-territorial rewards in exchange for military contributions, it should make recruiting allies easier. Potential bandwagoning allies will no longer need to be close enough to benefit territorially. While geographically proximate allies will likely still be the most advantageous for strategic reasons, more removed allies may be successfully courted. Additionally, territory is often one of the most difficult sorts of rewards to parcel out to potential allies, as any territory allotted to one ally, is no longer available to another or as a spoil of war for the original belligerents. Such negotiations over territory can be torturous and can derail potential alliances as was seen in the chapter on the First World War. Financial and other non-territorial spoils, however, should not cause such competition among allies. While these spoils are not limitless, from the potential allies' point of view, it is not a constant sum game. Spoils to one ally do not necessarily reduce those going to another by the same amount—or at all. Whether this increased ability to recruit allies affects the incidence of war is unclear as it could potentially both encourage and discourage potential aggressors, as both the aggressor and defender should be able to benefit from this greater ease in recruiting allies. This said, such non-territorial rewards are most likely to be able to be provided by great powers and wealthy states. Thus, it may increase their incidence of war to the extent that the ability to recruit allies affects their decisions about belligerency. It also means military success will not attract allies as in the past. Previously, potential bandwagoners may have waited to see which side was likely to win and thus if the promised territorial spoils were really available. Given the change in the nature of spoils, success on the battlefield will no longer be as important in swaying potential bandwagoners as it will say little about their potential rewards, though battlefield results may affect the costs bandwagoners will have to pay and the size of the rewards offered by their suitors. Thus, the likelihood that a state will bandwagon will still be somewhat connected to battlefield results, though far less than in earlier eras.

States engaged in balancing in the post-1945 era, however, act in much the same way that balancers did prior to 1945. Such states are deeply concerned about the outcome of the ongoing wars they are considering joining and hope through the use of force they can alter the outcome of those wars. Thus, events within those wars should still be causal of their decision to join and dictate the timing of their entry. The lack of territorial alterations should not greatly affect their behavior.

Indeed, such states are often trying to enforce the norm of territorial integrity.[128] Given their concern with the outcome of the war, the entry of balancers into ongoing wars is likely to be triggered by events within those wars.

The other major change was the enhanced role international institutions played in the spread of war. The Gulf War illustrated this nicely. The UN played an active and important role in justifying intervention and increasing the number of states that decided to join the Gulf War. While the US and several other states would have joined regardless of the UN's actions, the very large size of the coalition was dependent on UN action. The lack of UN action in Vietnam may help explain why the US failed in attracting European and Latin American allies to its side despite US efforts and some expression of allied interest. Certainly, the US had been able to attract such allies in the Korean War, a war fought under UN auspices. More clearly, the lack of a UN endorsement for the 2003 Iraq war is often cited as a reason that the US was unable to assemble the large anti-Iraq coalition in 2003 that it did in 1991. There is, however, essentially a chicken and egg dilemma with this phenomenon. Does UN involvement lead to widespread support and additional belligerents, or does widespread support lead to UN involvement? Certainly, widespread support—especially among attending veto members—is necessary in order to bring about UN actions. However, actions by international organizations may lend legitimacy to actions (Claude 1966; Hurd 1999). If this is in fact the case, UN actions could help bring fence sitters or states which want to appear to be acting in accordance with the international will into a conflict. Without the UN resolutions, it seems highly unlikely that Canada or any European state other than Britain would have sent troops to the Gulf even though many of these states opposed Iraq from the outset. These states were anxious to work multilaterally and saw the coalition against Iraq as far more legitimate because it operated under a UN mandate. As mentioned above, the reaction of these states to the current war in Iraq only serves to reinforce this conclusion.

The UN and other IGOs, such as the Arab League, GCFCG, EC, WEU, and GCC, certainly increased the speed and ease with which states coordinated their interventionist policies. The Gulf states coordinated their response through the GCC. Given that every GCC state participated in the conflict, even though many had paltry militaries and could not affect the outcome, it seems likely that the GCC helped reduce free riding. GCC coordination also allowed its members to present a united front at the Arab League summit and force through their preferred resolutions. Similarly, the European states coordinated their military and economic responses through the EC and WEU. Additionally, bandwagoners and enablers

128 One important difference, however, is that balancers are now very unlikely to receive even incidental territorial rewards for their efforts. For example, Britain joined the First World War with the primary intention of balancing against Germany and preserving the territorial status quo. However, Britain obtained territorial compensation in the form of League of Nations mandates after the war. Such compensation for balancing is much less likely to occur in the post-1945 era.

were enticed to join or at least not oppose the coalition through World Bank and GCFCG economic aid. Finally, while the Arab League was unable to resolve the issue peacefully or bring about a unified Arab response, its votes condemning the Iraqi invasion and authorizing a response greatly enhanced the legitimacy of GCC, Egyptian, Syrian, and Moroccan actions. Clearly, international institutions significantly expanded the conflict and altered the way states responded to it.

Thus, the nature of late joining has changed significantly since the Second World War. The decline in the availability of territorial spoils has decoupled the decision-making process of potential bandwagoners from the course of the war itself. Additionally, international institutions have played an increasingly important role in forming large coalitions to check attempts to alter the territorial status quo and thus bring even more states into ongoing wars. Whether these trends continue or the pre-1945 patterns of joining reemerge depends on staying power of the norm of territorial integrity and whether or not the trend toward multilateral institutionalism remains robust.

Chapter 8
Conclusions, Extensions, and Avenues for Future Research

War is a Contagion
–Franklin D. Roosevelt

There can be no doubt that why and when states join ongoing wars is an important topic. The entry of states into ongoing interstate wars has greatly affected the course of many wars, including wars that shaped and made the international system what it is today. The world would be a very different place had the US not entered either world war or if those wars had remained bilateral conflicts. The same can be said, albeit on a smaller scale, of the British and French entries into the Crimean War. History also could have been quite different if intervention had occurred in other wars. What would the 20th century have looked like if states had balanced against Prussia in either the Franco-Prussian War or Six Weeks War? Clearly, whether or not military interventions have occurred has played an important role in the course of history and in shaping the present international system. Furthermore, the conduct of wars is shaped by the prospect that non-belligerents may join them. For example, both the Entente and Central Powers crafted their strategies in the First World War with the hope of attracting allies, while Bismarck was careful to not provoke balancing against Prussia during its wars with Austria and France. Thus, even the prospect of intervention has shaped the course of international affairs in important ways.

Chapter 2 made it equally clear that the phenomena of joining had yet to be adequately explained in the literature. While a good start had been made about which states might be more likely to join, no progress had been made regarding which wars states were likely to join and when they likely would enter. This work proposed that revealed information explains when and why states join ongoing wars and which wars they will join. It is argued that new and revealed information is a good predictor of late joining because the information can shift states' acceptable bargaining ranges thereby potentially destroying the tacit agreements between warring and non-belligerent states.[1] Additionally, it was argued that new and revealed information also causes belligerents to reconsider their participation in wars and will often cause them to exit those wars. As discussed in Chapter 2, this hypothesis needs to take into account Goemans' (2000) hypothesis that mixed regimes gamble for resurrection delaying the termination of a war. Both

1 This excludes information confirming the estimates of sufficiently risk adverse states, a possibility that is discussed in Chapter 2.

hypotheses, that new and revealed information causes states to join wars and that it causes states to leave wars, were tested. They received strong support from both the large n study and from the case studies.

Summary of the Work's Main Findings

For the most part, the evidence presented in Chapters Three through Seven supported the hypotheses advanced in Chapter 2. In particular, the statistics in Chapter 3 provided strong support. They showed that the occurrence of an unexpected event in a given month or the proceeding two months substantially increased the likelihood a given non-belligerent would join in that month. The correlation held for both military events and political events. It was also shown that events of a higher magnitude were more likely to cause states to join than events of a lesser magnitude. Equally important was the finding that unexpected events cause states to leave wars and that the larger the event, the more likely the state was to leave. This was true for both political and military events. As unexpected events are a subset of revealed information, these findings support the revealed information hypotheses.

Additionally, the findings for when states exit wars fit with Goemans (2000) claim that mixed regimes gamble for resurrection when faced with negative battlefield results. While unexpected events which did not harm mixed regimes operated as predicted by the revealed information hypothesis, events which hurt mixed regimes either were not significantly correlated with exit or reduced the odds of exit. Only very high magnitude events which hurt mixed regimes increased the likelihood of exit, probably because even though the mixed regimes wanted to attempt to gamble for resurrection, they could not.

In addition to the findings relating to revealed information, several other hypotheses were confirmed. Among these was that geographic proximity to the conflict increased the odds a given state would enter that war. Specifically, either being contiguous by land to a war or being in the same region as a war substantially increased the chance a non-belligerent would enter a war. Also, receiving confirmation were previous findings that great powers were more likely to join ongoing wars and that all states were more likely to join if a great power had already joined the war. Finally, the statistics suggested that it was important to control for the involvement of the United Nations. They clearly show that in the Korean War and the 1990–91 Gulf War UN involvement played a major role in getting states to join those wars that would not have done so otherwise. Often these states were geographically distant minor powers, such as Ethiopia in the Korean War. Such states overall were highly unlikely to join ongoing wars, thus the involvement of the UN seems to almost have been a necessary condition for their involvement. The statistics were not, however, structured in a way as to allow for a true test of the hypothesis that collective security organizations generally lead to the spread of war if they fail to deter wars in the first place, as the statistics selected on the dependent variable of effective collective security. Future study of this question, however, may prove profitable. Thus, on the whole, the statistics offered strong support for the unexpected events hypotheses and confirmed some previously existing findings.

Other hypotheses were either disconfirmed or underwent modification. Specifically, the statistics contradicted the hypothesis that wars already involving at least one great power were more likely to experience intervention and there was no significant relationship between duration and the likelihood non-belligerents would join a war. Also, states with enduring rivals already in a war were no more likely to join than were other states nor were democracies any more likely to join wars involving fellow democracies. Additionally, prior joining by non-great powers did not significantly affect the likelihood states would intervene. Similarly, a non-belligerent already being in a war did not significantly affect its likelihood of joining another war. Faring somewhat better was the hypothesis that alliances tend to transmit wars between partners. It was confirmed, but only for the early stages of a war and only for defense pacts. Ententes and neutrality pacts were not correlated with the spread of war. This suggests that if alliances are to cause states to join wars, they must do so within the first month of war, but after this initial stage alliances cease to matter. In other words, alliances that are not honored quickly are alliances that are unlikely to ever be honored. This makes intuitive sense as alliances that exist antebellum would be factored into states' early decisions about joining. If the alliance is not sufficient to cause a state to join in a war's early stages, it is not clear why it would be a factor later on. This suggests the works of Siverson and Starr are essentially correct, but are far too general in their conclusions about the role alliances play in spreading war.

The case studies also supported the work's main hypotheses regarding revealed information. The battles of Sinope and Bashkadyklar in the Crimean War clearly triggered French and British intervention. These battles surprised the French and British—or at least British public opinion—not because they expected the Turks to be able to defeat the Russians, but rather because the Russians were not expected to act so aggressively. Similarly in the First World War, Bulgaria's entry was triggered by the unexpected success of the Gorlice-Tarnow offensive, while Romania joined as a direct result of the surprisingly successful Brusilov offensive. The US, too, joined because of revealed information—the resumption of unrestricted submarine warfare by the Germans and to a lesser extent the Zimmerman telegram. Italy entered the war in large part because of Austria-Hungary's defeats in Galicia in 1914 through early 1915 and the initial promise of the Gallipoli campaign. The entries of Greece and especially the Ottoman Empire illustrate how the interplay between revealed information and domestic politics can lead to joining, albeit often in indirect ways. Finally, in the post-World War Two era, balancers entered due to revealed information, though bandwagoners did not as they were seeking non-territorial spoils. The US escalated its involvement in Vietnam in directly response to the surprisingly rapidly deteriorating situation in South Vietnam in late 1964. Similarly, the US, Gulf Cooperation Council States, and Britain all entered the 1990–91 Gulf War in response to the unexpectedly aggressive actions of Iraq. Canada, France, Italy, Egypt, Syria, and Morocco all entered in part due to the surprise invasion and the further unanticipated threatening of Saudi Arabia by Iraq, though they needed additional factors in order to join. All of their entries were made more likely by the actions of international institutions—including but not limited to the UN and the Arab League—and the last three states were also induced to join by offers of non-territorial spoils. Thus, the cases as a whole offer strong support for the revealed information hypothesis.

In contrast to this strong support, the cases offer only slight support for the counter-hypothesis that non-belligerents delay entering a war in order to wait for some expected chain of events, such as rearmament, to occur. The counter-hypothesis does help explain Italy's entry into the First World War in conjunction with the revealed information hypothesis. In the spring of 1915, Italy believed it had an opportunity due to information revealed by Austria-Hungary's defeats in Galicia and was sufficiently rearmed, though as discussed in Chapter 5, both conclusions of the Italian government proved to be incorrect. Other than that single instance, the case studies do not lend support to the counter-hypothesis. In fact, Romania's entry into the First World War runs directly counter to it. Romania never addressed its armaments deficiencies to Brătianu's satisfaction, but joined anyway. Thus, it seems safe to conclude that the revealed information hypothesis predominates over the counter-hypothesis.

The case studies also highlight that some states join wars in order to obtain a seat at the conference table. This was a factor, if not the driving force, behind Sardinia's decision to enter the Crimean War and Romania's and the United States' decisions to enter the First World War. This sort of motivation cannot be derived from the revealed information hypothesis; however, this desire to obtain a seat at the conference table cannot explain the timing of intervention. Logically, such states would want to wait as long as possible before joining so as to avoid paying as many costs of the war while still getting the benefits of a seat at the conference table. Yet the two states which most clearly had this as a goal, the US and Romania, both clearly joined because of revealed information. Brătianu feared waiting too long before joining, because he felt that if Romania joined after the issue had been decided, Romania would lose its leverage at the peace talks or be excluded from them entirely. Using the information revealed by battles, Brătianu attempted to guess the right time to join when costs would be low, yet still early enough so the Entente would value Romania's contribution. The timing of the US's entry was not dictated at all by trying to get a seat at the conference table at the lowest cost. Wilson had not made a determination in early 1917 that the war was nearing its conclusion, rather he decided that the German U-boat campaign had gone too far in ignoring neutral rights. Thus, while states may factor the benefit of a seat at the conference table into their calculations about whether or not to join a war, the possibility of this benefit cannot by itself explain why states would enter the war in any given month. Thus, though it is important to note that states are often motivated by a desire to participate in the peace negotiations, such motivations do not minimize the importance of revealed information in determining why and when states change their calculations about whether to participate in the conflict nor the role of unexpected events in determining the timing of joining.

Just as important as the general confirmation that revealed information induces states to join ongoing wars, the case studies revealed that the actions of belligerents are strongly influenced by the possibility that other states will enter the war. Belligerents often attempt to prosecute wars quickly to reduce the opportunity for hostile balancing to occur and limit their demands to avoid hostile intervention. Prussian behavior in the Franco-Prussian War and the Six Weeks War illustrates both behaviors clearly. Belligerents may even directly appease non-belligerents and be coerced by non-belligerent threats. Russia's interaction with Austria during the Crimean War, especially in the war's latter stages, is a good example of a belligerent trying to appease a non-belligerent, but ultimately being compelled to the bargaining table by the non-belligerent's threats of intervention. Bismarck's diplomacy toward Russia and Britain in the latter stages of the Franco-Prussian War is another good example of a belligerent appeasing potential joiners. Nor is this the only way in which belligerents try to influence non-belligerents. Belligerents routinely try to induce friendly intervention through offers of spoils. They also try to win allies and deter potential enemies through displays of strength. The cases are full of examples of these sorts of behaviors. For example, in the First World War the Central Powers offered Romania Russian-held Bessarabia in hopes of luring Romania to their side, offered Italy territory in the Trentino in hopes of appeasing Italy and preventing Italy from joining the Entente, and finally threatened Romania with destruction in hopes of deterring Romania from joining the Entente. Likewise, the Entente offered spoils to Italy and Romania, threatened Greece, and altered their blockade policy to appease the US. In the Crimean War, Britain and France deterred Greece and Persia with threats and tried to cajole Austria into joining through a combination of inducements and threats.

Thus, the cases show that not only does the course of a war affect who joins, but that the course of a war is affected by the possibility of who may join. Belligerents are aware of this reciprocal causation, and therefore, craft strategies that account for the possibility of intervention and attempt to influence the behavior of potential joiners.[2] War-fighting strategies may at times focus on how they will affect non-belligerents, rather than how they will affect the state's enemies. An example of this is Britain delaying the Gallipoli campaign to avoid setbacks that might have discouraged Italian intervention even though this hurt the chances that the campaign would succeed. In discussing strategic interaction antebellum the larger literature has discussed this sort of interaction between soon to be warring states and third parties, but previous studies had not sharply focused on such interactions

2 Attempts to attract states through the offer of non-territorial spoils were also made, but these tended to not affect the course of wars. For example, in both the Vietnam and Gulf Wars, the US induced states to join its side by offering economic and military aid, but the US did little to change how it fought those wars.

between belligerents and potential joiners during the war itself, outside of the limited focus on alliance reliability.[3]

In addition to these findings about the spread of war, the case studies offered solid, though somewhat weaker, support for the hypothesis that revealed information causes states to leave wars. Russia's decision to agree to peace proposals in the Crimean War is the best example of such behavior. Both Austria's ultimatum to Russia and Sweden's alliance with Britain and France caught the Russians off guard. This caused Alexander II and his ministers, who previously had been optimistic about the upcoming 1856 campaign, to quickly agree to a peace conference and the main demands of their enemies.

The First World War also lends support to the hypothesis. The Russian Revolution, the Salonikan offensive, and the September 1918 offensives on the Western Front were all necessary to the departures of Russia, Bulgaria, Germany, and Austria-Hungary from the war. Additionally, Romania would not have left if not for Russia's exit. Equally important is that all of these events surprised contemporaries. A few short months before his ascension to power, Lenin had to go into hiding and his peace at any price formula had dismayed even his own followers. Likewise, the German military in general and Ludendorff in particular were still opposed to negotiating with the Entente prior to the Salonikan and September offensives. These offensives changed the German militaries expectations about the prospects of further resistance and led to Germany requesting negotiations for an armistice. Clearly, revealed information led to the termination of the First World War.

The actions of other belligerents in the cases provide considerably less support. France fought until near total exhaustion in the Franco-Prussian War. The peace treaty that terminated the Franco-Prussian War, as well as the treaties that ended Romania's and the Ottoman Empire's participation in the First World War, were essentially dictated terms rather than negotiated settlements. Thus, as has been widely argued in the war termination literature, revealed information may shift bargaining ranges to an extent that peace is possible.[4] Some wars, however, are fought well beyond the point where it is clear which side will win and by how much. They are fought until one or both sides have essentially reached exhaustion or near total military defeat.[5] Still, the revealed information hypothesis predominates. Perhaps further research can shed light on what type of wars follow each path.

The idea that revealed information could make joining even less attractive than it appeared prior to the event which revealed it was not testable using statistics.

3 Blainey 1973; Crawford 2003, 20.

4 Blainey (1973); Goemans (2000); Iklé (1971); Wittman (1979).

5 This might be because some states which are clearly losing a war hold out as long as possible hoping for an unexpected event to occur that would shift the course of the war back in their favor. This is essentially what Goemans (2000) calls "gambling for resurrection" and according to Goemans is more common in states where elites will be punished severely for a defeat. See the section on war termination in Chapter 2.

A state that never considered joining looks the same to a regression as a state that considered joining but was deterred from doing so by an unexpected event. Thus, the claim is best evaluated by case studies. The Franco-Prussian War provides very strong support for this hypothesis. Austria-Hungary, Italy, and Denmark all hoped to ally with a victorious France in order to pick up spoils at Prussia's expense. France's disastrous defeats at Rezonville, Wörth, and Sedan deterred these states. They wanted to bandwagon, not to balance. With France defeated, the prospect of easy spoils vanished. Similarly, in the First World War, many states looking for spoils were discouraged. Italy was initially frightened off by the German victories in the West. Bulgaria was temporarily dissuaded from joining the Central Powers by the Battle of the Marne and the Austrian disasters in Galicia in 1914. Likewise, Romania delayed joining the Entente after the success of the Gorlice-Tarnow campaign. In the Crimean War, Britain and France were initially convinced by the Ottomans' surprising early successes in the Balkans that it might not be necessary to enter the war. Thus, the hypothesis that revealed information can reduce as well as increase the likelihood third parties will join received strong support in the case studies.

On the whole the work offers strong support to the work's main hypotheses that revealed information causes non-belligerents to join wars, causes belligerents to exit wars, and can discourage intervention. Previous findings regarding the importance of geographic contiguity, regional proximity, and great power status in relation to the spread of war were confirmed, though the idea that wars involving great powers were more likely to experience joining and that states with a rival already in the war were more likely to join did not receive support. The hypothesis that alliances transmit wars from one ally to another was found to hold only for the initial stages of a war, not thereafter. Also, this relationship existed only for defensive pacts, not other types of alliances. In sum, the work confirmed eleven of the hypotheses advanced in Chapter 2—H1, H2, H4–7, H13, and H16–18—including all of the hypotheses concerning revealed information. It failed to support six hypotheses—H8–12 and H15. It suggested the modification of the hypothesis regarding alliances and found some evidence for the hypothesis regarding the UN, but was unable to structure a proper test of the hypothesis—H3 and H14 respectively.

Extensions

In addition to the confirmation of the work's main hypotheses and the disconfirmation of some previously existing hypotheses, the case studies suggested a number of extensions. The most obvious of these is the difference between potential balancers and potential bandwagoners. It becomes obvious from the case studies that potential balancers are more likely to join the war if the state they are prepared to balance against appears to be more of a threat than expected. This can happen if the threatening state either acts more aggressively than expected, as Russia did in the Crimean War, increases its demands, or does better than expected. If any of these events occur, the need for balancing becomes more acute. This makes it possible for belligerents to appease potential balancers in order to keep them neutral. By keeping their demands and actions within ranges acceptable to the non-belligerents, they can preserve the tacit agreement that exists between them and the potential balancers, thereby keeping the potential balancers neutral. During the First World War, Germany was able initially to keep the United States neutral by modifying, then temporarily halting, its submarine campaign. During the Franco-Prussian War, Bismarck constantly strove to keep from frightening the non-belligerent great powers. During the Crimean War, Russia might have been able to keep France and Britain neutral had it limited its war with the Ottoman Empire to border clashes and had it allowed its grievances to be resolved through arbitration. Britain and France were willing to accept many of Russia's demands prior to the widening of the war and had even encouraged the Turks to accept most of them. Of course, the Turks' fear of being forced to accept many of Russia's demands may have caused them to lure Russia into battle in order to induce Britain's and France's entry. Russia did keep Austria out of the war for several years through a series of concessions, before ultimately ending the war to avoiding fighting Austria.

While appeasement may prove successful in keeping balancers out, threats likely will not work. Potential balancers are not planning to join only if the war will be easy, but rather if crucial interests are threatened. They often anticipate a hard fight. The more aggressive the state they plan to balance against appears, the more likely they are to join. Thus, threats should backfire by making the aggressor appear even more dangerous, and therefore, should rarely be employed in this situation. In the cases examined, the only time threats were used against a potential balancer was when Russia threatened Austria during the Crimean War, but given Austria's weakness, this may be the exception that proves the rule. Austria could not afford to bear the full brunt of a war, and therefore, could not act like a traditional balancer. Even in this case, in the end Austria decided to enter despite Russia's bullying. Russian threats, even while successful, were always coupled with concessions to the Austrians. Only Russia's willingness to accept the Austrian ultimatum, an act of significant appeasement, prevented Austria's entry. More will be said about this censoring effect later.

Potential bandwagoners respond to events within a war and the actions of belligerents very differently than do potential balancers. Bandwagoners are more likely to join if their potential allies do better than expected as this indicates spoils can be readily and cheaply obtained. The cases, especially the Franco-Prussian War and the First World War, showed that potential bandwagoners have less choice about which side to join than is sometimes surmised in the political science literature. In the First World War, Italy and Romania could achieve most of their respective goals only by joining the Entente. Bulgaria had more flexibility, but it would have been very difficult for the Bulgarians to ally with Serbia, and thus, their alliance options were limited as well. Likewise in the Franco-Prussian War, it made sense for Austria, Italy, and Denmark to ally with France, not Prussia. If potential bandwagoners had a great deal of flexibility about which side to join, revealed information should very rarely deter them. Potential bandwagoners would just wait to see which side was likely to win and then join that side. Only an unexpected stalemate would deter fully flexible states looking to pick up spoils. For example, if in the First World War Romania had been in a position where joining either side made sense, Gorlice-Tarnow would not have reduced the likelihood Romania would join, but instead would have made it likely Romania would join on the side of the Central Powers. Given that non-belligerents often can join only one side or strongly prefer one side over the other, such events can deter potential spoilers.

Unlike with potential balancers, threats by a belligerent may be successful at deterring states looking to pick up easy spoils. In part this is because bandwagoners are often weaker states, but just as importantly it is because they are not looking for a hard fight. Certainly, British threats were able to deter Persia and Greece from joining the Russians during the Crimean War. German threats deterred Romania for a time during the First World War and Russian threats deterred Austria-Hungary and Denmark in the Franco-Prussia War.[6] Obviously, such threats work best when they are reinforced by military success. Appeasement may work as well, but this may require the cession of territory, not an attractive prospect during a war. Also, such cessions may simply whet the appetite of states looking for spoils. Certainly this was the assessment of many of the Germans and most of the Austro-Hungarians during the First World War when cessions to Romania and Italy were suggested.

The above is a logical extension of both Davis (1995, 2000) and fits well with Werner (2000). Recall, Davis argues threats of intervention are more likely to deter opportunistic states than states that are acting defensively, while Werner argues that belligerents can take actions to appease potential balancers. It makes sense then that if states actively engaged in wars are more sensitive to threats when they are acting opportunistically, that states considering joining wars will also be more sensitive to threats when they are acting opportunistically rather than defensively. In other words, threats should more easily deter bandwagoners than balancers. Thus, the type of revealed information that will trigger joining differs between potential balancers and bandwagoners. Unexpected defeats of potential allies will increase the likelihood of balancing, but decrease the likelihood of bandwagoning, while unexpected victories of potential allies will increase the likelihood of bandwagoning, but decrease the likelihood of balancing. Also, belligerents need to use different strategies to prevent the hostile entry of non-belligerents. States that may balance against a belligerent should be appeased, while states looking for spoils should be deterred.

Let us return to Russia's decision to agree to the Austrian ultimatum and end the Crimean War. This result suggests that joining may sometimes not occur because

6 Britain also threatened Denmark.

wars will end before it can happen. Belligerents threatened by potential balancers may agree to peace rather than fight new foes. Also, bandwagoners can potentially wait too long to join. If they wait until it is absolutely clear which side will win, the war may end before they can join. Additionally, the side they want to join may no longer need their aid, and therefore, will be unwilling to reward them with spoils. Though this did not happen in any of the cases examined, this fear clearly influenced the actions of both Italy and Romania during the First World War.

Finally, the case studies suggest that the less a state approximates a unitary actor, the more complex the process through which revealed information influences decisions about war and peace will be. The Ottoman Empire during the First World War and Britain during the Crimean War had governments divided as to the proper course of action. Both ultimately became belligerents because of revealed information. The events were important not because they convinced a unified government that joining the war would be beneficial, but rather because the events shifted the balance between pro- and anti-war factions within the states' governments. In each case, the determinant was the way in which pivotal members of the respective cabinets were influenced by events. In the Ottoman Empire, the actions of the British fleet in the Mediterranean and the seizure of Turkish ships in Britain persuaded Djemal Pasha to join the interventionist camp headed by Enver Pasha. This in turn allowed Enver to engineer the *fait accompli* that caused the Ottomans to join the First World War. In Britain during the Crimean War, Lord Clarendon was the key. He held the middle position in a divided cabinet and as events influenced him to favor joining, the cabinet inevitably followed. In both the British and Turkish cases, intervention did not immediately follow the events that caused key members to change their minds about war. In both cases, time was required to maneuver the more reluctant ministers into war, but the events were still just as casual as in cases in which belligerency was decided much more closely upon the heels of an event.[7]

Suggestions for Future Research

In addition to extensions discussed above, the statistical results and case studies raised questions that suggest two potential avenues for future research. The first is to look at why states join civil wars. Such intervention is not uncommon and is highlighted by the important role outside militaries played in the late civil

7 Domestic politics also played a prominent role in keeping Austria-Hungary and Italy out of the Franco-Prussian War and in causing Sardinia to join the Crimean War, though in these cases, domestic politics were acting separately from, rather than in conjunction with, revealed information. In Greece, conflict within the government about the war and other issues eventually split the state into rival factions and the decision on whether Greece should enter the First World War could not be ultimately settled until the contest between the Monarchist and Venizelist factions was resolved.

war in the Democratic Republic of the Congo which raged from 1998 to 2003. Undoubtedly, many of the reasons for joining discussed in this work will carry over to a study of why state join ongoing civil wars, but there also will likely be factors unique to civil wars that this work has not considered.

Second, this project intentionally ignores states that join in the first month of a war. Thus, by definition, this work cannot fully explain why states join ongoing wars. This leads to a second possible avenue of future research. It seems likely that there are several logics that may lead states to join wars, that these logics likely vary over the course of the war, and that they should fit with Fearon's (1995) schema on the rational causes of war.[8] Initially, states may join a war because of previous commitments such as alliances. They may have preferred not to fight a war at that given moment, hence they did not start the war, but given the existence of the war they may want to uphold their alliance commitments both to maintain their reputation and to protect the more tangible considerations that led to the formation of the alliance in the first place. For example, Russia was not eager for war in 1914, but given an Austro-Serbian war, it felt it had to intervene to uphold its reputation as a good ally and prevent Austria-Hungary from becoming dominant in the Balkans. These reasons for joining should quickly diminish in importance as the war progresses. A state's reputation will be quickly sullied if it does not readily honor its treaty commitments. Joining many months into a war likely will not do much to redeem a state's reputation. Likewise, if compelling material reasons to aid an ally exist antebellum, they will likely be acted on shortly after the outbreak of war. These sorts of logics should dictate whether or not states join roughly within a month of the war's outbreak. After this initial period, the logic outlined in this work should predominate. States that did not initially have an incentive to join may be induced to do so by the changing fortunes of war. As the logic of this course of action has been discussed extensively in Chapter 2, it will not be repeated here. Finally, near the end of wars, problems of indivisibility may arise. Problems of indivisibility of the stakes may prevent the war from ending and the introduction of an outside party may be necessary for a resolution to be found. This seems likely to be the least cause of joining, but a future comprehensive study of the causes of joining should consider it.

Thus, the questions of why and when states join ongoing wars should provide opportunities for fertile research for some time to come. Military intervention will likely remain a significant phenomenon in the future and should, therefore, be more extensively studied. This work has provided an explanation of what often causes states to join ongoing wars and when they choose to do so. The work, however, has not answered all questions about joining. Hopefully future works will shed even more light on why states join ongoing wars and perhaps these studies will help explain war initiation and war termination. This seems possible as this work and others have made it clear that war initiation, termination, and intervention are all intrinsically linked. Such studies may also lead to a better

8 See Chapter 2.

understanding of the spatial spread of other phenomena such as currency and trade regimes, financial crises, and regime types. Their spread unfortunately, much like the spread of war in the previous literature, has been compared to that of diseases or the diffusion of one liquid when poured into another. Like war, however, the spread of such phenomena is likely largely dictated by conscious decision-making and strategic interaction. Thus, a great deal more research can be undertaken, both on joining specifically and the spatial spread of political and social phenomena more generally.

Appendix: Coding for Unexpected Events, Regions, and Contiguity

As was mentioned in the main text, the descriptions and coding of the unexpected events variables need to be covered in detail, as these variables and their coding are crucial to the statistical results produced in Chapter 3. This appendix will describe the variables, discuss the rules and sources used for their coding, and describe each unexpected event in the data set.

Descriptions of the Unexpected Events Variables

Five variables indicating whether unexpected events happened during a particular war-month and the nature of those events are included in the dataset. They are UNEXP, MIL, POL, IMPMIL, and IMPPOL. UNEXP records whether an unexpected event occurred in the month in question. POL and MIL record whether the unexpected event in question was political or military in nature respectively. All three are dichotomous, zero/one variables. Additionally, all unexpected events were coded as being either political or military, thus if both POL and MIL are zero then UNEXP by definition will be zero as well. Likewise, if UNEXP is coded as a one, then either POL or MIL must be scored as a one as well. No single event was coded as being both political and military in nature. It is possible, however, for both POL and MIL to be coded as a one in the same month, as distinct unexpected political and military events do sometimes occur in the same war-month. IMPPOL and IMPMIL are ordinal variables ranging from zero to three and record the magnitude of the unexpected event that occurred in a given month. IMPPOL records the magnitude of political events while IMPMIL records the magnitude of military events. A value of three indicates an unexpected event of very great importance, while a one indicates a relatively minor event, but one with enough importance to be recorded. A score of zero indicates that no significant unexpected event occurred in that respective category. If either IMPPOL or IMPMIL are coded a one or greater, then by definition UNEXP will be coded as a one and either POL or MIL will be coded as a one, as is appropriate.

Coding Rules

As discussed above, UNEXP, POL, and MIL are simply dichotomous variables that are directly derived from the variables IMPPOL and IMPMIL. Thus, these three variables are not coded, but are merely the result of the coding of IMPPOL and IMPMIL. As such, their values depend entirely on the coding of IMPPOL and IMPMIL.

The coding of IMPPOL and IMPMIL involved three decisions: whether an unexpected event observable by outside states occurred; whether it was political or military in nature; and how significant was it. The easiest of these three questions to answer is the second. Political events include such things as assassinations, the fall of governments, revolts, riots, large or important protests, and revolutions, while military events include the introduction of new tactics or weapons, surprising battlefield results, and mutinies that remain largely apolitical in their nature. Obviously, the line between apolitical and political mutinies is somewhat fuzzy, but it is generally discernable. Political mutinies aim at revolution, overthrowing the government, or significant political change. Obviously, political mutinies may be sparked by more mundane matters than high politics. The question is, "Do politics become the focus of the mutiny?" Military mutinies tend to focus on improving the condition of the troops or a simple unwillingness to go into combat. The mutiny in the Black Sea fleet in 1905 is a good example of a political mutiny, while the mutiny in the French army in 1917 was basically apolitical, and therefore, would have been seen as a military event in this scheme of coding had the mutiny not been successfully kept a secret by the French. As it was kept a secret, it was not coded as an unexpected event as it was not observed by outside states. Only events which were observable by outside states, and hence revealed information to non-belligerents, were recorded.

Determining whether a significant unexpected event occurred was the most important part of the coding process. Obviously, in war and in politics, the unexpected is a daily occurrence. Many of these unexpected events, however, are trivial. An infantryman unexpectedly steps on a landmine, a sentry falls asleep at his post and is surprised, or a member of parliament votes differently than expected on a minor bill that has no effect on the standing of the government. These are not the sort of events that are recorded in IMPPOL and IMPMIL. They record nontrivial unexpected events. It is also important to remember that not all significant events are recorded. Only significant events that were surprises at the time are recorded. This question was always approached from the perspective of a contemporary statesman whose country was not involved in the war. For example, for the Franco-Prussian War, the coder would determine whether the events in the war would have surprised the British, the Italians, and so forth at that time. The initial outbreak of war is never coded as a surprise, though later interventions are coded as surprises when appropriate. This is because the study is not interested in why states initially join wars; thus whether the initial outbreak was a surprise or not is irrelevant. Later unexpected events, including an unanticipated entry of a non-belligerent, were relevant to the study.

Determining the magnitude of an unexpected event, if one occurred, was the most difficult part of the coding. Level three unexpected events are very decisive military results, unexpected revolutions, or radical changes in the direction of a government. Military results on the level of a three are battles which result in the surprising destruction of large portions of an army or fleet. Such victories do not have to knock a country out of a war, but they do have to result in serious damage to one side's capabilities, not just a retreat. Of course, just because a major crushing victory happens does not necessarily mean that it was an unexpected event. If such a large victory was anticipated, then it would not be an unexpected event at all and thus a zero would be recorded. The dramatic and surprising use of new and decisive weapons, such as the atomic bomb, also falls into this category. Clearly such events rarely occur, as events of this magnitude and decisiveness are rare on their own, and it is even rarer for them to be unanticipated.

Events that rate a one on the scale would be such things as a somewhat better or worse military showing than was expected by one side in a battle or series of battles fought over a short time span, small but surprising improvements in tactics or weapons, small scale protests, or an assassination or unexpected death of a leader that did not greatly alter the nature or expected actions of a government. Also, a state may do better in battle than expected, without necessarily winning. The state may have been expected to fight poorly, but in the event actually performed decently, despite still losing. An event of this level could also be a state winning more easily than was expected. An example would be a state being able to quickly defeat an opponent when most expected it to take longer.

Events on the level of a two are in between. Such events would be very significant battlefield surprises, though in such instances the defeated side would be able to retreat in relatively good order. They might also include unanticipated widespread protests or rioting against a government, but not of a scale that threatens to cause a revolution. It would also include the surprising fall of a government in a parliamentary system provided that it led to a significant change in policy. Without a significant change in policy, the event would be coded as a one. Obviously, some events are more surprising than others and part of this surprise comes not only from the magnitude of the event, but its degree of unexpectedness. This fact, the level of unexpectedness, also influenced the coding of IMPPOL and IMPMIL, though only to a limited extent.

The following procedure is used if two or more unexpected events occurred in the same month. As political and military events were coded separately, if one political and one military event occurred in the same month, both are recorded per the standard coding rules. If multiple unexpected events of the same type occurred in the same month—in other words, two or more political or two or more military events—the unexpected event with the greatest magnitude for its type is recorded. The events were not added together or otherwise aggregated.

One of the greatest coding difficulties is determining when an event ceased to be unexpected. Sometimes a series of events happen, such as long running demonstrations, which were initially unexpected, but over the course of time, became expected. Determining when they cease to be unexpected is difficult, but not impossible. Obviously, the onset of the event is coded as being unexpected. Any surprising changes in the level of intensity of the event are also recorded as unexpected. If the event was expected to stop, its continuation is coded as unexpected, but if it was expected to continue, then its continuation is not coded as unexpected.

Another challenge in coding unexpected events was the problem of hindsight. Hindsight is generally an advantage, but when determining whether something was unexpected, it is a decided disadvantage. Events that appear inevitable now, may have been largely or even completely unforeseen at the time. For this reason, the coding relied mainly on contemporary accounts. The *Annual Register* was the main source for the coding.[1] The *Register* is an annual compilation of year-end reports of events for each state in the world, often written by journalists or other in country observers. It is an excellent source and can generally be relied on, but it does have several weaknesses. First, the style of the writing in the *Register* does change over time as its contributors change. This is a minor problem, but still needed to be considered. Second, prior to the 20th century, the *Register* is quite Eurocentric, but as most of the interstate wars in the Correlates of War database in the 19th century involve at least one European power or the United States, this is not as serious of a drawback as it would first seem. Though its focus in this period is Eurocentric, it does cover many of the major non-European states such as the US, China and Japan. Still, it covers European events in more detail. This makes it tempting to overcode the number of unexpected events in European conflicts, relative to in other conflicts. COW can also be criticized for being Eurocentric, but that is a larger debate that this work does not seek to resolve. Another weakness of the *Register* is that it does, at times, have a British bias. This bias, however, is never overwhelming, though it is quite strong in the coverage of the Crimean War. Additionally, as the bias is consistently from a British perspective and generally mild, yet overt, it was not too difficult to manage and effectively control for the bias in the coding.

The final and main area of weakness in the *Annual Register* in this regard is its scanty coverage of Latin America in the 19th and early 20th centuries. This gap was filled by *Latin America's Wars* by Robert Scheina. Though not a contemporary source like the *Register*, it was the best source available in English. Other smaller wars also received limited coverage in the *Register*. The coding of these wars relied in large part on additional supplementary texts. They were as follows:

---

1 I am indebted to Charles Tilly for suggesting the *Annual Register*. I am also grateful to Ivan Savic who helped establish clear coding guidelines and aided with some of the more difficult coding. The final judgment was mine and any errors are my own.

– *War in Uganda: The Legacy of Idi Amin*, by Tony Avirgan and Martha Honey(1982)

– *The Israeli-Egyptian War of Attrition*, by Yaacov Bar-Siman-Tov (1980)

– *Australia's War*, by Joan Beaumont (1996)

– *By Reason or Force: Chile and the Balancing of Power in South America, 1830-1905*, by Robert Burr (1980)

– *Italo-Turkish Diplomacy and the War over Libya, 1911-1912*, by Timothy Childs (1990)

– *The Anatomy of a Small War: The Soviet-Japanese Struggle for Changkufeng/ Khasan*, by Alvin Coox (1977)

– *The Third Indochina War*, by Jaap Van Ginneken (1983)

– *Strategy*, by B. H. Liddell Hart (1991)

– *The Soviet Union and the Threat from the East*, by Jonathan Haslam (1992)

– *Chronology: New Zealand in the war, 1939-1946*, by Robin Kay (1968)

– *Turkish Diplomacy, 1918-1923*, by Salahi Sonyel (1975)

Thus, though the coding involved difficult decisions, a clear set of coding rules was followed. A description of the decision has been recorded allowing outside scholars to easily examine the coding. Thus, there are several checks to help assure that the coding was unbiased and fair. Obviously, no two people would code all events the same, but the process was done as objectively as possible. The coding rules discussed above are summarized as follows:

1. Did an unexpected event other than the outbreak of war occur? If no, code all variables as a zero and move to the next month. If yes, code UNEXP as a one and proceed to step two.

2. Was it political or military in nature? If it was political in nature code POL as a one. If it was military in nature code MIL as a one. All events are either military or political events and no event is both political and military in nature, however, multiple events can occur in the same month, thus it is possible to have both military and political events in the same month. Go to step three.

3. Determine the magnitude of the unexpected event. Small events are a one, medium events a two, and very important events a three. If the event in question was political in nature, record the magnitude under IMPPOL. If it was military in nature, record the magnitude under IMPMIL.

The results of the coding are listed in Table 9.1 below. For every unexpected event recorded, a short description of the event is included as well. Only months in which an unexpected event was record are included. Wars in which no event was recorded are omitted entirely. The entire database can be accessed at http://keep2.sjfc.edu/faculty/zshirkey/

Table 9.1 Descriptions of Unexpected Events

War	Year	Month	Impmil	Imppol	Description
1	1823	4	1	0	Unexpectedly light opposition from Spain
1	1823	5	2	0	Feeble resistance; Madrid falls
4	1828	5	1	0	Better Turkish defense of frontier than expected
4	1828	8	2	0	Vigorous Turkish defense of Shumla and Varna
4	1829	8	2	0	Turkish force routed at Selimno; Adrianople falls
7	1846	8	0	1	Santa Anna takes power in a coup
13	1848	5	1	0	Minor Danish victory
22	1853	11	2	0	Battle of Sinope
22	1854	10	2	0	Slow Allied progress; Battle of Balaklava
22	1854	11	2	0	Battle of Inkerman
22	1855	3	0	1	Nicholas I dies; French attack on Mamelon Vert repulsed
28	1859	4	0	1	Tuscan revolt; Modena occupied
40	1862	5	2	0	French advance halted at Puebla
40	1866	7	0	2	Prussia defeats Austria; France vulnerable
49	1866	9	2	0	Paraguay wins the Battle of Curupayti decisively
49	1866	11	0	2	Rebellion in the Argentine province of Mendoza
49	1868	2	1	1	Flores assassinated; Brazilian fleet runs past Humaita
52	1865	11	1	0	Spanish gunboat Covadonga and signal book captured
55	1866	7	2	0	Battles of Köninggratz and Lissa
58	1870	8	3	0	French beaten at Wörth and Rezonville
58	1870	9	2	3	Fall of Sedan; Declaration of the Third Republic
61	1877	7	2	0	Fall of Nicopolis; Russian defeat at Plevna
61	1877	8	1	0	Series of Russian defeats in Asia
61	1877	10	1	0	Catastrophic Turkish defeat in Asia
64	1879	4	1	0	Chile sinks the ironclad Independencia
64	1879	8	0	1	Chilean government forced out by protests
64	1879	10	2	0	Loss of the Peruvian ship Huascar
64	1879	12	0	1	Coups in Peru and Bolivia
67	1885	3	1	0	French successes on Formosa; Mixed honors in Tonkin
70	1885	3	3	2	President Barrios killed in surprising Guatemalan defeat
76	1897	4	1	0	Greeks easily defeated in Epirus and Thessaly
82	1900	6	1	0	Attempt to relieve Beijing legations rebuffed
85	1904	5	1	0	Japanese advance towards Port Arthur
85	1904	6	2	0	String of Japanese victories
85	1904	8	1	0	Port Arthur fleet destroyed: Vladivostok squadron damaged

85	1904	9	1	0	Japanese victory in the face of a superior force
85	1904	10	1	0	Russians defeated in Manchuria by outnumbered Japanese
85	1905	1	0	2	Port Arthur falls; Massacre in St. Petersburg; Japanese victory in Manchuria
85	1905	5	3	0	Massacres in Russian Poland; Battle of Tsushima Straits
85	1905	6	0	2	Mutinies in the Black Sea fleet; Riots in Baltic ports
85	1905	8	0	2	Tsar creates the Duma; Japanese take Sakhalin
94	1909	7	0	1	Attempted revolution in Barcelona; Civil war in Morocco; Moors attack Melilla
100	1912	7	0	1	Resignation of Grand Vizier Said Pasha; Insurrection in Albania becoming general
100	1912	10	2	0	Series of Turkish defeats
100	1912	11	1	0	Turkish defeats continue; Mass desertions of Christians from the Turkish forces
100	1913	1	0	2	Turkish coup
100	1913	3	0	1	Greeks and Bulgarians clash; Greek King assassinated
103	1913	7	1	1	Series of Bulgarian disasters; Romanians join war
106	1914	8	2	2	Germans occupy Belgium; Battle of the Mazurian Lakes
106	1914	9	3	0	Battle of the Marne; Russians defeated in East Prussia; Russians take L'viv
106	1914	12	2	0	Serbs crush an Austrian invasion
106	1915	2	0	1	British extend blockade; Unrestricted submarine warfare; Russia driven from East Prussia
106	1915	5	1	2	Gulflight and Lusitania sunk; Gorlice-Tarnow; Gallipoli Campaign begins to fail
106	1915	6	2	0	Russians badly mauled in Galicia and Poland
106	1915	10	1	0	Rapid collapse of Serbia
106	1916	6	2	0	Brusilov's offensive
106	1916	10	1	0	Romania crushed
106	1917	2	0	2	Resumption of unrestricted submarine warfare
106	1917	3	0	2	February Revolution
106	1917	7	2	0	Mass Russian desertions in Galicia; General advance by the Central Powers in the East
106	1917	10	2	0	Battle of Caporetto
106	1917	11	0	3	October Revolution; Tanks first used at Cambrai
106	1918	3	2	0	German Spring Offensive
106	1918	6	1	0	Allied offensive steadily successful
106	1918	9	0	1	Maximilian becomes Prime Minister in Germany; Secession attempt in Bohemia
106	1918	11	0	3	Riots and mutinies in, and collapse of, the Central Powers
109	1920	4	1	0	Major Polish offensive
109	1920	7	1	0	Russians retake Kiev; Series of Polish defeats
109	1920	8	3	0	Crushing Polish counter-attack

115	1921	2	0	1	Work stoppages throughout Greece
115	1921	9	1	0	Greek offensive checked
115	1922	8	3	0	Greeks routed
116	1920	4	1	0	French forced to retire
117	1920	7	1	0	Poles abandon Vilnius
117	1920	10	1	0	White Russian force captures Vilnius
121	1932	1	1	0	Unexpected Chinese resistance around Shanghai
121	1932	5	0	1	Prime Minister Inukai of Japan assassinated
121	1933	4	1	0	Nationalists beaten by the Communists
124	1932	9	2	0	Fall of Boqueron
124	1933	1	1	0	Bolivians fail in their attack on Nanawa
124	1933	12	2	0	Paraguayans capture Campo Via and many prisoners
124	1934	7	1	0	Paraguayan offensive fails
124	1934	11	0	3	Paraguayans capture Ballivian; Battle of El Carmen; Bolivian coup
124	1935	4	1	0	Paraguayans defeated in high country; Paraguay running out of men and material
127	1935	12	1	0	Ethiopian counter-attack successful
127	1936	2	2	0	Italians rout the Ethiopians
130	1937	12	0	1	USS Panay and HMS Ladybird attacked
130	1938	10	1	0	Fall of Wuhan and Guangzhou
130	1938	12	0	1	US and Britain grant China economic credits
130	1939	10	2	0	Japanese defeated in North Kiangsi and Northeastern Honan
130	1940	7	0	1	Militant government assumes power in Japan
130	1940	8	0	2	Japanese government restructured on fascist lines; US oil and metal embargo on Japan
130	1941	7	0	2	US and UK freeze Japanese assets; Embargo strengthened
130	1941	12	3	0	Pearl Harbor; Japanese attacks on British possessions
130	1942	1	2	0	Japanese advance on all fronts; Chinese win at Changsha
130	1942	5	1	0	Battle of the Coral Sea
130	1942	6	3	0	Battle of Midway
130	1943	5	1	0	Chinese victory at Ichang
130	1944	4	1	0	Japanese take Chengchow
130	1944	6	1	0	Battle of the Philippine Sea; Japanese take Changsha
130	1945	8	3	0	US drops atomic bombs on Japan
133	1938	8	1	0	Purge weakened Russians defeat Japanese
136	1939	7	1	0	Japanese repulsed despite more men and artillery
136	1939	8	2	0	Major Soviet offensive completely successful
139	1939	9	1	0	Poland overrun; speed of the operation surprising
139	1940	4	2	0	Denmark and Norway fall despite British control of the sea

139	1940	5	3	0	Germans triumphant in West
139	1940	6	0	2	France surrenders
139	1940	9	1	0	RAF gains the upper hand in the Battle of Britain
139	1940	11	1	0	Italian invasion of Greece fails; Taranto fleet sunk
139	1941	2	1	0	Benghazi falls; Italians defeated in the Horn of Africa
139	1941	3	0	2	Lend-Lease Act
139	1941	4	1	0	Germans overrun the Balkans; British beaten in Libya
139	1941	7	2	0	Rapid German successes against Soviets
139	1941	8	1	0	German advance remains rapid
139	1941	12	1	0	Soviet counter-attacks have decent success
139	1942	6	1	0	Significant German victory in Libya; Tobruk falls
139	1942	7	1	0	Sevastopol falls; Massive German offensive successful
139	1942	11	3	0	Battles of Stalingrad and El Alamein; Landings in Algeria
139	1943	4	1	0	The Battle of the Atlantic turns in favor of the Allies
139	1943	7	2	2	Battle of Kursk; Allies take Sicily; Fall of Mussolini
139	1944	6	1	0	Allied landings at Normandy
139	1944	8	1	0	American breakout from Normandy
139	1944	12	2	0	Battle of the Bulge
142	1939	12	2	0	Finns repel Soviet attacks; 163rd division destroyed
142	1940	1	1	0	Continued Soviet difficulties; 44th division destroyed
148	1948	7	1	0	Unqualified Israeli success
148	1948	10	1	0	Beersheba taken by the Israelis
148	1948	12	0	1	Riots in Cairo; Egyptian Prime Minister assassinated
151	1950	9	2	0	Inchon landings
151	1950	11	2	2	Chinese intervention and the defeat of UN forces
151	1952	6	0	1	Crisis in S. Korea over constitutional reform
151	1953	3	0	1	Death of Stalin
157	1956	11	0	1	UN and US pressure France and UK to withdraw
163	1966	3	0	2	Riots and lack of control in Hue and Da Nang
163	1967	5	0	1	Part of the Pentagon occupied by protesters
163	1967	10	0	1	10,000 demonstrate at the Pentagon for two days
163	1967	11	0	1	McNamara's resignation announced
163	1968	2	2	1	Tet offensive
163	1968	3	0	2	Johnson announces he will not seek another term
163	1968	6	0	1	Robert Kennedy assassinated
163	1968	8	0	2	Major disorder at Democratic Convention
163	1968	11	1	1	Bombing of North Vietnam suspended; Nixon elected

163	1969	3	1	0	Accelerated Pacification Program unexpectedly successful
163	1969	5	2	0	US intention to greatly reduce troop levels announced
163	1970	3	0	2	Overthrow of Prince Sihanouk of Cambodia
163	1970	4	1	1	Large US and S. Vietnamese forces enter Cambodia
163	1970	5	0	1	Kent State killings
163	1971	6	0	1	Release of the Pentagon Papers
163	1971	12	1	0	Successful NVA advance across the Plain of Jars in Laos
163	1972	3	2	0	Major conventional North Vietnamese offensive
163	1972	6	1	0	North Vietnamese offensive stalls
163	1975	1	0	1	Phuoc Long overrun; US rebuffs requests for aid
163	1975	3	2	2	Major NVA offensive; South's will collapses
169	1967	6	3	0	Israelis crush the Arabs in six days
172	1969	7	1	0	Israel escalates through the use of its air force
172	1970	1	1	0	Israel begins deep air raids into Egypt
172	1970	2	0	1	Russians decide to intervene
172	1970	6	1	0	Intervention by Soviet SAM crews becomes effective
187	1977	12	2	0	Major Vietnamese offensive
187	1978	1	1	0	Vietnamese offensive stalls; heavy Khmer Rouge casualties
187	1978	11	0	1	Vietnam joins Comecon; Gain explicit Soviet support
187	1978	12	2	0	Massive invasion of Cambodia is launched
189	1977	9	1	0	Somalis capture Marda Pass
189	1977	11	0	1	Ethiopia launches the internal "red terror" campaign
189	1978	3	1	0	Ethiopian counter-attack is completely successful
190	1979	3	2	0	Only token Ugandan resistance
199	1980	10	2	0	Initial Iraqi invasion stalls after only small gains
199	1981	3	0	1	Rioting in Tehran, President Bani-Sadr investigated
199	1981	6	1	2	Osirik raid; Iranian President Bani-Sadr impeached; New President and PM assassinated
199	1981	9	1	0	Iraqi withdrawals from Abadan and across the Karun
199	1982	3	1	0	Successful Iranian offensive
199	1982	6	0	1	Purges in the Iraqi government; Iraqi withdrawal from Iran
199	1984	10	1	0	Iranian offensive at the level of Baghdad defeated
199	1985	1	0	1	Iraqi Kurds begin to revolt
199	1986	2	1	0	Iranians capture Fao
199	1986	5	1	0	Iraqis capture Mehran
199	1986	7	1	0	Iranians recapture Mehran

199	1987	7	0	1	US reflags oil tankers; International mine sweeping effort follows
199	1987	9	0	1	US captures and sinks an Iranian mine layer
199	1988	4	2	1	USS Stark hits mine; US attacks Iranian assets in Gulf; Iraqis retake Fao
199	1988	5	1	0	Significant Iraqi successes around Basra
199	1988	7	0	1	USS Vincennes shoots down Iranian civilian airliner
202	1982	5	1	0	The General Belgrano sunk
205	1982	9	0	1	President Bashir Gemayel of Lebanon assassinated
208	1987	1	1	0	Fighting intensifies briefly
211	1990	8	0	1	Iraq overruns Kuwait; US sends troops to Saudi Arabia
211	1990	11	0	1	UN Resolution 678 allowing force passed
211	1991	2	2	0	Coalition ground assault is rapidly successful
220	1998	7	0	1	Ethiopia begins expelling ethnic Eritreans
220	1999	2	1	0	Ethiopia captures Badme; conflict intensifies
220	2000	5	1	0	Ethiopia captures Zalembessa, Bada, Senafe, and Barentu

Table 9.2 List of Regions

Regions	**COW Country Codes**
North America and the Caribbean	2–95
South America	100–165
Europe	200–395 and 640 (until 4/1913)
West Africa	402–484
Southern and East Africa	490–591
Middle East	600–698
Southern and Central Asia	700–705 and 750–790
Northeast Asia	365 and 710–740
Southeast Asia	800–850
Oceania	900–990

Table 9.3 List of the Foci of Interstate Wars

War	State Foci	Region
001	230	Europe
004	640	Europe; Middle East
007	70	North America
010	300 until 8/1848;	Europe
	325 from 3/1849	
013	390	Europe
016	327	Europe
019	160	South America
022	640 until 9/1854;	Europe
	365 from 9/1854	
025	630	Middle East
028	300	Europe
031	600	Middle East
034	327	Europe
037	329	Europe
040	070	North America
043	100	South America
046	390	Europe
049	150	South America
052	155	South America
055	300	Europe
058	220	Europe
061	640	Europe; Middle East
064	145;	South America
	155 until 4/1879;	
	135 after 5/1879	
067	816, 710	SE Asia; NE Asia
070	90, 92	North America
073	710	NE Asia
076	350, 640	Europe
079	40	North America
082	710	NE Asia
085	710	NE Asia
088	090	North America

091	091	North America
094	600	Middle East
097	620;	Middle East;
	640 from 4/1912	Europe after 4/1912
100	640	Europe
103	355	Europe
106	345;	Europe
	211, 220, 255, 300 from 9/1914;	
	640 from 10/1914;	
	325 from 5/1915;	
	355 from 9/1915;	
	360 from 8/1916–12/1917;	
	365 from 9/1914–12/1917	
109	365 until 7/1920;	Europe
	290 from 7/1920	
112	310	Europe
115	640	Middle East
116	640	Middle East
117	368	Europe
118	710	NE Asia
121	710	NE Asia
124	678	Middle East
127	530	Southern and East Africa
130	710;	NE Asia;
	775, 840, 850, 910, 983, 986 and 987 from 12/1941	SC Asia and Oceania from 12/1941
133	710	NE Asia
136	365, 712	NE Asia
139	290; 380, 385 from 4/1940;	Europe
	210, 211, 212, 220 from 5/1940;	M. East from 6/1940–5/1943
	350 from 10/1940;	SE Af. from 6/1940–6/1941
	345 from 4/1941	
142	375	Europe
145	811	SE Asia
147	750	South and Central Asia
148	666	Middle East
151	732;	NE Asia

	731 from 8/1950	
154	310	Europe
157	651	Middle East
160	750	South and Central Asia
163	816, 817	SE Asia
166	770	South and Central Asia
169	651, 652, 663, 666	Middle East
172	651, 666	Middle East
175	91, 92	North America
178	771	South and Central Asia
181	651, 652, 666	Middle East
184	352	Europe
187	811	SE Asia
189	530	Southern and East Africa
190	510 until 11/1978;	Southern and East Africa
	500 from 11/1978	
193	816	SE Asia
199	630, 645	Middle East
202	160	South America
205	660	Middle East
208	816	SE Asia
211	690	Middle East
	645 from 1/1991	
220	520	Southern and East Africa
230	750	South and Central Asia

Bibliography

Almeida, A. et al. (1917), *Plain Speaking: Reasons for the Military Intervention of Portugal in the European War* (London: Eyre and Spottiswoode).

Altfeld, M. and Bueno De Mesquita, B. (1979), 'Choosing Sides in War', *International Studies Quarterly* 23:1, 87–112.

Avrigan, T. and Honey, M. (1982), *War in Uganda: The Legacy of Idi Amin* (Westport: Lawrence Hill).

Axelrod, R. and Keohane, R. (1985), 'Achieving Cooperation Under Anarchy: Strategies and Institutions', *World Politics* 38:1, 226–54.

Balazs, J. and Wiberg, H. (1993), *Peace Research for the 1990s* (Budapest: Akademiai Kiado).

Barclay, G. (1988), *A Very Small Insurance Policy: The Politics of Australian Involvement in Vietnam, 1954-1967* (St. Lucia: University of Queensland Press).

Bar-Siman-Tov, Y. (1980), *The Israeli-Egyptian War of Attrition, 1969-1970* (New York: Columbia University Press).

Baumgart, W. (1981), *The Peace of Paris 1856: Studies in War, Diplomacy, and Peacemaking*. Tr. Saab, A. (Santa Barbara: ABC-Clio).

Beaumont, J. (1996), *Australia's War, 1939-45* (St. Leonards, NSW, Australia: Allen and Unwin).

Beck, N. (1991), 'The Illusion of Cycles in International Relations', *International Studies Quarterly* 35:4, 455–76.

Beck, N., Katz, J., Tucker, R. (1998), 'Taking Time Seriously: Time-Series—Cross-Section Analysis with a Binary Dependent Variable', *American Journal of Political Science* 42:4, 1260–88.

Bell, H. (1969), 'The Home Secretary in Foreign Affairs', in Gooch (ed.).

Bennett, D. and Stam, A. (2000), '*EUGene*: A Conceptual Manual', *International Interactions* 26:2 ,179–204.

Betts, R. (1992), 'Systems for Peace or Causes of War? Collective Security, Arms Control and the New Europe', *International Security* 17:1, 5–43.

Blackburn, R. (1994), *Mercenaries and Lyndon Johnson's "more flags": the hiring of Korean, Filipino, and Thai soldiers in the Vietnam War* (Jefferson: McFarland).

Blainey, G. (1973), *The Causes of War* (New York: Free Press).

Bosworth, R. (1983), *Italy and the Approach of the First World War* (London: MacMillan).

Boulding, K. (1962), *Conflict and Defense: A General Theory* (New York: Harper).

Bourgeois, E. (1969), 'Early Years of the Second Empire: Crimean War Origins' in Gooch (ed.).
Bragança-Cunha, V. (1938), *Revolutionary Portugal (1910-1936)* (London: James Clarke).
Bremer, S. (1982), 'The Contagiousness of Coercion: The Spread of Serious International Disputes, 1900-1976.', *International Interactions* 9:1, 29–55.
Brown, G. (1991), *Coalition, coercion and compromise: diplomacy of the Gulf Crisis, 1990-91* (Washington: Institute for the Study of Diplomacy).
Buehrig, E. (1955), *Woodrow Wilson and the Balance of Power* (Bloomington: Indiana University Press).
Bueno de Mesquita, B. and Lalman, D. (1992), *War and Reason: Domestic and International Imperatives* (New Haven: Yale University Press).
Bueno de Mesquita, B., Morrow, J., and Zorick, E. (1997), 'Capabilities, Perception, and Escalation', *American Political Science Review* 91:1, 15–27.
Buhaug, H. (2008), 'Contagion or Confusion? Why Conflicts Cluster in Space', *International Studies Quarterly* 52:2, 215–33.
Burr, R. (1980), *By Reason or Force: Chile and the Balancing of Power in South America, 1830-1905* (Millwood: Kraus Reprint).
Burstall, T. (1993), *Vietnam, the Australian Dilemma* (St. Lucia: University of Queensland Press).
Buzan, B. and Waever, O. (2003), *Regions and Powers: The Structure of International Security*. (Cambridge: Cambridge University Press).
Carnegie Endowment for International Peace. (1923), *Official German Documents Relating to the World War*. Vol. II. (New York).
Cederman, L. (2003), 'Modeling the Size of Wars: From Billiard Balls to Sand Piles', *American Journal of Political Science* 97:1, 135–50.
Chadefaux, T. (2005), 'Bargaining Rigidities and the Rationality of War', paper given at the annual meeting of the American Political Science Association, Washington: 1-4 September.
Chayes, A. and Chayes, A. (1993), 'On Compliance', *International Organization* 47:2, 175–205.
Childs, T. (1990), *Italo-Turkish Diplomacy and the War over Libya, 1911-1912* (New York: E.J. Brill).
Churchill, Winston. (1928), *The World Crisis*. Vol. 1. (New York: Scribner).
Claude, Jr., I. (1962), 'Collective Legitimization as a Political Function of the United Nations', *International Organization* 20:3, 367–79.
— (1966), *Power and International Relations* (New York: Random House).
Clausewitz, C. (1976), *On War* (Princeton: Princeton University Press).
Cooper, Jr., J. (2003), 'The United States' in Hamilton R. and Herwig H. (eds).
Coox, A. (1977), *The Anatomy of a Small War: The Soviet-Japanese Struggle for Changkufeng / Khasan, 1938* (London: Greenwood Press).
Correlates of War 2 Project. (2008), *State System Membership List*, version 2008.1. <http://www.correlatesofwar.org/COW2%20Data/SystemMembership/2008/states2008.1.csv>.

Crawford, T. (2003), *Pivotal Deterrence: Third Party Statecraft and the Pursuit of Peace* (Ithaca: Cornell University Press).
Cusack, T. and Stoll, R. (1991), 'Balancing Behavior in the Interstate System, 1816-1976', *International Interactions* 16:4, 255–70.
Davis, J. (1995), 'The Forgotten Variable: The Role of Promises in Deterrence', Dissertation (Columbia University).
— (2000), *Threats and Promises: The Pursuit of International Influence* (Baltimore: John Hopkins University Press).
Davis, W., Duncan, G., and Siverson, R. (1978), 'The Dynamics of Warfare: 1816-1965', *American Journal of Political Science* 22:4, 772–92.
Decsy, J. (1979), *Prime Minister Gyula Andrássy's Influence on Hapsburg Foreign Policy During the Franco-German War of 1870-1871* (Boulder: East European Quarterly).
De Meneses, F. (2004), *Portugal 1914-1926: From the First World War to military dictatorship*. (Bristol: HiPLAM).
Dewing, H. (1924), *Greece and the Great Powers: The Greek Struggle for National Unity During the Last Hundred Years* (Washington: American Friends of Greece).
Dickinson, F. (2003), 'Japan' in Hamilton, R. and Herwig, H. (eds.).
Diehl, P. (1991), 'Geography and War: A Review and Assessment of the Empirical Literature', *International Interactions* 17:1, 11–27.
Diehl, P. and Goertz, G. (2000), *War and Peace in International Rivalry* (Ann Arbor: University of Michigan Press).
Dillon, E. (1915), *From the Triple to the Quadruple Alliance: Why Italy Went to War* (London: Hodder and Stoughton).
Downs, G. and Rocke, D. (1994), 'Conflict, Agency, and Gambling for Resurrection: The Principal-Agent Problem Goes to War', *American Journal of Political Science* 38:2, 362–80.
Downs, G., Rocke, D., and Barsoom, P. (1996), 'Is the Good News about Compliance Good News about Cooperation?', *International Organization* 50:3, 379–406.
Ederington, L. and Mazarr, M. (1994), *Turning Point* (Boulder: Westview Press).
Edleston, R. (1915). *Italian Neutrality* (Cambridge: W. Heffer and Sons).
Edwards, R. (2004), *Military Encounters: Quotations on War and Peace* (New York: Barnes and Noble).
Emin, A. (1930), *Turkey in the World War* (New Haven: Yale University Press).
Faber, J., Houweling, H., and Siccama, J. (1984), 'Diffusion of War: Some Theoretical Considerations and Empirical Evidence', *Journal of Peace Research* 21:3, 277–88.
Falls, C., (1959), *The Great War: 1914-1918* (New York: Capricorn Books).
Fazal, T. (2004), 'State Death in the International System', *International Organization* 58:2, 311–44.
— (2007), *State Death: The Politics and Geography of Conquest, Occupation, and Annexation* (Princeton: Princeton University Press).

Fearon, J. (1994), 'Signaling versus the Balance of Power and Interests: An Empirical Test of a Crisis Bargaining Model', *Journal of Conflict Resolution* 38: 2, 236–69.

— (1995), 'Rationalist Explanations for War', *International Organization* 49:3, 379–414.

Filsen, D. and Werner, S. (2002a), 'The Dynamics of Bargaining and War', Manuscript (Emory University).

— (2002b), 'A Bargaining Model of War and Peace', *American Journal of Political Science* 46:4, 819–38.

Friedman, J., Bladen, C., and Rosen, S. (1970), *Alliance in International Politics* (Boston: Allyn and Bacon).

Fox, W. (1970), *How Wars End* (Philadelphia: American Academy of Political and Social Science).

Gartner, S. (1997), *Strategic Assessment in War* (New Haven: Yale University Press).

Gartner, S. and Siverson, R. (1996), 'War Expansion and War Outcome', *Journal of Conflict Resolution* 40:1, 4–15.

Gartzke, E. (1999), 'War is in the Error Term', *International Organization* 53:3, 567–87.

Gartzke, E. and Gleditsch, K. (2001), 'Balancing, Bandwagoning, Bargaining and War: Signaling and Selection Among Third-Party Joiners', paper given at the *Annual Meeting of the International Studies Association* (Chicago: 20–4 February).

Gartzke, E. and Simon, M. (1999), 'Hot Hand: A Critical Analysis of Enduring Rivalries', *Journal of Politics* 61:3, 777–98.

Gelpi, C. (1999), 'Alliances as Instruments of Intra-Allied Control', in Haftendorn, H., Keohane, R. and Wallander, C (eds).

Ghosn, F. and Palmer, G. (2003), 'Codebook for the Militarized Interstate Dispute Data Version 3.0', *Correlates of War* [website], <http://cow2.la.psu.edu>.

Gibbons, E. (1992), *Forging Consensus: The Western Alliance and the Invasion of Kuwait*. (Washington: Pew Charitable Trusts).

Ginneken, J. (1983), *The Third Indochina War: The Conflicts between China, Vietnam and Cambodia*. Tr. Smith, D. (Leiden: Psychological Institute, University of Leiden).

Gleditsch, K. (2002), *All International Politics is Local: The Diffusion of Conflict, Integration, and Democratization* (Ann Arbor: University of Michigan Press).

— (2003), 'Transnational Dimensions of Civil War', Manuscript (University of California San Diego).

Gleditsch, K. and Beardsley, K. (2004), 'Noisy Neighbors: Third Party Actors in Central American Conflicts', *Journal of Conflict Resolution* 48:3, 379–402.

Gleditsch, K. and Ward, M. (2000), 'War and Peace in Space and Time: The Role of Democratization', *International Studies Quarterly* 44:1, 1–29.

Gleditsch, N. and Hegre, H. (1997), 'Peace and Democracy: Three Levels of Analysis', *Journal of Conflict Resolution* 41:2, 283–310.

Gochal, J. and Levy, J. (2004), 'Crisis Mismanagement or Conflict of Interests? A Case Study of the Origins of the Crimean War', in Maoz, Z. et al (eds).

Goemans, H. (2000), *War and Punishment: The Causes of War Termination and the First World War* (Princeton: Princeton University Press).

Goertz, G. (1994), *Contexts of International Politics* (Cambridge: Cambridge University Press).

Goertz, G. and Diehl, P. (1995), 'The Initiation and Termination of Enduring Rivalries: The Impact of Political Shocks', *American Journal of Political Science* 39:1, 30–52.

Goldfrank, D. (1994), *The Origins of the Crimean War* (New York: Longman).

Gooch, B. (1969), *Origins of the Crimean War* (Lexington, MA: D.C. Heath and Company).

Goodman, A. (1992), *Diplomacy During the Persian Gulf War* (Washington: Institute for the Study of Diplomacy).

Gordon, M. and Trainor, B. (1995), *The Generals' War: The Inside Story of the Conflict in the Gulf* (Boston: Little, Brown and Company).

Gregory, R. (1971), *The Origins of American Neutrality in the First World War* (New York: W. W. Norton).

Gribler, D. and Sarkees, M. (2004), 'Measuring Alliances: the Correlates of War Formal Interstate Alliance Dataset, 1816-2000', *Journal of Peace Research* 41:2, 211–22.

Haftendorn, H., Keohane, R. and Wallander C. (1999), *Imperfect Unions: Security Institutions over Time and Space* (Oxford: Oxford University Press).

Haldi, S. (2003), *Why Wars Widen: A Theory of Predation and Balancing* (Portland: Frank Cass).

Hall, R. (1996), *Bulgaria's Road to the First World War* (Boulder: East European Monographs).

— (2003), 'Bulgaria, Romania, and Greece' in Hamilton, R. and Herwig, H. (eds.).

Halperin, S. (1961), 'Bismarck and Italian Envoy in Berlin on the Eve of the Franco-Prussian War', *Journal of Modern History* 33:1, 33–9.

— (1963), *Diplomat Under Stress: Visconti-Venosta and the Crisis of July, 1870* (Chicago: University of Chicago Press).

Hamilton, R. and Herwig, H. (2003), *The Origins of World War I* (Cambridge: Cambridge University Press).

Hamilton, R. and Herwig, H. (2003), 'Italy' in Hamilton, R. and Herwig, H. (eds.).

Hammerström, M. (1993a), 'Diffusion Effects of Military Conflict in Eastern Europe and the Balkans' in Pfetsch, F. (ed.).

— (1993b), 'The Diffusion of Military Conflict in the Middle East: Direct vs. Indirect Effects' in Balazs, J. and Wiberg, H. (eds).

— (1994), 'The Diffusion of Military Conflict: Central and South-East Europe in 1919-20 and 1991-92', *Journal of Peace Research* 31:3, 263–80.

— (1995), 'Diffusion Effects of Military Conflict in African Regions, 1945-1992: A Preliminary Assessment of Network Approaches', paper given at the *Second Pan-European Conference in International Relations,* Paris: 13–16 September.

Hammerström, M. and Heldt, B. (2002), 'The Diffusion of Military Intervention: Testing a Network Diffusion Approach', *International Interactions* 28:4, 355–37.

Hardin, J. and Hilbe, J. (2003), *Generalized Estimating Equations* (New York: Chapman and Hall / CRC).

Harris, J. (2003), 'Great Britain' in Hamilton, R. and Herwig, H. (eds).

Hart, B. (1991), *Strategy*. Second Revised ed. (New York: Meridian).

Haslam, J. (1992), *The Soviet Union and the Threat from the East, 1933-1941: Moscow, Tokyo and the Prelude to the Pacific War* (London: MacMillan).

Henderson, G. (1969), 'The Seymour Conversations, 1853' in Gooch, B. (ed.).

Herkless, J. (1972), 'Lord Clarendon's Attempt at Franco-Prussian Disarmament, January to March 1870' *The Historical Journal* 15:3, 455–70.

Hess, R. (1963), 'Italy and Africa: Colonial Ambitions in the First World War', *Journal of African History* 4:1, 105–26.

Hitchins, K. (1994), *Rumania, 1866-1947* (Oxford: Clarendon Press).

Hobkirk, P. (1992), *The Great Game: The Struggle for Empire in Central Asia* (New York: Kodansha International).

Holbraad, C. (1991), *Danish Neutrality: A Study in the Foreign Policy of a Small State* (Oxford: Clarendon Press).

Holden, A. (1976), 'Bulgaria's Entry into the First World War: A Diplomatic Study, 1913–1915', Dissertation (University of Illinois).

Hope, A. (1917), *Why Italy is with the Allies* (London: R. Clay and Sons).

Houweling, H. and Siccama, J. (1985), 'The Epidemiology of War, 1816-1980', *Journal of Conflict Resolution* 29:4, 641–63.

— (1988), *Studies of War* (Dordrecht: Martinus Nijhoff).

Howard, H. (1931), *The Partition of Turkey: A Diplomatic History, 1913-1923* (Norman: University of Oklahoma Press).

Howard, M. (1962), *The Franco-Prussian War: The German Invasion of France, 1870-1871* (New York: MacMillan).

Huth, P. and Russett, B. (1984), 'What Makes Deterrence Work? Cases from 1900 to 1980', *World Politics* 36:4, 496–526.

Hurd, I. (1999), 'Legitimacy and Authority in International Politics', *International Organization* 53:2, 379–408.

Iklé, F. (1964), *How Nations Negotiate* (New York: Harper and Row).

— (1971), *Every War Must End* (New York: Columbia University Press).

Jairazbhoy, C. (1914), *The Suicide of Turkey* (Bombay: Times Press).

Jervis, R. (1994), 'What Do We Want to Deter and How Do We Deter It?', in Ederington, L. and Mazarr, M. (eds).

Jomini, A. (1969), 'Diplomatic Study on the Crimean War' in Gooch, B. (ed.).

Jones, D. (1994), 'Balancing and Bandwagoning in Militarized Interstate Disputes', in Wayman, F. and Diehl, P. (eds).

Jones, W. (1986), *Denmark: A Modern History* (London: Croom Helm).

Kadera, K. (1998), 'Transmission, Barriers, and Constraints: A Dynamic Model of the Spread of War', *Journal of Conflict Resolution* 42:3, 367–87.

Kaur, K. (1994), *Gulf Crisis: US and the Emerging World Order* (New Delhi: Ashish Pub. House).

Kay, R. (1968), *Chronology: New Zealand in the war, 1939-1946* (Wellington: Historical Publications Branch, Dept. Internal Affairs).

Khadduri, M. and Ghareeb, E. (1997), *War in the Gulf, 1990-91: The Iraq-Kuwait Conflict and its Implications* (New York: Oxford University Press).

Kecskemeti, P. (1958), *Strategic Surrender: The Politics of Victory and Defeat* (Palo Alto: Stanford University Press).

Kegley, Jr., C. and Raymond, G. (1994), 'Networks of Intrigue? Realpolitik, Alliances and International Security', in Wayman, F. and Diehl, P. (eds.).

Kennan, G. (1951), *American Diplomacy, 1900-1950* (Chicago: University of Chicago Press).

Keohane, R. (1982), 'The Demand for International Regimes', *International Organization* 36:2, 325–55.

Keohane, R., Haftendorn, H. and Wallander, C. (1999), 'Conclusions', in Haftendorn, H., Keohane, R. and Wallander, C. (eds).

Keohane, R. and Nye, J. (1974), 'Transgovernmental Relations and International Organization', *World Politics* 27:1, 39–62.

Kim, D. (2002), 'Bargaining and War Initiation', Manuscript (Texas Tech University).

King, G., and Zeng, L. (2001), 'Explaining Rare Events in International Relations', *International Organization* 55:3, 693–715.

Knock, T. (1992), *To End All Wars: Woodrow Wilson and the Quest for a New World Order* (New York: Oxford University Press).

Lake, D. and Rothschild, D. (1998), *The International Spread of Ethnic Conflict: Fear, Diffusion, and Escalation* (Princeton: Princeton University Press).

— (1998), 'Spreading Fear: The Genesis of Transnational Ethnic Conflict', in Lake, D. and Rothschild, D. (eds).

Lansing, R. (1970), *War Memoirs of Robert Lansing* (Westport: Greenwood Press).

Larsen, S. and Collins, J. (1975), *Allied Participation in Vietnam* (Washington: Department of the Army).

Leeds, B. (2003), 'Do Alliances Deter Aggression? The Influence of Military Alliances on the Initiation of Militarized Interstate Disputes', *American Journal of Political Science* 47:3, 427–39.

— (2005), 'Alliances and the Expansion and Escalation of Militarized Interstate Disputes', in Mintz, A. and Russett, B. (eds).

Leeds, B., Long, A., and Mitchell, S. (2000), 'Reevaluating Alliance Reliability: Specific Threats, Specific Promises', *Journal of Conflict Resolution* 44:5, 686–99.

Leng, R. (1993), *Interstate Crisis Behavior, 1816-1980: Realism versus Reciprocity* (Cambridge: Cambridge University Press).

Leontartis, G. (1970), *Greece and the Great Powers* (Thessaloniki: Institute for Balkan Studies).

— (1990), *Greece and the First World War: From Neutrality to Intervention, 1917-1918* (Boulder: East European Monographs).

Leventoğlu, B. and Tarar, A. (2008), 'Does Private Information Lead to Delay or War in Crisis Bargaining?', *International Studies Quarterly* 52:3, 533–54.

Levy, J. (1982), 'Contagion of Great Power War, 1495-1975', *American Journal of Political Science* 26:3, 562–84.

— (1990), 'Preferences, Constraints, and Choices in July 1914', *International Security* 15:3, 151–86.

Liang, K. and Zeger, S. (1986), 'Longitudinal Data Analysis using Generalized Linear Models', *Biometrika* 73:1, 13–22.

Longmans, Green, etc. (1823–2000), *The Annual Register of World Events; a Review of the Year* Vols. 1823, 1828–29, 1846–49, 1851–7, 1859–71, 1877–85, 1893–95, 1897–98, 1900, 1904–07, 1909–22, 1929, 1931–45, 1948–53, 1956, 1962, 1965–88, 1990–95, and 1998–2000 (London).

Lord, R. (1966), *The Origins of the War of 1870: New Documents from the German Archives* (New York: Russell and Russell).

Lowry, H. (1990), *The Story Behind Ambassador Morgenthau's Story* (Istanbul: Isis Press).

Maoz, Z. et al. (2004), *Multiple Paths to Knowledge in International Relations: Methodology in the Study of Conflict Management and Conflict Resolution* (Lanham: Lexington Books).

Marie, Queen of Romania. (1935), *Ordeal: The Story of My Life* (New York: Charles Scribner's Sons).

Marshall, M. and Jaggers, K. (2007), *The Polity IV Project: Political Regime Characteristics and Transitions, 1800-2007* (Severn: Center for Systemic Peace).

May, E. (1959), *The World War and American Isolation, 1914-1917* (Cambridge: Harvard University Press).

— (1963), *The Coming of War, 1917* (Chicago: Rand McNally).

McEvedy, C. (1972), *The Penguin Atlas of Modern History* (New York: Viking Penguin).

— (1982), *The Penguin Atlas of Recent History* (New York: Viking Penguin).

Mélas, G. (1920), *Ex-King Constantine and the War* (London: Hutchinson).

Midlarsky, M. (1989), *Handbook of War Studies* (Boston: Unwin Hyman).

Miller, R. (1994), *Following the Americans to the Persian Gulf: Canada, Australian, and the Development of the New World Order* (Rutherford: Fairleigh Dickenson University Press).

Millman, R. (1965), *British Foreign Policy and the Coming of the Franco-Prussian War* (Oxford: Clarendon Press).

Ministry of Foreign Affairs of the Greek Government. (1919), *The Greek White Book: Supplementary Diplomatic Documents, 1913-1917* (New York: Oxford University Press).

Mintz, A. and Russett, B. (2005), *New Directions for International Relations: Confronting the Method-of-Analysis Problem* (New York: Lexington Books).

Mitrakos, A. (1982), *France in Greece During World War I: A Study in the Politics of Power* (Boulder: East European Monographs).

Morgenthau, Ha. (1973), *Politics Among Nations* (New York: Knopf).

Morgenthau, He. (1918), *Ambassador Morgenthau's Story* (New York: Doubleday, Page and Co.).

Most, B. and Starr, H. (1980), 'Diffusion, Reinforcement, Geo-politics and the Spread of War', *American Political Science Review* 74:4, 932–46.

— (1981), 'Theoretical and Methodological Issues in the Study of Diffusion and Contagion: Examples for the Research on War', paper given at the *22nd Annual Meeting of the International Studies Association,* (Philadelphia: March 18–21).

— (1990), 'Theoretical and Logical Issues in the Study of International Diffusion', *Journal of Theoretical Politics* 2:4, 391–412.

Most, B., Starr, H. and Siverson, R. (1989), 'The Logic and Study of the Diffusion of International Conflict', in Midlarsky, M. (ed.).

Moyal, J. (1949), 'The Distribution of Wars in Time', *Journal of the Royal Statistical Society* 112:4, 446–9.

Murray, W. (1984), *The Change in the European Balance of Power, 1938-1939: The Path to Ruin* (Princeton: Princeton University Press).

Newitt, M. (1981), *Portugal in Africa: The Last Hundred Years* (Harlow: Longman).

Nicholas, Prince of Greece. (1928), *Political Memoirs 1914-1917: Pages from My Diary* (London: Hutchinson and Co.).

Nyang, S. and Hendricks, E. (1995), *A Line in the Sand: Saudi Arabia's Role in the Gulf War* (Washington: PT Books).

O'Laughlin, J. and Anselin, L. (1991), 'Bringing Geography Back to the Study of International Relations: Spatial Dependence and Regional Context in Africa, 1966-1978', *International Interactions* 17:1, 29–61.

Oncken, H. (1928), *Napoleon III and the Rhine: The Origin of the War of 1870-1871* (New York: Russell and Russell).

Oneal, J. and Russett, B. (1999), 'Assessing the Liberal Peace with Alternative Specifications: Trade Still Reduces Conflict', *Journal of Peace Research* 36:4, 423–42.

Osgood, R. (1953), *Ideals and Self-Interest in America's Foreign Relations* (Chicago: University of Chicago Press).

Page, T. (1920), *Italy and the World War* (New York: Charles Scribner's Sons).

Park, J. (1981), *Korea's Return to Asia: An Analysis of New Moves in South Korean Diplomacy in the 1960s and 1970s* (New York: Columbia University).

Parker, C. (1907), *Life and Letters of Sir James Graham* (London: John Murray).

Pearson, F., Baumann, R. and Pickering, J. (1994), 'Military Intervention and Realpoltik', in Wayman, F. and Diehl, P. (eds).

Pemberton, G. (1987), *All the Way: Australia's Road to Vietnam* (Boston: Allen and Unwin).

Perry, J. (1996), *Arrogant Armies: Great Military Disasters and the Generals Behind Them* (New York: John Wiley and Sons).

Peterson, S. (1993), 'The Domestic Politics of Crisis Bargaining and the Origins of the Crimean War', in Snyder, J. and Jervis, R. (eds).

Petkov, P. (1991), *The United States and Bulgaria in World War I* (Boulder: East European Monographs).

Petrescu-Comnène, N. (2000), *The Great War and the Romanians: Notes and Documents on World War I* (Portland: Center for Romanian Studies).

Pfetsch, F. (1993), *International Relations and Pan-Europe: Theoretical Approaches and Empirical Findings* (Hamburg: Lit Verlag).

Pillar, P. (1983), *Negotiating Peace: War Termination as a Bargaining Process* (Princeton: Princeton University Press).

Powell, R. (1999), *In the Shadow of Power* (Princeton: Princeton University Press).

— (2004), 'Bargaining and Learning While Fighting', *American Journal of Political Science* 48:2, 344–61.

Pryce, R. (1954), 'Italy and the Outbreak of the First World War', *Cambridge Historical Journal* 11:2, 219–27.

Puryear, V. (1969a), 'Commercial Preliminaries of the Crimean War', in Gooch, B. (ed.).

— (1969b), 'New Light on the Origins of the Crimean War', in Gooch, B. (ed.).

Queen, I. (1997), 'Romania's Tenuous Neutrality', Thesis (University of Washington).

Questor, G. (1982), *American Foreign Policy* (New York: Praeger).

Raknerud, A. and Hegre, H. (1997), 'The Hazard of War: Reassessing the Evidence for the Democratic Peace', *Journal of Peace Research* 34:4, 385–404.

Rambaud, A. (1969), 'The Crimean War: Origins', in Gooch, B. (ed.).

Raymond, D. (1921), 'British Policy and Opinion During the Franco-Prussian War', Dissertation (Columbia University).

Reiter, D. (1995), 'Exploding the Powder Keg Myth: Preemptive Wars Almost Never Happen', *International Security* 20:2, 5–34.

Reiter, D. and Stam, A. (2002), *Democracies at War* (Princeton: Princeton University Press).

Renzi, W. (1968), 'Italy's Neutrality and Entrance into the Great War: A Re-examination', *American Historical Review* 73:5, 1414–32.

Renzi, W. (1987), *In the Shadow of the Sword: Italy's Neutrality and Entrance Into the Great War, 1914-1915* (American University Studies Series IX: History, Vol. 26; New York: Peter Lang).

Rich, D. (2003), 'Russia', in Hamilton, R. and Herwig, H. (eds).

Rich, N. (1985), *Why the Crimean War?: A Cautionary Tale* (Hanover: University of New England Press).

Richardson, Lo. (1999), 'The Concert of Europe and Security Management in the Nineteenth Century', in Haftendorn, H., Keohane, R. and Wallander, C. (eds).

Richardson, Le. (1960), *Statistics of Deadly Quarrels* (Chicago: Quadrangle).

Rosen, S. (1970), 'A Model of War and Alliances', in Friedman, J., Bladen, C. and Rosen, S. (eds).

— (1991), *Winning the Next War: Innovation and the Modern Military* (Ithaca: Cornell University Press).

Russett, B. (1968), 'Components of an Operational Theory of International Alliance Formation', *Journal of Conflict Resolution* 12:3, 285–301.

Russett, B. and Oneal, J. (2001), *Triangulating Peace: Democracy, Interdependence, and International Organizations* (New York: W. W. Norton).

Saab, A. (1977), *The Origins of the Crimean Alliance* (Charlottesville: University of Virginia Press).

Saab, A., Knaap, J., and Knapp, F. (1986), 'A Reassessment of French Foreign Policy during the Crimean War Based on the Papers of Adolphe de Bourqueney', *French Historical Studies* 14:4, 467–96.

Sabrosky, A. (1980), 'Interstate Alliances: Their reliability and the Expansion of War', in Singer, J. (ed.).

Saideman, S. (2001), *The Ties that Divide: Ethnic Politics, Foreign Policy, and International Conflict* (New York: Columbia University Press).

Salandra, A. (1932), *Italy and the Great War: From Neutrality to Intervention.* Pyne, Z (tr.). (London: Edward Arnold).

Sarkees, M. (2000), 'The Correlates of War Data on War: An Update to 1997', *Conflict Management and Peace Science* 18:1, 123–44.

Scheina, R. (2003), *Latin America's Wars.* 2 vols. (Washington: Brassey's).

Schelling, Thomas. 1966. *Arms and Influence.* New Haven: Yale University Press.

Schroeder, P. (1972), *Austria, Great Britain, and the Crimean War: The Destruction of the European Concert* (Ithaca: Cornell University Press).

Schultz, K. (1999), 'Do Democratic Institutions Constrain or Inform?', *International Organization* 53:1, 23–66.

Schweller, R. (1994), 'Bandwagoning for Profit: Bringing the Revisionist State Back In', *International Security* 19:1, 72–107.

Seaman, L. (1969), 'Causes of the Crimean War', in Gooch, B. (ed.).

Seligman, V. (1920), *The Victory of Venizelos: A Study of Greek Politics, 1910-1918* (London: George Allen and Unwin).

Seton-Watson, R. (1969), 'The Origins of the Crimean War', in *Origins of the Crimean War*, Gooch, B. (ed.).

Seymour, C. (1967), *American Neutrality, 1914-1917: Essays on the Causes of American Intervention in the World War* (Hamden: Archon Books).

Shirkey, Z. (1999), 'Power Transition Theory in a Sub-Regional Setting: A Case Study of the US-Mexican Dyad', *Michigan Journal of Political Science* 1:27, 1–50.

Silberstein, G. (1970), *The Troubled Alliance: German-Austrian Relations, 1914 to 1917* (Lexington: University of Kentucky Press).

Simmel, G. (1904), 'The Sociology of Conflict. I', *American Journal of Sociology* 9:4, 490–525.

Simowitz, R. (1998), 'Evaluating Conflict Research on the Diffusion of War', *Journal of Peace Research* 35:2, 211–30.

Simowitz, R. and Sheffer, M. (1998), 'Cumulation, Evaluation and the Research Process: A Response to Starr and Siverson', *Journal of Peace Research* 35:2, 238–44.

Simpson, F. (1969), 'Louis Napoleon and the Recovery of France: Crimean War Origins', in Gooch, b. (ed.).

Singer, J. (1980), *The Correlates of War II: Testing Some Realpolitik Models* (New York: Free Press).

Singer, J. and Small, M. (1972), *The Wages of War: 1816-1965* (New York: Wiley).

Singer, J. and Wallace, M. (1979), *To Auger Well* (Beverly Hills: Sage).

Siverson, R. and King, J. (1979), 'Alliances and the Expansion of War 1815-1965', in Singer, J. and Wallace, M. (eds).

— (1980), "Attributes of National Alliance Membership and War Participation, 1815-1965." *American Journal of Political Science* 24:1, 1–15.

Siverson, R. and Starr, H. (1989), 'Alliance and Border Effects on the War Behavior of States: Refining the Interaction Opportunity Model', *Conflict Management and Peace Science* 10:2, 21–46.

— (1990), 'Opportunity, Willingness, and the Diffusion of War', *American Political Science Review* 84:1, 47–67.

— (1991), *The Diffusion of War: A Study of Opportunity and Willingness* (Ann Arbor: University of Michigan Press).

Slantchev, B. (2002), 'The Power to Hurt: Costly Conflict with Completely Informed States', *American Political Science Review* 47:1, 1–11.

— (2003), 'The Principle of Convergence in Wartime Negotiations', *American Political Science Review* 97:4, 621–32.

— (2004), 'How Initiators End Their Wars: The Duration of Warfare and the Terms of Peace', *American Journal of Political Science* 48:4: 813–29.

Smith, A. (1995), 'Alliance Formation and War', *International Studies Quarterly* 39:4, 405–25.

— (1996), 'To Intervene or Not Intervene', *Journal of Conflict Resolution* 40:1, 16–40.

— (1998a), 'Fighting Battles, Winning Wars', *Journal of Conflict Resolution* 42:3, 301–20.

— (1998b), 'International Crises and Domestic Politics', *American Journal of Political Science* 92:3, 623–38.

Smith, A. and Stam, A. (2004), 'Bargaining and the Nature of War', *Journal of Conflict Resolution* 48:6, 783–813.
Snyder, G. (1997), *Alliance Politics* (Ithaca: Cornell University Press).
Snyder, J. and Jervis, R. (1993), *Coping with Complexity in the International System* (Boulder: Westview Press).
Sonyel, S. (1975), *Turkish Diplomacy, 1918-1923; Mustafa Kemel and the Turkish Nationalist Movement* (Sage Studies in 20th Century History; London: Sage).
Sorokin, P. (1937), *Social and Cultural Dynamics: Fluctuation of Social Relationships, War, and Revolution.* Vol. 3. (New York: American Book Company).
Spector, S. (1962), *Rumania at the Paris Peace Conference* (New York: Bookman Associates).
Starr, H. (1972), *War Coalitions* (Lexington: DC Heath).
Starr, H. and Most, B. (1976), 'The Substance and Study of Borders in International Relations Research', *International Studies Quarterly* 20:4, 581–620.
— (1983), 'Contagion and Border Effects on Contemporary African Conflict', *Comparative Political Studies* 16:1, 92–117.
— (1985), 'The Forms and Processes of War Diffusion: Research Update on Contagion in African Conflict', *Comparative Political Studies*. 18:1, 206–27.
Starr, H. and Siverson, R. (1998), 'Cumulation, Evaluation and the Research Process: Investigating the Diffusion of Conflict', *Journal of Peace Research* 35:2, 231–37.
Stevenson, D. (2005), '1918 Revisited', *Journal of Strategic Studies* 28:1, 107–39.
Strang, D. and Tuma, N. (1993), 'Spatial and Temporal Heterogeneity in Diffusion', *American Journal of Sociology*. 99:3, 614–39.
Swartz, R. (2004), *Diplomacy in a Time of War: The 1991 Persian Gulf War and the Interplay between War and Diplomacy*. Masters Thesis. (Missoula: University of Montana).
Tams, C. (1999), 'The Functions of a European Security and Defense Identity and its Institutional Forms', in Haftendorn, H., Keohane, R. and Wallander, C. (eds).
Taylor, A. (1969), 'End of the Holy Alliance, 1852-1853', in Gooch, B. (ed.).
Temperley, H. (1969), 'Responsibilities for the Crimean War', in Gooch, B. (ed.).
Theodoulou, C. (1971), *Greece and the Entente* (Thessaloniki: Institute for Balkan Studies).
Times Books. (1992), *Triumph Without Victory: The Unreported History of the Persian Gulf War* (New York).
Tobler, W. (1979), 'Smooth Pycnophylactic Interpolation for Geographic Regions', *Journal of the American Statistical Association* 74:367, 519–30.
Torrey, G. (1982), 'Romanian Historiography on the First World War', *Military Affairs* 46:1, 25–8.
— (1998), *Romania and World War I: A Collection of Studies* (Portland: Center for Romanian Studies).

Toynbee, A. (1991), *Turkey: A Past and A Future* (New York: J. C. and A. L. Fawcett).

Trachtenberg, M. (1990), 'The Meaning of Mobilization in 1914', *International Security* 15:3, 120–50.

Troubetzkoy, A. (1986), *The Road to Balaklava: Stumbling into War with Russia* (Toronto: Trafalgar Press).

Trumpener, U. (2003), 'The Ottoman Empire', in Hamilton, R. and Herwig, H. (eds).

Tuchman, B. (1966), *The Zimmerman Telegram* (New York: MacMillan).

Tuschhoff, C. (1999), 'Alliance Cohesion and Peaceful Change in NATO', in Haftendorn, H., Keohane, R. and Wallander, C. (eds).

United States Department of State. (1917), *Foreign Relations of the United States: 1917 Supplement* (Washington: Government Printing Office).

— (1928), *Papers Relating to the Foreign Relations of the United States, Supplement: The World War, 1915*. (Washington: Government Printing Office).

— (1964–68), *Foreign Relations of the United States, 1964-1968*. Vols. I–II. (Washington: Government Printing Office).

Vasquez, J. (1987), 'The Steps to War: Toward a Scientific Explanation of War Findings', *World Politics* 40:1, 108–45.

— (1993), *The War Puzzle* (Cambridge: Cambridge University Press).

Vopicka, C. (1921), *Secrets of the Balkans* (Chicago: Rand McNally).

Wagner, R. (2000), 'Bargaining and War', *American Journal of Political Science* 44:3, 469–84.

Wallander, C., and Keohane, R. (1999), 'Risk, Threat, and Security Institutions', in Haftendorn, H., Keohane, R. and Wallander, C. (eds.).

Wallensteen, P. and Sollenberg, M. (1998), 'Armed Conflict and Regional Conflict Complexes, 1989-97', *Journal of Peace Research* 35:5, 621–34.

Walt, S. (1985), 'Alliance Formation and the Balance of World Power', *International Security* 9:4, 3–43.

Ward, M. and Gleditsch, K. (2002), 'Location, Location, Location: An MCMC Approach to Modeling the Spatial Context of War and Peace', *Political Analysis* 10:3, 244–60.

Wawro, G. (2003), *The Franco-Prussian War: The German Conquest of France in 1870-1871* (Cambridge: Cambridge University Press).

Wayman, F. and Diehl, P. (1994), *Reconstructing Realpolitik* (Ann Arbor: University of Michigan Press).

Weber, F. (1970), *Eagles on the Crescent: Germany, Austria, and the Diplomacy of the Turkish Alliance, 1914-1918* (Ithaca: Cornell University Press).

Werner, S. (2000), 'Deterring Intervention: The Stakes of War and Third-Party Involvement', *American Journal of Political Science* 44:4, 720–32.

Werner, S. and Lemke, D. (1997), 'Opposites Do Not Attract: The Impact of Domestic Institutions, Power, and Prior Commitments on Alignment Choices', *International Studies Quarterly* 41:3, 529–46.

Wetzel, D. (1985), *The Crimean War: A Diplomatic History* (Boulder: East European Monographs).

— (2001), *A Duel of Giants: Bismarck, Napoleon II, and the Origins of the Franco-Prussian War* (Madison: University of Wisconsin Press).

Wittman, D. (1979), 'How War Ends: A Rational Model Approach', *Journal of Conflict Resolution* 23:4, 741–61.

Woods, F. and Baltzly, A. (1915), *Is War Diminishing? A Study of the Prevalence of War in Europe from 1450 to the Present Day* (Boston: Houghton Mifflin).

Wright, Q. (1965), *A Study of War*. 2nd ed. (Chicago: University of Chicago Press).

Yamamoto, Y. and Bremer, S. (1980), 'Wider Wars and Restless Nights: Major Power Intervention in Ongoing Wars, 1815-1965', in Singer, J. (ed.).

Yetiv, S. (2004), *Explaining Foreign Policy: US Decision-Making and the Persian Gulf War* (Baltimore: John Hopkins University Press).

Zacher, M. (2001), 'The Territorial Integrity Norm: International Boundaries and the Use of Force', *International Organization*. 55:2, 215–50.

Zipf, G. (1949), *Human Behavior and the Principle of Least Effort: an Introduction to Human Ecology* (Cambridge: Addison-Wesley Press).

Zorn, C. (2001), 'Generalized Estimating Equation Models for Correlated Data: A Review with Applications', *American Journal of Political Science* 45:2, 470–90.

Index